The Lexicon–Syntax Interface

Linguistik Aktuell/Linguistics Today (LA)

Linguistik Aktuell/Linguistics Today (LA) provides a platform for original monograph studies into synchronic and diachronic linguistics. Studies in LA confront empirical and theoretical problems as these are currently discussed in syntax, semantics, morphology, phonology, and systematic pragmatics with the aim to establish robust empirical generalizations within a universalistic perspective.

For an overview of all books published in this series, please see
http://benjamins.com/catalog/la

Volume 209

The Lexicon–Syntax Interface. Perspectives from South Asian languages
Edited by Pritha Chandra and Richa Srishti

The Lexicon–Syntax Interface

Perspectives from South Asian languages

Edited by

Pritha Chandra
Indian Institute of Technology New Delhi

Richa Srishti
Central Institute of Indian Languages Mysore

John Benjamins Publishing Company
Amsterdam / Philadelphia

The paper used in this publication meets the minimum requirements of the American National Standard for Information Sciences – Permanence of Paper for Printed Library Materials, ANSI z39.48-1984.

CIP data is available from the Library of Congress.

Linguistik Aktuell/Linguistics Today, ISSN 0166-0829 ; v. 209
ISBN 978 90 272 5592 1 (Hb ; alk. paper)
ISBN 978 90 272 7082 5 (Eb)

John Benjamins Publishing Co. · P.O. Box 36224 · 1020 ME Amsterdam · The Netherlands
John Benjamins North America · P.O. Box 27519 · Philadelphia PA 19118-0519 · USA

Table of contents

Acknowledgement

We wish to thank Werner Abraham and Elly van Gelderen for their interest in this project and considering it for the series that they are editing. Their constructive suggestions and criticisms carried this volume through various stages in its preparation. Thanks also to Kees Vaes, who patiently guided us through the entire publication process.

Of course, this volume would not have materialised without the help and perseverance of all our contributors, who met our demands untiringly over the last few months. We are also very grateful to Miriam Butt, Jessica Coon, Veneeta Dayal, Alice Davison, K.A. Jayaseelan, Omkar Koul, Rajesh Kumar, Andrew Nevins, Ivan Ortega-Santos and K.V. Subbarao for critical observations on the manuscript. Gurmeet Kaur and Anindita Sahoo deserve special mention for helping us with the copy-editing and indexing.

We also thank our respective partners for keeping us focussed when the path got difficult. Nothing however, counts more, than the faith the two toddlers – Homeyra and Sasha – put in their respective mothers. It is to them that we dedicate this volume.

The lexicon-syntax interface

Some issues

Pritha Chandra & Richa Srishti
Indian Institute of Technology Delhi and Central Institute of Indian Languages

1. Introduction

The lexicon in generative literature is generally taken as a repository of idiosyncrasies of a language that are used to build linguistic expressions in the syntax (cf. Chomsky 1995). Considering it as a list of exceptions suggests that the lexicon is unstructured and that it has no internal mechanisms and computations of its own. Its sole significance is in providing narrow syntax with lexical items (and relevant information coded in them) to construct structures. However, though a prevalent view, scholars are not unanimous on it. There are many who vouch that this component is more than a repository; it consists of mechanisms quite similar to those of narrow syntax – recursive structure building operations that help build words (see Selkirk 1982; Di Sciullo & Williams 1987 among others). For these scholars, syntax and morphology, as a theory of the lexicon, are both recursive definitions of sets of objects, albeit with different atoms as their members and different combinatorial rules. Levin and Rappaport Hovav (1995) is another pioneering work that helps develop a theory of lexical semantic representations and the linking procedures underlying the lexicon-syntax interface.

Minimalism however raises a different set of conceptual questions about the lexicon and the nature of its interface with narrow syntax. The substantive theory of minimalism demands that all attributes of the language organ should be recast either in terms of economy conditions or legibility constraints. The constructs used in narrow syntax, its principles and operations are all reanalyzed as emanating from the needs of the system itself or the requirements imposed by the two most crucial interfacing components – Articulatory-Perceptual (A-P) and Conceptual-Intentional (C-I) systems – dealing with sound and meaning respectively. Approaching the syntax-lexicon relation from this perspective, one is tempted to reduce the lexicon to bare essentials, transferring all possible computations for word formation to the syntax and rephrasing all conditions on mapping of lexical items into syntactic structures to the LF interface. Efforts in this direction have already been made and met with some success (see for instance Borer 2005; Harley 2011 among others). The war of course, is far from being over, as one can gauge from the copious research papers on this debate and related topics such as verb classifications, argument structure alterations, the redefinition of theta-roles, etc., based on data from many different languages.

In this chapter, we trace a necessarily brief and incomplete picture of pre-minimalist and minimalist conceptions of the lexicon and its interface with narrow syntax. Against this backdrop, we revisit previous and relevant studies in South Asian Languages (SALs) to understand the features of these languages better that also help us pose the right questions to guide future research.

We elaborate on questions related to the status of syntactic categories, verb classes and argument structure, causativization, passivization and case, theta-role and agreement correlations among others and suggest how the present volume, through its research papers dealing with various aspects of SALs, contribute in furthering our knowledge of the lexicon-syntax interface.

2. The pre-minimalist lexicon

The lexicon is introduced in Chomsky (1965) as simply an unordered list of all lexical formatives. Each lexical entry is taken as a pair (D, C), with D a phonological distinctive feature matrix and C a collection of specified syntactic features (a complex symbol). Chomsky however recognizes that this is not a sufficient representation for a category V(erb) as a complex symbol. Separate rules or more elaborate lexical entries must be provided to determine the transitive or intransitive nature of a V and for all other complex symbols. A rule like the following would be insufficient for representing a verbal formative in the lexicon (1).

(1) V → [+V, ±Progressive, ±Transitive, ±Abstract-Subject, ±Animate-Object]

Instead one requires context-sensitive rules like (2)–(3) for complete representations; the occurrence of the category symbol V and its substitution by a complex symbol containing the feature [+Transitive] are contingent on its environment. V is transitive only if it occurs in the environment of a noun phrase and intransitive otherwise.

(2) V → [+V, [+Transitive]/___NP]

(3) V→ –Transitive/___#

Similarly, for all other lexical features (e.g. Abstract-Subject, Animate-Object etc.), that are involved in the statement of varied contextual restrictions. They must each occur in the grammar via a context-sensitive rewriting rule. Moreover, even for different choices of subcategories of verbs, different rules need to be postulated. As for instance, verbs that occur in the contexts of adjectival predicates (*grow old*) must be separately specified from those that appear with nominal predicates (*become a president*).

But, as the cautious reader may have already noticed, postulating such rules as the above, though formally adequate, makes the grammar extremely clumsy. Moreover, in the process, we also miss out on important generalizations. The existence of different rules for different subcategories of verbs misleads us into believing that there are no commonalities underlying these verbal formatives.

In lieu of such unjustified complexity, Chomsky suggests contextual features or subcategorization features as more natural and revealing expressions of these processes. The feature specification [+Transitive] is taken as merely a notation suggesting the appearance of a verbal formative in the environment of a noun phrase. This context could be more appropriately symbolized as the notation "__ NP", for instance for a verb like *eat* (4). Intransitive verbs like *sit* on the other hand would be restricted from appearing in such environments (5). Pre-adjectival verbs such as *grow, feel* would be positively specified for the contextual feature [__ Adjective] as depicted in (6).

(4) Eat [+V, +–NP]

(5) Sit [+V, __#]

(6) Grow [+V, +–NP, +__#, +–Adjective]

Each lexical formative, instead of being introduced by separate context-sensitive rewriting rules, would be designated in the form [X – Y], with X and Y strings (perhaps null) of symbols.

Other selectional restrictions are also coded via similar notational devices. Features such as +abstract subject or +animate object would get representations like the following (7).

(7) [+V] → CS/[+Abstract]Aux –, [–Abstract] Aux –, –Det [+Animate], –Det[Animate]

Along with subcategorization and selectional restrictions, each entry in the lexicon also contains information that establishes the mapping between the syntax and the semantics of predicates. Argument structure of an entry is the information of its arity and the manner in which its arguments should be mapped onto syntactic representations. It is a level of syntactic description where the arguments of a predicate are denoted as members of a set, each corresponding to a particular theta-role. Thus a transitive verb *hit* with its two arguments and their respective theta-roles is represented as follows:

(8) Hit_V [1 2]
Agent Patient

What argument structure effectively does is enable the lexical head (the verb here) to project its arguments in the correct positions in the hierarchical syntactic structures. Following Williams' (1981), there is a special position for each predicate, which functions as the 'head thematic role' of the argument structure as a whole. This thematic role, which is assigned outside the maximal projection of its predicate, corresponds to the 'external argument.' Given standard conventions about feature percolation and the notion 'head of a word' the index of the external thematic role is passed on to the maximal projection of its predicate. All remaining thematic roles including the one corresponding to the 'internal argument' remain only within the first projection of the predicate. The thematic index of the internal theta role or the internal argument does not percolate to the VP node, but is assigned within the first projection of the predicate. Such assignment is realized under government, i.e. mutual c-command.

In pre-minimalist theories, there exists a separate level of representation – D-structure – where the mapping between lexical information and syntactic representations gets checked via some constraints. These constraints are:

(9) a. Projection Principle-Representations at each syntactic level are projected from the lexicon, in that they observe the subcategorization properties of lexical items, and

b. Theta-criterion: Each argument bears one and only one theta-role, and each theta-role is assigned to one and only one argument.

However, something else is needed to get the order of arguments (listed as part of argument structure) correctly reflected in syntactic hierarchy. To this effect, Baker (1988) proposes UTAH (10) as a means to constrain lexical-syntax mapping in a tight way.

(10) The Uniformity of Theta Assignment Hypothesis (UTAH)
Identical thematic relationships between items are presented by identical structural relationships between those items at the level of D-structure.

As Baker (1996) reflects, "[p]art of Baker's [1988] motivation for introducing this principle was to put teeth into the generative theory of that time (the early 1980s). Generative theory then as now aspired to achieve explanatory adequacy by having a very tightly constrained view of what syntax could do. However, in practice, the result of this approach was often not deeper analyses of interesting phenomena, but rather a banishing of those phenomena from the domain of syntax – typically into the realm of the lexicon. Within the terms of the theory, this seemed regrettable: if one is going to have a non-trivial syntax at all, then that syntax should be required to pull its own weight. The UTAH, then, was an attempt to identify a domain in which the answer to analytic questions must be a syntactic one."

Baker's quote above is suggestive that the debate on the division of labor between the lexicon and the syntax is not a new one. Even prior to minimalist theorizing, questions were raised about the structure of the lexicon, its interactions with syntax and the status of its constructs (e.g. theta-roles). Baker's is a representative view of a more syntactico-centric approach, where constraints on the lexicon-syntax mapping are more syntactic in nature than lexical. There is already a tension whether to attribute more to the syntax than to the lexicon, a view that goes against approaches that conceptualize the lexicon as a separate recursive structure-building component (Selkirk 1982; Di Sciullo & Williams 1987 among others). If the lexicon indeed is an independent component with similar computational capacities as the syntax, one need not shy away from conducting all word-related tasks in its workspace. But the set of atoms that the lexicon uses, its constructs such as theta-roles have been under the radar for long. Questions have been raised regarding their primitive status. Moreover, many of the lexical operations (e.g. argument structure alterations) seem to overlap quite extensively with the syntactic ones, which going by the Occam Razor Principle of scientific inquiry, should be reduced to only one set of operations. Since syntax is non-trivial, the obvious choice of reduction is the lexicon. These and related problems become more obvious once we step into the paradigm of minimalism. Minimalism, with its fresh set of assumptions, redefines most of these questions, as we elaborate below.

3. Toward a minimal lexicon

There have been attempts, some past and some recent ones, to minimize the lexicon, by either eliminating some of its constructs or transferring its operations to the syntax. We will start by detailing some works questioning the existence of theta-roles in the grammar, thereby, indirectly questioning notions like argument structure.

One notable study in this regard is that by Ladusaw and Dowty (1988). They observe that theta-theory is principally a diacritic theory. Its use in the GB grammar is to constrain theta-role assignment to arguments, thereby helping to delimit possible structures and rule applications on them. Their complaint is that though widely used, there has never been an attempt to ask whether theta-roles are intrinsic parts of the grammar. If they are shown to follow from language-external factors, there will be no justification for including them in the grammar.

They cite the following examples to defend their point.

(11) Fido chased Felix.

(12) Felix was chased by Fido.

According to Ladusaw and Dowty, *Fido* remains an agent in both sentences because of the relation that it has with the event described, not because of the grammatical category or function of anything in the sentence. The lexical semantics of the predicate *chase* is such that for any situation that it describes, certain things are entailed or presupposed about *Fido* qua dog. The agentive semantics of the said NP follows naturally from the lexical semantics of the verb. Hence, there is no motivation for postulating independent constructs like theta-roles. Similarly, for the control examples (13)–(14) cited in Nishigauchi's (1984) work, proposed originally in Jackendoff (1972) and Grimshaw (1979).

(13) Bill bought for Susan$_i$ a large flashy car [PRO$_i$ to drive].

(14) John$_i$ received from Susan a book [PRO$_i$ to read].

Nishigauchi observes that the controller in both cases is the goal NP, irrespective of whether it occupies the object or the subject position of the matrix sentence. In Ladusaw and Dowty's alternative understanding of theta-roles, this restriction follows from three things: (a) the entailment relation between the semantics of the purpose clause and the action denoted by the infinitive (the former entails that the action denoted by the lower infinitive is the purpose behind the action of the main clause), (b) Bach's (1982) observation that "a necessary condition for you to do something with an object, or use it to some end …, is that you have it available, or in your control, or that it be in your 'control space'", and (c) the semantics of the purpose clause is placed temporally after the action of the main clause. These three factors together purport to make the NP Goal as the controller, "as the Goal is, by definition, the person in whose possession the Theme resides when the actions entailed by the main clause are over, and therefore the person in whose possession the referent of the Theme will be at the later time that the purpose clause refers to." (Ladusaw & Dowty).

Given that thematic roles emerge from the entailment relations evident between predicates or events, Ladusaw and Dowty are led to believe that they are properly understood as labels of clusters of verb entailments and presuppositions. Theta-roles are not primitives to the grammar.

Theta roles have also been conceptualized as entities playing a conceptual role in the individuation of events (Carlson 1984), or as purportedly derivable from inherent features such as causes (Zubizarreta 1989) or even as entities that help sentences to modify cognitive representations (Emonds 1991).

Syntactic alternatives to theta-roles have also been put on the table in pre-minimalist times, though a radical lexicon-free picture of a grammar was yet to be proposed. One notable study in this regard is that by Hale and Keyser (1993) who try to provide an explanation for the restricted number of theta-roles in the grammar. Their contention is that the few theta roles we have in natural language actually emerge from the limited structural configurations at our disposal. Theta roles for nouns are determined by the structural positions they occupy in a given sentence. An agent is the interpretation, for instance given to an argument projected in the specifier of Event Phrase (see Travis 1994; Harley 1995; Kratzer 1996). Theme is the interpretation given to any argument projected as a sister of the Root.

Hale and Keyser, following Clark and Clark (1979), also observe that denominal verbs such as *shelve* appear in structures that closely resemble their nominalized counterparts. Relevant examples are provided below.

(15) The librarian put the books on the shelf.

(16) The librarian shelved the books.

They argue that though the convention is to relate these pairs via a morphological relationship in the lexicon, there is an alternative way to do the pairing and that is by using the vocabulary of syntax. "Thus, for example, if established principles of syntax function to constrain denominal verb derivations, then the simplest assumption to make is that these derivations are, in fact, syntactic in nature."

They then go on to introduce a new level in the grammar by suggesting that syntax may be divided between S-syntax (syntactic syntax) and L-syntax (lexical syntax). However note that L-syntax is not narrow syntax; it is a separate level of the grammar from syntactic syntax and is a part of the lexicon. The lexicon, in their account, gets more structure and computations, some of them very similar to those in syntax.

Reinhart (1996, also see Reinhart 2002) is another interesting endeavor to fit theta-roles into the system, but this time via formal features. Reinhart, while agreeing with many others that theta-roles are not primitives of the grammar, claims that they are constituted of formal features, which also govern theta-selection and linking/mapping operations. In her system, each theta-role is a feature cluster (of 'c' = cause, 'm' = has a mental state). Consider (17).

(17) a. [+c, +m] = agent
b. [−c, +m] = experiencer
c. [+c, −m] = instrument/cause
d. [−c, −m] = affected patient/theme

The interesting addition in Reinhart's framework is the Theta System, an interface of the System of Concepts and the Computational System (Syntax) as illustrated below.

(18) Conceptual System (Central System) -> Theta System (Lexicon) →
Computational System (Syntax)

The outputs of the Theta System – the theta-feature clusters among others – are inputs to the Computational System or narrow syntax. These features are legible to the interfaces and hence are not erased in the computational workspace. Other outputs of the theta-system like indices or accusative case are of a different category – they are not readable at the interfaces – and hence are used and, then erased by narrow syntax.

The Theta System contains the theta-specification of a given lexical verb-entry as well as the instructions for the merging of arguments in the syntax. It also consists of a number of thematic arity operations that enable shifting the semantic meaning of a given verb with thematic-specification effects. More precisely, thematic arity operations alter the number of theta-roles or clusters that the predicate carries.

In other works (Reinhart & Siloni 2003, 2005), thematic arity operations are also allowed in the Computational System. Languages are given a choice whether to apply them in the Theta System or in the Syntax. Hence, the Lex-Syn Parameter (19):

(19) The Lex-Syn Parameter
UG allows thematic arity operations to apply in the Lexicon or in Syntax.

English, Hebrew and Dutch are some of the languages that choose the lexicon as the ground for arity changing operations, while French, Italian and German go for the syntactic option.

Though technically different, both frameworks (Hale & Keyser 1993; Reinhart 1996, 2002) allow for a second generative component of the grammar besides syntax, namely the lexicon. Hale and Keyser suggest an L-syntax level for word-level computations while Reinhart takes a further step and redefines the lexicon itself as a computational workspace dealing with the same kinds of formatives that the syntactic computational system uses, i.e. formal features. The lexicon and the syntax in these approaches are not radically distinct from each other, though they are independent components of the grammar.

With the advent of minimalism, certain methodological compulsions persuade us to reconsider postulating two separate generative components of the grammar. As Harley (2011) opines, "The division of labor between two generative components – syntactic and lexical, each with its own primitive operations – ran counter to the central notion of employing the minimally conceptually necessary set of tools for constructing complex constituents." Methodological minimalism demands that the grammar employs mechanisms that are non-redundant and are most economical. In that light, postulating two components with very similar properties appears extremely redundant and costly.

Previously lexicon-free theories have been shown to be possible. Halle and Marantz's (1993, 1994) Distributed Morphology framework is one such illustration, where the entire load of the lexicon is distributed through various other components. This work holds the potential to moot the entire debate on the division of labor between the lexicon and the syntax, by simply eliminating the former.

Instead of going the Distributed Morphology way, one could also simply try to shift the lexical operations, principles and mapping constraints to one of the existing three (syntax, LF and PF) systems. Harley (2011) has a similar observation to offer below.

"It is in fact trivially simple to establish that the basic functions of GB's theta-theoretic module are subsumed within a modern understanding of the interpretation of LF representations. In the semantic architecture of the Fregean program, as described in Heim and Kratzer (1998), predicates are functions, which must compose with arguments in order to achieve interpretability at LF. Unsaturated predicates, or extra arguments which cannot compose with predicates, will result in type mismatch and interpretation failure…Given that something like Fregean semantic composition is needed to understand the behavior of quantifiers and adverbial and adjectival modification in any case, it would be emphatically non-minimalist to propose a specific interpretive mechanism and set of principles to capture the observation that predicates require arguments and vice versa. Within minimalism, and given a Fregean view of the LF interface, the single Full Interpretation requirement can do the work of the Theta Criterion and Projection Principle within minimalist theory."

In addition, all kinds of arity-changing operations, such as those found with passives, middles, causative, inchoatives, etc. should be part of the syntactic computational system. The lexicon is therefore rendered completely redundant; all that was once attributed to it could be shown to follow from narrow syntactic computations or at the interfaces.

These aforementioned practices, we believe, are all geared towards methodological minimalism. Methodological Minimalism or the "weak minimalist thesis" constitutes a necessary aspect of every scientific inquiry; we try to build systems that are simple, economical and non-redundant. However, there is a "strong minimalist thesis" (Chomsky's (2001) 'substantive thesis of minimalism' or Martin and Uriagereka's (2000) 'ontological minimalism') that tries to go beyond explanatory adequacy and ask not what the properties of language are, but why they are that way. It is an understanding of the Faculty of Language (FL) from the viewpoint of its usability on the part of its interfaces.

Talking of interfaces, the Conceptual-Intensional (C-I) system is under focus when one talks about lexical entries and the semantic information they carry. Whatever enters into C-I via the syntactic component are virtually conceptually necessary constructs, i.e. those that are motivated for semantic interpretation. There should be nothing semantic-related in the syntax that is considered illegible at C-I. The strongest hypothesis would be that semantic structures have syntactic correlates; they have a common set of features.

Ramchand (2008, 2011) has an interesting thesis worth mentioning here in this regard. Her contention is that there is a small set of basic argument relations that are implicated in the linguistic construction of eventive predication, tied to the syntactic representation. The systematicity and recursion one finds at this level is very reminiscent of syntactic representations. It would seem that whatever C-I requires, is made available from existing syntactic constructs, thus making the lexicon a highly suspicious part of the grammar.

According to Ramchand, there are three important subevental components at the level of event predication: (a) a causing subevent, (b) a process denoting subevent and (c) a subevent corresponding to result state. They are hierarchically organized thus:

(20) $[_{initP}$ DP-3 init $[_{procP}$ DP-2 proc $[_{resP}$ DP-1 res XP]]]

What Ramchand's structures also do is to derive a set of core argument roles, based on the predicational relations formed at each level. More precisely, the following argument roles fall out naturally from the tree above:

(21) a. initP introduces the causation event and licenses the external argument ('subject' of cause = INITIATOR)
b. procP specifies the nature of the change or process and licenses the entity undergoing change or process ('subject' of process = UNDERGOER)
c. resP gives the 'telos' or 'result state' of the event and licenses the entity that comes to hold the result state ('subject' of result = RESULTEE)

With these structures and the relations emanating from them, Ramchand is able to discard the lexicon completely from the system. All instructions one may need for the C-I interface come solely from the syntax.

Pietroski (2011) is another, and perhaps a clearer exposition, of the instructions that syntax provides for semantics. For him, expressions generated by I-language procedures are recursively combinable instructions for building concepts that constitute the interface between the human faculty of language (HFL) and other cognitive systems. This consorts with Chomsky's (1995, 2001, among others) assumption that each human language represents a certain state of HFL, generating expressions that pair phonological structures PHONs with semantic structures SEMs. These are minimal units facilitating the interaction between HFL and other cognitive systems. Pietroski takes the radical step in assuming that SEMs are instructions to assemble concepts, and meanings are associated with such instructions in the following sense: "to have a meaning is to be a certain kind of instruction, and thus to have a certain 'fulfillment' condition, and semantic theories for human languages are theories of the concept assembly instructions that HFL can generate." (Pietroski 2011). SEMs, for Pietroski therefore are, "Janus-faced": they are grammatical objects composed through formal operations like concatenation and labeling; yet they are what underlie the construction of concepts that are described in terms of semantic operations like saturation or conjunction.

What is interesting about Pietroski's conceptualization of the syntax-semantic interface is that it allows the possibility of postulating an independent component like the lexicon while delimiting its role to providing the syntax with information needed to construct "minimal instructions" for concept formation. However, since the instructions take the shape provided by core syntactic operations like concatenation/merge and labeling, the input from the lexicon will have very little impact on their shapes. But with that, we are once again, back to square one on whether the lexicon is a recursive generative component in the same sense that syntax is. If concepts or word meanings are based on syntactic configurations, we have no motivation left to confer the lexicon with computations to build recursive structures, even if they are restricted to forming words.

In any case, we believe that the jury is still out on the debate. Ultimately, in linguistics, theory-internal problems and data questions both count. The nature of the lexicon-syntax interface is both a theoretical question as well as an empirical one. We need empirical support from diverse languages to determine whether changes in verb-classes can be universally accounted for by syntactic processes or by lexical ones, whether passivization is of the same type in all languages, if causativization bears special features in some languages etc. (see Abraham & Leisiö 2006, Reuland, Bhattacharya & Spathas 2007, for some answers). These are some of the many questions that one needs to answer before getting a fuller view of the lexicon-syntax problem.

4. Features of South Asian Languages (SALs)

In this section, we put forward a few issues/questions that we feel are very relevant to ask to get a better picture of the syntax-lexicon interface. We list them below one by one, giving reasons for why we think studying them from the perspective of SALs is significant for the topic under discussion.

(i) The Status of Syntactic Categories

The literature generally assumes that syntactic categories like nouns, verbs, etc. are primitives of the grammar; they are found in all languages without exception. Hale and Keyser (1993), in their attempt to derive thematic functions from the LRS projected by lexical categories, assume a four-level distinction, Nouns (N), Verbs (V),

Adjectives (A) and Pre/post-positions (P) corresponding to the semantic types of entities, events, states and relations respectively. However, several studies reveal that these categories may not be universal and are not easily isolated from each other even within a given language (see Baker 2003 for detailed discussion).

The same problem persists in some SALs. As Amritavalli (2003) notes, it has long been a contentious issue whether Adjectives constitute a separate category in Kannada and more generally in the Dravidian language family. Additionally, postpositions in Kannada and Malayalam resemble nouns, or even verbs, which lead some to assume that these languages may have only two categories N and V. Amritavalli's contention is that the other two (P and A) are derived categories, possibly emerging from operations on case-markers. To elaborate, during the course of syntactic change, case-markers either transform into a new syntactic category P or get incorporated or absorbed into existing lexical categories – into V (e.g. into *be* to give *have*); or even into N to yield A. If that is true, languages with case markers will not have Ps as primitives much as they will be unable to host the verb *have*. Similar arguments go for As.

For Munda (Austro-Asiatic) too, the noun-verb distinction, if it exists, is very weak. This point has been convincingly made for several North Munda languages like Santhali, Mundari and Ho where nominal and verbal functions can be undertaken by any lexeme of the language (Hoffman 1903; Bodding 1929; Deeney 1975; Neukom 2001). Peterson (2007) makes a similar argument for Kharia by suggesting that the four-level syntactic category distinction should be replaced instead by a two class distinction in the lexicon: open (lexical) morphemes and closed (grammatical morphemes). The implication of his study is that syntactic categories are not universals and hence not primitives.

Since syntactic categories have a positive correlation with the nature of predicates and their argument structures in any given language, it is pertinent that one studies their cross-linguistic variations in detail. These studies can shed light on the nature of the lexicon – on its primitives – as well as any operations (lexical or syntactic) that may underlie the production of categories in languages. If incorporation of case-markers, as Amritavalli suggests, into lexical heads, yields Ps and As, it indicates that syntactic operations, rather than lexical ones, are at play here. For SALs that show similar patterns, detailed expositions of syntactic categories are therefore desirable.

(ii) Verb Classes and Argument Structures

Verb classes and their argument structures in SALs provide another domain to investigate. It has been observed that SALs like Hindi-Urdu have their verb classes derived from each other. Bhatt and Embick (2003) for instance show that this language has two set of verbs – the AA class, where the transitive forms have an overt suffix *-a*, and the NULL-class that is without any overt suffix. There is a single rule of Vowel Simplification (shortening of the vowel) that operates to derive transitives from intransitives in the AA class and intransitives from transitives in the NULL class. But, what is interesting to note is that these two classes cannot be differentiated from each other syntactically or semantically. Additionally, morphology fails to serve as a reliable cue in determining whether roots are at base transitive or intransitive. In other words, arguments from morphology cannot be the bases to decide which forms are derived and which are basic.

Similarly, the diagnostics for the unaccusative/unergative distinction also tend to yield different results in different languages. As is well known, Levin and Rappaport Hovav (1995) argue that a convincing unaccusative diagnostic must test for a syntactic property because unaccusativity is essentially a *syntactic* property, even as it is also semantically predictable. Some of the diagnostics are causative alternation, passivization, use of auxiliary *be*, *ne*-cliticization, incorporation, resultative constructions and the use of perfective participle as reduced relatives. However, for SALs like Hindi-Urdu, Mohanan (1994) has a different set of criteria based on the case of the subject. She divides Hindi-Urdu verb classes into three, independently of transitivity (in given aspectual conditions) – (a) those taking only nominative subjects, (b) those with only ergative subjects and (c) those with either nominative or ergative subjects. She argues that ergativity should not be associated with transitivity as done by Srivastava (1969), McGregor (1972) and Kachru (1980). More recent works (Bhatt 2003; Richa 2011) have however tried to provide syntactic diagnostics for verb class recognition. Some like passivization are common across languages but others like imperfective participles occurring with genitive markers on the agent, ergativity and light verb selectional restrictions are specific to Hindi-Urdu. Richa also contends that the evaluation of the unaccusative diagnostics vis-à-vis Hindi-Urdu verb classes show that most of the verb classes behave as unaccusatives; only agentive manner of motion verbs show unergative behaviour. Some others show variable behavior.

Similar studies have to be undertaken for other SALs, to understand how verbs are grouped together in the language and the nature – syntactic or semantic – of the criteria used for classifying them.

(iii) Causativization

Studies on argument structure also help in understanding the phenomenon of causativization in SALs. As argued by Levin (1993), internally caused verbs are monadic in terms of their lexical semantic representation. These verbs do not participate in the causative alternation and need not be agentive as they are internally caused. In Hindi-Urdu, too, purely internally caused verbs do not form transitives and hence, no causatives are also available for them. This generalization is applicable to other SALs.

Harley (1995, 2009) takes an iterated-vP approach where the causativizing morpheme instantiates a v head introducing the causer as an external argument. This head takes as its complement a second agentive vP which introduces the causee as an external argument in its specifier. Following Kratzer (1996), Pylkkänen (2002, 2008) proposes a CAUSE head that combines with non-causative predicates and introduces a causing event in the causative constructions. CAUSE can either be independent of θ_{EXT} or can be grouped together into a syntactic head, resulting in cross-linguistic variation in the expression of causation. These accounts have been extended to SAL causatives in recent works, albeit with some modifications. Richa (2011) for instance, suggests a VoiceP as an additional eventive layer that introduces the causee argument, which is independent of θ_{EXT} also see Bhatt and Embick (2003). In Manipuri, the causative suffix – *han\-hal* is also evidenced as heading a VoiceP (Richa & Nandaraj 2011). The Kashmiri causative morpheme -*InAv* is however argued to head a CAUSEP (Manetta 2011).

This suggests that SAL causatives may bear special features. These differences and their implications for the analysis of causativization in particular, and for the theory of grammar in general, must therefore be focused on. There are other related interesting typological as well as theoretical issues that demand our attention. For instance, even though it appears that causativization in general adds a new argument to the existing argument structure of the predicate, the status of the added element – i.e. whether it is an argument or an adjunct – remains unclear, with interesting typological variations. Similarly, the nature of the causative morpheme and the kind of eventive structure it introduces, varies from one language to the other and therefore needs to be dealt with in some detail.

(iv) Passives, Middles and De-transitivizing Operations

Passivization is another phenomenon which has received some much-deserved attention in SALs, especially given its differences from widely studied passive structures in English and other western languages. In the Principle & Parameters (P & P) framework (See Chomsky 1982; Jaeggli 1986; Roberts 1987, Baker 1988; Baker, Johnson & Roberts 1989 and others), it was proposed that the English passive suffix -*en* absorbs the accusative Case and external theta-role of the verb, making it necessary for the internal argument to move to the subject (i.e. Spec, IP) position. There were, however, at least two problems posed by this analysis. The first was a lack of clarity as to how the passive participle was to be morphologically and syntactically distinguished from the homophonous active past participle. The second problem arose from the fact that the external theta role was assigned in two different positions in active and passive constructions, leading to a violation of the Uniformity of Theta Assignment Hypothesis/UTAH (Baker 1988).

To solve these problems, Collins (2005) proposes an analysis that combines aspects of both the *Syntactic Structure* and the P & P analysis. He argues that the active past participle suffix and the passive participle suffix are not different. Neither absorbs the external theta role or accusative Case. In his analysis, the participle morpheme *-en* heads a PartP that selects VP and this PartP is the complement of v. He also claims that there is movement of PartP to Spec, VoiceP in passives. Roberts (2008) exploits Chomsky's (2008) proposal of feature inheritance and reformulates Collins's disassociation theory in terms of it. Thus, Roberts claims that because Voice selects v*P, the feature of Voice is inherited by v*in actives, but is withheld by Voice in passives.

With regard to passives in SALs, it is important to highlight their differences from the widely studied passives in English before proposing an alternative analysis. Mahajan (1994) argues that the passive construction in Hindi-Urdu is only passive-like and not actually a passive. He terms it ACTIVE Passive as he claims that the underlying object does not become the surface subject and at the same time, the underlying subject remains an active subject. To prove this, he applies some tests based on anaphor binding, pronominal coreference, control, etc. (mostly based on Keenan 1976); also see Richa (2011).

Recent studies have shown that these features are not unique to Hindi-Urdu, but rather extend to other SALs like Oriya, Malayalam and Kharia as well. Many SALs appear to have ACTIVE Passives that are different from both actives and passives, while languages belonging to the Tibeto-Burman language family seem to avoid them completely (Sahoo 2011, in progress). Typological differences aside, passivization also raises interesting questions such as (a) do detransitivizing operations take place in the lexicon or in the grammar, (b) are suitable predicates listed separately as actives and passives etc.? Similar questions also come up for middles, yet another instance of detransitivized predicates. Studying passives, middles and other detransitivized predicates in SALs will help us understand whether the lexicon is an active ground for such operations or whether we should restrict all such operations to narrow syntax alone.

(v) Case, Agreement, Theta-Role Connections

A different topic, though connected to the lexicon-syntax debate, is the case, agreement and theta-role correlations found in languages. Many of the modern Indo-Aryan languages have ergative (or split-ergative) case systems, where intransitive subjects and transitive objects are marked similarly. This is different from the purely nominative-accusative languages like English, German, etc. where the subjects are consistently marked in direct opposition to the objects. However, ergative marking on subjects and corresponding agreement patterns vary from one SAL to another (Deo & Sharma 2007). In Hindi-Urdu, the perfect subject is morphologically marked with the ergative postpositional clitic *-ne* in all persons and numbers. The language in general disallows verbal agreement with all overtly case-marked DPs, and hence ergative agreement is also not an option here. Nepali on the other hand, has overt case-marking on the subject, but there is no such constraint on agreement with morphologically marked arguments. Gujarati is similar to Hindi-Urdu and Nepali in that it allows subject marking in all three persons, but its distinctive feature is its nominative-ergative case-syncretic forms for first and second person plural subjects. Moreover, it allows object agreement irrespective of whether it is in the nominative or the accusative.

Another important research theme in generative theories has been the determination of the domains in which case and theta-theory apply. A recurrent question has been whether case is parasitic on theta-roles and whether any correlation that one finds between them is decided in the lexicon or emanates from the structural configuration that a DP occupies in a structure. There is no clear consensus on this matter, with some opting for a dissociated approach where the domains for each are kept separate while some others choosing syntax as the determining factor. SALs with their split-case marking systems, varying agreement patterns and visible case-markers can contribute immensely to our understanding of this complex correlation. It has been observed for instance, that the instrumental/ablative case marker *-se* in Hindi-Urdu appears on the agent of inabilitative passives, on the causee argument of the causatives, and with an instrumental adjunct. One could ask whether this can be brushed aside as merely accidental homophony or if we should provide a more principled analysis that explains, rather than just describes the relation between the three. This homophony is found in other SALs too. In Nepali as well as in Manipuri, the ergative and the instrumental markers are phonetically similar. Haryanvi has the same case morpheme for ergative, dative and accusative.

Case and theta-role connections in SALs could therefore provide some interesting insights into the lexicon-syntax debate. Moreover, the agreement connection complicates the process further since agreement is a structural, context-sensitive phenomenon; it takes place in the syntax. How this connection between what could apparently be called a lexical phenomenon (case-theta role relation) and a syntactic one (case-agreement relation) comes about constitutes one of the very important questions for present day theoretical research.

5. The contribution of the present volume

All research papers included in this volume take up one or more of the above mentioned questions and try to answer them with the help of some hitherto unnoticed data from a SAL. The main points of each paper are highlighted below.

Mythili Menon, in her paper 'Property Concepts and the Apparent Lack of Adjectives in Dravidian', takes up the contentious issue of Adjectives in Malayalam again and tries to provide an alternative account for them. She argues that Dravidian lacks an adjective category lexically and also fails to derive one in the syntax. She assumes that the lexicon comprises of uninflected roots, following Marantz (1997), Borer (2005), and these cannot be manipulated in Malayalam to create the adjective category. Instead, Malayalam uses relativization and nominalization to express meaning generally expressed by adjectives in English-type languages. Roots in the language combine with the relative clause marker or the nominalization marker, and are analyzed as primitive property concepts with kind reference.

Saurov Syed's paper 'Adjective-fronting for evidence as focus and topic within the Bangla nominal domain' has two goals. The first is to elaborate on the syntax of adjectives in Bangla and suggest a hierarchy of functional projections where Adjective phrases are manifest as specifiers. The second goal is to show the presence of Focus and Topic phrases within the nominal domain. The author presents evidence from adjective fronting to claim that there is a fixed FocP immediately above the Bangla DP, with one or more TopP placed above FocP. A broad theoretical claim of this paper is that principles of phrase and clause composition are same in all languages. Languages also share functional make-up and the hierarchies of functional projections that dominate VP, AdjP, and NP among others are universal.

R. Amritavalli, in 'Rich Results' presents first-phase event structures of two verbs found in Kannada dative experiencer constructions, namely *bar-* 'come' and *aag-* 'happen, become'. She argues, contrary to Ramchand (2008), that stative verbs may project "rich" results and "poor" processes. The paper also distinguishes the "rich" result phrase from the resultative construction (a diagnostic of unaccusativity) that characterizes accomplishment verbs, adopting Higginbotham's (1999) idea that achievement verbs allow telicity by "classifying events that are themselves already results." This analysis of the dative experiencer construction assimilates it to the double object possessive construction, suggesting that it is limited neither to "psych" verbs nor to South Asian languages. In contrast, English lacks the dative experiencer/possessor construction because it does not tolerate a weak or a poor process verb as Kannada does, assuming that a language impoverished in adjectives needs to designate states by a category (or a combination of categories) other than adjectives. Another difference between these languages is the availability of the verb *have*, and hence of dative case to signal a possessional relation.

In 'Lexical Semantics of Transitivizer light verbs in Telugu', Rahul Balusu examines the semantic contribution made by a certain variety of light verbs in Telugu called transitivizer light verbs. Both verbal and nominal complex predicates involving these light verbs have inceptual meanings, which suggest inception or beginning, continuation or progression, and completion or end-point. Balusu proposes that these meanings are derived directly from the underlying structural representation. The verbal domain, following the First Phase Syntax framework of Ramchand (2008), is decomposed into initP (introducing causation), procP (specifying process) and resP (producing results). Interaction between these three layers gives rise to the inceptual meanings. Balusu also argues against positing the 'Light Verb Constraint' that states that a verb can be used as a light verb only when all its category features Agree with some other verbal element in its complement domain in the grammar, arguing that it is nothing but a stipulation in Ramchand's system. He shows that Telugu light verbs function as transitivizers, and can combine with unaccusative main verbs.

Shiti Malhotra, through her paper 'Ditransitive Structures in Hindi/Urdu' explores two kinds of ditransitive constructions in the language, appearing in *to*-datives and double object constructions in English. Separating the two kinds of ditransitives from each other is difficult in Hindi/Urdu given that they do not display distinct word-orders. Investigating their thematic structures, Malhotra, however, presents evidence to argue that despite apparent similarities, there are two distinct forms corresponding to two distinct sets of ditransitive predicates in the language: "show" type verbs and "send" type-1 and type-2 verbs. These two types of verbs involve two different argument structures, which correspond to the PDC and the DOC constructions in English respectively. The "show" type verbs take an experiencer as their IO and, have a high applicative structure. The "send" type-1 verbs have a possessor as their IO and involve a low applicative structure, whereas the send type-2 verbs take a locative and have a structure similar to PDC. However, some language-specific properties (like obligatory movement of the theme to the outer Spec of vP for Case/Agreement reasons) make this difference between the two verbs less apparent in Hindi/Urdu.

In their paper, 'Is Kashmiri Passive Really a Passive?', Richa Srishti and Shahid Bhat assess Kashmiri passives with an intention to find out if these resemble English-like passives or behave on par with Hindi-Urdu Active-passives. In Kashmiri passives, the internal argument of the transitive verb surfaces as the subject of the sentence with the passive morpheme *-nI* attached to the verb root, followed by a periphrastic auxiliary *yun* 'to come' in perfective form. The agent is optional. Two primary questions with regard to these passives therefore are, (a) are objects actually derived subjects, and (b) are the subjects, given their optionality, adjuncts or arguments of the predicate? Srishti and Bhat use tests based on anaphora binding, pronominal co-reference, control, etc. to show that just like Hindi-Urdu passives, there are no derived subjects in Kashmiri passives. The objects fail to move as high as the subject position. Even more interestingly, the external arguments, though optional, are the real subjects of these constructions, suggesting an interesting divide between English-kind passives and SAL-passives. The broad theoretical claim of this work is that passive voice is universal in languages, though it may manifest differently in different languages.

Pritha Chandra's paper 'Middles in the Syntax' is on Hindi-Urdu middles. It is well-known that some languages have middle-passive overlap while some others mark them differently. This has led some researchers to claim that this cross-linguistic variation can be accounted for by allowing languages to generate their middles either in the lexicon or in the syntax. Chandra presents evidence that Hindi-Urdu middles are morphologically very different from passives and comparatively more restricted. However, the language productively generates different construction types with middle/generic interpretations. Chandra then presents problems with the two-modular approach and proposes a syntactic analysis for all middles. Her main contention is that while Hindi-Urdu chooses a middle non-active voice head that fails to project a higher aspectual head hosting an external argument, other languages like Italian and Serbo-Croatian choose the same non-active voice for both passives and middles. The truncated structure in Hindi-Urdu middles makes them different from passives, in both morphological form and syntactic behavior.

Richa Srishti's paper 'Not so High: The Case of Causee in South Asian Languages (Hindi, Kashmiri, Punjabi and Manipuri)' looks at the case marker on causees in causatives that are homophonous with an instrumental/ablative adjunct. Srishti questions whether this is a case of accidental homophony or whether there are underlying similarities between the two. Her paper argues that the causee is an argument that is merged to the Voice head as its specifier and is valued with structural case. However, this position, though outside vP, is not high enough to warrant subjecthood-status to these arguments. Srishti further claims that in causative Voice, the head withholds its features from v; the verbal head is phi-incomplete. Voice-v feature inheritance, for her, is comparable to C–T feature inheritance. In cases where v appears to be the phase head, it must be the case that Voice has transferred the relevant features to v. This proposal thus lends support to Robert's (2008) claim that Voice is uniformly present in all constructions, quite unlike Collin's (2005) claim that it is present only in passives.

The paper 'Agreement and Verb Types in Kutchi Gujarati', by Patrick Grosz and Pritty Patel-Grosz studies the phi-agreement system with transitive and psych predicates and modal auxiliaries. Their main contention is that Kutchi Gujarati has two agreement probes, with T hosting the higher (number/person) probe and v/Asp hosting the lower (gender/number) probe. This bifurcation of the probes leads to the phenomenon of split-ergative agreement in canonical transitive constructions, and can also explain agreement patterns with other verb types.

Emily Manetta's paper 'Markedness and Syncretism in Kashmiri Differential Argument Encoding' deals with differential argument encoding (DAE) in Kashmiri, in which the case-marking of objects in non-perfective aspects is dependent on a person-hierarchy, with a further interesting correlation with the clitic system of the language. Following Aissen (1999, 2003) among others, Manetta contends that DAE be considered a phenomenon of the morphology-syntax interface that results through a combination of underspecification of vocabulary items and impoverishment operations. She suggests that Kashmiri verbal marking requires us to consider Kashmiri DAE as a non-zero/non-zero alternation, and the underspecification of clitic morphemes allows us to understand an otherwise mysterious set of clitic syncretism, including the overlap in the marking of ergative subjects and bare (accusative) objects. This paper further suggests that the intricacies of the highly complex Kashmiri case/cliticization system (and presumably the ways in which it contrasts with those of related languages, e.g. Poguli) can be best understood as operating in optimality-theoretic competitions in the morphological component that serve to reduce the syntactic input to morphological realization.

6. Conclusion

The chapters in this collection bring out many interesting and hitherto unnoticed features of SALs that shed light on the lexicon-syntax interface. The first is that categories like adjectives in Dravidian languages may not be primitives of the grammar; they are neither lexically nor syntactically derived in these languages. Adjectival meanings are instead expressed via syntactic mechanisms like nominalization and relativization. On the other hand, certain Indo-Aryan languages like Bangla have elaborate nominal and adjectival phrases with functional layers at par with those found with v, T and C.

Dravidian languages also present intriguing cases of verb semantics, which can be understood only when their intricate structural representations are probed into. First phase syntactic frameworks seem to be extremely fruitful in bringing out these verbal idiosyncrasies.

Verb variations also show up in the ditransitive domain in Hindi-Urdu. The argument structures of predicates determine whether a PDC or a DOC construction is generated in the language. These two constructions are therefore not derivationally linked, contrary to what has been observed for other languages.

As far as arity-changing operations like passives and middles are concerned, data from SALs highlight both similarities and differences with non-SAL languages. Passives are shown to manifest as Active Passives while hosting the same (universal) passive head as in other languages. Middles, on the other hand, are demonstrated to generate in the syntax, and rely on the kind of non-active voice head selected by any given language.

Causatives present another puzzling case in SALs like Hindi-Urdu, where the argument structure of the involved predicates are shown to host an additional argument, that is otherwise marked as an instrumental DP. There is also evidence to suggest that these arguments dislocate from their original positions.

Finally, given SALs' intricate case and agreement systems, we may further our understanding of the domain in which each applies by looking closely at their interactions in these languages. Split agreement systems are shown to emerge in certain languages like Kutchi Gujarati from differences in (T and v) probes, an analysis that also nicely extends to non-transitive predicates and modal auxiliaries. Additionally, we learn that case and agreement syncretism need not be results of pure syntactic operations. Rather optimality theoretic computations at the morphology-syntax interface can also explain how these systems work in different languages.

References

Abraham, Werner & Leisiö, Larisa (eds). 2006. *Passivization and Typology. Form and Function* [Typological Studies in Languages 68]. Amsterdam: John Benjamins.

Aissen, Judith. 1999. Markedness and subject choice in optimality theory. *Natural Language and Linguistic Theory* 17: 673–711.

Aissen, Judith. 2003. Differential object marking: Iconicity vs. economy. *Natural Language and Linguistic Theory* 21: 435–483.

Amritavalli, Raghavachari. 2003. Syntactic categories and lexical argument structure. *Language in India* 3(5 May).

Bach, Emond. 1982. Purpose clauses and control. In *The Nature of Syntactic Representation*, P. Jacobson & G. K. Pullum (eds), 35–57. Reidel: Dordrecht.

Baker, Mark C. 1988. *Incorporation: A Theory of Grammatical Function Changing.* Chicago: University of Chicago Press.

Baker, Mark. C. 1996. On the structural position of themes and goals. In *Phrase Structure and the Lexicon*, J. Rooryck & L. Zaring (eds), 7–34. Dordrecht: Kluwer.

Baker, Mark C. 2003. *Lexical Categories: Verbs, Nouns, and Adjectives.* [Cambridge Studies in Linguistics 102]. Cambridge: Cambridge University Press.

Baker, Mark C., Johnson, Kyle & Roberts, Ian. 1989. Passive arguments raised. *Linguistic Inquiry* 20: 219–251.

Bhatt, Rajesh. 2003. Topics in the syntax of the modern indo-aryan languages. Causativization. http://web.mit.edu/rbhatt/www/24.956

Bhatt, Rajesh & Embick, David. 2003. Causative derivations in Hindi. http://people.umass.edu/bhatt/papers/bhatt-embick-caus.pdf (2003)

Bodding, Paul O. 1929/1952. *A Santal Grammar for the Beginners.* Benagaria: Santal Mission of the Northern Churches.

Borer, Hagit. 2005. *Structuring Sense II: The Normal Course of Events.* Oxford; New York: Oxford University Press.

Carlson, Greg N. 1984. Thematic roles and their role in semantic interpretation. *Linguistics* 22(3): 259–279.

Chomsky, Noam. 1965. *Aspects of the Theory of Syntax.* Cambridge MA: MIT Press.

Chomsky, Noam. 1982. *Some Concepts and Consequences of the Theory of Government and Binding.* Cambridge, Mass: MIT Press.

Chomsky, Noam. 1995. *The Minimalist Program*. Cambridge MA: MIT Press.

Chomsky, Noam. 2001. Derivation by phase. *MIT Working Papers in Linguistics*. Cambridge, Mass.: MIT Press.

Chomsky, Noam. 2008. On phases. In *Foundational Issues in Linguistic Theory. Essays in Honor of Jean-Roger Vergnaud*, R. Freidin, C. P. Otero & M. L. Zubizarreta (eds), 133–166. Cambridge: MIT Press.

Clark, Eve V. & Clark, Herbert H. 1979. When nouns surface as verbs. *Language* 55: 767–811.

Collins, Chris. 2005. A smuggling approach to the passive in English. *Syntax* 8(2): 81–120.

Deeney, John. J. 1975. *Ho Grammar and Vocabulary*. Chaibasa: Xavier Ho Publications.

Deo, Ashwini & Sharma, Devyani. 2007. Typological variation in the ergative morphology of Indo-Aryan Languages. *Linguistic Typology* 10(3): 369–418.

Di Sciullo, Anna M. & Williams, Edwin. 1987. *On the Definition of Word*. Cambridge, Mass.: The MIT Press.

Emonds, Joseph E. 1991. Subcategorization and syntax-based theta-role assignment. *Natural Language and Linguistic Theory* 9: 369–429.

Grimshaw, Jane. 1979. Complement selection and the lexicon. *Linguistic Inquiry* 10: 279–326.

Hale, Kenneth & Keyser, Samuel J. 1993. On argument structure and the lexical expression of syntactic relations. In *The View from Building*, 20. *Essays in Linguistics in Honor of Sylvain Bromberger*, K. Hale & S. J. Keyser (eds), 53–109. Cambridge, Mass.: MIT Press.

Halle, Morris & Marantz, Alec. 1993. Distributed morphology and the pieces of inflection. In *The View from Building*, 20. *Essays in Linguistics in Honor of Sylvain Bromberger*, K. Hale & S. J. Keyser (eds), 111–176. Cambridge, Mass.: MIT Press.

Halle, Morris & Marantz, Alec. 1994. Some key features of distributed morphology. In *Papers on Phonology and Morphology* [MIT Working Papers in Linguistics 21], A. Carnie, H. Harley & T. Bures (eds), 275–288. Cambridge: MIT Press.

Harley, Heidi. 1995. *Sase* bizarre: The structure of Japanese causatives. In *Proceedings of the Canadian Linguistic Society Meeting*, P. Koskinen (ed.), 221–232. Toronto: Toronto Working Papers in Linguistics.

Harley, Heidi. 2009. Compounding in distributive morphology. In *Oxford Handbook of Compounding*. Rochelle Lieber & Pavol Stekauer (eds), 129–144. Oxford: Oxford University Press.

Harley, Heidi. 2011. A minimalist approach to argument structure. In *The Oxford Handbook of Linguistic Minimalism*, C. Boeckx (ed.), 427–448. Oxford: Oxford University Press.

Higginbotham, James. 1999. Accomplishments. In *Proceedings of the Nanzan GLOW, the Second GLOW Meeting in Asia*, Mamoru Saito et al. (eds), 131–139. Nagoya, Japan: Nanzan University.

Heim, Irene & Kratzer, Angelika. 1998. *Semantics in Generative Grammar*. Oxford: Blackwell.

Hoffmann, Johann. 1903. *Mundari Grammar.* Calcutta: Bengal Secretariat Press.

Jackendoff, Ray. 1972. *Semantic Interpretation in Generative Grammar.* Cambridge, MA: MIT Press.

Jaeggli, Osvaldo. A. 1986. Passives. *Linguistic Inquiry* 17: 587–622.

Kachru, Yamuna. 1980. *Aspects of Hindi-grammar.* New Delhi: Manohar Publications.

Keenan, Edward. 1976. Towards a universal definition of subject. In *Subject and topic*, C. N. Li (ed.), 303–333. New York: Academic Press.

Kratzer, Angelika. 1996. Severing the external argument from its verb. In *Phrase Structure and the Lexicon*, Johann Rooryck & Laurie Zaring (eds), 109–137. Kluwer Dordrecht: Academic Publishers.

Ladusaw, William. A. & Dowty, David. R. 1988. Towards a nongrammatical account of thematic role. *Syntax and Semantics* 21: 61–73. Academic Press.

Levin, Beth. 1993. *English Verb Classes and Alternations.* Chicago: University of Chicago Press.
Levin, Beth & Rappaport Hovav, Malka. 1995. *Unaccusativity at the Syntax-Semantics Interface.* Cambridge. Mass: MIT Press.
Mahajan, Anoop. 1994. Active passives. In *Proceedings of the Thirteenth West Coast Conference on Formal Linguistics*, R. Aronovich, W. Byrne, S. Preuss & M. Senturia (eds). Stanford University: CSLI Publications.
Manetta, Emily. 2011. *Peripheries in Kashmiri and Hindi-Urdu.* The Netherlands: John Benjamins.
Marantz, Alec. 1997. No escape from syntax: Don't try morphological analysis in the privacy of your own lexicon. In *Proceedings of the 21st Annual Penn Linguistics Colloquium* [Penn Working Papers in Linguistics 4:2], A. Dimitriadis et al. (eds), 201–225.
Martin, Roger & Uriagereka, Juan. 2000. Some possible foundations of the minimalist program. In *Step by Step: Essays in Minimalist Syntax in Honor of Howard Lasnik*, R. Martin, D. Michaels & J. Uriagereka (eds), 1–29. Cambridge: MIT Press.
McGregor, R. S. 1972. *Outline of Hindi Grammar.* Oxford: Clarendon Press, Gloucestershire Ltd.
Mohanan, Tara. 1994. *Argument Structure in Hindi.* Stanford: CSLI Publications.
Neukom, Lukas. 2001. *Santali.* München: LINCOM Europa.
Nishigauchi, Taisuke. 1984. Control and the thematic domain. *Language* 60: 215–250.
Peterson, John. 2007. Languages without nouns and verbs? An alternative to lexical classes in Kharia. In *Old and New Perspectives on South Asian Languages. Grammar and Semantics*, Colin P. Masica (ed.), 274–303. Delhi: Motilal Banarsidass.
Pietroski. Paul. 2011. Minimal semantic instructions. In *The Oxford Handbook on Linguistic Minimalism*, C. Boeckx (ed.), 472–498. Oxford: Oxford University Press.
Pylkkänen, Liina. 2002. Introducing Arguments. Doctoral Dissertation, Massachusetts Institute of Technology.
Pylkkänen, Liina. 2008. *Introducing Arguments.* Cambridge MA: MIT Press.
Ramchand, Gillian. 2008. *Verb Meaning and the Lexicon: A First Phase Syntax.* Cambridge: CUP.
Ramchand, Gillian. 2011. Minimalist semantics. In *The Oxford Handbook of Linguistic Minimalism*, C. Boeckx (ed.), 449–471. Oxford: Oxford University Press.
Reinhart, Tanya. 1996. Syntactic effects of lexical operations: Reflexives and unaccusatives. *UiL-OTS Working Papers.* Utrecht: University of Utrecht.
Reinhart, Tanya. 2002. The theta system – An overview. In *Theoretical Linguistics* 28, W. Sternfeld (ed.), 229–290. Berlin: Mouton.
Reinhart, Tanya & Siloni, Tal. 2003. Thematic arity operations and parametric variations. *OTS Working Papers in Linguistics.* University of Utrecht.
Reinhart, Tanya & Siloni, Tal. 2005. The lexicon-syntax parameter: Reflexivization and other arity operations. *Linguistic Inquiry* 36: 389–437.
Reuland, Eric J., Bhattacharya, Tanmoy & Spathas, Giorgos. 2007. *Argument Structure.* Amsterdam: John Benjamins.
Richa. 2011. *Hindi Verb Classes and their Argument Structure Alternations.* Newcastle Upon Tyne: Cambridge Scholars Publishing.
Richa & Nandaraj, Amom. 2011. *The Status of Causee in Manipuri and Hindi.* Mysore: Central Institute of Indian Languages.
Roberts, Ian. 1987. *The Representation of Implicit and Dethematized Subjects.* Foris: Dordrecht.
Roberts, Ian. 2008. *Smuggling, Affectness and Argument Structure Alternation.* University of Cambridge.
Sahoo, Anindita. 2011. Oriya passives with ditransitives. In *Papers from Lancaster University Postgraduate Conference in Linguistics and Language Teaching 2010*, K. Kaufhold, S. McCulloch & A. Tominc (eds), 173–200. UK: Lancaster University.

Sahoo, Anindita. in progress. Passives in Some South Asian languages: A Comparative Study. PhD Dissertation, Indian Institute of Technology Delhi.

Selkirk, Elizabeth O. 1982. *The Syntax of Words* [Linguistic Inquiry Monograph 7]. Cambridge, Mass: The MIT Press.

Srivastava, Vishwajit N. 1969. A Structural Study of Hindi Phrases. PhD Dissertation, Agra University.

Travis, Lisa. 1994. Event phrase structure and a theory of functional categories. In *Proceedings of the 1994 Annual Conference of Canadian Linguistics Society*, P. Koskinen (ed.), 559–570.

Williams, Edwin. 1981. On the notions of "lexically related" and "head of a word". *Liinguistic Inquriy* 12.2: 245–274.

Zubizarreta, Maria L. 1989. *Levels of Representation in the Lexicon and in the Syntax*. Amsterdam: John Benjamins.

Property concepts and the apparent lack of adjectives in Dravidian*

Mythili Menon
University of Southern California

Dravidian lacks an adjective category lexically and neither does it derive one in the syntax. The primary data comes from Malayalam where unlike what previous accounts suggest (Bhat 1994; Amritavalli & Jayaseelan 2003; Jayaseelan 2007), the lexicon comprises of uninflected primitive roots (Marantz 1997; Borer 2003). These roots are property concept roots and they combine with null verbal and nominal heads to derive structures. The syntax derives structures, which in English-type languages would be expressed with an adjective. Relativization and nominalization are the two routes to arrive at meanings expressed by adjectives in other languages.

Keywords: adjective; Dravidian; relativization; nominalization; feature sharing

1. Introduction

One of the tasks of generative theory over the years has been to find and explain language universals. One such apparent universal is the notion of primitive lexical categories, namely Noun (N), Verb (V), Adjective (A) and Preposition (P) (Chomsky 1970). It is often believed that every language has words belonging to these four classes, and they are listed and categorized as such in the lexicon. In early generative grammar, these four categories were characterized in terms of binary distinctions of N and V features. An adjective in this view is [+N, +V]. Currently the most prominent contender for the Universalist approach to lexical categories is probably Baker (2003, 2005) who argues that at least N, V, and A, are universal, although A can be quite varied in realization.

* I would like to thank Roumyana Pancheva, Andrew Simpson, Hajime Hoji, Audrey Li, Akira Watanabe, Uli Sauerland and the audience at Glow-in-Asia IX, Japan for valuable discussions, and three anonymous reviewers for their extensive comments and suggestions. Any errors are solely mine.

Recently this Universalist view has been challenged from data pertaining to variations found cross-linguistically across A and P. Particularly, in the Dravidian literature the question of whether the language family indeed has a separate lexical category of adjectives has remained controversial (see e.g. Zvelebil (1990: 27)). More recently from a functional perspective, Bhat (1994) has argued that Dravidian does lexicalize the adjectival category. On the contrary, Amritavalli and Jayaseelan (2003), Jayaseelan (2007) argue in a Lexical Relational Structure (LRS) approach (Hale & Keyser 1993) for an incorporation account of adjectives. For them universally, adjectives are created with the incorporation of a noun into a preposition or a Case head.[1] Thus, the Dravidian literature is still divided amongst the view as to whether there is a separate lexical category for adjective.

This paper contributes to this debate by arguing with data from Malayalam that an adjective category cannot be universal since there is no independent class of adjectives in Malayalam. More specifically, adjectives are not found in the lexicon nor are they created in syntax. An adjectival-like[2] construction can be syntactically created for the purpose of attributive modification and predication. With the help of null verbal and nominal heads, a relativization structure is created for attributive modification, and a nominalization structure is created in the case of predication. Crucially, the lexicon comprises only of primitive property concept roots (as in a distributed morphology framework).

The paper is organized as follows. In the next section I will introduce the basic paradigm concentrating on data from Malayalam and other related Dravidian languages and then look at the status of adjectives in Korean, Japanese, and some Bantu languages. In § 3.0, I will sketch my analysis regarding the semantics and the syntactic representations. In § 4.0, I conclude.

2. Missing adjectives in Malayalam and other languages

In this section, I will review the two classes of property concept roots in Malayalam by considering their morphology and their different syntactic distributions. On the basis of this, I will argue that Malayalam does not lexicalize an adjective neither does it derive an adjectival category in the syntax.

---

1. See Amritavalli (2008) for a detailed illustrative exposition of this account.

2. Any use of the term adjective refers to the lexical category of adjectives as found in English-type languages. I am not committed to whether the lexical A comes out of the lexicon as an A or whether it is a root combining with a lexically specified *a* head.

2.1 The basic paradigm in Malayalam

There are two classes of roots in Malayalam that look adjectival, by which I mean they participate in positions in which English would have an adjective – Class1 or Relativizing roots and Class2 or Nominalizing roots. A brief look into the history of these roots suggests that Class1 roots have a verbal origin (See Jayaseelan 2007) and they could be deverbal (as suggested in Anandan 1985). Class2 roots are borrowed roots, mostly from Sanskrit. A representative list is given in (1) and (2).

(1) **Class 1** (*-a* ending relativized roots)
*valiy**a*** big, *ceriy**a*** small, *puthiy**a*** new, *nall**a*** good, *pacc**a*** green,
*velutt**a*** white, *maṇṇ**a*** yellow, *pazhay**a*** old

(2) **Class 2** (*-am* ending nominalized roots)
*santosh**am*** happiness, *sankat**am*** sadness, *prayas**am*** difficulty,
*pokk**am*** tallness, *bedh**am*** better, *madhur**am*** sweetness

Probing into the morphological make up of Class 1 forms gives the indication that the forms based on Class1 roots all end in *-a* which is also the Proto-Dravidian relative clause marker derived from a shortening of the distal determiner *aa* 'that'.

(3) a. pazhay-**a** 'that which is old' Tamil, Malayalam
b. p–**a** 'that which is old' Kodagu, Todi
c. par-**a** 'that which is old' Tulu
d. hos-**a** 'that which is new' Kannada, Tulu
e. pedd-**a** 'that which is great' Telugu

The idea that the forms found in the Class1 category are reduced relative clauses was first suggested by Anandan (1985). On the other hand, Class2 roots are borrowed mostly from Sanskrit.[3] Malayalam has a phonological restriction on the coda position of a syllable. The only sounds that can appear in this position are vowels and the bilabial nasal /m/ and the alveolar nasal /n/.[4] Notice that the Sanskrit roots in Class2, illustrated in (2) mostly end in an obstruent before the suffixation of the *-am* marker. This phonological coda restriction entails that the nominal morpheme *-am* is employed to turn the Class2 roots into something more native-like. Malayalam also has a nominalizer *atə* which is used to nominalize only clauses or verbal elements as we will see below.

3. Among the Dravidian languages, Malayalam borrowed the most from Sanskrit.

4. Even though Malayalam has the maximum number of nasals in any Indian language, only these two nasals can occur in the coda position.

Class1 roots can undergo nominalization with the nominalizing morpheme *atə* whereas Class2 roots cannot, since they are already nominals; neither can they be relativized using the *-a* marker.

(4) a. *valiy-**atə**, ceriy-**atə***
big-NOML, small-NOML

b. **valiya-**am**, *ceriya-**am***
big-NOML, small-NOML

c. **santosh**am-a**, *sankat**am-a***
happiness-REL, sadness-REL

d. **santosh**am-atə**, *sankat**am-atə***
happiness-NOML, sadness-NOML

The data illustrated so far suggests that Class 2 roots end up as nominals whereas Class 1 roots behave similar to reduced relative clauses. At least from morphology, we have no evidence suggesting that indeed words formed from Class 1 and Class 2 roots behave similar to adjectives. In the next section, I will look at the syntactic distribution of the Class 1 roots and Class 2 roots looking specifically at the attributive and the predicative positions.

2.1.1 *Distribution of Class1 and Class2 roots*

Class1 and the Class2 roots differ in their syntactic behavior. Relativized Class1 roots can appear in attributive positions whereas Class2 roots can appear in attributive positions only with the mediation of a non-finite copula (*uLL*, the verb 'to exist') and the relative marker *-a*.

(5) a. *valiy**a** kutti* [Class1]
big child
'Big child' (Lit: child being big)

b. *santosh**am** uLLa kutti* [Class2]
happy COP-REL child
'Happy child'(Lit: child (to whom) there being happiness)

This strategy is also found in other languages such as Wolof as reported by McLaughlin (2004). The relative clause marker in Wolof is /Cu/ where C is a noun class marker which shows concord with the noun. In the particular example in (6), the relative clause marker is /bu/.

(6) a. *xale bu rafet* **Wolof**
child REL pretty
'A pretty child'

b. *xale bu xam*
child REL know
'A child who knows'

Slave and Ika (belonging to the Athapaskan language family) also admit adjectives in the attributive position only if there is an obligatory copula present on the adjective. Examples are from Baker (2003).

(7) a. *yenene* *(be-gho)* *sho* *hili* **Slave**
woman 3-of proud/happy 3-is
'The woman is happy/proud (of him/her).'

b. *aná?nuga* [*awʌn?* *(*kawa*)] *guákʌ-ža* **Ika**
animal big seem kill-MED
'It kills big animals.'

The use of the non-finite copula in Malayalam (*uLL*) ties in with the fact that relative clauses in Malayalam are non-finite (See Jayaseelan 2011 for a detailed analysis). A question begs itself at this point, why can't the relative clause marker attach directly to the borrowed roots, i.e. why doesn't the language allow words as in (8).

(8) a. *pokk-**a** 'tall'
b. *santosh-**a** 'happiness'[5]

If both Class1 and Class2 roots are identical then what makes the relative clause marker attach only to certain roots? Class2 roots as we saw before are borrowed roots. Moreover there is no prohibition in a word ending in a vowel (as Class1 illustrates). The answer lies in the patterns exhibited by the two classes of roots. The morphology module admits both the relativization and nominalization as routes to realizing an adjectival meaning. The Class1 roots are deverbal, the Class2 roots are not deverbal. The relative clause marker *-a* is always looking for a verbal element. Class2 roots are borrowed and upon borrowing they have to go through the nominal morphology stage prior to the *-a* suffixation. In a morphological parser this can be achieved by ranking the relativization module after the nominalization module. Informally put,

i. If a √ is native, then skip the nominalization and attach the *-a* marker.
ii. If a √ is borrowed, then first nominalize with the *-am* marker.

5. Interestingly, this form is attested only in one usage- the 'Happy birthday' equivalent in Malayalam which is:

(i) *santoshajanmadinam* *kutti-kkə*
happy born day child-DAT
'Happy birthday to the child'

Presumably, this is because 'santoshajanmadinam' is a compound and the /m/ in the coda of 'santosham' is deleted.

The fact that the relative clause marker *-a* is always looking for a verbal element is exemplified in the attributive position of the Class2 adjective, they always need the non-finite copula as support for the *-a* attachment. *-a* attaches to verbs and never to nouns.

(9) a. [*njaan* ___ *kaNT-***a**] *kutti*
I see-REL child
'The child that I saw'

b. [[*njaan* ___ *kaNT-u ennə*] *ningal parayunn-***a**] *kutti*
I see-PAST COMP you say-REL child
'The child that you say that I saw'

In English, the relativizers move from an argument position to a non-argument position. The Malayalam *-a* is different in that respect. The behavior of *-a* is different from the English 'who' in that *-a* does not open up any argument positions. *-a* doesn't contribute anything semantically, since the root has already been changed into an $\langle e,t \rangle$ with a null verbal head in the case of Class1 and by the overt non-finite copula in Class2.

Turning to the predicative position, we find that neither Class1 nor Class2 roots can appear as predicative modifiers unless they are nominalized. Class1 roots appear in relative clauses, which now modify a pronominal. This is seen by the number and gender marking on the relativized Class1 root that combines with the so-called equative copula, whereas Class2 roots can appear as the complement of an existential copula triggering the appearance of dative case on the subject/experiencer.

(10) a. *avan nalla-***van** *aaNə* [Class1]
he good-M.SG EQ
'He is good' (Lit: he is one being good)

b. *avaL nalla-***vaL** *aaNə*
she good-F.SG EQ
'She is good' (Lit: she is one being good)

(11) a. *avan-ə* ***pokkam*** *uNTə* [Class2]
he-DAT tall EX
'He is tall' (Lit: to him there is tallness)

b. *kutti-***kkə** ***dukham*** *uNTə*
child-DAT sad EX
'The child is sad' (Lit: to the child there is sadness)

Class1 and Class2 appear in predicative positions with different copulas. While Class1 uses the equative copula *aaNə*, Class2 uses the existential copula *uNTə*. In Class1 roots, there is the appearance of the nominalization morphemes adhering to the number and gender features of the subject and the subject appears in nominative case. Class2 are nominals to begin with, hence, there is no reappearance of the nominal markers found in (10). The strategy that is at use here is what I call the 'possessive strategy'. The dative case in (11) exemplifies this overtly. The meaning is akin to saying the subject 'he' possesses 'tallness' or 'height'. A summary of the different morphological processes undergone by the Class1 and Class2 roots are illustrated below.

Table 1. Morphosyntactic combinations possible with Class 1 and Class 2

(12)	CLASS1: NATIVE ROOTS	CLASS2: BORROWED ROOTS
a. Nominalization	$\sqrt{1}$ + *atə*$_{\text{noml}}$	$\sqrt{2}$ + *am*
b. Attributive	$\sqrt{1}$ + *a*	$\sqrt{2}$ + *am* EX$_{\text{non-finite}}$ + *a*
c. Predicate	$\sqrt{1}$ + *a* + AGREQ	$\sqrt{2}$ + *am* EX; $\sqrt{2}$ + *am* EX$_{\text{non-finite}}$ + *a* +AGREQ

2.2 Missing predicative adjectives in Dravidian

The fact that adjectives do not exist as a separate lexical class is not just an anomaly of Malayalam, but it is true of most other Dravidian languages as well. Although we know of many languages which do not allow adjectives in attributive position (such as Korean, Japanese a.o), not many languages disallow adjectives in the predicative position as well. The starting empirical observation in this paper is that Dravidian does not admit adjectives in the attributive position nor in the predicative position. I include the four major Dravidian languages- Telugu, Tamil, Kannada, and Malayalam and also other lesser-known Dravidian languages. I will divide Dravidian into two sets:

A. South Dravidian – Tamil, Malayalam, Kannada, Tulu
B. South-Central Dravidian – Telugu, Gondi, Kui, Kuvi

In South Dravidian, on their own adjective-like roots cannot occur attributively or predicatively (data from Krishnamurthi 2003). In the attributive position for Tamil, Kannada there is an obligatory particle suggesting these are actually participial clauses. In Malayalam, either there is a copula used to host the relative clause marker or the adjective has to be a participial clause.

Attributive:

(13) a. *azhak-*(aNa) poNNu* **Tamil**
beauty-PART woman
'The woman who has beauty'

b. *ganam *(uLL-a) kaNNati* **Tamil**
heavy COP-REL mirror
'The mirror that has heaviness'

c. *bhaŋŋi *(uLL-a) sthri* **Malayalam**
beauty COP-REL woman
'The woman who has beauty'

d. *sundaram-*(aaya) rathri-kaL* **Malayalam**
beauty-PART night-PL
'The nights that are beautiful'

In the predicative position, the adjective appears with a nominalizing morpheme which is actually dependent on the Person Number and Gender features (PNG) of the subject.

Predicative:

(14) a. *avan periy-a-van* **Tamil**
he big-REL-AGR
'He is a big man'

b. *avan viTu peri-cu* **Tamil**
he house big-AGR
'His house is big'

c. *kutti nall-a-van aaNə* **Malayalam**
boy good-REL-AGR COP
'The boy is a good one'

d. *avanu cikk-a-vanu* **Kannada**
he small-REL-AGR
'He is a small man'

In South-Central Dravidian, adjectives cannot appear attributively without the obligatory presence of a particle similar to that used in South-Dravidian but they can appear predicatively without being nominalized.[6] In this paper, I will leave aside a detailed discussion of South-Central Dravidian, concentrating only on South-Dravidian, specifically Malayalam.

6. In this paper, I will not deal with the semantics of the adjectival constructions in South-Central Dravidian since adjectives appear in the predicative position without an overt nominal marker, and (16a) is not grammatical without the degree modifier 'cala'. This suggests a primary difference between the extent of 'tallness' in terms of scales in South-Central Dravidian and South Dravidian.

Attributive:

(15) a. *andam-*(ayna) pilla* **Telugu**
beauty-PART girl
'A girl who has beauty'

b. *kas-*(ta) eer* **Gondi**
hot-PART water
'Water that is hot'

Predicative:

(16) a. *atanu cala podugu* **Telugu**
he a lot tall
'He is quite tall'

b. *negi-k-a* **Gondi**
good-1SG-COP
'I am a good person'

Similar to South-Dravidian, there are other languages which also do not allow adjectives to appear in attributive position. Some of the well-known languages are Japanese, Korean, Slave, Ika, and other Bantu languages belong to this category. In Japanese, which we turn to presently, the status of adjectives is as controversial as it is in the Dravidian literature.

2.3 Japanese adjectives

There are two kinds of adjectives discussed in the literature. The first one is called the true adjective (Miyagawa 1987; Murasagi 1990) and in Chomsky's (1970) terms is categorized as [+N, +V]. The other category comprises of the "verbal adjective" which is categorized as +V ([±N, +V]).

(17) **True Adjective** **Verbal Adjective**
a. Kirei 'beautiful' b. Utsukushi 'beautiful'

It is often assumed that the adjectives belonging to (17a) can appear as attributive modifiers without the help of any additional morphology. Verbal adjectives, on the other hand, can appear only with the help of a copula in the attributive position.

(18) *utsukushi-*(i) onna* **Japanese**
beautiful-PRES woman

Baker (2003) notes that the presence of the copular element makes (18) a relative clause structure and *-i* does not signal an attributive modifier. However, he wishes to maintain the view that (17b) type verbal adjectives in fact behave like attributive modifiers and are not similar to the characteristic functions of verbs. The diagnostics include resultative secondary predications (RSPs), the complement position of a degree word such as 'too', 'as', and unaccusativity predicates. In English, only adjectives can appear in RSPs. Nouns and verbs are unable to do so.

(19) a. I beat the metal flat (AP)
b. *I beat the metal broke (VP)
c. *I beat the metal (a) sword (NP)

Utsukushi-type adjectives as in (18) can appear in RSPs suggesting they are adjective-like in their behavior and unlike verbs in that sense (Ohkado 1991; Washio 1997).

(20) a. *Taroo-ga kami-o mizika-ku kit-ta.*
Taro-NOM hair-ACC short-AFF cut-PST
'Taro cut the hair short.'

b. #*Taroo-ga kami-o ochi(-te) kit-ta*
Taro-NOM hair-ACC fall-AFF cut-PAST
'Taro cut the hair so that it fell.'

In English, the complement position of dedicated degree words such as 'too' and 'as' necessarily has to be occupied by an adjective. Similarly, Utsukushi-type adjectives can appear in the complement position of a degree word suggesting their behavior is unlike that of verbs or nouns.

(21) a. Mary is *too* smart (to make such a mistake).
b. *Mary is *too* (a) genius (to make such a mistake).

(22) a. *Hanako-ga totemo utsukusi-i.* (A)
Hanako-NOM very beautiful-PRES.
'Hanako is very beautiful.'

b. **Hanako-ga totemo sensei-da.* (N)
Hanako-NOM very teacher-COP
'Hanako is very (much a) teacher.'

c. **Hanako-ga totemo okasi-o tabe-ru.* (V)
Hanako-NOM very sweets-ACC eat-PRES
'Hanako very (much) eats sweets.'

A point however which he does not make is the fact that even (17a) needs the presence of a particle (in traditional grammar this could be a copula)[7] to obligatorily be present in order for the adjective to attributively modify a noun. Thus, for our purposes it is important to note that without the mediation of an extra particle, attributive modification is not possible for either type of adjective in Japanese.

7. Hajime Hoji p.c.

(23) *kirei-*(na) onna* **Japanese**
beautiful-PRT woman
'Beautiful woman'

Similar to the claims for Japanese, Korean too admits only a relative clause structure in the attributive position (Kim 2002). Traditionally, however, Korean has been analyzed as having adjectives but as seen in (24) the adjective 'yeppu' is realized as a participial form and the relative clause marker 'ten' attaches to the entire constituent.

(24) *Ce [e1 yeppu-ess]-ten1 yeca* **Korean**
that [pretty-PRT]-REL woman
'that woman who used to be/was pretty'

Returning to Dravidian, among the Dravidian languages Malayalam is the only language which does not have overt verbal agreement. This is particularly relevant to the theory put forward by Baker (2003, 2005) to account for why adjectives cannot appear in the attributive position in some languages. Baker (2003) appeals to phi-feature agreement. Consider the Romance sentences below where the nominal modifiers show agreement with phi-features (number, gender) and case:

(25) a. *este libro; estas mesas* (Demonstratives, **Spanish**)
this(M.SG) book(M.SG); these(F.PL) tables(F.PL)

b. *el libro rojo; las*
the(M.SG) book(M.SG) red(M.SG); the(F.PL)
mesas rojas (Adjectives)
tables(F.PL) red(F.PL)

Baker (2003) accounts for the lack of attributive adjectives in Japanese-type languages[8] by assuming that Romance languages have phi-feature agreement but not Japanese-type languages, which he states in a formal statement, reproduced below (Baker (2003) pg. 14).

(26) Modifiers can be adjoined to Nx only if they agree with Nx in phi-features.

Crucially for Baker (2003), English type languages allow adjectives in the attributive position and he assumes covert agreement morphology for English-type languages. Where does Dravidian stand in this respect? Recall that Malayalam is the only outlier among the Dravidian subset of languages we considered

8. I will use Japanese-type languages as an umbrella term for Japanese, Korean, Slave, Ika and the Bantu languages that do not allow adjectives in the attributive position.

with respect to agreement. However, all the other languages I have considered do not have adjectives in the attributive position either despite showing overt agreement. Thus, Dravidian is similar to Japanese-type languages. Baker (2003) assumes Japanese type languages to lack adjectives in the attributive position since Japanese adjectives lack phi-features. Supposing then that Dravidian languages are similar to Japanese type languages in lacking phi-features, then we also expect Dravidian to behave similar to Japanese-type languages in the placement of measure phrases.

I will argue against Baker's phi-feature agreement theory showing that it is empirically undesirable because of the conflicting results and assumptions and agreement cannot be used as an indication of whether adjectives can appear in the attributive position or not. Another recent theory relying on agreement is Watanabe (2011). Unlike Baker (2003), he analyzes dimensional adjectives in the predicative position. In looking at placement of measure phrases in dimensional adjectives, Watanabe crucially assumes English and Dutch to be similar to Japanese type languages in that they show no overt agreement in predicative dimensional adjectives as opposed to Romance where there is overt phi-feature morphology as discussed before (25). Thus, in Romance, the dimensional adjective precedes the measure phrases, this is seen as predicate inversion preempted by phi-feature agreement. In English, Dutch which lack phi-features, the adjective follows the measure phrase.

(27) a. *La voiture est longue de deux me`tres.* **French**
the car is long of two meters (Corver 2009: (33a))

b. *Gianni e’ alto due metri.* **Italian**
Gianni is tall two meters (Corver 2009: (89))

(28) a. John is six feet tall. **English**

b. *Dit brood is drie dagen oud.* **Dutch**
this bread is three days old (Corver 2009: (42a))

For Baker (2003), thus, it is necessary to posit phi-feature agreement (abstractly) in English because attributive modification is possible in English-type languages. For Watanabe (2011), both English and Japanese type languages do not have phi-feature agreement. The difference is only in the measure phrase placement. The prediction of Watanabe's (2011) parametric typology for the placement of the measure phrase and the adjective would put Dravidian type languages without phi-feature inflection to behave like Japanese (Watanabe's (22b.ii)).

(29) ^{OK}[GP AP G [FP MP F *t* AP]] (e.g. Japanese)

(29) predicts that in Dravidian the adjective phrase (AP) should precede the measure phrase (MP). This is so because we established Dravidian behaves similar to

Japanese in not allowing adjectives to appear in the attributive position. Baker (2003) relates this to the fact that Japanese adjectives do not have phi-features that are needed to establish agreement relations with the noun in the attributive modification, or in other terms, to allow attributive modification. However, this prediction is not borne out. In Dravidian, the measure phrase precedes the dimensional adjective.

(30) a. *john-inə andjə aTi pokkam uNTə*
john-DAT five feet tall EX
'John is five feet tall'

b. [GP AP G [FP MP *andjə aTi* F AP *pokkam*]]

What indeed Dravidian displays is the parametric option which is true of English and Dutch where the measure phrase precedes the AP.

(31) ^{OK}[GP G [FP MP F AP]] (e.g. Dutch, English)

Note that this is potentially problematic for Baker (2003). The two theories crucially rest on very different assumptions, namely the presence and absence of phi-features, whether overt or covert.[9] For Baker (2003), Japanese does not allow attributive modification because Japanese adjectives do not have phi-features. Crucially then Baker (2003) needs to assume covert phi-features for English, since English does allow adjectives in attributive positions. On the contrary, for Watanabe (2011), English has no phi-features either covertly or overtly. In fact, the only languages that do have phi-features are Romance type languages. Japanese and Dravidian would thus behave similar to English and Dutch in having no phi-features.

In § 3.2, I will reevaluate the role and nature of agreement overall for attributive and predicative positions arguing that agreement in the sense of Baker (2003) indeed can not be the forerunner in determining whether an adjective can appear in the attributive position. The syntactic role of AGREE, however, is necessary in evaluating the predicative position where it interacts with the feature sharing mechanism. In the next section, I will propose a theory to account for the syntactic distribution of Class 1 and Class 2 roots as discussed in § 2.1.

9. Note, however, that Baker (2003) looks at attributive adjectives whereas Watanabe (2011) looks at adjectives in the predicative position.

3. The analysis

My core proposal is that Dravidian never lexicalizes an adjective, in other words, an *A* does not exist in the lexicon of Dravidian nor does it derive one in the syntax. Primitive property concept roots combine with null verbal and nominal heads in order to derive structures that can participate in adjectival-like positions and this happens in the syntax-morphology interface. Crucially, I assume that the lexicon comprises only of roots (similar to Halle & Marantz 1993; Marantz 2004; Borer 2003) as in the Distributed Morphology tradition. These roots are prototypical 'property concepts' and refer to *kinds* of a different sortal type. An adjectival meaning is expressed by either a reduced relative clause structure (in the attributive position) or as a nominalization (in the predicative position). The two routes to the adjectival meaning are mediated by possessive semantics.

I will assume a functional lexicon consisting of featural specifications such as ϕ-features, tense features, case features and √ (roots) which are place holders for content words to be inserted post syntactically. This is illustrated for the example below:

(32) a. John slept
b. Functional Lexicon:
[+R] [{P:3, N:sg, G:m}] [+Past] √ √
c. Syntax:
$[_{CP}C\ [_{TP}\ [_{DP}\ [+R]\ [_{NUMP}\ [_{NUM}\ \{P{:}3, N{:}sg, G{:}m\}\ [_{NP}\ \surd\ ]]]\ [_{T}[\ +\ Past]]\ [_{VP}\ \surd\ ]]]]$
d. After post syntactic lexical insertion
$[_{CP}\ C\ [_{TP}\ [_{DP}\ \text{John}\ ]\ T^0\ [_{VP}\ \text{slept}\ ]]]]$

Keeping the lexicon devoid of any inflectional morphology, i.e. the morphological particles exist in the functional lexicon but they are not attached to the roots, allows many one-to-many mismatches to surface only in the morpho-syntactic module. Derivations are syntactic and can be seen as additional functional structure which contribute to interpretation. Class1 and Class2 roots start out as category-neutral expressions. In the morpho-syntactic module they undergo complex derivational processes that enable them to function as words, thus word formation is always in the syntax. These processes are motivated using null verbal and nominal heads.

3.1 Derivation of Class1 words

Recall, Class1 roots have been traditionally assumed to be deverbal (See Old Malayalam data in Jayaseelan 2007). They can only be merged in the complement position of a vP which has a null verbalizer head. The root first composes with the null head. I will argue that this is essential and the only way for the relative clause marker -*a* to attach to the root. It can never combine directly with the root without the mediation of this extra functional layer. The -*a* marker can only attach to verbal predicates. This also explains why -*a* can never attach to Class2 roots directly, because they are nominals to begin with.

In the attributive position, the Class1 root can appear as a reduced relative clause. -*a* is itself not an A' operator but a morpheme on the verb that marks what argument has been relativized (See Groenendijk & Stokhof 1982; Caponigro & Polinsky 2008; Caponigro & Polinsky 2011). Crucially, relative clause markers such as 'who' in English move from an already created argument position and in some languages there is a requirement that only the subject position can be relativized. However, the semantics of the relative clause marker in the Class1 roots cases is simply to make the Class1 verbalized root into a reduced relative clause. I assume the following semantics for the null verbalized element. This is a modification of the semantics of the possessive 'ka' in Ulwa (see Francez & Koontz-Garboden 2010). Π is a metavariable over property concept denoting expressions.

(33) $[\![\varnothing_v]\!] = \lambda\Pi.\ \lambda d.\ \lambda x.\ [x \text{ has } \Pi \text{ to } d]$

(33) is the semantics of the null verbalizer for Class1 roots. The metavariable Π ranges over entities that have a kind reference, a.k.a roots. The calculation proceeds thus (to be modified in §3.1.1):

(34) **Step 1:** Combination with the null verbalizer
$[\sqrt{\textit{nall}} + \varnothing]_v = \text{nall}_{\langle e,t\rangle}$
Step 2: Combine with the relative clause marker
$[\text{nall}_{\langle e,t\rangle} + \text{-a}]_{\text{rel}} = \text{nalla}_{\langle e,t\rangle}$

Note that the relative marker does not change the semantic type of the predicate, but allows for syntactic function as an attributive modifier. A verb cannot function as such on it's own. The derivation is represented as tree diagrams below:

(35) **Step 1:** Combination with the null verbalizer

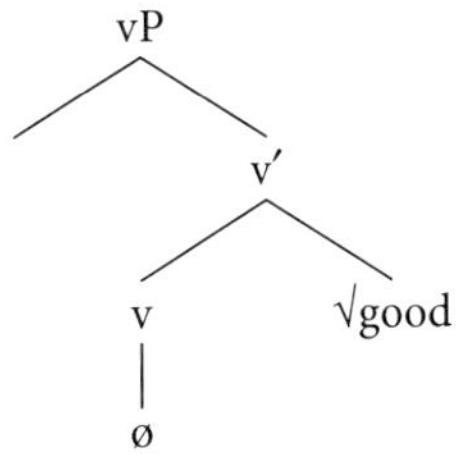

Step 2: Combine with the relative clause marker

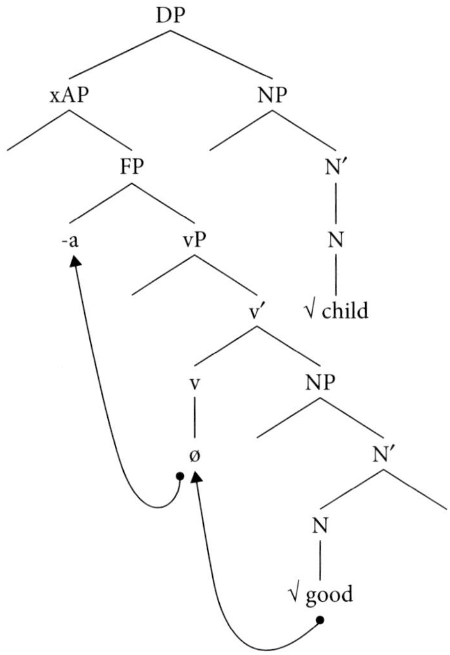

The fact that attributive Class1 roots are always reduced relative clauses is given further support by the absence of non-intersective readings. In English, (36) below is ambiguous between an intersective reading and a non-intersective reading (Siegel 1980) whereas the Malayalam counterparts in (37) only show an intersective reading suggesting they are actually reduced relative clauses.

(36) Olga is a beautiful dancer
Reading 1: Olga is a dancer who is beautiful *intersective*
Reading 2: Olga dances beautifully *non- intersective*

(37) *Sita oru ceriya nrithakkari aaNə*
Sita a small dancer EQ
'Sita is a small dancer'
Reading 1: Sita is a dancer who is small *intersective*
Reading 2: Sita is small and Sita is a dancer *≉non-intersective*

Adjectives inside an English relative clause behave like the Malayalam examples in (37) in displaying only the intersective reading. This lends support to the reduced relative clause analysis. Semantically, the null verbalizer converts the root into a predicate of type ⟨*e*,*t*⟩. The semantic role of the *-a* is only to make the predicate into a reduced relative clause.

The predicative position, I noted, also requires a nominal. The verbalized roots cannot appear in this position without the help of additional nominal morphology – and as relative clauses they cannot appear there either. This nominalization is sensitive to the number and gender of the subject (cf. (10) and (11)). Baker (2003) in analyzing predicative adjectives assumes they check selectional features of the PRED head. Similarly, the predicative head [+PRED] in Dravidian is marked for nominal features and these features have to be checked off by the operation [AGREE]. The appearance of the nominal features is only a reflex of the checking operations.

It is plausible for the *-a* marked root to appear in the predicative position since it is already a predicate however, syntactically relative clauses are not standalone predicates. Moreover, the clause structure of Dravidian is very restricted and conservative (see Jayaseelan 2011 for a recent discussion of this idea). Jayaseelan (2011) takes this conservativity to be seen as the inability to "hive-out" positions in the clause architecture. Supposing that what I have said is on the right track and there are indeed no adjectives in Dravidian, then we expect only a nominal element as the complement of the verb. The inability of the *-a* marked root to appear as the complement of the verb suggests that only a nominal can appear in the complement position of the verb. If this theory is correct, it makes two predications:

a. Comparative constructions formed with Class1 roots are always nominalized, since there can only be nominal comparatives. Presumably verbal comparatives should also be allowed. Adjectival comparatives should be missing.
b. Secondary predications of the kind found in English should not be possible.

Indeed (a) and (b) is borne out in Malayalam as seen in sections below.

3.1.1 *Comparative constructions*

Research in comparative constructions has largely concentrated on the syntax and semantics of the adjectival constructions. Considerably less work has been done in the nominal and verbal domains. One of the immediate consequences of the theory outlined above is the lack of adjectival comparative constructions in Dravidian. Dravidian comparatives are always nominal or verbal comparatives. This brings about interesting questions about the semantics of the "adjectival-like" expressions. The normal treatment of adjectives takes into account a degree theoretic semantics for adjectives. They relate a degree to a particular individual. This can be seen in the lexical entry below (following Kennedy 1998 a.o).

(38) $[\![\text{tall}]\!] = \lambda d\ \lambda x\ [\text{x's height} \geq d]$

In Dravidian, indeed if there are no adjectives then crucially the lexical entry for the roots will be different. In particular, Class1 and Class2 roots after the *-a* suffixation is a predicate of type ⟨*e,t*⟩ and a nominal of type *e* respectively. How then does this affect the syntax and semantics of adjectival comparatives found in English-type languages? Malayalam comparatives are always nominal, verbal or adverbial comparatives (Menon 2012). This can be seen by the distribution of the overt comparative marker (see, Menon 2013 for a recent exposition).

In Class1 roots, the degree argument is saturated by the positive morpheme. Thus, Class1 roots are norm-related. The positive morpheme has the following semantics and the derivation is in (40):

(39) $[\![\text{POS}]\!] = \lambda g_{\langle d, \langle e,t\rangle\rangle}. \lambda x. \exists d\ [g(d)(x) \text{ and } d > d_s]$

(40) a. $[[[\sqrt{nall} + \varnothing_v]_v + \text{POS}]_v\ \text{-}a]_{rel} = \text{nalla}_{\langle e,t\rangle}$ [Class1]
Lit. 'having a degree of goodness that exceeds the standard'

b. $\lambda x. \exists d\ [x \text{ is good to d and } d > d_s]$

Class1 roots can appear in the predicative position only with the appearance of agreement markers which have been equated to a strategy of nominalization (Hany Babu 1996). This suggests that Class1 roots can only appear as nominals in comparative constructions, i.e. the relative clause which is the output of (34) has to be nominalized before using it in a predicative comparative construction (41).

(41) *anil* komalan-e kaaḷ-um *valiya-van aaNə* [Class1]
anil komalan-ACC than-UM big-NOML EQ
'Anil is bigger than Komalan' (Lit. Anil is one who has bigness than Komalan)

In (41), the *than*-phrase marks the standard of comparison 'Komalan' who is compared against 'Anil' on the scale of bigness 'valiya-van'. Here, the Class1 root 'valiya' appears with number and gender marking 'van' suggesting that the only comparison possible is when Class1 reduced relative clause structures are nominalized.

3.1.2 *Lack of secondary predications*

Resultative secondary predications are normally taken to be an indication of an adjective position. In Dravidian, if the theory is correct in that Dravidian lacks an adjectival category then resultative secondary predications should be missing from the syntax. Indeed this prediction is borne out.

(42) a. *anil meSa vritthi-*(aaki) tudacc-u*
anil table clean-PART wipe-PAST
'Anil wiped the table clean'

b. *komalan mudi ceruta-*(aaki) muricc-u*
komalan hair small-PART cut-PAST
'Komalan cut his hair short'

The resultative secondary predictions in (42) can appear only with the obligatory participial marker suggesting again that Class1 roots actually can combine only with a null verbal head in order to participate in attributive modification. 'aaki' is the past participle form of the *be* verb.

3.2 Class1 roots in predicative position

I have established why the Class1 roots have to appear with nominal morphology in the predicative position. I will now proceed to my assumptions on AGREE and the presence of the nominalization morpheme. The model assumed is closest to recent modifications of Chomsky's original AGREE model proposed in Frampton and Gutmann (2006) and Pesetsky and Torrego (2007), henceforth FG and PT. They propose a feature-sharing model where the probe can evaluate and check features of the probe by multiple AGREE. In looking at Icelandic data which show agreement on the pronoun as well as the matrix participle, FG's analysis would entail the feature sharing mechanism whereby the participle first agrees with the pronoun and then subsequently the matrix *v* can check and assign case to the pronoun and this case is shared with the participle. The pronoun is in some sense linked to the participle.

For Dravidian, the Class1 roots are realized as participials in that they are reduced relative clauses having very little structure. I already noted the requirement of the Dravidian verbal predicate to have a nominal in its complement position. Adopting FG and PTs feature sharing approach enables us to explain why the Class1 root in the predicative position always appears with a nominal marker sensitive to gender and number. I will assume a [+PRED] head that has {N, G} features. The probe on the [+PRED] head is looking for some element to saturate its feature. The reduced relative clause cannot saturate this without the help of the nominalization morpheme- *van*, *vaL*, and *tə*. These rudimentary agreement markers have phi-features that can saturate the [+PRED] head.

(43) a. [$_{PRED}$ nalla [$_{vP}$ COP]]

b.

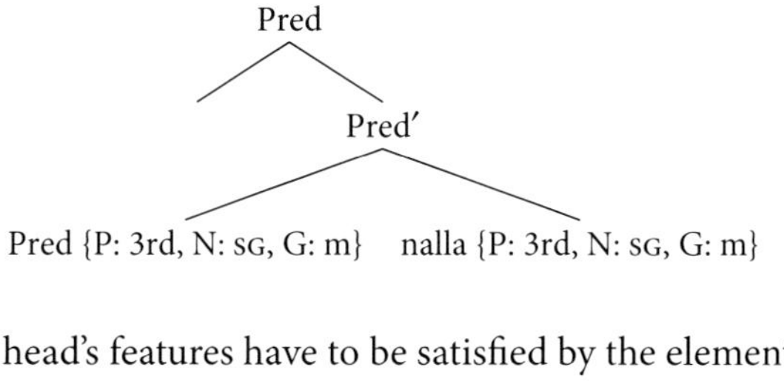

The [PRED] head's features have to be satisfied by the element in the complement position. This is done by the feature sharing mechanism since this is reflected in the case assignment patterns as well. The nominative case is a feature assigned as a result of the feature sharing by the probe and goal. Thus, the subject in the case of the Class1 predicative constructions is assigned nominative case (which is always null marked). The feature sharing mechanism sketched here is different from Baker's agreement checking story for the lack of adjectives in the attributive position in Japanese. Baker's (2003) story relies on feature checking where the adjective has to be specified for uninterpretable features in order for the feature checking to happen. In this case, it is not about checking off uninterpretable features, rather the need to share features in connection with the fact that only a nominal can appear in the complement position of the predicative head that triggers the feature checking mechanism. In the absence of a lexical category of adjectives, the fact that the complement of the [PRED] head is a nominal is indeed not surprising. The derivation is below:

(44) a. [$_{CP}$ [$_{TP}$ John-ø [$_{PRED}$ [$_{PRED'}$ nalla-*van* [$_{COP}$ aaNə]]]]

b.

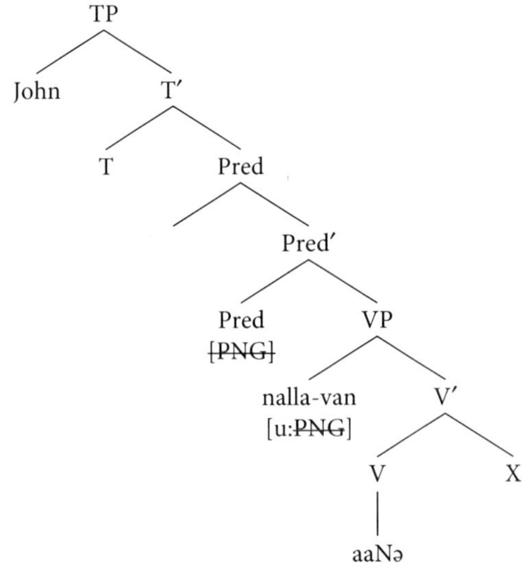

I am assuming the Spec of the VP to host the xAP projection as shown in (35: Step2). The Class1 root first combines with the null verbalizer which then combines with the relative clause head. This is then merged into the Spec of the VP. The probe on the [PRED] head sends out the probe which then agrees with the xAP. The movement of the root from lower down in this projection to the Spec of the xAP (as seen in 35:Step2) is motivated precisely because of this AGREE relation. Only the edge of the projection is visible to the probe. Depending on the PNG features, the inflection on the relativized root changes. This thus creates a nominal predicate. Further evidence comes from adjectival ordering restrictions.

3.2.1 *Lack of adjectival ordering restrictions*

If there are no adjectives, then we do not expect the word order restrictions exhibited by English-type adjectives as in (45).

(45) a. The small square house
b. *The square small house

This is unlike the nature of relative clause modification since relative clauses can be stacked in any order in English and Japanese (Sproat & Shih 1991).

(46) a. The house that's small that's square
b. The house that's square that's small

(47) a. *maru-i aka-i e*
round red picture
b. *aka-i maru-i e*
red round picture

Similarly, in Dravidian there are no adjectival ordering restrictions which is an immediate consequence if the Class1 roots are reduced relative clauses.

(48) a. *cuvanna valiya vahanam*
red big vehicle
'The red big vehicle'
b. *valiya cuvanna vahanam*
big red vehicle
'The big red vehicle'

There might be ordering restrictions between Class1 and Class2 roots which I will not consider at this point, but the crucial point to note is that within the classes there are no restrictions between the different roots.

3.3 Class2 roots

Class2 roots are borrowed roots. These roots normally end in a stop or a fricative. Malayalam coda is restricted in that only a bilabial nasal, an alveolar nasal or a vowel can appear in the coda position. The roots are nominalized after being borrowed with the nominalizing morpheme *-am*. Note that the other nominalizing morpheme 'atə' is not available for Class2 roots, because 'atə' is a true nominalizer and can appear only on verbal and clausal elements whereas *-am* is a nominal morpheme and appears in other non-borrowed nominal roots as well.

(49) a. pazh**am** 'banana'
b. veLL**am** 'water'

A question that comes up automatically is why the Class2 roots cannot undergo relativization, unlike the Class1 roots. The relative clause is not attaced directly to the root, it attaches to the null verb. Therefore the null v cannot attach to Class 2 roots. Class2 roots, unlike Class1 roots, thus start out as nominals. There is no syntactic restriction prohibiting the attachment of the relative clause marker onto the borrowed root, the constraint is purely phonological. Borrowed roots have to undergo the nominalization because of the coda restriction. Recall that the relative clause marker, I argued in § 3.1 can attach only to a verbal predicate. Thus, the only way for the relative clause marker to attach to the Class2 roots is by converting the Class2 roots into a verbal predicate. However, this is not the strategy that is commonly used for borrowing.

The Class2 roots, similar to the Class1 roots start out as *kinds* of a different sortal type. Addition of the nominal morpheme *-am* turns the roots into *e*. The nominal morpheme is the head of an *n*P. The semantics of the word created by the *-am* suffixation behaves like any other nominal in the language. Given that Class2 roots end up as nominals and not as predicates, attributive modification is not possible at all. The only way to use a nominal predicate in an attributive position is to employ a copula. Malayalam uses the non-finite existential copula *uLL* for this purpose. The non-finite copula turns the nominal predicate into an $\langle e,t \rangle$ to which the relative clause marker *-a* can then attach to. The use of the non-finite copula is consistent with the view that relative clauses are non-finite in Dravidian. This non-finite copula is the overt form of the null verbalizer employed for the Class1 roots. Thus, Class2 roots have the morphology spelt out overtly whereas Class1 roots only have it covertly. The calculation proceeds thus:

(50) a. **Step 1:** Combination with the nominal morpheme
$[\sqrt{pokk} + \text{-}am]_{\text{n}} = \text{pokkam}_{e}$

b. **Step 2:** Combine with the non-finite copula
$[\text{pokkam}_{e} + \text{uLL}]_{\text{v}} = [\text{pokkam uLL}]_{\langle e,t \rangle}$

c. **Step 3:** Final merge with the relative clause marker
$[\text{pokkam uLL}_{\langle e,t \rangle} + \text{-a}]_{\text{rel}} = \text{pokkam uLL}\mathbf{a}_{\langle e,t \rangle}$

Note that *-a* is merging with a non-finite verbal head in this case the non-finite copula 'uLL'. The syntactic derivations are show below:

(51) **Step 1:** Combination with the nominal morpheme

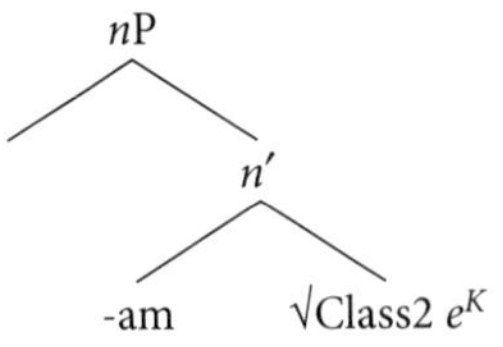

Step 2: Combine with the non-finite copula

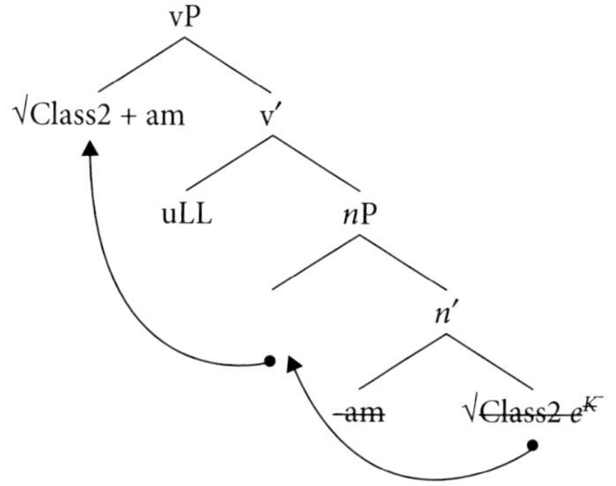

Step 3: Final merge with the relative clause marker

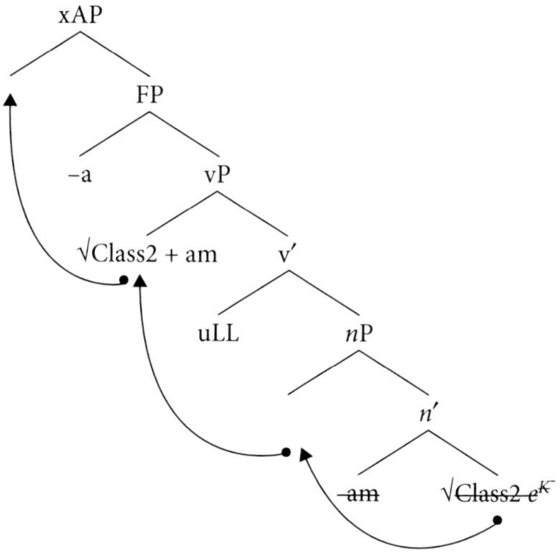

In the predicative position, unlike the Class1 roots, there are two strategies that Class2 roots employ. Either the derivation can proceed similar to the Class1 roots, whereby the Subject gets nominative case and the Class2 predicate gets nominalized or the Class2 root can stay as in Step 1 of (51) and the subject can receive dative case. I will appeal to the feature sharing mechanism and show that this much-discussed "dative experiencer" construction receives a simple explanation under this theory. It is a by product of feature sharing as well as the semantics of the possession which I have discussed under the rubric of what it means to be in an attributive or predicative position.

When the Class2 root remains as a relative clause, it has to appear with the nominalizing morphemes pertaining to person, number, and gender. This is similar to the predicative position in a Class1 root. The [PRED] head is marked for features and there has to be obligatory feature sharing between the head and the Class2 root. The entire relative clause is nominalized. This would seem a bizarre strategy considering that the Class2 root was a nominal after the first morphological merge unlike the Class1 root (which ends up verbal). However, there is an option to use the nominal first created after the morphological merge as well which is the experiencer dative construction.

In the case of the first strategy, the [PRED] head sends down the probe which then agrees with the relative clause upon the affixation of the nominal morpheme. The AGREE relation shares the features on the subject NP and the relative clause which gets the nominalized forms.

(52) a. $[_{CP}$ $[_{TP}$ John-ø $[_{PRED}$ $[_{PRED'}$ pokkam uLLa-*van* $[_{COP}$ aaNə]]]]

b.

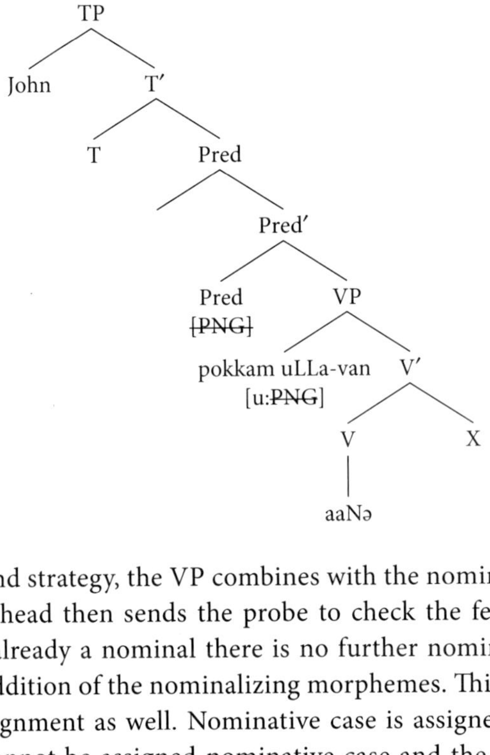

In the second strategy, the VP combines with the nominal belonging to Class2. The PRED head then sends the probe to check the features on the nominal. Since it is already a nominal there is no further nominalization required and hence no addition of the nominalizing morphemes. This feature sharing results in case assignment as well. Nominative case is assigned to the predicate. The "subject" cannot be assigned nominative case and the only other option is to assign dative.

(53) a. *John-inə pokkam uNTə*
John-DAT tall EX
'John has tallness'

b.

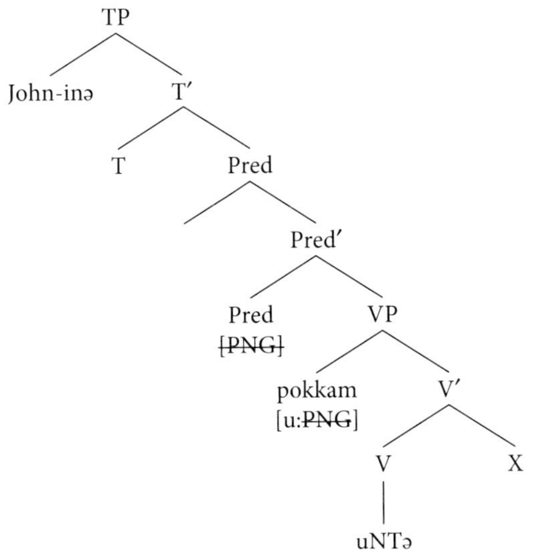

4. Conclusion

In this paper, I have shown that Malayalam does not have an adjective category either lexically or derivationally in the syntax. The two routes taken to derive adjectival-like meaning are relativization and nominalization. The lexicon comprises of primitive property concept roots which combine with different *v* heads and *n* heads in the syntax to derive the relevant structures. These roots start out as *kinds* of a different sortal type. The adjective category is therefore not a primitive category in Malayalam.

References

Amritavalli, Raghavachari. 2008. The origins of functional and lexical categories: Tense-aspect and adjectives in Dravidian. *Nanzan Linguistics* 4: 1–20.

Amritavalli, Raghavachari & Jayaseelan, Karattuparambil A. 2003. The genesis of syntactic categories and parametric variation. Paper presented at the *4th Asian GLOW Colloquium* at Seoul, August 2003.

Anandan, Kaattuparambil Narayanan. 1985. Predicate Nominals in English and Malayalam. M.Phil Dissertation, CIEFL: Hyderabad.

Baker, Mark. 2003. Verbal adjectives as adjectives without phi-features. In *Proceedings of the Fourth Tokyo Conference on Psycholinguistics*, Yukio Otsu (ed.), 1–22. Keio University.

Baker, Mark. 2005. *Lexical Categories: Verbs, Nouns, and Adjectives.* Cambridge: Cambridge University Press.

Bhat, D.N. Shankara. 1994. *The Adjectival Category: Criteria for Differentiation and Identification*. Amsterdam: John Benjamins.

Borer, Hagit. 2003. Exo-skeletal vs. endo-skeletal explanations: Syntactic projections and the lexicon. In *The Nature of Explanation*, M. Polinsky & J. Moore (eds), 31–67. Chicago: Chicago University Press (distributed by CSLI).

Caponigro, Ivano & Polinksy, Maria. 2008. Almost everything is relative in the Caucasus. *Semantics and Linguistic Theory (SALT) 18*, Amherst, MA.

Caponigro, Ivan & Polinsky, Maria. 2011. Relative embeddings: A Circassian puzzle for the syntax/semantics interface. *Natural Language and Linguistic Theory* 29(1): 71–122.

Chomsky, Noam. 1970. Remarks on nominalization. In *Readings in English Transformational Grammar.* R. Jacobs & P. Rosenbaum (eds), 184–221. Waltham, MA: Blaisdell.

Corver, Nobert. 2009. Getting the (syntactic) measure of measure phrases. *The Linguistic Review* 26(1): 67–134.

Frampton, John & Gutmann, Sam. 2006. How sentences grow in the mind: Agreement and selection in efficient minimalist syntax. In *Agreement Systems*, Cedric Boeckx (ed.), 121–157. Amsterdam: John Benjamins.

Groenendijk, Joroen & Stokhof, Martin. 1982. Semantic analysis of Wh-complements. *Linguistics and Philosophy* 5(2): 175–233.

Hale, Kenneth & Keyser, Samuel Jay. 1993. On argument structure and the lexical expression of syntactic relations. In *The View from Building 20: Essays in Linguistics in Honor of Sylvain Bromberger*, S. Hale & S. Keyser (eds), 53–110. Cambridge, Mass: MIT Press.

Halle, Morris & Marantz, Alec. 1993. Distributed morphology and the pieces of inflection. In *The View from Building 20: Essays in Linguistics in Honor of Sylvain Bromberger*, Ken Hale & Samuel Jay Keyser (eds), 111–176. Cambridge, Mass: MIT Press.

Jayaseelan, Karattuparambil A. 2007. The argument structure of the dative construction. In *Argument Structure*, E. Reuland, T. Bhattacharya & G. Spathas (eds), 37–48. Amsterdam: John Benjamins.

Jayaseelan, Karattuparambil A. 2011. Coordination and finiteness in Dravidian. Invited talk at FiSaL in Universitat of Tromsø, June 09–10 2011.

Kim, Min-Joo. 2002. Does Korean have Adjectives. Ms. Umass Amherst.

Koontz-Garboden, Andrew & Francez, Itamar. 2010. Possessed properties in Ulwa. *Natural Language and Linguistic Theory*, 197–240.

Krishnamurthi, Bhadriraju. 2003. *The Dravidian Languages*. Cambridge: Cambridge University Press.

Laughlin, Fiona. 2004. Is There an adjective class in Wolof? In *Adjective Classes: A Cross Linguistic Typology*, R.M.W. Dixon & Alexandra Y. Aikhenvald (eds), 242–262. Oxford: Oxford University Press.

Marantz, Alec. 1997. No escape from syntax: Don't try morphological analysis in the privacy of your own lexicon. In *Proceedings of the 21st Annual Penn Linguistics Colloquium: Penn Working Papers in Linguistics 4*: 2, Alexis Dimitriadis et al. (ed.), 201–225.

Menon, Mythili. 2012. Adverbial comparatives: Evidence from Malayalam. In *Proceedings of Sinn und Bedeutung 16 vol. 2, MIT Working Papers in Linguistics*, Ana Aguilar, Anna Chernilovskya & Rick Nouwen (eds), 461–474. Cambridge: MIT Press.

Menon, Mythili. 2013. Comparison in the Absence of Adjectives: The Case of Malayalam. Talk at FASAL 3, University of Southern California. March 9–10 2013.

Miyagawa, Shigeru. 1987. Lexical categories in Japanese. *Lingua* 73: 29–51.

Ohkado, Masayuki. 1991. On the status of adjectival nouns in Japanese. *Lingua* 83: 67–82.

Pesetsky, David & Torrego, Esther. 2007. The syntax of valuation and the interpretability of features. In *Phrasal and Clausal Architecture*, S. Karimi, V. Samiian & W. Wilkins (eds), 1–31 Amsterdam: John Benjamins.

Siegel, Muffy. 1980. *Capturing the Adjective*. New York: Garland.

Sproat, Richard & Shih, Chilin. 1991. The cross-linguistic distribution of adjective ordering restrictions. In *Interdisciplinary Approaches to Language*, C. Georgopoulos & R. Ishihara (eds), 565–593. Dordrecht: Kluwer.

Watanabe, Akira. 2011. Adjectival inflection and the position of measure phrases. *Linguistic Inquiry* 42, 490–507.

Washio, Ryuichi. 1997. Resultatives, compositionality and language variation. *Journal of East Asian Languages* 6: 1–49.

Zvelebil, Kamil. 1990. *Dravidian Linguistics: An Introduction*. Pondicherry, India: PILC (Pondicherry Institute of Linguistics and Culture).

Adjective-fronting as evidence for Focus and Topic within the Bangla nominal domain

Saurov Syed
University of Southern California

The goal of this paper is twofold. First it talks about the syntax of adjectives in Bangla, and argues in favor of the idea that there is a fixed hierarchy of functional projections where Adjective phrases are manifest as specifiers. It takes the stance that the adjectives are part of the lexicon; they are taken from the lexicon during a computation, and mapped into the syntax, forming an Adjective Phrase (AdjP). Secondly, the paper argues for Focus and Topic phrases within the nominal domain, thus extending Rizzi's original proposal of a split CP to DPs (cf. Rizzi 1997). Specifically the paper uses evidence from adjective fronting to claim that there is a fixed FocP immediately above the DP in Bangla, and at least one TopP above the FocP. The constituent bearing such a topic/focus feature needs to move up in a local checking configuration with the relevant functional head that has the matching feature, thus explaining the attested adjective-fronting.

Keywords: Bangla; adjective-fronting; focus; topic; nominal-domain

1. Introduction

Adjectives in Bangla are argued to occupy the specifier of NP in Bhattacharya (1998). However, in this paper I assume a cartographic approach to the syntax of adjectives (cf. Cinque 1999; Scott 2002, among others), and show the mileage gained by such an account. Furthermore I use this account along with facts related to word order of demonstrative and multiple adjectives to argue for an extended nominal domain (or the 'left periphery' of the nominal domain, to use Rizzi (1997)'s term) in Bangla.

Cinque (1999) in his seminal work on adverbs and functional heads, proposes a correlation between adverbs and functional projections that are associated with tense, aspect, modal force, etc. He argues for a fixed universal hierarchy of clausal Functional Projections (FPs), and claims that Adverb phrases are overt manifestations of the specifiers of these FPs. In other words, according to his analysis, each adverbial class occurs in the Specifier position of a phonologically null or 'empty-headed' FP,[1] to which the adverbial class is semantically related.

Following Cinque's idea that such cartographic approach can be taken in the case of adjectives as well, there has been research attempting to extend this approach towards adjectives; Sproat and Shih (1990) and Scott (2002) argue for a similar universal hierarchy of functional projections of which AdjPs are manifest as overt specifiers. There is a huge list of FPs proposed cross-linguistically; I shall not go into the details of argumentation for these projections, but rather give the final proposed order given in Scott (2002),[2] shown in Figure 1.

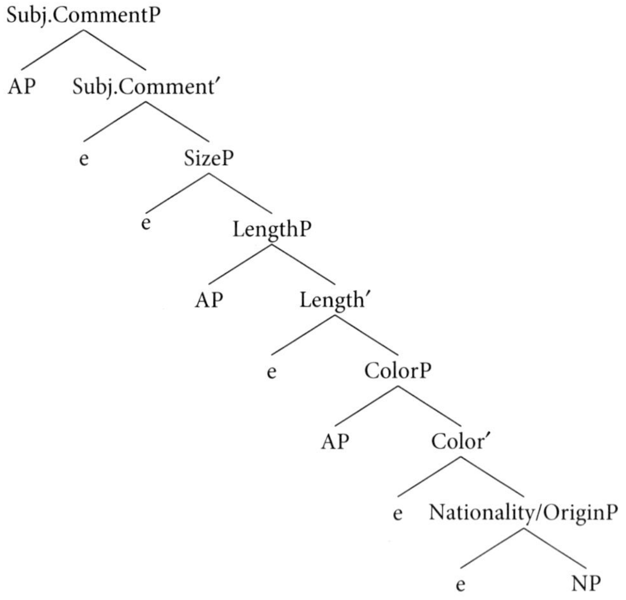

Figure 1. The hierarchy of Functional Projections in Scott (2002)

Adopting such a view can account for the fact that Bangla allows multiple adjectives before the noun, and that there is a fixed order occurence of the adjectives. Consider the following examples.

(1) *ami ekta choto sobuj chine fuldaani kinlam*
I one-CL small green Chinese vase buy-past-1P
'I bought a small green Chinese vase'

1. FP stands for Functional Projection here, and not a Focus Phrase.

2. For a detailed discussion on each of these nodes, and many more sub-nodes for each of these functional projections, see Scott (2002).

(2) **ami ekta sobuj choto chine fuldaani kinlam*
I one-CL green small Chinese vase buy-PAST-1P
'I bought a small green Chinese vase'

(3) **ami ekta chine choto sobuj fuldaani kinlam*
I one-CL Chinese small green vase buy-PAST-1P
'I bought a small green Chinese vase'

(4) **ami ekta chine sobuj choto fuldaani kinlam*
I one-CL Chinese green small vase buy-PAST-1P
'I bought a small green Chinese vase'

(5) **ami ekta sobuj chine choto fuldaani kinlam*
I one-CL green Chinese small vase buy-PAST-1P
'I bought a small green Chinese vase'

(6) **ami ekta choto chine sobuj fuldaani kinlam*
I one-CL small Chinese green vase buy-PAST-1P
'I bought a small green Chinese vase'

The Examples (1)–(6) show that any attempt to change the order of adjectives in Example (1) results in unacceptability. Taking a similar line of thought as in Scott (2002), I take these examples to suggest that the restriction in terms of the order of the adjectives is because there is a universal hierarchy of the Functional Projections. Bangla shows the same hierarchy of *size>color>provenance* as claimed universal in Scott (2002). Specifically, one needs to say that there are different types of functional projections named SizeP, ColorP, ProvenanceP, and the AdjP 'small', 'green', and 'Chinese' are generated in the specifier positions of these respective functional projections. And because the order of the functional projections is fixed, the order of the AdjPs automatically is fixed as well. Such an account can explain occurrence of multiple adjectives in a fixed order in Bangla.

Before moving any further, I will make a terminological point here. Throughout this paper, the higher functional projections that occur in a fixed order and that house AdjPs in their specifier positions will be labeled as aP.[3] Restating things in the light of the new terminology, there are multiple levels of aP, with a fixed universal hierarchy. The aP can be a SizeP, a ColorP, or a ProvenanceP etc, and the AdjP 'small', 'green', and 'Chinese' are in the specifier positions of these aPs.

It is pertinent to note here that generating adjectives in the Spec, NP position will fail to account for the ordering restriction observed in Bangla. To account

3. This is just a change in label from 'FP' in Scott (2002), and has no theoretical consequences. I change the label to avoid any confusion that might arise with FocP (focus phrase) that I make use of later.

for multiple adjectives, a *Spec, NP*-approach has to resort to multiple adjunctions of the adjectives in the specifier position; however adjunction can happen in any order, and thus will not be able to account for a fixed order of adjectives.

If one compares Bangla with Hindi, there is another view that one can take, namely adjectives as Specifiers of an AgrP (and positing the possibility of multiple AgrP-s) right above the NP. In Hindi, there is gender agreement, and the adjectives agree in gender with the noun it qualifies. See (7) and (8).

(7) *choti* *mez*
small-fem table

(8) *chota* *computer*
small-male computer

To account for such Hindi data, one can follow the line of thought in Giusti (1997), and argue that for the agreement pattern, there has to be an AgrP within the DP, and the Adjectives are generated in the specifier of this AgrP. The adjective is in Spec-Head relationship with the Agr-head, and thus gets agreement. If there are more than one adjective, one can further assume that there can be as many AgrP-s as needed, to accommodate as many adjectives as present. A schematic representation of the theory looks like Figure 2 below.

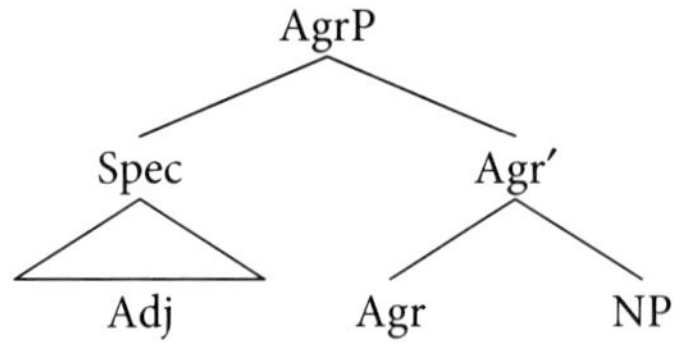

Figure 2. An AgrP-based approach

In Bangla, there is no overt agreement between adjectives and nouns. One can, however, argue that Bangla being close to Hindi, also has Agrp (or AgrP-s) hosting the adjectives in their specifiers, but the Agr-head has to be null.[4] This proposal, much as the Spec, NP approach, will also not be able to explain why multiple adjectives cannot occur in any free order.

4. This is, as an anonymous reviewer has pointed out, similar to the idea that such difference between Bangla and Hindi agreement is a PF process. In lines of work done by Sigurðsson, it can be said that whenever Merge/Agree and subsequent matching applies, the possibility of agreement arises; Hindi makes a (PF) choice to morphologically signal such instance of Merge/Agree/matching, where Bangla does not (for a detailed discussion about the system, see Sigurðsson 2006).

To sum up, I assume adjective phrases to be generated in the specifiers of functional projections that are higher than the NP, and I provide arguments to show that this account is better than a couple of alternative approaches to explain the Bangla facts.

2. Phrasal movement within the nominal

It has been proposed in Bhattacharya (1999) that there is phrasal movement within the nominal domain in Bangla. As this phrasal movement within the nominal will be crucial for my analysis, I will spend some time here to show the existence of such a movement.

Let me quickly take you through the structure proposed in Bhattacharya (1999). He analyzes *Adj+Noun* as an NP; he fuses the number and the quantifier as a complex head QP, has the classifier 'ta' as a cleft to the number 'two' in the Q head, and has the adjective generated in the Spec of the NP. An overall schematic representation, without going into the details of his argumentation, looks like Figure 3.

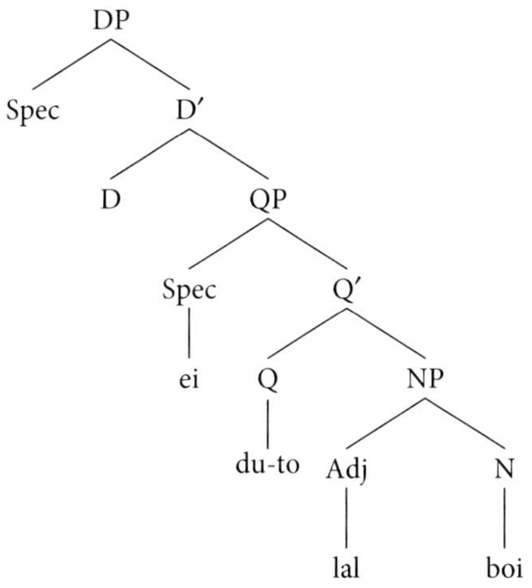

Figure 3. The structure of the Bangla DP in Bhattacharya (1999)

To show phrasal movement within the DP, I will present what Bhattacharya (1998) calls the 'NP Object Shift'. Consider the following data:

(9) *du-to boi*
two-CL book
'two books'

(10) *boi* *du-to*
book two-CL
'the two books'

The examples above show movement of 'boi' across the Num-Cl. This cannot be an N-movement as more structure is allowed within the moved portion. Consider the following set:

(11) *du-to* *lal* *boi*
two-CL red book
'two red books'

(12) *lal* *boi* *du-to*
red book two-CL
'the two red books'

The data shows that the unmarked order is *Num>adj>book*, and that *Adj-N* can front before the *Num*. This is evidence that something more than an *N* is moving here, and Bhattacharya takes it to be an example of *NP-movement*. I agree to him to the extent that it is at least an NP-movement, but I suggest that this phrasal movement involves more than an NP. In other words, I take the examples are good enough to show *phrasal movement* within the DP, but the phrase moved is not NP, but rather an aP. The broad schema for the movement in Example (12) is shown below in (13).

(13) $[_{aP}$ lal boi $]_i$ du-to t_i

More specifically, this movement looks like (14).

(14) $[_{ColorP}$ lal $[_{NP}$ boi $]]_i$ duto t_i

With a bigger phrase with multiple adjectives, I suggest that the highest aP (which includes the other aPs) moves up across the NumP. This is shown in the data in (15) and the schema of the movement is given in (16).

(15) *choto* *sobuj* *chine* *fuldani* *du-to*
small green Chinese vase two-CL
'the two small green Chinese vases'

(16) $[_{SizeP}$ choto $[_{ColorP}$ sobuj $[_{ProvenanceP}$ chine fuldani $]]]_i$ du – to t_i

2.1 Against a couple of alternative ways of explaining the phrasal movement

There are two alternative ways of deriving this surface order of adj-adj-adj-N-Num-Cl in (15). One is to posit movement of each adjective from the specifier of each aP to a landing site higher up. The schema of this idea will look like (17).

(17) $choto_i$ $sobuj_j$ $chine_k$ fuldani du-to t_i t_j t_k

This does not sound a very appealing idea, as it will require exact number of landing sites up in the tree as the number of adjectives. It is hard to argue for that many number of available specifier positions, where all these adjectives move up to.

There is yet another way of deriving the same order. This is to posit a head-movement of the noun *fuldani* across the NumP, and then pied-piping the remnant of the highest aP. Schematically it will look like (18):

(18) $[\text{choto sobuj chine}]_j$ $fuldani_i$ du-to t_j t_i

The problem with this idea is constraints on head-movement; a head while moving up cannot skip a head. In other words, a head will block any head-movement across it. There is a Num-head *two* present here, and the movement of the head noun *fuldani* across it should be blocked.

I take this as a suggestion that given the current evidence we have, the idea of the entire aP moving up[5] seems like the most plausible way of deriving the attested surface order.

3. FocusP and TopicP within the nominal domain

Bhattacharya (1998) argues for a Focus Phrase (FocP) within the DP; however I suggest this FocP to be above the DP (thus above the Dem) instead of a lower FocP.[6] I suggest this based on evidence from data where a demonstrative can co-occur with multiple adjectives. Adopting the standard view in the literature that a demonstrative is in the D^0 position (that is, the head of the functional projection DP),[7] word order variation with respect to aP-raising and the demonstrative can be used to reveal further structure within the nominal domain. Consider the following example.

5. It is perhaps important to spend a few lines on the motivation of such an aP-movement, even though it's not a central part of the paper. For Bhattacharya, the phrasal movement shown in (10) is due to reasons of specificity; I believe such movement as well as aP-raising is motivated by the need to achieve definiteness (also suggested in Dayal 2012), as by virtue of such movement the nominal expression obligatorily becomes a definite one.

6. I shall remain agnostic to if there is a need for a lower FocP; but rather advocate for the presence of a higher FocP above the DP.

7. This view is however not unchallenged. Bhattacharya (1999) generates Dem as specifier of QP.

(19)

ei	*lal*	*boi*	*du-to*	*amar*	*pochondo*
this	red	book	two-CL	my	like-noun

'these two red books are of my liking'

Here, presumably the aP has moved up across the Num-CL but lower than the Dem *ei*, as shown in the schematic representation below.

(20) ei [$_{aP}$ lal boi]$_i$ du-to t$_i$ amar pochondo[8]

I show in (21) that an adjective can be extracted out of the raised aP, and moved further up across the Dem, and thus above the DP (as I Dem is the head D^0). Crucially, this is possible ONLY when the extracted adjective is stressed and interpreted as being in focus. That is, empirically the moved element has to bear stress; if the moved adjective does not bear stress, it renders the expression ungrammatical, as shown in (22).

(21)

LAL$_j$	*ei*	[$_{aP}$ *t*$_j$	*boi*]$_i$	*ta t*$_i$	*amar*	*pochondo*
red	this		book	CL	my	liking

'this red book is of my liking'

(22)

**lal*$_j$	*ei*	[$_{aP}$ *t*$_j$	*boi*]$_i$	*ta t*$_i$	*amar*	*pochondo*
red	this		book	CL	my	liking

'This red book is of my liking'

This clearly suggests that the adjective moves to a focus position above the DP.

3.1 Evidence for a fixed Focus position

In (21), there is only one adjective present. Now let's consider an example where there are multiple adjectives, in the universal order, as shown in the following example.

(23)

ei	[$_{aP}$ *choto*	*lal*	*boi*]$_i$	*du-to*	*t*$_i$
this	small	red	book	two-CL	

'these two small red books'

Fronting of multiple adjectives is observed. From the order in (23), both the adjectives *choto* and *lal* can move further up across the Dem *ei*. However, when there is fronting of more than one adjective, only one of these is ever stressed, and it is

8. It is interesting to note here that the non-raised aP form of the data in (20) is also a definite expression; if indeed aP-raising is motivated by definiteness as mentioned in Footnote 6, then it is curious how a nominal is still definite where the aP has not raised up. However, to address this puzzle is beyond the scope and relevance of this paper.

always the second adjective in the adjective sequence, the one adjacent to the Dem that gets the stress.[9] This is shown in (24)–(27).

(24) *choto*$_i$ *LAL*$_k$ *ei* $[_{aP}$ t_j t_k *boi*$]_i$ *du-to* t_i
small red this book two-CL
'this small RED book'

(25) **CHOTO*$_i$ *lal*$_k$ *ei* $[_{aP}$ t_j t_k *boi*$]_i$ *du-to* t_i
small red this book two-CL
'this small red book'

(26) *lal*$_k$ *CHOTO*$_j$ *ei* $[_{aP}$ t_j t_k *boi*$]_i$ *du-to* t_i
red small this book two-CL
'this red small book'

(27) **LAL*$_k$ *choto*$_j$ *ei* $[_{aP}$ t_j t_k *boi*$]_i$ *du-to* t_i
red small this book two-CL
'this red small book'

The ungrammaticality of (25) and (27) shows that there is a fixed focus position which is immediately above the DP; the second adjective which moves out across the DEM but does not land in this position does not get stress.

That is, I claim that there is one FocP within the nominal domain, and the FocP is right above the DP. Theoretically, this position provides a landing site for the phrasal movement of adjectives across the Dem, and it also accounts for the empirical fact that whenever such a movement occurs with one adjective, that adjectives gets stressed, and when two adjectives move out, the lower one (close to the Dem) gets the stress.

I will argue here that in case of movement of multiple adjectives across the Dem, each adjective from the order in (23) separately moves out, as opposed to both the adjectives moving out as a chunk. The movements that I am arguing for and against can be schematized as follows, shown in (28) and (29).

(28) choto$_i$ lal$_j$ ei $[_{aP}$ t_i t_j boi] du-to

(29) *[choto lal]$_i$ ei $[_{aP}$ t_i boi] du-to

Let me present my reasons for assuming the movement in (28), and not the one in (29). See (23) repeated as (30) below.

9. In cases where the focused adjective has a modifier, the modifier can bear the stress when both the adjective and the modifier are fronted. This means that the stress is not always at the right edge of a focus constituent, something that an anonymous reviewer has pointed out to be an interesting topic for future research.

(30) *ei* [$_{aP}$ *choto lal boi*]$_i$ *du-to* t_i
this small red book two-CL
'these two small red books'

Notice that the adjectives *choto* and *lal* within the aP are in the universal order of *size* and *color*. In case of multiple adjective fronting, if the adjectives moved as a chunk, then the order predicted after the movement is *choto lal*. However, I have shown in (26) that the order after the movement can be *lal choto*. I take this as evidence that the adjectives move out independently across the Dem where multiple adjective fronting takes place.[10] The movement will look like (31).

(31) choto$_i$ [$_{FocP}$LAL$_j$ [$_{DP}$ei [$_{aP}$ t_i t_j boi]$_k$ du-to t_k]]

Now that I have argued that only one of the moved adjectives land in the FocP, and that both the adjectives move independently across the Dem, I will argue that the non-focused adjective moves higher up than the FocP, and lands in the TopP above the FocP.

3.2 TopicP within the nominal domain

See (31) repeated as (32) below:

(32) choto$_i$ [$_{FocP}$ LAL$_j$ [$_{DP}$ ei [$_{aP}$ t_i t_j boi]$_k$ du-to t_k]]

This expression can only be uttered when the adjective *small* (*choto*) is part of background information. That is, it is a situation where the information about the size of the book is already available, namely the fact that the book is small; then an additional information or a contrastive information is given in terms of the color of the book, in this case the color being *red* (*lal*). In this case, if someone asks a question which of the small books one wants, one can answer by uttering (34). This conversation is shown in (33)–(34).

(33) *kon choto boi du-to tomar chai?*
which small book two-CL you want
'which of the small books do you want?'

10. An anonymous reviewer has pointed out that generally it is assumed that adjectives cannot undergo A′-movement because of Left Branch Condition, which states that the leftmost item of an NP cannot be moved out of that NP. However, the relevant adjective-movement in this paper suggests that A′-movement is allowed within the nominal domain. Ross (1967) notes that there are Left Branch Condition violations in a number of languages (for example, Russian); the data shows that Bangla adds to the number of such languages.

(34) *choto LAL oi boi du-to amar chai*
small red those book two-CL I want
'I want those two RED small books'

In the literature *topic* is often described as the background information of an utterance. Taking that as a standard notion of a topic, I suggest that *choto* in (34) is a topic. That is, the adjective *choto* moves further up than the FocP, and lands in the TopP. In other words, I claim there is a TopP within the Bangla nominal domain, and it is above the FocP, and the adjective *choto* in this case raises there. The relevant final structure of the Bangla nominal phrase, according to this paper, is shown below in (35).

(35) $[_{TopicP}$ choto$_k$ $[_{FocP}$ LAL$_j$ $[_{DP}$ ei $[_{aP}$ $t_j t_k$ boi$]_i$ du-to t_i $]]]$

The final structure can be schematically shown in (36).

(36) $[_{TopicP}$ Adjective2$_k$ $[_{FocP}$ Adjective1$_j$ $[_{DP}$ DEM $[_{aP}$ $t_j t_k$ N$]_i$ Num-Cl t_i $]]]$

It is pertinent to note that focus and topic are optional functional heads in the extended nominal domain. That is, focus and topic projections will be activated only when they are needed. Furthermore, it seems that regarding adjective fronting, there is parametric variation if some language will allow focus or topic movement. Russian, for example, allows adjective fronting to a FocP but does not allow a topic movement. Consider (37)–(39).

(37) *eta bolshaya krasnaya kniga*
this big red book
'this big red book'

(38) *KRASNAYA eta bolshaya kniga*
red this big book
'this big RED book'

(39) */?*bolshaya KRASNAYA eta kniga*
big RED this book

Example (37) shows multiple adjectives before the noun *kniga*; (38) shows fronting of *red* across the D^0 head *eta*, suggesting movement to a fixed focus position above the DP; (39) shows that Russian does not allow movement of the second adjective across *eta*, suggesting that topic-movement is not allowed in the language.

3.3 Evidence that Focus and Topic are not outside the nominal domain

I have shown movement of adjectives across the DEM, and into higher functional projections, and I have argued that these landing sites are FocP and TopP. Now one can posit a concern that the FocP and the TopP where the adjectives move to are outside the nominal domain. That is, in other words, I need to show that the FocP and the TopP that I discussed are indeed within the nominal domain, and the adjectives are not moving to the clausal Focus or Topic phrases.

Consider (40) and (41). The expression 'lal CHOTO ei boi-ta' may either occur below or above the subject 'I'. The different possible positions with respect to the subject show that it constitutes a single nominal expression. If it is a single nominal, then there is only one nominal domain here, and any movement within this whole expression has to be within the nominal domain itself. I take this is as sufficient evidence that the movements of the adjectives to the Focus and the Topic positions take place within the nominal domain, and not to any sentential/clausal Focus/Topic positions.

(40) ***ami*** *[lal CHOTO ei boi-ta] porechi*
I red small this book-CL have read
'I have read this red small book'

(41) *[lal CHOTO ei boi-ta]* ***ami*** *porechi*
red small this book-CL I have read
'I have read this red small book'

3.4 Mechanism

In this section, I talk about the mechanism of the movement of adjectives to the focus and topic positions. I have shown earlier, regarding focus, that the constituent in Focus is marked by prosodic prominence; that is, it bears the primary stress. I will side with Aboh (2010) in that the information structure of a sentence is pre-determined in the numeration. In other words, topic and focus are functional categories that are selected as lexical choices in the numeration. In Aboh's words, "a numeration N pre-determines the Information Structure of a linguistic expression". The constituent that bears the feature related to the Information Structure then needs to move up in a local checking configuration with the relevant functional head that has the matching feature (cf. Rizzi 1997). *Criteria*, a set of principles, constrain such local checking configurations; it requires that a Specifier/Head agreement relation obtains between the criterial functional head and the corresponding features of relevance, say, topic or focus. In more precise terms, the functional projection XP and the relevant head must have the same feature F (where F is focus or topic), and XP_F and X_F must be in a spec head configuration. *Criteria* then triggers the movement, in the sense that it gives an attraction capacity to the X_F, and thus the XP moves up and lands in the specifier position of the X_F.

In the case in hand, namely in (35), the adjective *lal* is marked with Focus feature, and the adjective *choto* is marked with Topic feature. Recall that I argued that an adjective is an AdjP; that is, *lal* is an XP with the feature focus marked in the numeration, and *choto* is an XP with the feature topic marked in the numeration.

Criteria triggers the focus movement, when the covert Foc^0 attracts the XP_{focus}, and thus *lal* moves to the specifier of the FocP, and is in a Spec-Head configuration with the Focus head. The topic movement is triggered in a similar way by *criteria*, and the Top^0 attracts the AdjP *choto* (which has Topic feature marked), and thus *choto* moves up to the specifier of the TopP, and is in a Spec-Head relation with the Topic head. I take the focus movement to be a representative case and show it in a tree diagram in Figure 4; the topic movement happens in the same fashion.

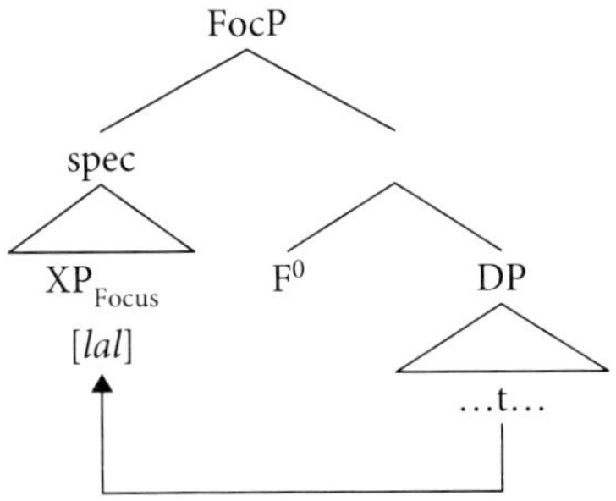

Figure 4. Mechanism of Focus Movement

3.5 Comparison with the clausal domain

Since Rizzi (1997) it is a well-known idea in the literature that the left periphery of a clause (CP) has finer divisions, and has higher functional projections like Topic phrases, Focus phrases, Fin phrases etc. If DP is taken as the counterpart of IP in the nominal domain, in this paper I have shown that there are higher projections within the nominal domain as well; namely FocP and TopP above the DP. My evidence from Bangla adjective fronting extends Rizzi's core proposal to the nominal domain, and adds to the recent research that focuses on the parallelism between the two domains.

Choudhury (2010) looks into focus and topic structure in the clausal domain of Bangla, and she argues for a FocP above the IP in Bangla, and for a TopP above the FocP.[11] If we assume the parallelism hypothesis,[12] then the clausal and the nominal domain of Bangla should be parallel. This paper provides evidence on the parallelism in the discourse-related sub-domain (CP in case of the clause); assuming Choudhury (2010) in terms of the position of focus and topic in the clausal part, I show that the Focus and the Topic present in the nominal domain are exactly

11. This proposal differs from a lower focus phrase right above the VP proposed for some other Indian languages in Jayaseelan (2008).

12. The Parallelism Hypothesis will state that the structure of a clause [CP… [IP… [VP]]] should be parallel to the nominal domain as well.

parallel to the clausal structure. In other words, the IP in the clausal domain is the DP in the nominal domain. I showed in the paper that there is a fixed Focus position right above the DP, and a Topic phrase above the FocP, which is what Choudhury (2010) argues for the clausal counterpart. This is shown schematically in (42).

(42) Clause: TopP...FocP...IP
Nominal: TopP...FocP...DP

4. From the 'lexical'-'functional' and 'syntactic' perspective

This paper is in the line of cartographic research, attempting to draw a right structural map for natural language syntax. A lot of functional heads were identified in the syntax literature over the years; X-bar theory was extended to functional elements of the clause as a CP-IP-VP syntactic mapping; and the idea started to be accepted that other configurations like nominal expressions can also be in a hierarchical structure with a lexical projection embedded within a functional structure (Abney's 1987 DP-hypothesis).

It is now almost unanimously believed that clauses and phrases are formed by a lexical and a higher functional structure, and following Chomsky's 'Uniformity Principle',[13] this paper assumes that the principles of phrase and clause composition in all languages are the same, and so is the functional make-up. That is, the hierarchies of functional projections that dominate VP, IP, NP, AdjP, PP are universal in the type of heads and specifiers that they involve.

Valois (1991) points out that the structure of the DP is parallel to CP; that is, NP is the nominal counterpart of VP, and DP is the nominal counterpart of CP. Assuming this view, once the array of functional projections within the clausal domain were argued to exist, it follows that the hierarchy of adverbs suggested by Cinque (1999) should also have nominal counterparts. This is what Scott (2002) works out, and I take his stance that the nominal domain has a fixed hierarchy of functional projections, which I have shown in the paper as aP-s. To put the idea in a nutshell, the adjectives are part of the lexicon. They are taken from the lexicon during a computation, and mapped into the syntax, forming an Adjective Phrase (AdjP).[14] An AdjP is generated in the specifier position of a higher functional

13. "In the absence of compelling evidence to the contrary, assume languages to be uniform, with variety restricted to easily detectable properties of utterances."

14. A reviewer raised a question on the lexical status of adjectives, suggesting another possibility (cf Leu 2008) that what is in the lexicon is rather 'adjectival roots', which later is 'made' into an adjective in the syntax. Whether adjectives are primitives is an issue well beyond the scope of this paper; however there is no empirical indication in Bangla, unlike

projection aP, the hierarchy of these higher functional categories is in the UG (universal grammar). Such an analysis where an adjective is in the specifier of an aP associated with its respective semantic class gives a very 'articulated correspondence between universal semantic properties and the syntax'.[15] Then extending the parallelism between the clausal and the nominal domain, this paper shows that there are higher functional projections TopicP and FocusP above the DP, which is already well argued for in the clausal domain in the literature (the split CP of Rizzi 1997). I assume that the information structure of an utterance is pre-determined in the numeration (Aboh 2010), which is to say that the functional categories of topic and focus are selected as lexical choices in the numeration. Once this is lexically determined, the constituent marked with such information about information structure needs to move up in a local checking configuration with the relevant functional head that has the matching feature; and how this mechanism works I have discussed previously in 5.5.

5. Conclusion

The paper discusses the syntax of adjectives in Bangla, and argues that adjectives are specifiers of universal functional projections. Using data of multiple adjective fronting, I argue that there is a focus and a topic projection within the nominal domain of Bangla. I discuss how a feature driven analysis can explain such adjectival movement to higher discourse-related functional projections. This is parallel to the general clausal structure proposed in Rizzi (1997), and also to an existing account of focus and topic positions in the clausal domain of Bangla (Choudhury 2010).

6. Further research

An anonymous reviewer has correctly pointed out that the next step of this research is to investigate if DP is a phase or not. If one takes a strong parallelism

many Dravidian languages (cf. Zvelebil 1990; Bhat 1994; Amritavalli & Jayaseelan 2004; Menon 2013 for various arguments and attempts to address the controversial status of adjectives in Dravidian) that the status of adjectives is confusing. For lack of any strong evidence on the contrary, I will go with the standard view where adjectives are part of the lexicon. It is important to note that even with an account claiming adjectives are actually primitive roots, which are then made into adjectives, there will be movement needed to the focus and topic positions to account for the relevant word order discussed in this paper, and thus the analysis provided here would remain unchanged.

15. In the words of G.J Scott (2002).

hypothesis regarding the nominal and clausal domain, then a priori one should expect arguments for two phases within the nominal domain, as VP and CP are known to be phases in the clause.

Furthermore, it would be interesting to see if there are counterparts of an ForceP and FinP in the nominal domain, as they are argued to be functional projections the extended left periphery of Rizzi (1997).

Acknowledgements

I would like to thank Dr. Andrew Simpson, Priyanka Biswas, Arunima Choudhury, Caitlin Smith, Dasha Henderer, Antonina Barankevich, and two anonymous reviewers for valuable comments, suggestions, and data/judgments.

References

Aboh, Enoch Oladé. 2010. Information structuring begins with the numeration. *Iberia* 2(1): 12–42.

Amritavalli, Raghavachari & Jayaseelan, Karattuparambil A. 2004. The genesis of syntactic categories and parametric variation. In *Generative Grammar in a Broader Perspective: Proceedings of the 4th GLOW in Asia 2003*, Hang-Jin Yoon (ed.), 19–41. Hankook: Seoul.

Bhat, DN Shankara. 1994. *The Adjectival Category: Criteria for Differentiation and Identification* 24. Amsterdam: John Benjamins.

Bhattacharya, Tanmoy. 1998. DP-internal NP movement. *UCL Working Papers in Linguistics* 10: 225–251.

Bhattacharya, Tanmoy. 1999. Specificity in Bangla DP. In *Yearbook on South Asian Languages and Linguistics* 2, Rajendra Singh (ed.), 71–99. SAGE Publications.

Choudhury, Arunima. 2010. Study of Focus in Bangla. MA thesis, University of Southern California.

Cinque, Guglielmo. 1999. *Adverbs and Functional Heads: A Cross-linguistic Perspective*. Oxford: Oxford University Press.

Dayal, Veneeta. 2012. What can South Asian Languages tell us about classifier systems? Talk given at FASAL2, MIT.

Giusti, Giuliana. 1997. The categorical status of determiners. In *New Comparative Syntax*, Iliiane Haegeman (ed.), 95–124. London: Longman.

Jayaseelan, Karattuparambil A. 2008. Topic, focus and adverb positions in clause structure. *Nanzan Linguistics* 4: 43–68.

Leu, Thomas. 2008. *The Internal Syntax of Determiners*. ProQuest.

Menon, Mythili. 2013. The apparent lack of adjectives in Malayalam and other related languages. In *Proceedings of Glow-in-Asia IX 2012: The Main Session*, Nobu Goto, Koichi Otaki, Atsushi Sato, Kensuke Takita (eds), 157–171. Japan: Mie University.

Rizzi, Luigi. 1997. The fine structure of left periphery. In *Elements of Grammar: Handbook of Generative Syntax*, Liliane Haegeman (ed.), 281–337. Springer.

Ross, John. 1967. Constraints on variables in syntax. PhD thesis, Massachusetts Institute of Technology.

Scott, Gary-John. 2002. Stacked adjectival modification and the structure of nominal phrases. In *Functional structure in DP and IP: The Cartography of Syntactic Structures,* vol. 1, 91–120. Oxford: OUP.

Sigurðsson, Hálldor Ármann. 2006. Agree in syntax, agreement in signs. In *Agreement Systems*, C. Boeckx (ed.), 201–237. Amsterdam: John Benjamins.

Sproat, Richard & Shih, Chilin. 1990. The cross-linguistic distribution of adjective ordering restrictions. In *Interdisciplinary Approaches to Language: Essays in Honor of S.-Y. Kuroda*, C. Georgopoulos & R. Ishihara (eds), 565–593. Dordrecht: Kluwer Academic Publishers.

Valois, Daniel. 1991. The Internal Syntax of DP. PhD dissertation, University of California, Los Angeles.

Zvelebil, Kamil. 1990. *Dravidian Linguistics: An Introduction*. Pondicherry, India: PILC (Pondicherry Institute of Linguistics and Culture).

Rich results

R. Amritavalli
The English & Foreign Languages University

The first-phase event structure of two verbs typical of the Kannada dative experiencer construction, *bar-* 'come' and *aag-* 'happen, become,' suggests (differently from Ramchand 2008) that stative verbs may project "rich" results and "poor" processes. The properties of *bar-* are explored vis-à-vis English 'come.' *Bar-* and *aag-* allow telicity by "classifying events that are themselves already results" (Higginbotham 1999). The result event is a small clause with experiencer and experience in a possession relation, as in the English double object construction; with the difference that Kannada encodes possession with dative case, whereas possessional *to* in English incorporates into *be* to yield *have* (Kayne 1993 [2000]). The dative argument occupies the RESULTEE position; arguments in higher event structure positions (UNDERGOER or INITIATOR) are nominative in Kannada.

Keywords: event structure; dative of possession; experiencer; telicity; stativity

1. Introduction[1]

The experiencer dative construction in South Asian languages has received the attention of linguists for about half a century now (Verma & Mohanan 1990; Shibatani 1999; Bhaskararao & Subbarao 2004). This investigation has centered mainly on the subject-like properties of the experiencer dative argument. Amritavalli and Jayaseelan (2003, and related papers; henceforth A&J) turned their attention to the experience-denoting noun in the predicate. In this paper, I examine the verb in the predicate. I begin with an account of the event structure projection, in terms of the first-phase syntax of Ramchand (2008), of the verbs *bar-* 'come' and *aag-* 'happen, become' in Kannada that are typical of the construction.

A&J pointed out a significant, if neglected, fact about the dative experiencer construction: its predicate categorially expresses the experience as a noun, whereas nominative experiencer constructions express it as an adjective. Not all four of the

1. I thank Rahul Balusu, Shruti Sircar and K. A. Jayaseelan for helpful discussion, and two anonymous referees for useful comments.

syntactic categories N, V, A and P, which correspond respectively to the semantic types of entities, events, states and relations, are universal; many languages lack A and P (Hale & Keyser 1993). The impoverishment of the category A in the Dravidian languages correlates with the prevalence of the experiencer dative construction in them. A&J postulated a "floating" dative case in experiencer constructions with *be*, which appears on the experiencer in Dravidian, or (in languages like English) is absorbed by the experience N to yield the syntactic category Adjective.

I shall here widen the inquiry to verbs other than *be*, and argue that the experiencer and experience denoting nouns in the dative construction are in a "possession" relation expressed by dative case. They occur in a small clause in the result projection of the event structure of the verb. Kannada *bar-*, like English *come*, is an activity or accomplishment verb when it occurs with nominative subjects. But in the dative experiencer construction, it is a presentational verb – a light verb that projects a "rich" result and a "poor" process (Ramchand 2008: 148). The structure it occurs in is that of double object verbs in English, minus the *init* projection. My account of *bar-* is consistent with the proposal in Higginbotham (1999) that achievement verbs allow telicity by "classifying events that are themselves already results."

Turning to the verb *aag-*, I show that its paraphrases *become* and *happen* follow from the nature of its small clause complement. A copular small clause complement yields the *become* interpretation via "incorporation" of the copula into the process verb; in this case, *aag-* has a nominative subject. A dative small clause argument yields the *happen* reading; dative case in Kannada does not "incorporate" into the verb, and the experiencer dative construction results. This structurally derived alternation in the meanings of *aag-* in its occurrences with a dative experiencer or nominative subject argues against traditional accounts of experiencer dative case as a "governed" or "quirky" case assigned semantically by a class of "psychological" predicates.

The paper is organized as follows. Section 2 sets out the main theoretical assumptions in this paper: a first-phase syntax of event structure that facilitates a "rich" result sub event, and a dative case with the semantics of possession that is overt in Kannada, but covert in *have* languages like English. Section 3 is an exploration of the event structures projected by *bar-* in its occurrences with nominative subjects and dative experiencers, and proposes an event structure for the latter. Section 4 addresses issues in the representation of stative verbs that arise out of my analysis. I distinguish the result phrase that I posit from resultatives of accomplishment verbs, and outline Higginbotham's account of telicity in achievement verbs. Section 5 presents an analysis of the verb *aag-* as 'come to be,' 'come to pass' or 'come to have;' and Section 6 concludes with the argument that the experiencer dative construction is the sub part of the double object construction that does not project the causative sub event.

2. Theoretical assumptions

2.1 A first phase representation of eventive predicates

Ramchand (2008) is a recent account within minimalist assumptions of how lexical items are mapped into the syntax. Verbs have argument structure, their arguments have recognizable thematic roles, and there are identifiable regularities in the thematic-syntactic mapping. Such grammatically relevant aspects of lexical meaning can be thought of as arising out of the computational system in syntax. Ramchand proposes an event-building phase in the syntax (the 'first phase'), taking into account core predicational relations and syntactic argument types. The event-building portion of a proposition is assumed to be prior to case marking/checking, agreement or tense (op. cit.:16, n.4). In her system of event structure, an event is decomposed into three sub event types. There is a causing projection *init*P whose subject is the external argument, the INITIATOR; a process-denoting projection *proc*P, whose subject is the UNDERGOER; and a result state *res*P whose subject is the RESULTEE. The category label V(erb) is correspondingly decomposed into [init], [proc] and [res], and a lexical item can project these features to form a predication.

Let me add (at a reviewer's instance) a word about the choice of this "complex and costly" framework for a construction that has been much analyzed "using more 'standard' approaches." My exploration of some non-obvious properties of a construction long viewed as an areal/typological phenomenon of "quirky" or "governed" case assigned by a semantically identifiable class of predicates, and earlier, even speculated to reflect an "experiential" rather than "agentive" world view (Klaiman 1986), aims at an explanatory account of it in terms of parametric variation in the categorial representation of stative predications, and the expression of the possession relation. In the absence of Adjectives, a predicate Noun designates the experiential state of the experiencer, and a possession-denoting case relates the two. The principled and restrictive account of the syntactic projection of various aspectual categories of verbs in the first phase is what prompts and facilitates this analysis.

The idea that syntax represents sub lexical units, i.e. of lexical decomposition in the syntax, allows us to unify the possession relation in the experiencer dative construction with the same relation in an apparently different construction in a genetically and typologically unrelated language: namely, the double object construction in English. The postulation of an abstract preposition of possession in the latter (Harley 2002, building on Pesetsky 1995; Richards 2001) was consequent on Kayne's (2000[1993]) decomposition of possessive *have* into *be* and a dative case. (An earlier attempt at a parametric approach to the experiencer dative construction, Jayaseelan 1990, cast in the mould of pro-drop and scrambling, had postulated a "complex predicate" formed by the experiencer and the experience but left unspecified the nature of the relation between them.) Lexical decomposition receives a natural implementation within Distributed Morphology (which allows "late" lexical insertion, after syntactic trees have been built up). The decomposition of transitive/ causative verbs into *v* and V (Chomsky 1995: 315ff.; Kratzer 1996) is now part of the standard generative machinery, even as *v* has later been split into various *ad hoc* 'flavours.'

First phase syntax is built up by Merge. A verb may be specified for more than one of the features [init], [proc] and [res]; the system allows it to project a feature and Merge with its argument, then project again and Remerge. Remerge is a way of implementing "head movement" in this framework; it also follows from a copy theory of movement. A single argument can now have more than one thematic role (a "composite role"), as it can be remerged into more than one projection, depending on the verb's event structure. A second novel idea is Underassociation. A lexical item bears multiple features and associates with multiple nodes: it lexicalizes chunks of trees. Its features may be a superset of the sequence to be spelled out; thus, it can have Underassociated features, which have to be independently identified and linked with it under specific conditions.

Ramchand's main concern is with eventive predicates, and her suggestions about how to represent stative predicates are much more programmatic. I will return to these in the sections where I present my analysis, following my explication of the Kannada data. Here, I only illustrate briefly her treatment of verbs of the *come* class. For Levin and Rappoport-Hovav (1995; henceforth L&RH), *come* is an unaccusative verb of inherently directed motion (L&RH: 111). Ramchand, however, treats as unaccusative only such intransitive (inchoative) verbs like *break* that have causative forms (2008: 78, n.6).[2] In her system, *come*, like the intransitive verbs *arrive* and *fall* that she discusses, would project all three of [init, proc, res]; the single argument of these verbs would have this composite thematic role. The telicity of these verbs, their having an end state, argues that they project [res]. They must also (argues Ramchand) project [init], because (i) they do not allow causativization, and (ii) unlike "the true unaccusatives," they do not allow their *-en* participle to occur pre-nominally (contrast *the broken stick* with **the arrived train*, **the come guests*). The possibility of *the recently arrived train* (moreover) suggests that "modification related to the initiation portion of the event is required" because the argument of *arrive* is an INITIATOR as well as an UNDERGOER or RESULTEE. The sentence *Michael arrived* thus has the representation (1) (=her (34), p. 79).

2. Intransitive *break* projects [proc] and [res]. The two "subjects," UNDERGOER and RESULTEE, share a subscript to mark their identity. The causative counterpart of *break* projects [init].

(1)

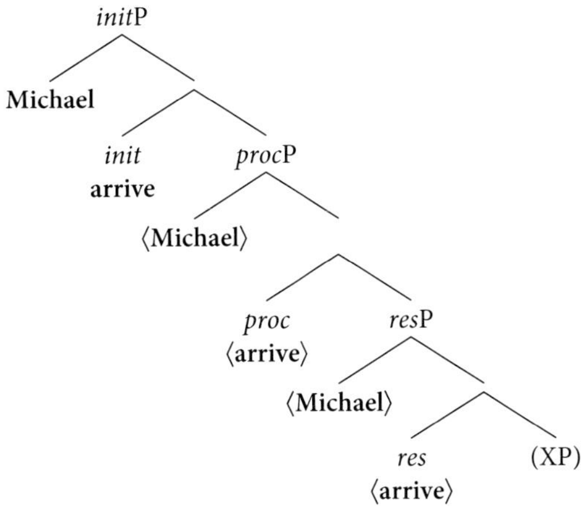

2.2 Light predicates and rich results

More pertinent to my analysis of the dative experiencer construction is a suggestion Ramchand offers about "light verbs" in complex predicate constructions in Indic. This construction is the counterpart of the verb-particle construction in English. Compare (2–3). The particle in (2), and the second verb in (3), force a resultative reading.

(2) She ate the mango up.

(3)

avaLu	*maavinahaNNu*	*tindu*	*haakidaLu/*	*biTTaLu.*
she	mango	eat.PST PPL.	put.PST.3F.SG./	leave.PST.3F.SG.

'She ate up the mango.'

In (2), the particle *up* identifies the [res] projected by the verb, and it is 'light:' i.e. it has "a fairly general and abstract semantics" (Ramchand op.cit.: 136). The sub events into which the eating event is decomposed are here separately lexically identified by the verb and the particle. So *eat* must underassociate its [res] feature, and unify its "lexical-encyclopedic" content with *up* (by a process like Agree). In this scenario, one of the unifying items is forced to be 'light;' in (2), the particle is light ("plausibly one of the salient properties of particles in English" (loc. cit.)).

In (3), a verb does the duty of the particle in English; the second verb is semantically 'light.' Interestingly, it is this verb and not the content verb *eat* that carries tense and agreement. Ramchand argues from the head-finality of the Indic languages that the *proc* head must (at some level) follow the *res* head. Taken together, these facts argue that the light verb is the *proc* head (and where projected, the *init* head) of the complex predicate. Therefore, the verb *eat*, which is encyclopedically rich, is the *res* head in (3); and indeed, it is realized as a perfect participle in

Kannada and Bangla. Standardly, the light verb has been considered to add telicity to the predicate; however (Ramchand points out) this "descriptive statement can easily be reconciled with the facts once we realize that it is the light verb that selects for a *res*P in this structure" (p. 146); "the crucial contribution of the tensed verb here is as the process descriptor … that selects the *res*P."

First phase predicate decomposition, thus, accounts for "result augmentation" in the verb-particle and complex predicate constructions. The difference between (2) and (3) lies in "how rich the lexical-encyclopedic content of each part of the first phase syntax is." In the verb-particle construction (2), "the main verb provides the bulk of the real-world content, and the particle representing the result is fairly abstract, or impoverished." In the complex predicate (3), the *res* head is rich in encyclopedic content, but the *proc* element is a light verb. In English as well, argues Ramchand (p. 148), cases "can be detected, whereby a 'light' verb joins forces with a richly contentful final state to create a complex predication:"

(4) (=her (96) Rich *res*, poor *proc*:
She got her boyfriend arrested.

Notice that (4) instantiates "causative" *get*, and not its unaccusative counterpart, *Her boyfriend got arrested*. Ramchand's discussion of "result augmentation" is limited to accomplishment verbs, i.e. verbs that have a causal subevent. The literature on resultatives has considered achievement verbs to not allow result phrases. I shall argue in Section 4.2 that the "rich *res*, poor *proc*" account be extended to achievement verbs.

2.3 Dative possessors and the have~be alternation

Kannada expresses inalienable possession with a "dative of possession" construction. There is no verb *have* in this language.

(5) *naayi-ge baala ide.*
dog-DAT. tail be.3SG.N.
'The dog has a tail.' (lit. 'To the dog is a tail.')

A&J note that English, which expresses possession with the verb *have* in (6a), has a vestigial and restricted dative of possession construction (6b) which corresponds word-for-word (*modulo* word order and expletive *pro*) to the Kannada "dative of possession" (7).[3]

(6) a. This must have a lid (to it).
b. There must be a lid to this.

3. The possessor must be inanimate, and the possession non-referential, in this construction in English: **There are ears to the dog*, **This is the lid to this.*

(7) *ida-kke ondu muccaLa ira beeku*
this-DAT. one lid be must
'(There) must be a lid to this.'

The idea that *have* is derived from *be* by the incorporation of a prepositional dative case (Kayne 2000 [1993]; also Freeze 1992) explains these data. The *be* and *have* sentences in (6) are related by the incorporation of the prepositional dative in (6b) into the verb in (6a), which surfaces as *have.*[4] Kannada has no verb *have* because dative case does not incorporate into *be* in Kannada; this case surfaces instead on the possessor.

In Ramchand's framework, the dative of possession can be simply expressed as an XP headed (in Kannada) by dative case *ge-*, which relates two entities: a possessor and a possession. (Following Antisymmetry (Kayne 1994), the representations for Kannada are in the head-complement order, though nothing crucial hinges on this.)

(8)
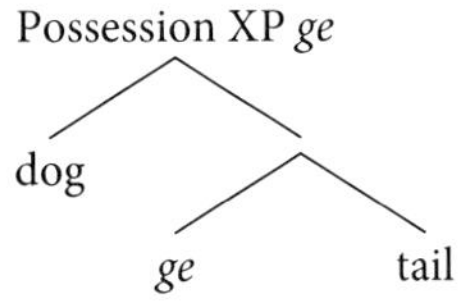

A counterpart has been proposed in English to the overt dative case in (8): a covert preposition of possession P_{HAVE} in the English double object construction (Harley 2002, following Pesetsky 1995; cf. also Richards 2001). P_{HAVE} is covert because the English preposition *to* has lost possessional meaning, this sense of *to* incorporating obligatorily into *be* to yield *have.*[5] (Ramchand analyzes *to* as a path head or a

4. Kayne builds on Szabolcsi's (1983) analysis of the Hungarian possessive construction, where *John has a sister* surfaces as *To John is a sister*. This construction originates with a copula (*van* in Hungarian) taking a single DP complement containing the possessor DP, to the right of and below D^0:

$$\ldots \textit{van} \; [_{DP} \text{ Spec } D^0 \; [\; DP_{poss} \ldots]].$$

The possessor may move to the left of the D head and surface as dative; it can then move out of the larger DP entirely, retaining dative case. (If the larger DP is definite, the possessor can also remain in situ and be marked nominative.)

For an account of the optional "to it" in (6a), cf. A&J p. 64, n. 1.

5. When not merged into the clausal functional architecture, *to* expresses possession, cf. the fragments in birth announcements *To John, a sister*; *sister to John*. *She is a sister to me* patterns with the examples in (6) above: *to* forces a non-referential reading for *a sister*, signaling the absence of a real relation.

result head.) Harley's "alternative projection" approach to the double object construction opposes Larson's (1988) account deriving it from the *to*-dative structure. For Harley, a verb like *give* selects different prepositional complements in the *to*-dative and the double object constructions. In the latter (… *give Mary a letter*), it selects $P_{HAVE.}$

(9) (=her 3b)

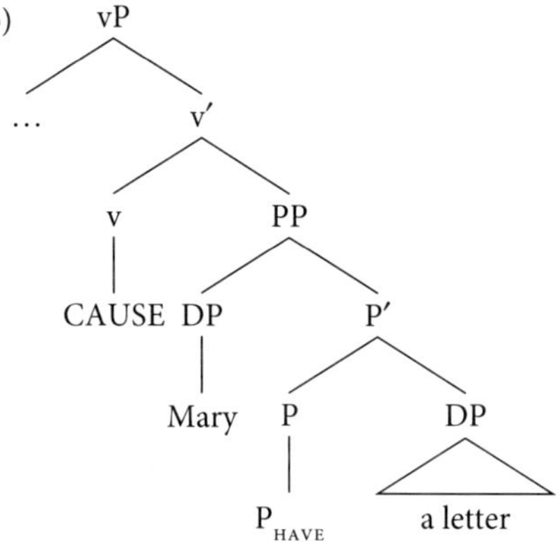

Ramchand adapts (9) to her more articulated clause structure: (10) below is her (74), p. 103. The verb *give* projects the causal subevent *init* (that perhaps corresponds to *v*'), and identifies *proc* and *res*. The possession PP is not *res*, but the complement of *res*. This PP does not have a specifier; the possessor is generated as the specifier of *res*P. Thus Ramchand adds a layer of structure between the possessor and P_{have}.

(10) Alex gave Ariel the ball.

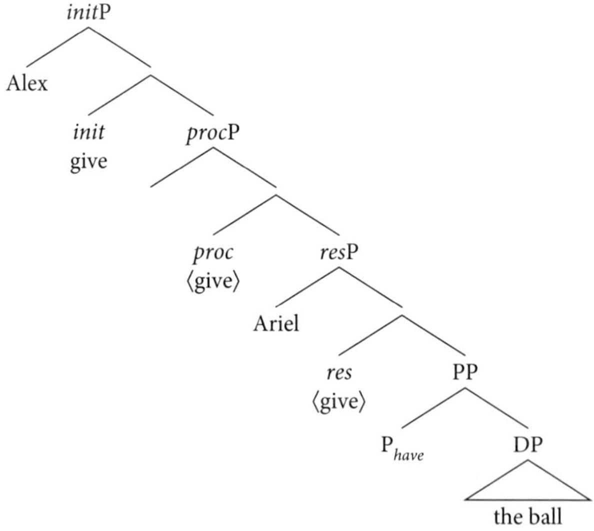

Kayne (2010) suggests that *BE* rather than *HAVE* is more likely the silent element in (the French counterpart of) such possessive constructions, because matrix *be* is left unpronounced in many languages, whereas a silent matrix *have* is unattested; then the possessor "already has, within the small clause, its dative Case." If so, the Kannada and the English/French dative-of-possession constructions are completely parallel.

To sum up this section, there is a PP of possession that occurs as a complement to a copula, yielding either the dative of possession, or the verb *have*. This PP of possession occurs also in the double object construction. I shall argue that yet another occurrence of it is what gives rise to the dative experiencer construction. In the structure I propose in (21), the verb (*bar-* or *aag-*) is the head of a *proc* phrase which takes a dative case possession phrase as its complement. (I revert to Harley's structure for the possession phrase in preference to Ramchand's.)

3. A first phase account of *bar-* 'come'

I explore the event structure projected by *bar-* in the nominative and experiencer dative constructions by teasing out differences between the Kannada verb and its English counterpart in their privileges of occurrence: i.e. the types of subjects and complements each allows. Where the verb meaning in the two languages maps into identical event structure projections, the Kannada sentence translates into English almost literally, *modulo* word order and case realizations. Kannada locutions that fail to thus converge in English show us the fault lines between these languages in the mapping from verb meaning to syntax.

3.1 *bar-* as a verb of self-initiated directed motion

In its prototypical use as a verb of physical motion with a nominative subject, the Kannada verb *bar-* corresponds to the English verb *come*.

(11) i. *naanu mane-ge bande.* Kannada
I.NOM. house-DAT. come.PST.1SG.
'I came home.'

ii. *gaaDi sTeeshan-ge bantu.*
train.NOM. station-DAT. come.PST.3SG.N.
'The train came to the station.'

(12) i. I came home. English
ii. The train came to the station.

We have seen that in Ramchand's system, English *come* is a [proc] verb that also projects [init]. In (12), the argument of *come* is plausibly an initiator. *Come* is also punctual, incorporating a [res] or result phrase: 'John will come in a minute/ *for a minute;' 'The pizza boy comes in 20 minutes/ *for 20 minutes.'[6]

A similar characterization is possible of Kannada *bar-* in (11) as [init, proc, res]. Consider first the [init] feature. Kannada *bar-* has a morphological causative form *bar-is-*, which may appear to argue that the causative morpheme realizes [init], and not the verb *bar-*. However, (11) (which has a nominative subject that is a plausible initiator of the movement) does not in my judgment allow the causativizing morpheme to occur.[7]

(13) i. **avaru nann-annu mane-ge bar-is -id-aru.*
they I-ACC. house-DAT. come-CAUS -PST.-3PL.
*'They made me come home, they brought me home.'

ii. **Draivaru gaaDi-yannu sTeeshan-ge bar-is -id-anu.*
driver train-ACC. station-DAT. come-CAUS -PST-3SG.M.
*'The driver brought the train to the station.'

bar- is also punctual: it allows adverbial adjuncts of time headed by *-alli* 'in,' and disallows the bare or the *-hottu* 'time' adjunct that has the durative interpretation:

(14) i. *avanu ondu ganTe-yalli bandanu.*
he one hour-IN come.PST.3M.SG.
'He came in an hour.'

ii. **avanu ondu gaNTe (hottu) bandanu.*
he one hour (time) come.PST.3M.SG.
*'He came for an hour.'

3.2 *bar-* in the experiencer dative construction

How should the verb *bar-* be analyzed in its occurrences in the experiencer dative constructions (15) and (16)? A literal rendering of these examples is that a memory or thought "comes" in (15); in (16), anger, sleep or wisdom "comes." But clearly,

6. These *for*-phrases can occur with the meanings 'John will stay for a short while,' or 'the pizza boy habitually hangs around for 20 minutes' (as a reviewer points out). The paraphrases indicate that what is modified is not the process of coming ('the pizza boy's coming will last for 20 minutes'), but its result (the "staying" or "hanging around"); strengthening the claim that *come* is punctual.

7. A magical situation, where movement could be externally induced, is imaginable with the causative *bar-is*. We may treat this as an instance of the "underassociation" of the causative feature of *bar-* when it is embedded under a causative morpheme (Ramchand op. cit:172 ff., 181).

none of these can be said to initiate a process of coming. I conclude that *bar-* in (15–16) must lack an [init] feature.

(15) i. *nan-age ondu gnyaapka/ nenapu bantu.*
I-DAT. one remembrance/ memory come.PST.3N.SG.
'A memory came to me.'

ii. *nan-age ondu yoocane bantu.*
I-DAT. one thought come.PST.3N.SG.
'A thought occurred to me.'

iii. *ivan-ige yeenu bantu?*
he-DAT. what come.PST.3N.SG.
'What has come over him?'

(16) i. *nan-age koopa bantu.*
I-DAT. anger come.PST.3N.SG.
'I felt/ got angry.'

ii. *nan-age nidde bantu.*
I-DAT. sleep come.PST.3N.SG.
'I felt/got sleepy.'

iii. *nan-age buddhi bantu.*
I-DAT. wisdom come.PST.3N.SG.
'I got wisdom/ I became wiser.'

iv. *nan-age ii kanassu bantu.*
I-DAT. this dream come.PST.3N.SG.
'I had this dream.'

Where *bar-* lacks [init], we expect [init] to be independently lexically realizable when projected. Indeed, the causative verb *bar-is* occurs most naturally in examples corresponding to (16 i–ii):

(17) i. *avaru nan-age summane koopa bar-is-utt-aare.*
they I-DAT. for no reason anger come-CAUS-NONPST-3PL.
'They always make me get angry.' (=they tease me)

ii. ii *maatre nan-age nidde bar-is-utt-e.*
this pill I-DAT. sleep come-CAUS-NONPST-3N.SG.
'This pill makes me sleepy.'

Insofar as the Kannada examples (15–16) have well-formed English counterparts, an inference that [init] need not always be projected by the English verb *come* either, seems to be warranted.[8] We do not of course expect straightforward

8. If *bring* in English is 'cause to come' (*John brought his new girlfriend to the party*), *come* does not inevitably lexicalize [init]. (L&RH report a suggestion in Chierchia (1989) to this effect.)

correspondences in English for the occurrences of *bar-* in the experiencer dative construction (henceforth "dative *bar-*"), since English is known to lack the construction. Yet some instances of dative *bar-* lend themselves more readily to an English rendering than others. Compare the sets (18–19). (The dative experiencer corresponds to a *to*-object, and the predicative noun in Kannada to the subject, in English). I judge the English examples in (19) less acceptable than those in (18). The examples in (19) improve when the parenthesized elements are included; these are elements that modify and enhance the process component.

(18) i. A memory came to me (of roses and champagne).
ii. A(nother) thought came to me.
iii. What has come over him?

(19) i. *Anger came to me.
ii. Sleep came to me (unheralded, unaided by pills …) (Cf. also *Sleep eluded me*, *Sleep would not come to me*)
iii. ?Wisdom came to him (late in life).
iv. ?This dream came to me.

The less acceptable English examples in (19) are more obviously stative than (18). In English, the semantic type of state is encoded by the predicative category Adjective, and the most natural way in English to express the states in (19) is with adjectival predicates, as in the translations of (16): 'I felt/ got angry;' 'I felt/got sleepy;' 'I got wise/ I became wiser.' Kannada, we have noted, is impoverished in adjectives, and so relies on nouns to designate states. Now in (18) as against (19), the nouns that are the subjects of *come*, though not sentient, are individualized and therefore conceivable as entities that undergo a process of coming; it is easier to visualize 'thinking' or 'remembering' as an event, than 'sleeping' or 'being angry.' This explains why (19ii–iii) improve when elements that modify the *proc* projection are included; they foreground the process of "coming." The process-enhancing elements include, but are not limited to, manner adjuncts in (19ii) (*unheralded, unaided by pills*), or a time adjunct in (19iii) (*late in life*). The acceptability of *elude* relative to *come* in (19ii) is perhaps because the lexical meaning of *elude* encodes manner of motion, i.e. avoidance of pursuit. Negation, i.e. the not-coming of sleep, may also play a role: the relative acceptability of *Sleep would not come to me* as against ?*Sleep came to me* suggests that the not-coming of sleep is eventive compared to the stativity of sleep "coming" to someone. Conversely, example (19iv) improves if its stativity is enhanced by specifying a locational source for a generic subject: <u>*Dreams*</u> *come to us* <u>*from the collective unconscious*</u>.

In short, dative *bar-* differs from English *come* in that it tolerates a weaker *proc* element. It encodes a state that is the end result of a process. Hence, it more readily allows the semantic type of state in its nominative argument, which denotes the state that the dative argument is in. Dative case here thus signifies simply a relation between two nouns. We know that dative case encodes possession in Kannada. Now it is well-known that the possession relation serves merely to relate two nouns in a somewhat unspecified, or typical, relationship. Thus, the experiencer dative construction is in fact a (dative-of)-possession construction. Indeed, we find that the relation expressed by dative case in the experiencer construction is, in a range of corresponding English examples, expressed by the verb of possession *have*. We have already seen this in (16iv) (repeated below as (20i): the dream-state conveyed by *bar-* translates into English as *I had this dream*, i.e. the dreamer "possesses" the dream. The other examples in the set elaborate this point.

(20) i. *nan-age ii kanassu bantu.*
I-DAT. this dream come.PST.3N.SG.
'I had this dream.'

ii. *avan-ige ondu khayile/ rooga/ jvara/ negaDi bandide.*
he-DAT. one illness/ disease/ fever/ cold has.come
'He has an illness/ a disease/ a fever/ a cold.'

iii. *avan-ige English bar-utt-e.*
he-DAT. English come-NONPST-3N.SG.
'He knows English;' cf. 'He has (no) English, 'English comes to him easily.'

iv. *nan-age dhairya baral-i*
I-DAT. courage come.INF.-modal (permissive)
'Give me courage' (lit. 'Let courage come to me')

The last example, translated as a double object dative in English, does not have an overt *have*. But it is of a natural class with possessives, cf. (9–10) above.

3.3 *bar-* as a stative verb

We have seen that dative *bar-* has no [init], and tolerates a weak [proc]. It encodes a state that is the end result of a process. Dative *bar-* is then like a verb of appearance or existence, with a relational element in the predicate. This relational element is dative case, which designates a possession relation between the experiencer and the experience. I, therefore, represent dative *bar-* in (21) as a process head that has a result phrase, a small clause. The head of the small clause is dative case, which relates the experiencer (the holder or possessor of a result state) and the experience-denoting noun in the rheme position.[9]

9. The rheme is characterized as the object of a stative verb, where there is "no dynamicity/ process/ change involved in the predication" (Ramchand op. cit: 33), only a "predicational asymmetry." The rheme is part of the description of the state predicated of the subject.

(21) *nan-age koopa bantu / nan-age ondu yoocane bantu.*
I-DAT. anger came / I-DAT. one thought came
'I got angry' 'I had a thought'

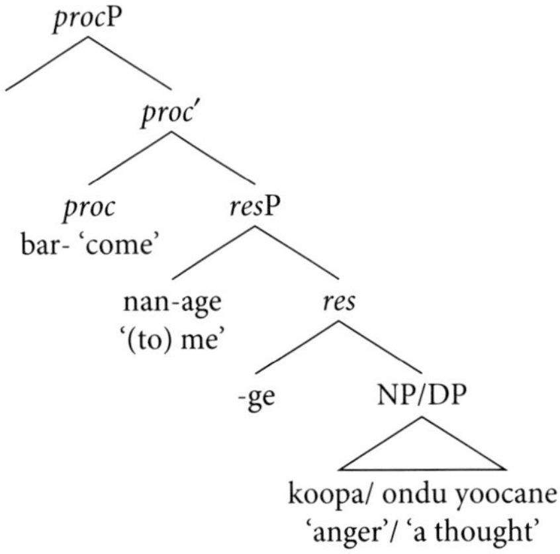

This structure is akin to the relevant subpart of the English double object structure. Ramchand's structure for it was illustrated in (10) above. A difference is that I have allowed *bar-* to underassociate its *res* feature, with dative case instantiating *res*. Ramchand has the verb identify both *proc* and *res* to show that the result of giving is "cotemporaneous" with the act of giving. (In contrast, in her *to*-dative construction the verb underassociates and unifies its semantics with *to*, which heads *res*.) Since dative *bar-* does not denote an action or process that brings about the result, but only "presents" the result, I choose not to project the additional layer of structure required if *res* were not headed by dative case.[10] Dative *bar-* thus underassociates its *res* feature and unifies its conceptual content with the *res* head *ge*, in the manner of the complex predications discussed in Section (2.2). The possessor/experiencer is merged as the specifier of the dative head, as in Harley (2002).

4. The representation of stative verbs

This analysis of dative *bar-* raises some questions about the representation of stative verbs, including verbs of appearance and existence, and the licensing of

10. That dative case can head *res*, even as *to* can, is suggested by the dative adjunct below, interpreted as a result. Compare the Kannada with its literal English translation: 'To our misfortune, they happened to see us.'

namma duradriST-akke avaru nammana nooDi-biTTaru.
our misfortune-DAT. they us see.PPL.-left.asp.

result phrases by them. Stative verbs, in Ramchand's system, have no *proc* element (op.cit.:55), as *proc* is "the hallmark of dynamicity" (p. 106). This accords well with our observation that *proc* is attenuated in dative *bar-*; but it also militates against this projection for it. What, then, would *bar-* project in Ramchand's system, as a stative verb?

4.1 The init projection

For Ramchand, stative verbs "consist simply of an *init* projection, with rhematic material projected as the complement of *init* instead of a full processual *proc*P" (p. 55). Thus, *Katherine fears nightmares* (her example (33)) has the structure (22) (=her (34)), where Katherine is "straightforwardly interpreted as the holder of the state:"

(22)

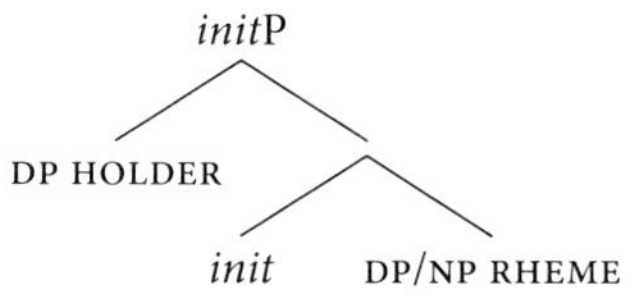

Ramchand concedes that "notating the first-phase syntax of statives as '*init*' is not strictly necessary, since we could simply assume an independent verbal head corresponding to an autonomous state," but prefers to "unify the ontology" of stative and dynamic verbs because Burzio's generalization (that verbs that assign accusative case license an external argument) applies to both.[11]

The considerations from Burzio's generalization do not, of course, straightforwardly carry over to the experiencer dative construction. The experience argument in Kannada is never marked accusative.[12] Therefore, nothing forces an external argument in this construction. The initiator is a primitive that distinguishes the external argument. It is defined for intransitive unergatives as "an entity whose properties/behavior are responsible for the eventuality coming into existence" (p. 24; e.g. *he stank*). This definition is indeed appropriate for the nominative subject of *bar-* in (23a), but not for the dative experiencer in (23b).

11. It is not obvious that *be* in English (e.g.) has an "object" with accusative case. As Ramchand notes (p. 34), DP objects of stative verbs are 'Rhematic Objects' that are part of the description of the predicate, and RHEMES can be PPs and APs as well as DPs.

12. Mahajan (2004:286) in fact argues that "constructions in which (the) non-nominative subjects appear (in Hindi, RA) lack a source for accusative case." Tamil, however, is claimed to allow accusative case in the dative experiencer construction.

(23) a. *idu vaasane bar-utt-ide.*
this.NOM. smell come-NONPST.-3N.SG.
'This is stinking.'

b. *nan-age vaasane bar-utt-ide.*
I-DAT. smell come-NONPST.-3N.SG.
'I am getting a smell.'

For statives, the initiator is claimed to be "the entity whose properties are the cause or grounds for the stative eventuality to obtain" (p. 107). Again, this characterization is more appropriate to the external argument in (23a) (where the decaying subject is giving rise to a stink), than to (23b).

The argument that (22) is not the appropriate representation for all stative verbs can be made purely on the basis of English. The English verb *come*, like dative *bar-*, occurs as a verb that presents a result state. Consider first the metaphoric contexts in (24).

(24) We came to a conclusion/ a decision/ an impasse.

Ramchand intends "the abstract structuring principles behind all eventive predications … to cover changes and effects in more subjective domains as well" (op. cit. 54). So *come* in (24) must be an [init, proc, res] verb. But the information content of (24) resides chiefly in the *res* part of the predication, as evident in the informational richness of the negation of (24):

(25) We haven't (yet) come to a conclusion/ a decision.

Another way of saying this is that in these examples, there is a "rich *res*, poor *proc*;" or that *come* in (24–25) is a light verb.[13] Consider now (26):

(26) i. I have come to understand/ realize that …
ii. I have come to know that …
iii. I have come to believe that …

The infinitive in (26) that denotes a state of belief, knowledge, or understanding, contrasts with the purposive *to* infinitive in (27).

13. In adjuncts, i.e. in the absence of the first phase functional projections, *come* merely presents a state or event.

i. Come September, the clouds will be here. (=when it is September, …)
ii. Come what may, you must contest the election. (=Whatever happens, …)
iii. How come you're here? (= how does it happen/ how has it come about that …)

Come also occurs with presentational *there* (*There comes a time when* …).

(27) I have come to see you.

Correspondingly, in (27) the subject is the initiator of the movement of coming, in (26) it is not. Thus, in the paraphrase (28) of (26b), the subject position of *come* is not thematic.

(28) It has come to my knowledge that …

I do not claim a one-to-one correspondence between the verbal and nominal complements of *come* in (26) and (28) (cf. *It has come to our notice/attention/*belief/ *understanding*); the point is that the subject of *come*, which is clearly not thematic in (28), is arguably not thematic in (26) either. This suggests a raising structure (29) for *come* in (26):

(29) come [I to know that …]

Now this is very close to the structure suggested in (21) for Kannada *bar-*: *come* has a clausal internal argument that encodes a result state, a mental state that the subject is in. The difference is that *bar-* has a small clause complement, and *come* an infinitival complement (but cf. (33) below). Infinitival complements to *bar-* can have only a purposive, eventive reading (thus the Kannada counterpart of (26iii) has the odd reading 'I have come (somewhere) in order to believe that …'), due to the more general fact that Kannada does not allow subject raising out of infinitive complements.[14]

14. E.g. to *seem* or *appear*:

i. **avanu*$_i$ [*t*$_i$ *baruvud* -*akke*] *tooruttaane* /*kaaNuttaane*.
he come.NONFIN. -DAT. seems /appears
'*He seems/ appears to have come.'

On the other hand, (28) corresponds word for word to the Kannada (ii), except that Kannada lacks expletive *it*; and a non-clausal subject can occur in this structure in both English and Kannada (iii):

ii. [… *anta*] *namma tiLivaLike-ge/ gamana-kke bandide.*
[… that] our knowledge-DAT./ notice-DAT. has.come

iii. *ii viSHaya namma tiLivaLike-ge/ gamana-kke bandide*
this matter our knowledge-DAT./ notice-DAT. has.come
'This matter has come to knowledge/notice.'

In (ii–iii) the dative NP is not an experiencer. Dative case has here the semantics of English *to*, specifying a *res* and a location (cf. Section (5)). As in (6) above, English allows parallels to Kannada in the absence of the semantics of possession.

4.2 A result phrase for achievement verbs

We must distinguish the "rich" result postulated in the complement of a light verb *come* or *bar-* from the resultative constructions discussed in the literature on unaccusatives, such as the following:

(30) i. John wiped the table clean. [resultee: transitive object]
ii. John shouted himself hoarse. [resultee: reflexive object of unergative]
iii. The bottle broke open. [resultee: unaccusative subject]
iv. John ran his shoes ragged. [resultee: unselected object of unergative]

L&RH (p. 34) define a resultative phrase as "an XP that denotes the state achieved by the referent of the NP it is predicated of *as a result of the action denoted by the verb* ..." (emphasis added, RA). The result state in this construction is *caused* by the predicate: "the state denoted by the resultative XP is part of the core eventuality described in the VP" (p. 49). Resultatives are "expressions in which both the causing event and the change of state are specified, each by a different predicate" (p. 107). In Van Valin's (1990) system of predicate decompositions, an activity predicate that causes a change of state derives an accomplishment predicate, and the resultative in (30 i–iv) is diagnostic of accomplishments.[15]

L&RH point out (pp. 55–56) that the resultative as they define it does not occur with verbs of inherently directed motion such as *come*, *go* and *arrive*: (31) does not mean (32).

(31) Willa arrived breathless. (≠ (32))

(32) Willa became breathless as a result of arriving.

The nonexistent meaning is clearly an accomplishment reading (i.e. if the activity of arriving resulted in breathlessness, *arrive* would be an accomplishment verb; compare *shout* in (30ii) above). L&RH also observe that verbs of existence and appearance, "though cited as bonafide unaccusative verbs, are like unergative verbs in generally lacking causative uses" (p. 81). I.e. we do not have the usages "The magician appeared the rabbit" or "God be-ed the universe." (Recall that this

15. Clause (d) of Van Valin's (1990) system of predicate decompositions (from L&RH p. 167) derives an accomplishment predicate from an achievement predicate, via an activity that causes the achievement.

a. STATE: **predicate'** (x) or (x, y)
b. ACHIEVEMENT: BECOME **predicate'** (x) or (x, y)
c. ACTIVITY (± Agentive): (DO (x)) [**predicate'** (x) or (x, y)]
d. ACCOMPLISHMENT: φ CAUSE ψ, where φ is normally an activity predicate and ψ an achievement predicate

is why Ramchand analyses these verbs as projecting [init] as well as [proc] and [res].) Again, what is nonexistent is an accomplishment reading.

The claim that verbs of inherently directed motion are incompatible with resultatives is contested by Tortora (1998). I briefly summarize below Tortora's argument, before turning to its refutation by Higginbotham (1999), who provides an account of the telicity of achievement predicates that supports my analysis of dative *bar-*.

L&RH attribute (p.58) the putative inability of verbs of inherently directed motion to accommodate resultatives to Tenny's (1987) claim that "an eventuality may be associated with at most one delimitation." Since "verbs of inherently directed motion are achievement verbs; they specify an achieved endpoint," a resultative, which is a delimiter, cannot again occur with these verbs. Tortora points out (however) that

i. atelic verbs of inherently directed motion are also incompatible with resultatives: **The gas rose cool*, **The meteorite fell hot*, but the single-delimitation explanation is inapplicable to them;
ii. the single delimitation constraint would prohibit also *The bottle broke open*, except for a qualification (due to Tenny) that the second delimiter can be a "further specification of the result already inherent in the verb's meaning" (Tortora 1998: 341). **The vase broke worthless* violates the "further specification" constraint, whereas *The bottle broke open* respects it.

Tortora argues that the ungrammaticality of **Willa arrived breathless* may be due to a violation of the further specification constraint. Then this example has no bearing on the incompatibility of *arrive* with resultatives. Verbs like *arrive* do occur with goal phrases (*We arrived at the airport*), which are delimiters. Tortora concludes that the goal phrase delimiter meets the "further specification" condition; and that "there does not seem to be a way to straightforwardly maintain that *open* in [*The bottle broke open*] is a resultative but *at the airport* in [*We arrived at the airport*] is not" (p. 343).

Higginbotham (1999: 134) deems this a conclusion "that would be unfortunate if true," because there are languages (e.g. the Romance languages) that lack resultatives of the *break XP open* type but have constructions of the type *arrive at XP*. Kannada is like the Romance languages; it by and large lacks resultatives of accomplishment predicates. The solution Higginbotham proposes is to regard *arrive* as a predicate applying to (instantaneous) events of being at a place, which constitute the terminus or telos of events of journeying to that place, formally as:

arrive (x, e) ⟨-⟩ (Ep [at (x, p, e) & (Ee') (e' is a journey by x & (e', e) is a telic pair)

> If so, then the adjunct [*at the airport* in *They arrived at the airport*, RA] does not express the result of the arrival, but simply identifies the place in question. Furthermore, *arrive* does not admit a resultative, since it classifies events that are themselves already results. (loc. cit.)

A "telic pair" is a mode of semantic interpretation through composition. A telic predicate "makes some reference to the notion of an end;" it may be "the end of a process given by the predicate itself," as with accomplishment predicates; or "recovered by implication" for an achievement predicate (Higginbotham op.cit. 132). In the latter case, the predicate presents a situation that has come into existence (recall that achievement predicates are BECOME predicates that take a state as complement).

I have characterized as a weak [proc] what Higginbotham characterizes as an "instantaneous event." The observation that *arrive* "classifies events that are themselves already results" is particularly pertinent to my analysis of dative *bar-* as a verb that presents or encodes a result state. Kannada incidentally does not distinguish *arrive* from *come*: both translate as *bar-*.[16] In English as well, *come* and *arrive* overlap in meaning. *Arrive*, like *come*, can take metaphoric locations as complement (*arrive at a conclusion*). *Come*, like *arrive*, presents the result of metaphorical events located in a PP complement: *What has come over him? He came into (a lot of) money. His efforts have come to grief/come to naught*), suggesting that like dative *bar-*, *come* can take a small clause complement:

(33)

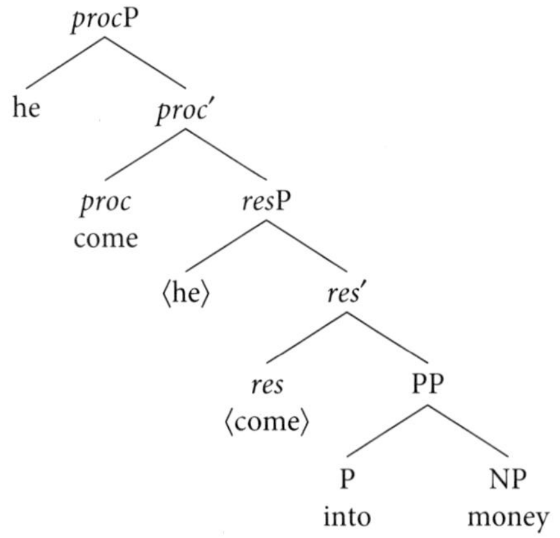

16. A serial verb *bandu-seeru* (lit.'come-join') can specifically signify *arrive*, but also "to join a group." The claim that verbs that classify "events that are themselves already results" do not admit resultatives may need to be thought out further, given the causativization of stative datives in (17) above.

5. *Aag-* as 'come to be,' 'come to pass' or 'come to have'

A second verb typical of the dative experiencer construction is *aag-*. I assume that like *bar-*, *aag-* projects a weak [proc] and a rich [res] ('to me fear') in (34).

(34) *nan-age bhaya aayitu.*
I-DAT. fear happened.3N.SG.
'I felt afraid.'

Other psychological predicates that occur with *aag-* are *aascarya* 'surprise,' *dukkha* 'sadness,' *gaabari* 'fear,' *santooSHa* 'happiness,' and *yoocane* 'worry.'

Aag- is commonly translated into English as a pair of verbs 'happen, become.' The 'become' reading is seen in (35).

(35) *ivanu uddakke aaguttaane.*
he.PROX tall become.NONPST.3M.SG.
'This boy will become tall.'

The 'happen' reading is seen in (36).

(36) *ondu durghaTne aagide.*
one accident has.happened.
'An accident has happened.'

aag- thus means both *come to be* (=*become*), and *come to pass* (=*happen*), which I shall analyze as *come to be at* (= *take place*). *aag-* also means *come to have,* i.e. *get*:

(37) *avar-ige makkaLu aagiddaare/ makkaLu aagilla.*
they-DAT children have.happened 3PL./ children have.not.happened.
'They have got/have not got children.'

5.1 The '*happen*' and '*become*' interpretations of *aag-*

Consider the examples below. They form minimal pairs with respect to the *happen* and *become* readings of *aag-*. These readings are contingent on a dative argument on the *happen* reading, and a nominative subject on the *become* reading.

(38) *nin-age yeenu aayitu?*
you-DAT. what happened 3N.SG.
'What happened to you?'

(39) *niinu yeenu aade?*
you.NOM. what became.2SG.
'What did you become?'

(40) *avan-ige ondu magu aayitu.*
he-DAT. one child happened 3N.SG.
'He had a child.'

(41) *avanu ondu magu aada.*
he one child became.3M.SG.
'He became a child.'

This alternation is clear evidence that dative case is not a "governed" case, i.e. a semantic case assigned by a particular class of "psychological predicates." It suggests that the distinction between the dative and nominative case frames for *aag-* derives from the *happen-become* distinction that *aag-* straddles.

This distinction lies in the head of the small clause *res* complement to *aag-*. The small clause head is a copula on the *become* reading, and dative case on the *happen* reading. When a copula heads the small clause, *be* "incorporates" into *aag-*. In Ramchand's framework, incorporation (head movement) is effected by underassociation of the incorporating element, and remerge. I analyze *aag-* as projecting both *proc* and *res*, informally notating these as 'come' for process and 'be' for stativity. Let us assume 'be' to reflect the minimum or barest possible content, the least encyclopedically rich instance, of the stativity head *res*. When the result complement of *aag-* is headed by (the features of) a copula, the semantics of the lexical copula are non-distinct from the features of the *res* head that *aag-* identifies. This allows the copula to underassociate in *res* – to be identified by *aag-* under Agree, and unify content with it, as required (Ramchand op.cit: 98). In this case, underassociation exhausts the features of the copula, and so it is not spelt out separately as a lexical item. The "subject" (Specifier) of *res* is now remerged as the "subject" of *proc* (in its Specifier). This is shown in (42).

(42) 'He became a child'(=41)/'He became tall'(=45, 46)

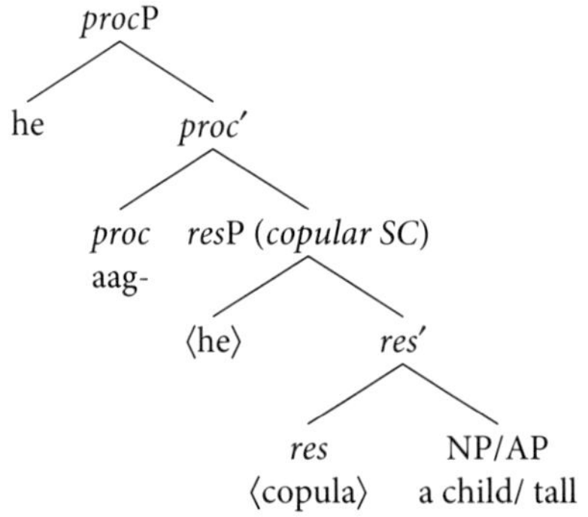

We must note that copular sentences in Kannada may have the copula overt or covert (or perhaps absent). What concerns us here is that according to whether it is overt or covert, the category of the complement to the copula varies. When there is an overt *be*, its complement is adjectival (cf. (43)).[17] When the copula is covert, the complement is nominal (cf. (44)).

(43) *avanu udda-kke iddaane.*
he height-DAT. be.PRES.3M.SG.
'He is tall.' (lit. 'He is to a height')

(44) *avanu udda.*
he height
'He is tall.' (lit. 'he height')

aag- permits either type of complement. Thus, the rheme in (45) is adjectival and corresponds to (43), and the rheme in (46) is a noun and corresponds to (44).

(45) *avanu udda-kke aagiddaane.*
he height-DAT. has.become
'He has become tall.'

(46) *avanu udda aagiddaane.*
he height has.become
'He has become tall.'

Thus *aag-* must have the full range of features that the copula in Kannada has, allowing it to take either nominal or adjectival complements.

The subject of *aag-* in (42) is remerged into *proc*P, by the underassociation of the copula and the identification of *res* by *aag-*. Hence, it is an UNDERGOER (of a process sub event; it undergoes some sort of identifiable change/transition (Ramchand op.cit: 28)). In Ramchand's system, INITIATORS and UNDERGOERS both end up as nominative case marked subjects (the former, classical external arguments; the latter, subjects of unaccusative verbs). *aag-* thus has a nominative subject on the 'become' reading.[18]

The subject of *aag-* in (42) is perhaps remerged again as high as *initP*. i.e. *aag-* in the sense of 'become' probably projects all three of [init, proc, res]. The evidence for [init] is that purposive adjuncts may occur with this sense of *aag-*,' as they may with *become* in English: *avanu raajanannu kondu raaja aada*, 'he king-ACC. kill-PST.PPL. king became,' 'He became King by killing the King.'

17. Here, a dative case-marked noun. Dative case derives A (Adj./Adv.) from N in Kannada; cf. Amritavalli and Jayaseelan (2003).

18. English *become* may also be decomposed as the "incorporation" of *be* into a weak process verb *come*, although *become* is taken to be a primitive in the predicate decomposition of achievement verbs in the tradition of Dowty 1979; Van Valin 1990 and Vendler 1957[1967].

When the small clause head is dative *ge-*, a *happen* reading obtains, which corresponds to the eventive reading of English *happen* as well as the possession reading of English *have*. Consider first the latter reading. The *res* phrase here is identified by dative case *ge-*, which encodes not only a *res* state, but adds the semantics of possession to it. This is a lexical-encyclopedic content of dative case that we have extensively illustrated. *aag-* lacks the semantics of possession. So *ge-* cannot "incorporate" into it. Instead, *aag-* underassociates its *res* feature.

(47) avanige hasivu aayitu 'he-DAT. hunger happened' 'He felt hungry.'

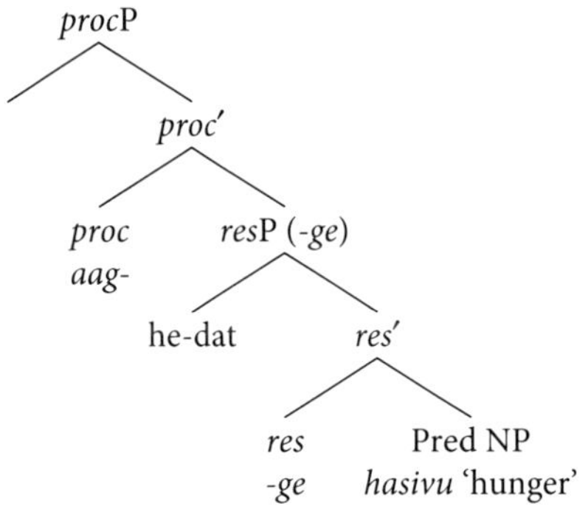

On the 'happen' or 'come to pass' reading, *aag-* may surface with a single argument (48), but this argument is required to be eventive (49).

(48) *yeenu aagide?*
what has happened?
'What has happened?'

(49) **onde kaaru aagide.*
a car has happened
*'A car has happened.'

Taken together with (50) where a dative argument surfaces, this suggests that there is indeed a small clause in the complement of *aag-* in (48), headed by dative case. I take dative case here to encode a location for a result: as *to* does in English, specifying PLACE as well as *res* (Ramchand op. cit: 118).[19] Informally, we may notate this content of *ge-* as BE AT.[20]

19. For Ramchand, *to* "has a *res* feature in addition to its specification for PLACE" (p. 118). The place head may be filled with *in* and *on*; underassociation of *to*'s place feature yields *into* and *onto*.

20. Dative case can indicate a point of time: *ondu gaNTe-ge*, 'at one o'clock.' The *res* of *aag-* may covertly signify the temporal location of an event (AT OVER/AT NOW, identified by the tense of the verb), cf.

(50) *nin-age yeenu aagide?*
you-DAT. what has.happened
'What has happened to you?'

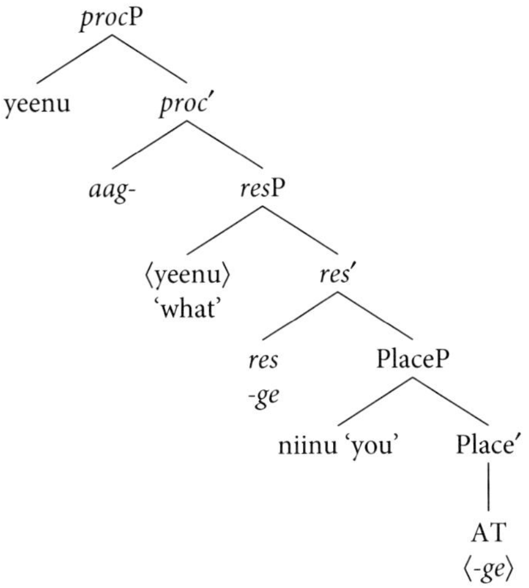

6. The possessor/experiencer as RESULTEE

6.1 A double object construction in Kannada

The structure I have proposed in (21) for the experiencer dative construction is essentially that of the English double object construction (minus the changes in Ramchand 2008), with the difference that the verb in the experiencer construction does not project an *init*P. Consider now (51), a canonical ditransitive sentence interpreted as the transitive or causative counterpart of the experiencer dative sentence (52).[21]

(51) *avanu nan-age tondare koTTanu.*
he.NOM. I-DAT. trouble gave.3M.SG.
'He gave me trouble.'

(52) *nan-age (tumba) tondare aayitu.*
I-DAT. (a lot of) trouble happened.3N.SG.
'I had (a lot of) trouble.'

(i) uuTa aay-it-aa? 'Is lunch over?' (Lit. 'Did lunch happen?')
(ii) uuTa aag-ide-yaa? 'Is lunch ready?' (Lit. 'Has lunch happened?')

21. As Shibatani (1999: 54) notes, "many languages provide transitive and intransitive pairs" (canonical transitive counterparts to the dative experiencer construction).

The simple addition of an *init* projection to the experiencer dative structure gives us the structure for (51). The verb *koDu-* 'give' lexicalizes an *init* projection in addition to the *proc* and *res* projections lexicalized by *aag-* (47), as shown in (53).

(53)

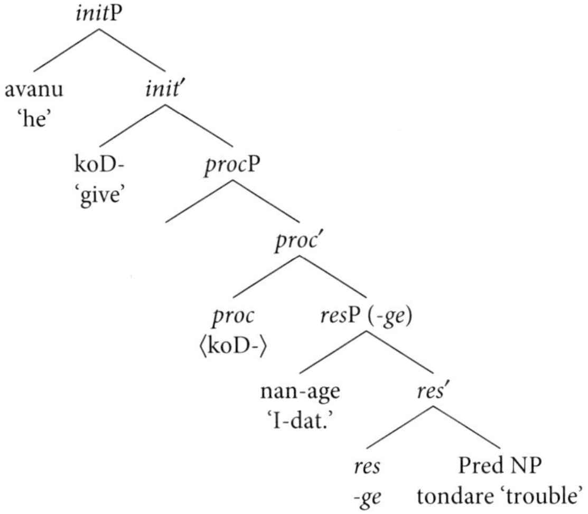

(53) (the structure of (51)) is a double object construction. This suggests that Kannada has a double object construction in addition to, and different from, the standard goal-dative construction in (54).

(54) *avanu nan-age ondu pustaka-vannu koTTanu.*
he.nom. I-DAT. one book-ACC. give.PST.3M.SG.
'He gave a book to me.'

Up until now, (54) has not been differentiated from (53). There is no difference in the word order. However, while it is possible to mark the direct object with an overt accusative case in (54), it is not possible to so mark the predicative noun in (53). This has so far remained a stipulative observation.[22]

Up until now (again), the double object construction (51) and the experiencer dative construction (52) have been thought to differ radically, in that (52) is a "dative subject" construction, whereas (51) is a "nominative subject" construction with a dative (indirect) object. On my analysis, (51) and (52) differ only in the *init* projection, which is lexicalized by the Kannada verb 'give' but not by 'happen.' Such a relation between English *give* in its double object occurrence, and *get/take*, is supported by the classical argument of shared idioms (Richards 2001).

22. This NP, being non-referential, must remain indefinite and non-specific (Jayaseelan 2004: 240).

The idioms *The Count gives everyone the creeps, You get the creeps (just looking at him)* suggest a component *have the creeps* common to both these occurrences. This in turn argues for the Harleyan double object structure with its sub lexical preposition of possession (notated as *HAVE*), that occurs also in the complement of unaccusative *get*: [$_{vP}$ The Count [$_{v'}$ CAUSE [$_{PP}$ everyone *HAVE* the creeps]]], [$_{vP}$ You [$_{v'}$ BECOME [$_{PP}$ *HAVE* the creeps]]].

Richards does not mention the possibility of a pleonastic subject for this idiom in the double object construction: *It gives me the creeps* (*when he does that/ to think that* ...) (= *I get/ have the creeps when* ...).[23] This example (and others like it, e.g. *It gives me great pleasure to...*) suggest that in English as in Kannada, the double object construction does not necessarily project an *init*P. Then the structures for *The Count gives me the creeps* and *It gives me the creeps* ... are related precisely as the structures for *koD-* and *aag-* are in (51–52), *modulo* the requirement of a pleonastic subject for the latter in English: [$_{initP}$ The Count [$_{init'}$ give [$_{procP}$ [$_{proc'}$ ⟨give⟩ [$_{resP}$ me *HAVE* the creeps]]]]], [$_{procP}$ *e* [$_{proc'}$ give [$_{resP}$ me *HAVE* the creeps]]].

6.2 The experiencer as RESULTEE

The argument in the preceding sections identifies the dative experiencer construction with the sub component of the double object construction that depicts a *res* complement to a *proc* head. If so, in the event structure projected by *bar-* or *aag-*, the dative experiencer is a RESULTEE argument. Experiencer objects of eventive verbs like *depress* (*The weather depressed John*) are also RESULTEES (Ramchand 2008: 54), as are possessors in the double object construction. The RESULTEE position in event structure is plausibly thus the canonical position for experiencers/ possessors.

I analyze the dative experiencer as a RESULTEE but not an UNDERGOER, even as Ramchand does the goal or possessor in the double object construction (op. cit.:103–4). The RESULTEE is the holder of a result state. The experiencer dative and the double object dative both hold the state of possession. But neither appears to "undergo" the process designated by the verb (the experiencer does not undergo the process of *bar-*, i.e. 'coming,' or *aag-*, i.e. 'happening;' and in (10) above, *Alex gave Ariel the ball,* Ariel does not undergo the process of 'giving').

To add to the argument that the dative experiencer is a RESULTEE, and not an UNDERGOER, recall that when *aag-* takes a copular complement, its subject is remerged at least as high as in the specifier of the *proc* head, if not the *init* head; i.e. it is either an UNDERGOER or an INITIATOR. This subject is nominative. When

---

23. My thanks to a reviewer for drawing my attention to Richards' squib in the context of this example.

the small clause has a dative of possession head, a dative marked NP is the most prominent argument. Nothing suggests that this argument has a role other than RESULTEE, and it surfaces with dative case.

This correlation between nominative case and an event structure position higher than RESULTEE is seen again in the following data. Some predicate nouns that occur with *aag-* occur also in a nominative experiencer construction with the verb *paD-* 'experience, undergo:'

(55) *avaru* *aascharya/santooSHa/bhaya* *paTTaru*
they.NOM. surprise/happiness/fear underwent.3PL.
'They felt surprise/ happiness/ fear.'

The verb *paD-* has a causative form *paD-is*, arguing that it allows an initiator to be projected. Thus *aascharya paD-isu* 'surprise' (transitive) ('surprise caus-undergo') has an initiator that causes the state, and therefore, an undergoer that receives the process of causation as well as experiences the resultant state. No such roles are available for *aag-*, which no causative form **aag-is*. Modals arguably related to the *proc* subcomponent occur with *paD-* but not with *aag-*: *kaSHTa paD beeku* 'One should take trouble (lit. should undergo difficulties),' **kaSHTa aag beeku* *'Difficulties should happen.' All this suggests that RESULTEE arguments that are not remerged in higher event projections surface with dative case in Kannada.

What are the consequences of these claims for case marking, and the subject-like properties of the dative experiencer (to address a reviewer's concern)? The arguments distinguishing the dative object from the dative experiencer that impute subject-like properties to the latter are well-known: e.g. control of a null participial subject, or control of anaphora. On the other hand, its very case marking argues that the dative experiencer is not in the "subject position," if that designates a nominative case-marking position in the syntax. Now a property of the double object construction is that the goal argument c-commands the theme argument. This suggests that the subject-like properties of the dative experiencer may derive from it being the most prominent argument in the clause, which c-commands all other arguments.[24]

Coming to case marking, Ramchand assumes that the inflectional head is responsible for nominative, and *init* for internal structural case (p. 62); and that all three sub event "subjects" must be licensed by these two cases. Thus (she points out) in her descriptions of English verb types, the specifiers of *init*, *proc* and *res* are not all three ever full, for Case reasons (loc. cit.).

24. That the dative experiencer does not occupy the canonical subject position but is a scrambled non-subject argument is argued in Jayaseelan (1990). The possibility of *naanu meeri-ge$_i$ avaLanne$_i$ tooriside* 'I Mary-dat. herself showed' 'I showed Mary herself,' in contrast to **naanu avaLanne$_i$ meeri-ge$_i$ tooriside*, argues that a dative argument on the left c-commands the accusative to its right.

In both the English double object structure (10) and the dative experiencer structure (21), the specifier of *proc* is empty. What is the case of the RESULTEE? In English, it is standardly assumed to receive accusative case, which is plausible if *init* is projected. We, have, however noted the possibility of an expletive subject in this construction – i.e. *init* may not be projected. If so, the RESULTEE case may in fact be dative (cf. Kayne's (2010) suggestion cited in Section 2.3). This would be as in Kannada, where (I suggest) the RESULTEE retains the dative case it receives within its small clause. In the Kannada experiencer dative structure (21), the external argument (the specifier of *proc*) may be an expletive *pro* (Jayaseelan 1990), or it may not be projected at all (perhaps a structural reflex of Kannada tolerating a weak *proc*). The predicate noun controls verb agreement. Early analyses, therefore, assumed it to be a subject, in addition to the dative "subject." I suggest that agreement in this construction is an instance of "inverse" agreement with a predicate when the subject is empty, as in existential *there*-constructions in English.

6.3 Conclusion

I have argued that experiencer datives in Kannada are RESULTEE arguments of verbs that project a weak or poor process and a rich result. This implies that there are stative verbs (achievements) that merely present a result state, in a kind of resultative construction noticed in Higginbotham (1999). My analysis of the dative experiencer construction assimilates it to the possession subpart of the double object construction, limiting it neither to "psych" verbs nor to South Asian languages. English lacks the dative experiencer/possessor construction because it does not tolerate weak or poor process verbs. Kannada must do so, as it is impoverished in adjectives, and nouns in this language designate states that are "in the possession of" experiencers. A second difference between these languages is in the signaling of possession with the verb *have* or dative case. Finally, RESULTEE arguments that are the sole "subject" argument in the first phase surface with inherent dative case in Kannada.

References

Amritavalli, Raghavachari & Jayaseelan, Karattuparambil A. 2003. The genesis of syntactic categories and parametric variation. In *Generative Grammar in a Broader Perspective: Proceedings of the 4th GLOW in Asia 2003*, Hang-Jin Yoon (ed.), 19–41. Hankook: KGGC and Seoul National University.

Bhaskararao, Peri & Subbarao, Karumuri Venkat (eds). 2004. *Non-nominative Subjects*, vol. 1 [Typological Studies in Language 60]. Amsterdam: John Benjamins.

Chierchia, Gennaro. 1989. A Semantics for Unaccusatives and its Syntactic Consequences. Ms., Cornell University.

Chomsky, Noam. 1995. *The Minimalist Program*. Cambridge, MA: MIT Press.

Dowty, David. 1979. *Word Meaning and Montague Grammar*. Dordrecht: Reidel.

Freeze, Ray. 1992. Existentials and other locatives. *Language* 68: 553–595.
Hale, Ken & Keyser, Samuel J. 1993. On argument structure and the lexical expression of syntactic relations. In *The View from Building 20: Essays in Honor of Sylvain Bromberger*, K. Hale & S. J. Keyser (eds), 53–109. Cambridge, MA: MIT Press.
Harley, Heidi. 2002. Possession and the double object construction. *Yearbook of Linguistic Variation* 2: 29–68.
Higginbotham, James. 1999. Accomplishments. In *Proceedings of the Nanzan GLOW, the Second GLOW Meeting in Asia*, Mamoru Saito et al. (eds), 131–139. Nanzan University: Nagoya, Japan.
Jayaseelan, Karattuparambil A. 1990. The dative subject construction and the pro-drop parameter. In *Experiencer Subjects in South Asian Languages*, M. K. Verma & K. P. Mohanan (eds), 269–283. Stanford: CSLI.
Jayaseelan, Karattuparambil A. 2004. The possessor-experiencer dative in Malayalam. In *Non-nominative Subjects,* vol. 1, P. Bhaskararao & K. V. Subbarao (eds), 227–244. Amsterdam: John Benjamins.
Kayne, Richard. 1994. *The Antisymmetry of Syntax.* Cambridge, MA: MIT Press.
Kayne, Richard. 2000. Toward a modular theory of auxiliary selection. In *Parameters and Universals*, R. Kayne (ed.), 107–130. New York: Oxford University Press, and *Studia Linguistica* [1993]. 47: 3–31.
Kayne, Richard. 2010. The DP-internal origin of Datives. Paper at the *4th European Dialect Syntax Workshop* in Donostia/San Sebastian.
Klaiman, Miriam. 1986. Semantic parameters and the South Asian linguistic area. In *South Asian Languages: Structure, Convergence and Diglossia*, Bh. Krishnamurthy, C. P. Masica & A. K. Sinha (eds), 179–194. Delhi: Motilal Banarsidass.
Kratzer, Angelika. 1996. Severing the external argument from the verb. In *Phrase Structure and the Lexicon*, J. Rooryck & L. Zaring (eds), 109–137. Dordrecht: Kluwer.
Larson, Richard. 1988. On the double object construction. *Linguistic Inquiry* 19(3): 335–391.
Levin, Beth & Rappoport-Hovav, Malka. 1995. *Unaccusativity: At the Syntax-Lexical Semantics Interface.* Cambridge, MA: MIT Press.
Mahajan, Anoop. 2004. On the origin of non-nominative subjects. In *Non-nominative Subjects,* vol. 1, P. Bhaskararao & K. V. Subbarao (eds), 283–299. Amsterdam: John Benjamins.
Pesetsky, David. 1995. *Zero Syntax: Experiencers and Cascades.* Cambridge, MA: MIT Press.
Ramchand, Gillian. 2008. *Verb Meaning and the Lexicon: A First-phase Syntax.* Cambridge: Cambridge University Press.
Richards, Norvin. 2001. An idiomatic argument for lexical decomposition. *Linguistic Inquiry* 32(1): 183–192.
Shibatani, Masayoshi. 1999. Dative subject constructions twenty-two years later. *Studies in the Linguistic Sciences* 29(2): 45–76.
Szabolcsi, Anna. 1983. The possessor that ran away from home. *The Linguistic Review* 3: 89–102.
Tenny, Carol. 1987. Grammaticalizing Aspect and Affectedness. Doctoral dissertation, MIT.
Tortora, C.M. 1998. Verbs of inherently directed motion are compatible with resultative phrases. *Linguistic Inquiry* 29(2): 338–345.
Van Valin. 1990. Semantic parameters of split intransitivity. *Language* 66: 221–260.
Vendler, Zeno. 1957/1967. Verbs and times. In *Linguistics in Philosophy*, Z. Vendler, 97–121. Ithaca: Cornell University Press.
Verma, Manindra K. & Mohanan, Karuvannur P. 1990. *Experiencer Subjects in South Asian Languages.* Stanford: CSLI.

Lexical semantics of transitivizer light verbs in Telugu

Rahul Balusu
EFL University, Hyderabad

This chapter examines the kind of meanings that are uniformly present in constructions involving a certain variety of light verbs in Telugu – transitivizer light verbs. The meanings that are inalienably constant in both the verbal and the nominal complex predicates that these light verbs form are the inceptual meanings- emphasizing inception or beginning, continuation or progression, and completion or end-point. These meanings can be directly linked, and are further evidence for the structural decomposition of the verbal domain into 3 subparts or projections (First Phase Syntax, Ramchand 2008) – *initP* (introduces causation), *procP* (specifies the process), and *resP* (gives the result state). The semantics of this structure is what I claim gives rise to the inceptual meanings.

Keywords: complex predicates; inceptual meaning; first phase syntax; argument structure; Dravidian

1. Introduction[1]

Researchers agree that verb meaning is of two kinds – structural meaning and lexical-conceptual meaning. Ramchand (2012) calls the first type, *skeletal* meaning – a hierarchically structured representation of abstract actional factors that are directly correlated with linguistic generalizations concerning argument structure realization in the syntax – and the second type, *flesh-and-blood* meaning – conceptually rich information that provides detailed expression to highly specific named events. One question that arises is which meaning components of a verb are part of the structural meaning and which are lexical-conceptual.

---

1. A preliminary version of this paper was presented at the workshop on Complex Predicates in South Asian Languages held in EFLU, Hyderabad, January 2012. I would like to thank the audience for helpful discussion and comments. The present paper has greatly improved from the painstaking criticisms of two anonymous reviewers of this volume, whom I wish to thank.

Light verbs (Jespersen 1965) are a good place to look for this separation because they are bleached or abstract versions which carry only the skeletal meaning, whereas their heavy counterparts which act as full verbs carry both structural and conceptual meanings. By examining the meanings that remain in the light verb use, we can identify the meaning components that are structural and clues to the structure itself.

In this paper, I examine the kind of meanings that are uniformly present in constructions involving a certain variety of light verbs in Telugu – transitivizer light verbs. The meanings which are inalienably constant, in both the verbal complex predicates and the nominal complex predicates that these light verbs form, are the inceptual meanings- which emphasize inception or beginning, continuation or progression, and completion or end-point. I propose that these meanings can be directly linked, and are further evidence for the structural decomposition of the verbal domain into 3 subparts or projections (First Phase Syntax, Ramchand 2008) – *initP* (that introduces causation), *procP* (that specifies the process), and *resP* (that gives the result state). This achieves a close match between the phrase structure and the compositional semantic primitives that are structural.

Ramchand (2008) proposes the *Light Verb Constraint*: A verb can be used as a light verb only when all of its category features Agree with some other verbal element in its complement domain. This constraint is at best a stipulation in the system. The Telugu data examined shows that the stipulation is unnecessary and the possible combination that the compositional system allows is actually attested. In Telugu, light verbs also function as transitivizers. According to the light verb constraint, the transitivizer light verbs should not compose with unaccusative main verbs, which do not have an [init] feature to license the [init] feature of the transitivizer light verbs. But they do. What we see here are instances of direct lexicalization of the Spec of *InitP*, thus licensing the [init] feature of the light verbs. The transitivizers in Telugu are thus light verbs which exhibit direct lexicalization of the *init* head. The paper also examines other selectional restrictions and combinatorial possibilities between light verbs and nominal and verbal elements, and between light verbs and the causative morpheme.

The paper is organized as follows. Section 2 briefly sets out the theoretical framework of first phase syntax. Section 3 explores the meaning and composition of aspectual light verbs in Telugu to arrive at their event structure projection properties. In Section 4 I postulate a structure for transitivizer light verbs in Telugu. In Section 5 the interaction of the transitivizer light verbs with the causative suffix is explored. In Section 6 the composition of the transitivizer light verbs with nominal elements to form Nominal complex predicates is presented. Section 7 is the conclusion.

2. The theoretical landscape: First Phase Syntax

2.1 Functional decomposition of verbs

Ramchand's (2008) First Phase Syntax is characterized by the functional decomposition of verbs into three distinct heads, each corresponding to a primitive element of events. The internal structure of the verbal phrase contains the following three subevent projections: init[iation]P, proc[ess]P, and res[ult]P. The first (init) and the third (res) are stative heads, while the second – proc – is the hallmark of dynamicity. Every dynamic verb, then, contains the *proc* head in its decomposition. The stative *init* and *res* heads, however, can be missing in the case of dynamic verbs. Each subevent head enters in a predicational relation with its specifier position, where we find the "subject" of the event. The maximal decomposition of the verb phrase is given in (1). InitP introduces the causation event and licenses the external argument – the Initiator. ProcP specifies the process or the nature of the change and licenses the internal argument – the Undergoer. ResP introduces the result state and licenses the holder of the result state – the Resultee.

(1)

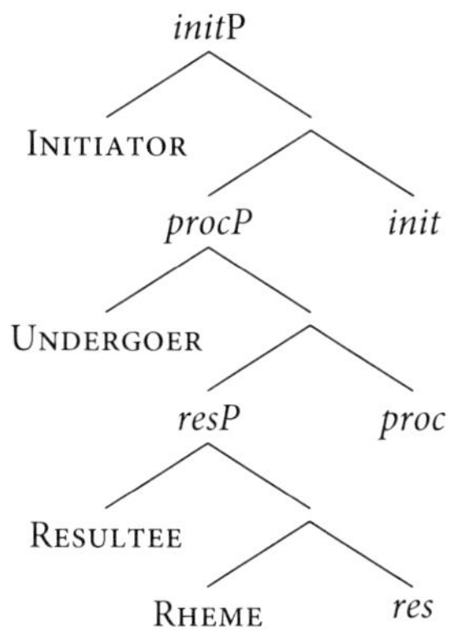

In this model, verbs come in the lexicon with a categorial feature specification which determines which subevents they lexicalize. For example, a verb specified as ⟨init, proc⟩ will spell out both the *init* and the *proc* head simultaneously. Depending on which subevent heads a verb lexicalizes, it belongs to a particular verb class. Thus, there is the class of ⟨init, proc⟩ verbs, the class of ⟨init, proc, res⟩ verbs, the class of ⟨proc, res⟩ verbs, etc. If we are to connect these classes to the traditional aspectual classes, then activities are characterized by the features ⟨init, proc⟩ or only ⟨proc⟩, achievement verbs are specified as ⟨init, proc, res⟩ or ⟨proc, res⟩, statives have only the feature ⟨init⟩, etc. When it comes to argument structure, unergatives are verb that are specified with the feature ⟨init⟩, while unaccusatives lack this feature.

Composite roles arise when the same DP argument occupies two (or more) specifier positions. This happens when a DP raises from the specifier of a lower subevent head to the specifier of a higher subevent head. In such cases, we have the roles of Initiator-Undergoer, Undergoer-Resultee, and Initiator-Undergoer-Resultee. The first one arises when the same argument is the holder of the initiational stage and undergoes the process/change (e.g. the sole argument of the verb run). The second one arises when the same argument undergoes the process/change specified by the *proc* head and holds the result state (e.g. the direct object of break). The third one arises when the same argument initiates the event, undergoes the process/change and is the holder of the result state (e.g. the argument of arrive). The composite thematic roles of the participants in the event are encoded in the lexical entry of the verb, that is, the verb determines whether a certain DP will raise from one specifier to another or not.

An event head can have not only another subevent phrase as its complement but also non-verbal material (DP, AP, PP, etc.) occupying its complement position – called Rheme. Rhemes are not subjects of events but part of the description of the predicate. A DP in the rheme position builds one joint predication with the verb. A DP in the specifier position of a subevent head is a verbal argument.

2.2 Lexical insertion as phrasal spell-out

Lexical items are not inserted under terminal nodes. Syntactic features correspond to distinct heads. Lexical items are associated with groups of category features, so they need to spell-out multiple heads in the functional sequence. An articulated theory of lexical insertion is developed by Starke (2009, 2011) and Caha (2007). The Superset Principle, argued for by Caha (2007) states that "The phonological exponent of a Vocabulary item is inserted into a node if the item matches all or a superset of the grammatical features specified in the node. Insertion does not take place if the Vocabulary item does not contain all features present in the node. Where several Vocabulary items meet the conditions for insertion, the item containing fewer features unspecified in the node must be chosen." Fabregas (2007) states the principle of Exhaustive Lexicalization "Every node in the syntactic representation must be identified by lexical content." So while all the functional sequence in the syntax has to be exhaustively lexicalized, category features on a particular lexical item may remain 'underassociated' because these principles do not prohibit lexical items from inserting even if all of their features are not matched in the syntactic tree. But this makes the system too unconstrained, allowing for many lexical items to spell out a small chunk of structure, and underassociating the rest of their categorial features. To constrain this, Ramchand (2008) proposes the following constraints on Underassociation: If a lexical item contains an underassociated category feature, (i) that feature must be independently identified within the phase and linked to the underassociated feature, by Agree; (ii) the two category features so linked must unify their lexical encyclopedic content.

Agree of subevental features is possible only if the lexical conceptual content of two 'agreeing' features can unify conceptually without infelicity. This can happen only if one of the lexical items has a fairly general and abstract semantics, that is it is 'light' in a semantic sense, so that it can conceptually unify with a more specific lexical item, in a kind of hyponymous relation. Category features on a lexical item can fail to directly be associated with syntactic structure and instead be underassociated with the feature in the syntactic structure. Features on a lexical item may be underassociated when they are in an Agree relation with a feature of the same kind that is syntactically present. Underassociated features have to be licensed in the same phase by Agree. The underassociated features remain semantically active and facilitate the presence of certain adjuncts. So Merge and Agree are both possibile as operations to satisfy the category requirements of a lexical item.

3. Aspectual light verbs in Telugu

There are 3 aspectual/completive light verbs in Telugu, *poo* 'go', *veyyi* 'throw', and *paDa.veyyi* 'fall throw', that occur in V–V complex predicates, as shown in (2)–(4), with the full or heavy verb version given in (b) along with the light verb version in (a). The light verb bears tense and agreement. The main verb appears as a perfective/conjunctive participle with the marker *-i*. The light verb has a very abstract semantics. The semantic content of the complex predicate comes from the main verb.

(2) a. **poo 'go'**
siita paD-i-poo-indi
Sita fall-PERF-go-PST.3FSG
Sita fell (fully).

b. *siita america poo-indi*
Sita America go-PST.3FSG
Sita went to America.

(3) a. **veyyi 'throw'**
siita pustakam cad-i-vees-indi
Sita book read-PERF-throw-PST.3FSG
Sita read the book (fully).

b. *siita banti vees-indi*
Sita ball throw-PST.3FSG
Sita threw the ball.

(4) a. **paDa.veyyi 'fall throw'**
siita pustakam cadiv-i-paDees-indi
Sita book read-PERF-fall.throw-PST.3FSG
Sita read the book (totally).

b. *siita banti paDees-indi*
Sita ball fall.throw-PST.3FSG
Sita dropped the ball.

Of these three verbs, *poo* 'go' is unaccusative; and *veyyi* 'throw', and *paDa.veyyi* 'fall throw', are transitive, as can be seen from their full verb use given above. These category labels are analysed in First Phase terms as shown in (5).[2]

(5) TRANSITIVE: init, proc, (res)
UNACCUSATIVE: proc, (res)

3.1 Selectional restrictions on the aspectuals

There are strict selectional restrictions between the light verbs and the main verbs that they can compose with. Of the three light verbs, *poo* 'go' which is unaccusative can only combine with unaccusative main verbs. It cannot compose with transitive or unergative main verbs. This is shown in (6).

(6) a. **poo + unaccusative**
icu karig-i-poo-indi
ice melt-PERF-go-PST.3FSG
The ice melted.

b. **poo + unergative**
**siita navv-i-poo-indi*
Sita laugh-PERF-go-PST.3FSG
Intended: Sita laughed.

c. **poo + transitive**
**sita cadiv-i-poo-indi*
Sita read-PERF-go-PST.3FSG
Intended: Sita read.

2. A reviewer points out that Ramchand (2008) provides evidence for the positing of *init*, *proc* and *res* for the lexical classes. In this paper no independent evidence is being presented that would justify the lexical semantic analyses being proposed. Rather I take over Ramchand's existing verb classes for Bangla.

Veyyi 'throw', and *paDa.veyyi* 'fall throw', which are transitive, can only combine with transitive and unergative main verbs. They cannot combine with unaccusative main verbs. This is shown in (7) and (8).

(7) a. **veyyi + unaccusative**
**icu karig-i-vees-indi*
ice melt-PERF-throw-PST.3FSG
Intended: The ice melted.

b. **veyyi + unergative**
siita navv-i-vees-indi
Sita laugh-PERF-throw-PST.3FSG
Sita laughed.

c. **veyyi + transitive**
siita cadiv-i-vees-indi
Sita read-PERF-throw-PST.3FSG
Sita read

(8) a. **paDa.veyyi + unaccusative**
**icu karig-i-paDa.vees-indi*
ice melt-PERF-fall.throw-PST.3FSG
Intended: The ice melted.

b. **paDa.veyyi + unergative**
siita navv-i-paDa.vees-indi
Sita laugh-PERF-fall.throw-PST.3FSG
Sita laughed.

c. **paDa.veyyi + transitive**
siita cadiv-i-paDa.vees-indi
Sita read-PERF-fall.throw-PST.3FSG
Sita read.

So an aspectual light verb in Telugu has a requirement on the category or argument structure of the main verb that it combines with.

3.2 A First Phase Analysis of the selectional restrictions on the aspectual complex predicates

Complex predicates like these have been analysed in First Phase Syntax terms as underassociation of the main or heavy verb features under the light verb (Ramchand 2008). This is shown for the Telugu data given in (2)–(4) above, in the syntactic structures in (9). The heavy verb lexicalizes or occupies the rheme position. Together they form one joint predication.

(9)

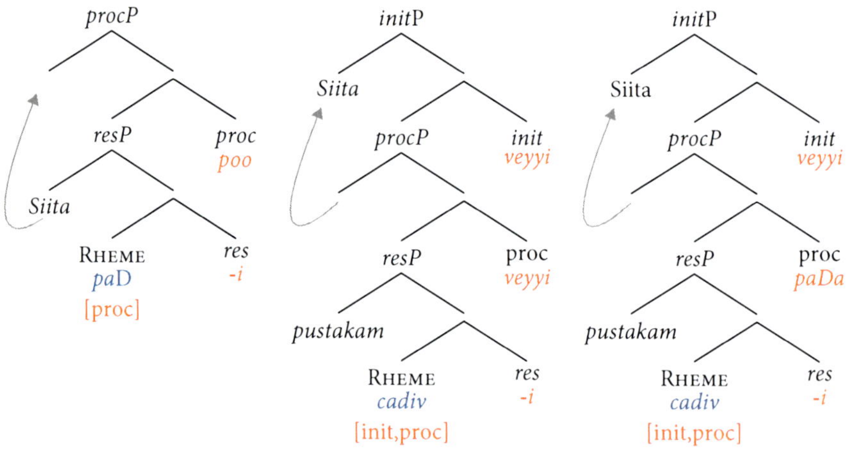

The subevent feature specification of the light verb is the same as the subevent specification of that verb when it is used as a heavy verb, an assumption that Ramchand (2012) bases on Butt's Generalization, given in (10). Based on historical evidence, Butt and Lahiri (2012) show that the light version and the full version of a verb are very closely tied together: When a verb is lost, both light and main verb versions are lost simultaneously. There is also no evidence for progressive grammaticalization of the main verb into a light verb, as has been documented with auxiliaries.

(10) Butt's Generalization (Butt 2003, 2010; Butt & Lahiri 2012):
Unlike auxiliaries which may become grammaticalized over time to have a purely functional use, light verbs always have a corresponding full or 'heavy' version in all the languages in which they are found.

The constraints on underassociation that Ramchand (2008) derives from analyzing complex predicates in Bangla and Hindi are the following: (1) Underassociation of category features of any 'main verb' is possible, constrained by Agree. (2) Agreeing categorial features must unify their conceptual content.

A verb is light when its categorial features are in Agree relation with an element in its complement position. For the conceptual content of the agreeing features to unify, one of the verbal elements must have extremely light or abstract lexical content.

In the case of *poo* 'go', the unaccusative light verb, the light verb lexicalizes [proc], and the main verb lexicalizes only the [res] head through the perfective ending *-i* so that all its other category features remain underassociated. Should the main verb contains an [init] feature, the structure will not converge because it will not be licensed – either by AGREE or by direct lexicalization. This explains the selectional restrictions on *poo*.

(11) **siita cadiv-i-poo-indi*
Sita read-PERF-go-PST.3FSG
Intended: Sita read (fully).

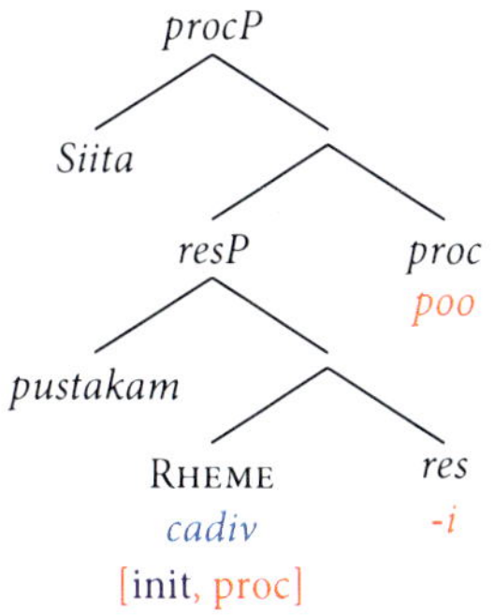

In the case of the transitive light verbs, *veyyi* 'throw' and *paDa.veyyi* 'fall.throw', the light verb lexicalizes both [init] and [proc] in the first phase structure. This should allow both kinds of verbs – those with only [proc], and those with both [proc] and [init] – to lexicalize the [res] and RHEME position, thus permitting all verb types to form complex predicates with these light verbs. But the transitive light verbs do not compose with unaccusative main verbs.

(12) **icu karig-i-vees-indi* **icu karig-i-paDees-indi*
ice melt-PERF-throw-PST.3FSG ice melt-PERF-fall.throw-PST.3FSG
Intended: The ice melted (fully). Intended: The ice melted (fully).

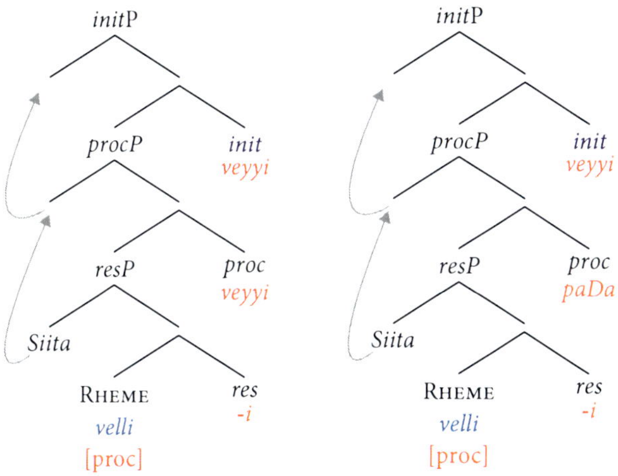

To explain the ungrammaticality of unaccusatives combining with the transitive light verbs, Ramchand (2008) proposes the light verb constraint, given in (13), which enforces matching in the other direction, from the light verb to the main verb, which requires all of the features of the light verb to be linked to another verb by means of Agree.

(13) The Light Verb Constraint: A verb can be used as a light verb when all of its category features Agree with some other verbal element in its complement domain

To conclude, of the 3 aspectuals in Telugu, *poo* is an unaccusative verb ([init]-less in First Phase terms) and selects for other unaccussative verbs. The other two have an [init] head and select for verbs with [init]. The [init]-less light verb cannot select [init] verbs and the [init] light verb cannot select [init]-less verbs as shown in (14) with the non-converging structures given in (15), because if two lexical items combine to lexicalize an event structure skeleton, then their conceptual contents must be able to unify without contradiction. The Telugu data is further evidence for the constraints on underassociation and the selectional restrictions of light verbs that Ramchand (2008) identifies from Bangla data.

(14) a. **poo + [init] V**
**siita cadiv-i-poo-indi*
Sita read-PERF-go-PST.3FSG
Intended: Sita read.

b. **veyyi + [init]-less V**
**siita america vell-i-vees-indi*
Sita America go-PERF-throw-PST.3FSG
Intended: Sita went to America.

c. **paDa.veyyi + [init]-less V**
**siita america vell-i-paDees-indi*
Sita America go-PERF-fall.throw-PST.3FSG
Intended: Sita went to America.

(15)

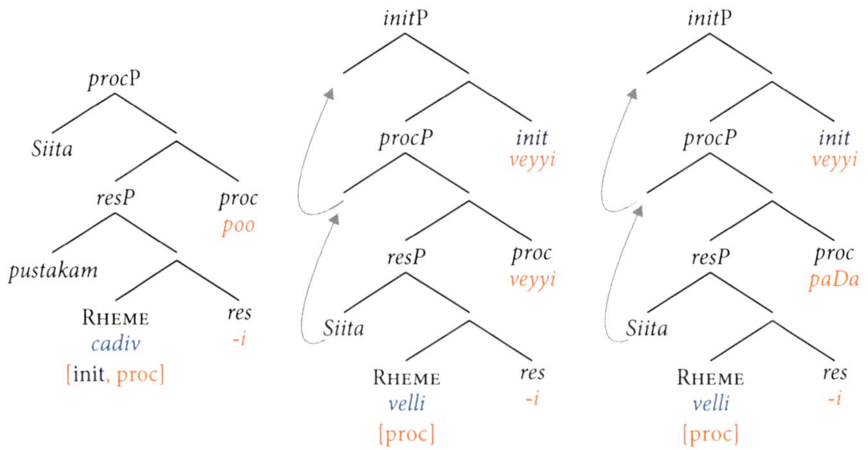

4. The 3 transitivizer light verbs in Telugu

In Telugu, light verbs also function as transitivizers. This is shown in (17)–(19), where each of the 3 transitivizer light verbs, *veyyi* 'throw', *peTTu* 'put', and *koTTu* 'hit', combine with the two unaccusative main verbs *aaru* 'dry' and *karugu* 'melt', and the resulting complex predicates take an agent DP. The unaccusative constructions are shown in (16).

(16) a. **aaru 'dry'**
baTTalu aari-niyyi
clothes dry-PST.3FPL
The clothes dried.

b. **karugu 'melt'**
icu karig-indi
ice melt-PST.3FSG
The ice melted.

(17) a. **veyyi 'throw'**
siita baTTalu aar-a-vees-indi
Sita clothes dry-INF-throw-PST.3FSG
Sita put the clothes to dry.

b. *siita icu karag-a-vees-indi*
Sita ice melt-INF-throw-PST.3FSG
Sita melted the ice.

(18) a. **peTTu 'put'**
siita baTTalu aar-a-peTT-indi
Sita clothes dry-INF-put-PST.3FSG
Sita put the clothes to dry.

b. *siita icu karag-a-peTT-indi*
Sita icu melt-INF-put-PST.3FSG
Sita melted the ice.

(19) a. **koTTu 'hit'**
siita baTTalu aar-a-koTT-indi
Sita clothes dry-INF-hit-PST.3FSG
Sita put the clothes to dry.

b. *siita icu karag-a-koTT-indi*
Sita icu melt-INF-hit-PST.3FSG
Sita melted the ice.

Going by Butt's Generalization, stated in (10), we should find heavy versions of the 3 transitivizer light verbs in Telugu. These are shown in (20a)–(20c).

(20) a. **veyyi 'throw'**
siita banti vees-indi
Sita ball throw-PST.3FSG
Sita threw the ball.

b. **peTTu 'put'**
siita banti akkaDa peTT-indi
Sita ball there put-PST.3FSG
Sita put the ball there.

c. **koTTu 'hit'**
siita banti koTT-indi
Sita ball hit-PST.3FSG
Sita hit the ball.

As noted in §3.2, to account for Butt's Generalization, Ramchand proposes that the skeletal structure of the light verb is always the same as that of the heavy verb counterpart. By identifying the lexical specification of the heavy verb, we can identify the lexical specification of the corresponding light verb. From (20a)–(20c), we can conclude that the lexical categorial specifications of the three transitivizer light verbs are as shown in (21).

(21) *veyyi, peTTu, koTTu*: [init, proc, res]

4.1 A First Phase analysis of the transitivizer complex predicates

The event schema of the 3 transitivizers in their heavy verb use in the constructions in (20) is shown in (22).

(22)

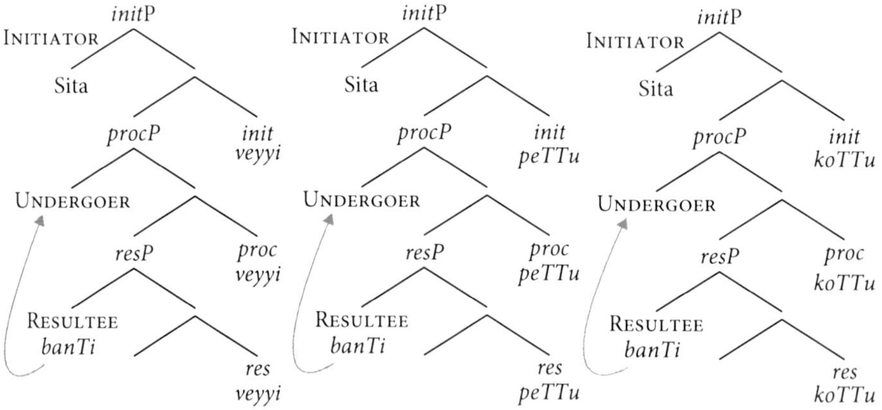

Applying the compositional principles of the aspectual complex predicates in §3.2 to the transitivizer complex predicates, the corresponding structures for the transitivizer complex predicates in the sentences in (17)–(19) in First Phase syntax terms are shown in (23).

(23)

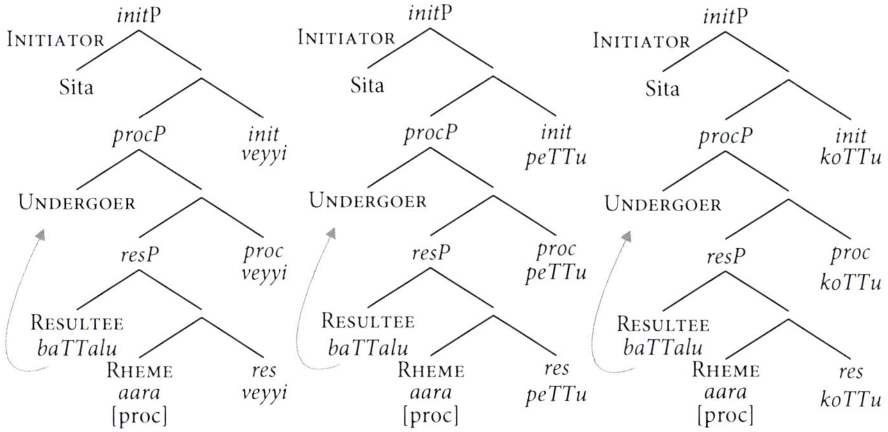

But according to the light verb constraint discussed in §3.2, all of the features of the light verb should Agree with features on the main verb in a complex predicate. So the three transitivizer light verbs in Telugu should not compose with unaccusative main verbs which do not have an [init] feature to license the [init] feature of the transitivizer light verbs.

What we see here are instances of direct lexicalization of the Spec of *init*, thus licensing the [init] feature of the light verbs. This is show in (24). This is a possible composition, which the First Phase Syntax system allows, but was ruled out as a stipulation by Ramchand (2008) because there were no instances of this found in the data in Bangla. The Telugu data here shows that the stipulation is unnecessary and the possible combination that the compositional system allows is actually attested.

(24)

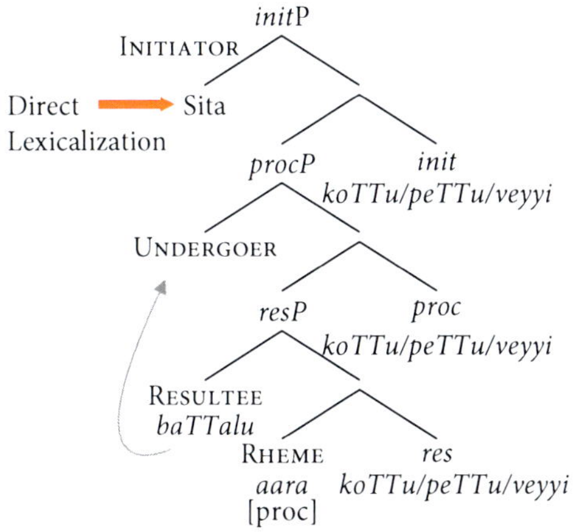

4.1.1 paDa.veyyi: *Aspectual light verb formed using a transitivizer*

The aspectual light verb *paDa.veyyi* discussed in §3, after understanding the composition of the transitivizer light verbs, can now be itself analyzed as a composite light verb formed by the transitivization of the unaccusative verb *paDu* 'fall' with the transitivizer light verb *veyyi* 'throw'. This is shown in (25).

(25) a. **paDu 'fall' = unaccusative**
pustakam paD-indi
book fall-PST.3FSG
The book fell.

b. **paDa.veyyi = unaccusative + transitivizer light verb**
siita pustakam paD-a-vees.indi
Sita book fall-INF-throw-PST.3FSG
Sita dropped the book.

c. **cadivi.paDa.veyyi = main verb + aspectual light verb**
siita pustakam cadiv-i-paD-a-vees-indi
Sita book read-PERF-fall-INF-throw-PST.3FSG
Sita read the book (fully).

4.2 The 3 transitivers have 3 inceptual meanings: Inception, Continuation, and, Completion

While any of the 3 transitivizers can be used to transitivize the unaccusative main verbs as shown in (17)–(19), there are subtle semantic differences between the 3 constructions. The 3 transitivizers – *veyyi* 'throw', *peTTu* 'put', and *koTTu* 'hit', emphasise 3 different parts of the action: inception, continuation and completion, respectively. For example in (26)–(28), the main semantic content of the event remains the same, an event of drying, but the transitivizers impart the subtle semantic notion of inception, ongoing, and completion.

(26) **veyyi 'throw'**
siita baTTalu aar-a-veesindi
Sita clothes dry-INF-throw-PST.3FSG
Sita put the clothes to dry (the clothes have begun drying).

(27) **peTTu 'put'**
siita baTTalu aar-a-peTT-indi
Sita clothes dry-INF-put-PST.3FSG
Sita put the clothes to dry (the clothes are in the process of drying).

(28) **koTTu 'hit'**
siita baTTalu aar-a-koTT-indi
Sita clothes dry-INF-hit-PST.3FSG
Sita put the clothes to dry (the clothes have finished drying).

The transitivizers manifest the same components of first phase syntax but with different parts emphasized. In the initiative light verb, the [init] projection has richer lexical content focusing on the beginning of the event, in the continuative verb, the [proc] projection has richer lexical content focussing on the process of the event, and in the completive transitivizer the [res] projection has rich lexical content focussing on the result of the event. This is shown in a non-formalized way in (29). I put aside the technical details of how to implement this distinction here.[3]

(29) Initiative transitivizer: *veyyi* ⟨**init**, proc, res⟩
Continuative transitivizer: *peTTu* ⟨init, **proc**, res⟩
Completive transitivizer: *koTTu* ⟨init, proc, **res**⟩

4.3 Inceptual meanings: Evidence from Bangla

Inceptual meanings in light verbs have been noticed for some time. Previous literature on complex predicates (Alsina et al. 1997) in South Asian languages have documented the various meanings contributed by the light verb to the complex predicate (Hook 1974, 1993; Dasgupta 1977; Verma 1993; Mohanan 1994; Krishnamurti 1992; Uma Maheshwara Rao 1994; Rajyarama 1998). Butt (1995) identified that semantic information like inception/completion is contributed by the light verb in Hindi.

Paul (2004) observes that in Bangla "The V2 oTha 'rise' implies the commencement of the V1 event when the two verbs combine. The resultant CV expresses inceptive aspectual information." Paul (2004) examines the nuances of meaning that the light verb contributes to the complex predicate. She observes the three inceptual meanings of inception, continuity, and result, for the light verbs given in (30). (Paul 2004:82)

(30)

V1	V2	CV	Semantic Overtone
hasha 'laugh'	oTha 'rise'	hesh-e-oTha	Focus on inception
hasha 'laugh'	jaoa 'go'	hesh-e-jaoa	Focus on continuity
hasha 'laugh'	phaela 'drop'	hesh-e-phaela	Focus on result

3. A reviewer points out that the *init*, *proc* and *rec* subevents are events which have not been located in time or mapped to a time axis. This is something that usually happens in AspP or TP. So one can tie the inception, continuation, and completion readings to another piece of the structure, like AspP. This requires the analysis presented here to be extended, and which I leave out for future exploration.

Basu & Wilbur (2010) make an exhaustive list of light verbs in Bangla that contribute inceptual meanings. This is given in (31)–(32). (Basu & Wilbur 2010: 6)

(31)

Meaning	phel	di	ni	por	tul	uth	bosh
endpoint	+	+	+	+	+	–	–
inception	–	–	–	–	–	+	+
ongoing	–	–	–	–	–	–	–

(32)

Meaning	path	rakh	ash	mor	chol	ja	bera
endpoint	–	–	–	–	–	–	–
inception	–	–	–	–	–	–	–
ongoing	+	+	+	+	+	+	+

They note that the inceptual light verbs uTh 'rise' and boS 'sit' mark the sudden, unexpected initiation of an event, they impart the meaning of blurting out something unexpectedly. This is shown in (33).

(33) **uTho 'rise'**
ram kotha-Ta bol-e-uTh-lo
Ram words-CLF say-PERF-rise-PST.3
Ram said those words (unexpectedly).

Continuation light verbs, Basu & Wilbur (2010) note, "impart meaning of ongoing repeated iterations of the same event over a period of time. Most of these verbs are semantically 'go' type motion verbs that mean something happening over a period of time." An example is given in (34).

(34) **ja 'go'**
meye-Ti kotha bol-e-ja-cchi-lo
girl-CLF word say-PERF-go-be-PST.3
The girl was going on talking.

An example of a completion light verb in Bangla is given in (35).

(35) **ni 'take'**
ram chiThi-Ta likh-e-ni-lo
Ram letter-CLF write-PERF-take-PST.3
Ram wrote the letter (finished it).

So just like the 3 transitivizers in Telugu emphasize 3 different parts of the action (inception, continuation and completion), light verbs in Bangla also contribute inceptual meanings that add one of the 3 semantic nuances (inception, continuation, completion) to the action denoted by the main verb.

4.3.1 *Structural meaning vs. Lexical-conceptual meaning*

As Ramchand (2012:7) notes "If light verbs were functional elements and their heavy counterparts were roots, there would be no ready explanation of the fact that certain types of meaning (event structural) carry over from one use to the other." She takes the selectional restrictions of light verbs and the entailment from Butt's Generalization regarding the properties of the light verb arising from its properties as a heavy verb to indicate that all verbs come with both structural and lexical-conceptual meanings. She takes the abstractness of the light verb uses to indicate that their lexical-conceptual meanings are systematically defeasible. Ramchand (2012) comes to the conclusion that causation (Rappaport-Hovav & Levin 2010), event structure, and abstract path related meanings (Talmy 2007) are skeletal.

From the data and the analysis of the transitivizer light verbs in §4.2 it is clear that the inceptual meanings are tied to the skeletal or structural meaning. They mark initiation, ongoing and completed telic sub-events. This has been investigated and documented for Bangla light verbs (Paul 2003, 2004; Basu 2005) and this chapter presents the data and analysis for Telugu transitivizer light verbs.

However, we still have a number of major questions to address before we can have a satisfying story for Butt's Generalization and the pattern of loss that turns main verbs into light verbs.

5. Transitivizer light verbs vs. Causative suffix

The causative suffix in Telugu is *-inc* or *-imp* as shown in (36)–(38) and the structure in (39a). An unaccusative verb, as in (36), can be transitivized using the causative as shown in (37) with the structure given in (39b). It can causativize further with underassociation as shown in (38) and the structure given in (39c).

(36) *daaram teg-indi*
thread snap-PST.3FSG
The thread snapped.

(37) *siita daaram te-mp-indi*
Sita thread snap-CAUS-PST.3FSG
Sita snapped the thread.

(38) *siita daaram raamu-too te-mp-inc-indi*
Sita thread Ram-with snap-CAUS-CAUS-PST.3FSG
Sita made Ram snap the thread.

(39)

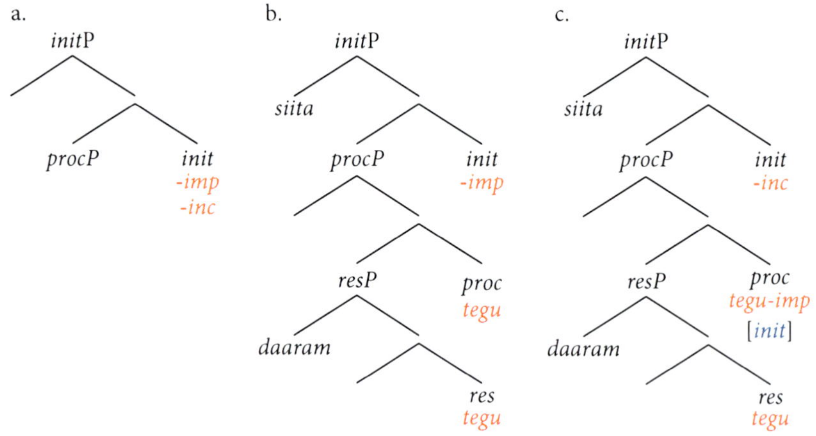

5.1 Causative suffix *-inc* and aspectual light verbs

The causative cannot co-occur with an unaccusative (⟨init⟩-less) light verb, but it can co-occur with a transitive (init) light verb, as shown in (40). This is because the [init] feature of *-inc* cannot underassociate with the ⟨init⟩-less light verb, whereas it can underassociate with ⟨init⟩ light verbs, as predicted by the constraints on underassociation. This is shown in (41).

(40) a. ***-inc* + poo 'go'**
**siita icu karig-inc-i-poo-indi*
Sita ice melt-CAUS-PERF-go-PST.3FSG
Intended: Sita melted the ice (completely).

b. ***-inc* + veyyi 'throw'**
siita icu karig-inc-i-vees-indi
Sita ice melt-CAUS-PERF-throw-PST.3FSG
Sita melted the ice (fully).

c. ***-inc* + paDa.veyyi 'fall.throw'**
siita icu karig-inc-i-paDees-indi
Sita ice melt-CAUS-PERF-fall.throw-PST.3FSG
Sita melted the ice (fully).

(41) karig.incu vs. *karig-inci-poo vs. karig-inci-veyyi

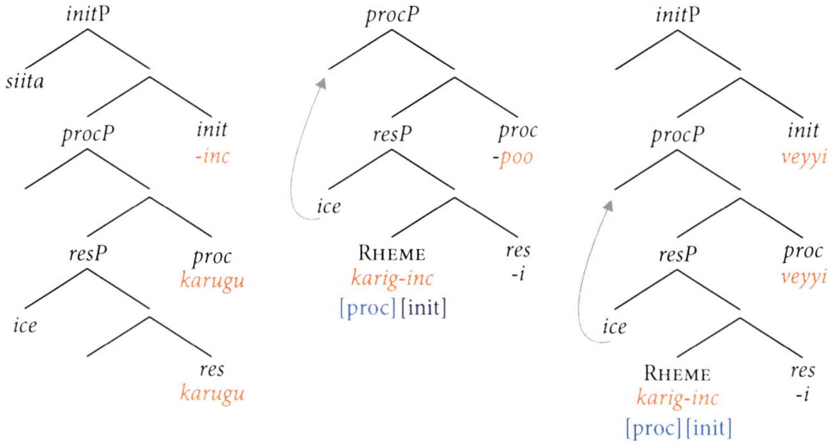

So the causative suffix can occur with an unaccusative main verb but cannot occur with an unaccusative light verb. This is because of the Agree constraint on under-association in the formation of complex predicates which does not apply in causative suffixation of simple main verbs.

5.2 Transitivizing using *-inc* vs. light verbs

An unaccusative verb can be transitivized using either the causative suffix or a transitivizer light verb (Krishnamurti 1992). This is shown in (42). In (42a) the unaccusative is transitivized using the causative morpheme, and in (42b) and (42c) it is transitivized using the transitivizer light verbs.

(42) a. **unaccusative + -inc**
siita cigarette kaal-c-indi
Sita Cigarette burn-CAUS-PST.3FSG
Sita smoked a cigarette.

b. **unaccusative + peTTu 'put'**
siita cigarette kaal-a-peTT-indi
Sita Cigarette burn-INF-put-PST.3FSG
Sita burnt the cigarette.

c. **unaccusative + veyyi 'throw'**
siita cigarette kaal-a-vees.indi
Sita Cigarette burn-INF-throw-PST.3FSG
Sita burnt the cigarette.

The two combinations however differ in their semantics.The transitivizer light verb brings its inceptual meaning along with it. The causative suffix -inc is only [init] whereas the light verbs are [init, proc, res] thus building in the semantic properties of the structure into the meaning of the complex predicate. This is shown in (43).

(43)

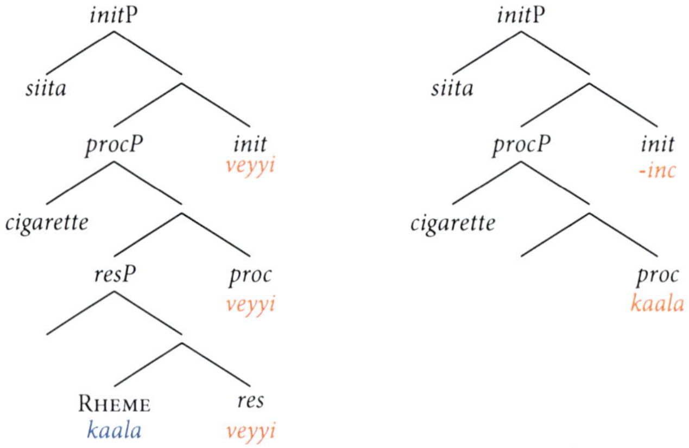

6. Transitivizer light verbs in nominal complex predicates

6.1 Nominal complex predicates in Telugu

In the nominal complex predicates, the light verb acts as the verbalizer. It is a very productive way of forming predicates in the language, especially incorporating loan words into the lexicon. Some examples are given in (44).

(44)

Light verb:	**ceyyi 'make' & koTTu 'hit'**			**peTTu 'put'**	**avvu 'happen'**		
Loan word:	print	phone	ready	effort	surprise	sad	defeat
	call	defeat	type	leg	shock	happy	begin
	post	apply	hurt	blood	excite	tired	

In First Phase syntax terms, in nominal complex predicates, the light verb lexicalizes the subevent heads and provides the argument structure skeleton (Pantcheva 2008, 2010), just as it does in verbal complex predicates. The preverb (Lazard 1957) or the nominal element lexicalizes the rheme. Together they form one joint predication. This is shown in (45).

(45) *baya paDu*
fear fall
'be afraid'

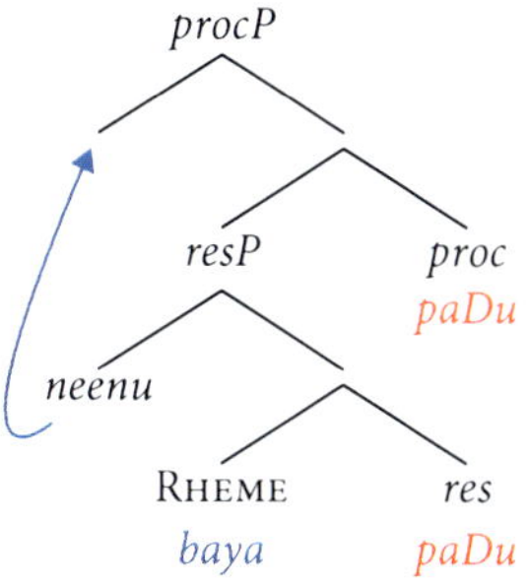

kampu koTTu
stink hit
'to stink'

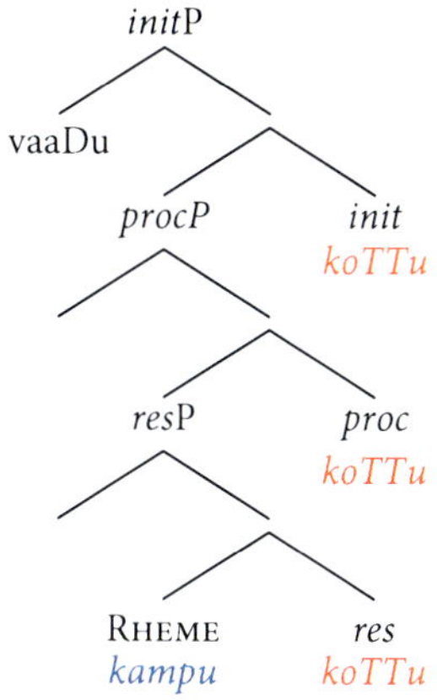

As the light verb lexicalizes the verbal heads, the argument structure should depend entirely on the categorial specification of the light verb. Karimi-Doostan (1997) divides Persian light verbs into two classes: *initiatory* and *transition* light verbs. Telugu light verbs that enter into nominal complex predication also fall into these two groups as shown in (46). In First Phase Syntax terms, *initiatory* light verbs have an [init] specification, *transition* light verbs are without an [init] subevent head. The choice between these light verbs determines agentivity in the complex predicates formed.

(46)

[init] light verbs		**[init]-less light verbs**	
ceyyi 'make'	ivvu 'give'	paDu 'fall'	avvu 'happen'
peTTu 'put'	tiyyi 'remove'	kalugu 'arose'	tegu 'break'
koTTu 'hit'	aaDu 'play'	poo 'go'	digu 'go down'
veyyi 'throw'	cuupincu 'show'	ekku 'go up'	maaru 'change'

In Telugu, a fairly systematic way to transform a complex predicate without an external argument into one with an external argument is to change the light verb from the [init]-less type to the [init] type, thus providing the Spec of InitP for the initiator. When the [init] light verbs compose with a nominal element, they have an initiatory meaning with an external argument. When the [init]-less light verbs combine with a nominal element, they have an experiential meaning only. This is shown in (47) and (48).

(47) **paDu**
neenu booltaa paDD-aanu
I flip fall-PST.1SG
I flipped.

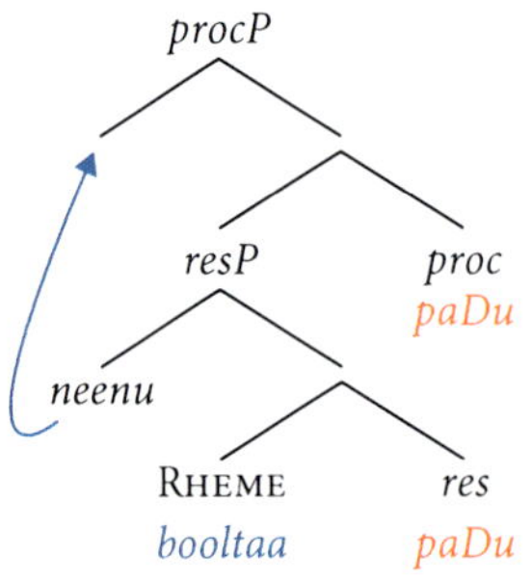

koTTu
neenu booltaa koTT-eenu
I flip hit-PST.1SG
I did a cartwheel.

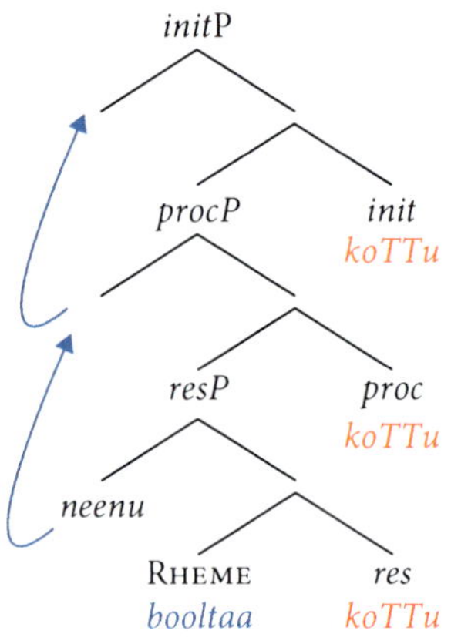

(48) **[init]-less = experiential**
baya paDu 'get scared'
pedda avvu 'grow up'
muuta paDu 'get closed down'
moosam poo 'get deceived'

[init] = agentive
baya peTTu 'scare someone'
pedda ceyyi 'bring up'
muuta veyyi 'close down'
moosam ceyyi 'deceive'

Further evidence for this comes from passivization. The [init]-less predicate cannot be passivized, but the [init] version can. This is shown in (49)–(50).

(49) **[init]-less Complex predicate + Passive suffix**

a. *dukaanam muuta-paD-indi*
shop lid-fall-PST.3FSG
The shop got closed down.

b. **dukaanam muuta-paDa-baD-indi*
shop lid-fall-PASS-PST.3FSG
Intended: The shop got closed down.

(50) **[init] Complex predicate + Passive suffix**

a. *siita dukaanam muuta-vees-indi*
Sita shop lid-throw-PST.3FSG
Sita closed the shop down.

b. *dukaanam muuta-veyya-baD-indi*
shop lid-throw-PASS-PST.3FSG
The shop got closed down.

Nominal predicates enter into constructions only with corresponding verbal predicates. This is shown in (51a)–(51c). The nominal complex predicate behaves syntactically like the light verb that constitutes it. A mismatch is not allowed in terms of sub-event heads. This is shown in (52). This further strengthens the argument that the light verb contributes the argument structure.

(51) a. **poo 'go'**
siita baya-paD-i-poo-indi
Sita fear-fell-PERF-go-PST.3FSG
Sita got afraid.

b. **veyyi 'throw'**
sita guraka-peTT-i-vees-indi
Sita snore-put-PERF-throw-PST.3FSG
Sita snored away.

c. **paDa.veyyi 'fall.down'**
siita sutti-koTT-i-paDees-indi
Sita hammer-hit-PERF-fall.throw-PST.3FSG
Sita talked boringly.

(52) a. **[init]-less NomCPr + [init] verb**
**siita baya-paD-i-vees-indi*
Sita fear-fall-PERF-threw-PST.3FSG
Intended: Sita got afraid.

b. **[init] NomCPr + [init]-less verb**
**Siita sutti-koTT-i-poo-indi*
Sita hammer-hit-PERF-go-PST.3FSG
Intended: Sita talked boringly.

6.2 Transitivizer light verb + Nominal element

When the transitivizer light verbs compose with nominal elements to form nominal complex predicates, they again bring their inceptual meanings into the constructions as shown in (53)–(54).

(53) ***baTTalu* 'clothes' + *veyyi/peTTu/koTTu***
a. *baTTalu veyyi*
clothes throw
'put on clothes'

b. *baTTalu peTTu*
clothes put
'gift clothes'

c. *baTTalu koTTu*
clothes hit
'steal clothes'

(54) ***kannu* 'eye' + *veyyi/peTTu/koTTu***
a. *kannu veyyi*
eye throw
'throw a glance'

b. *kannu peTTu*
eye put
'keep an eye'

c. *kannu koTTu*
eye hit
'wink'

In (54a), it is the inceptual meaning of the transitivizer light verb *veyyi* that composes with the noun, to deliver the meaning of the complex predicate. In (54b), the continuative meaning of the transitivizer light verb *peTTu*, composes with the noun *kannu*, so that the phrase means 'keep an eye'. In (54c), the completive meaning of the transitivizer light verb *koTTu* is what gets added, to form the phrasal meaning 'wink'.

So the properties of the transitivizer light verbs are the same in nominal complex predicates as they are in the verbal complex predicates.

7. Conclusion

The aspectual light verbs in Telugu compose based on selectional restrictions. Selection can be captured by the underassociation of category features constrained by Agree. The transitivizer light verbs instantiate direct lexicalization of the Spec of [init]. There are inceptual meanings associated with the transitivizers. The meanings obtained when they compose with unaccusatives are different from when the causative morpheme composes with unaccusatives. They also bring their inceptual meaning into nominal predicates that they form. When the same nominal element composes with the 3 transitivizers, the predicate so formed, takes on the meaning based on the inceptual meaning of the light verb that it combines with.

Where does the inceptual meaning for the transitivizers come from? Is this structurally dependent? I propose that the inceptual meanings – inception, continuation, and completion are linked to the 3 structural heads of verbs – ⟨init⟩, ⟨proc⟩ and ⟨res⟩. There must be some way of encoding the primacy of one of these heads in each of the transitivizers in the system of verb meaning. By association with particular subevental heads, structure is linked with an abstract meaning. When the verb is excoriated of its lexical-encylopaedic semantic content, and only its functional skeleton is left, it still preserves its inceptual meaning, which is inalienably linked to each sub-event head.

References

Basu, D. 2005. Complex predicates in Bangla: An event based analysis. MA thesis, Purdue University.

Basu, Debarchana & Wilbur, Ronnie. 2010. Complex predicates in Bangla: An event based analysis. In *Rice Working Papers in Linguistics* 2.

Butt, M. 1995. *The Structure of Complex Predicates in Urdu* [Dissertations in Linguistics]. Stanford CA: CSLI.

Butt, Miriam. 2003. The light verb jungle. In *Proceedings of the Workshop on MultiVerb Constructions, Trondheim Summer School.* Trondheim: Norwegian University of Science and Technology.

Butt, Miriam. 2010. The light verb jungle: Still hacking away. In *Complex Predicates in Cross-Linguistic Perspective,* M. Amberber, M. Harvey & B. Baker (eds), 48–78. Cambridge: CUP.

Butt, Miriam & Lahiri, Aditi. 2012. Diachronic pertinacity of light verbs. *Lingua.* ⟨http://dx.doi.org/10.1016/j.lingua.2012.11.006⟩

Caha, Pavel. 2007. The Superset Principle. Ms, University of Tromsø.

Dasgupta, Probal. 1977. The internal grammar of compound verbs in Bangla. *Indian Linguistics* 38(3): 68–85.

Fábregas, Antonio. 2007. The exhaustive lexicalisation principle. *Tromsø Working Papers on Language and Linguistics: Nordlyd* 34(2).

Hook, P.E. 1974. *The Compound Verb in Hindi.* Ann Arbor MI: Center for South and Southeast Asian Studies, The University of Michigan.

Hook, Peter E. 1993. Aspectogenesis and the compound verb in Indo-Aryan. In *Complex Predicates in South Asian Languages.* M. K. Verma (ed.), 97–113. Stanford CA: CSLI.

Jespersen, Otto. 1965. *A Modern English Grammar on Historical Principles,* Vol. VI: *Morphology.* London: George Allen and Unwin.

Karimi-Doostan, Gholamhossein. 1997. Light Verb Constructions in Persian. PhD dissertation, University of Essex.

Krishnamurti, Bhadriraju. 1992. Complex predicates in Telugu. *Bulletin of The Deccan College Post Graduate and Research Institute: S.M. Katre Felicitation Volume,* 314–327.

Lazard, Gilbert. 1957. *Grammaire du Persan contemporain.* Paris: Librairie C. Klincksiek.

Mohanan, Tara. 1994. *Argument Structure in Hindi.* Stanford CA: CSLI.

Pantcheva, Marina. 2008. Noun preverbs in Persian complex predicates. *Tromsø Working Papers on Language and Linguistics: Nordlyd* 35: 19–45.

Pantcheva, Marina. 2010. First phase syntax of Persian complex predicates: Argument structure and telicity. *Journal of South Asian Linguistics* 2(1): 51–70.

Paul, Soma. 2003. Composition of compound verbs in Bangla. In *Proceedings of the Workshop on Multi-Verb Constructions, Trondheim Summer School,* D. Beermann & L. Hellan (eds). Trondheim: Norwegian University of Science and Technology.

Paul, Soma. 2004. An HPSG Account of Bangla Compound Verbs with LKB Implementation. PhD dissertation, University of Hyderabad.

Rajyarama, Koppaka. 1998. A Study on Some Aspects Of Derivational Morphology in Telugu with Special Reference to Compounds. PhD dissertation, University of Hyderabad.

Ramchand, Gillian C. 2008. *Verb Meaning and the Lexicon: A First Phase Syntax.* Cambridge: CUP.

Ramchand, Gillian C. 2012. On structural meaning vs. conceptual meaning in verb semantics. In *Workshop on Complex Predicates in South Asian Languages*. Hyderabad: EFLU.

Rao, Uma Maheshwar G. 1994. On certain aspects of word formation process: A case study of Telugu. In *National Seminar on Word formation in Indian Languages*. Hyderabad: Osmania University.

Rappaport-Hovav, Malka & Levin, Beth. 2010. Reflections on manner/result complementarity. In *Syntax, Lexical Semantics, and Event Structure*, ch. 2, M. Rappaport-Hovav, E. Doron & I. Sichel (eds), 21–37. Oxford: OUP.

Starke, Michal. 2009. Nanosyntax: A short primer to a new approach to language. In *Nordlyd* 36(1): Special issue on *Nanosyntax*, P. Svenonius, G. Ramchand, M. Starke & T. Taraldsen (eds). Tromsø: Universitetet i Tromsø.

Starke, M. 2011. Towards an Elegant Solution to Language Variation: Variation Reduces to the Size of Lexically Stored Trees. Ms. University of Tromsø. ⟨ling.auf.net/lingBuzz/001183⟩

Talmy, Leonard. 2007. Lexical typologies. In *Language Typology and Syntactic Description*, vol. 3, ch. 2, T. Shopen (ed.), 66–168. Cambridge: CUP.

Verma, Manindra K. (ed.). 1993. *Complex Predicates in South Asian Languages*. New Delhi: Manohar.

Ditransitive structures in Hindi/Urdu

Shiti Malhotra
Northeastern University

This chapter makes the following two language specific claims; (a) Hindi/Urdu involves two types of ditransitive constructions, corresponding to the prepositional dative constructions and the double object constructions as in languages like English, and (b) the two constructions are not derivationally connected, and are a result of two distinct ditransitive verbs in Hindi/Urdu, namely the "send" type verbs and the "show" type verbs. The two types of verbs have different argument structures and as a consequence two different verb phrase structures. The difference between the two types of verbs however doesn't get reflected in the word – order in Hindi/Urdu because of the feature-driven movement of the objects to the edge of the vP.

Keywords: ditransitives; Hindi/Urdu; thematic structure; hierarchical relation; VP-structure

1. Introduction

Ditransitive structures are one of the basic constructions of all languages, and yet there is no consensus regarding the structure of a ditransitive construction. From the good old days of the *phrase structure* representation to the *Minimalist* paradigm, the ditransitive constructions have remained a challenge. As a result, issues have been brought forward both related to the status of the two objects in the structural configurations as well to the thematic hierarchy among them.

This chapter contributes to the current debate regarding Ditransitive structures through its investigation of Hindi/Urdu ditransitives. In this exploration, it makes the following two language specific claims; (a) Hindi/Urdu involves two types of ditransitive constructions, corresponding to the prepositional dative constructions and the double object constructions as in languages like English, and (b) the two constructions are not derivationally connected, and are a result of two distinct ditransitive verbs in Hindi/Urdu, namely the "send" type verbs and the "show" type verbs. The two types of verbs have different argument structures and as a consequence two different verb phrases. The difference between the two types of verbs however doesn't get reflected in the word-order in Hindi/Urdu because of the feature-driven movement of the objects to the edge of the vP.

The analysis proposed here for Hindi/Urdu is an extension of Malhotra (2005, 2011) and is in line with the work done on ditransitives in other verb-final languages like Japanese (Matsuoka 2003 and Miyagawa & Tsujioka 2004) and Bangla (Bhattacharya & Simpson 2011). This paper shows that these analyses can account for Hindi/Urdu facts as well. In this exploration, it provides further evidence for the proposal that verb final languages also involve more than one ditransitive structures.

2. The status of the two objects

The status of objects in the VP structure directly corresponds to the relation that the verb bears to its arguments. In view of the fact that verbs differ in the number of arguments that they require, they also differ in the structural arrangements of these arguments. Since theta theory assigns the semantic meaning to these arguments on the basis of selectional criteria of the verb, the structures are accordingly represented. In the structural arrangement of the arguments, the condition of *locality*, is an important factor which demands proximity between the arguments and the verb.

In the case of ditransitives, the verb takes more than one internal argument. Therefore both the theta theory and the *locality* condition require the closest relation between the verb and its arguments. One possibility is to assume that the two arguments are the sisters of the verb (1).

(1) [VP verb [NP argument1] [NP argument2]]

Hale and Keyser (1994), on the basis of the Single Complement Hypothesis (SCH), argued that a verb can permit only one complement as a consequence of the binary branching representations. A similar point was made by Kayne (1994), which suggests that it is not permissible for a head to have more than one complement, since the two complements would asymmetrically c-command subparts of each other and produce a violation of anti-symmetry. This poses an interesting problem: What is the status of the second object in a ditransitive construction? Given this restriction, the structure would only allow the first argument to be the sister of the verb and not the second. This not only challenges the condition of locality but also imposes a restriction on the argument structure of the verb.

Much later, this issue was raised again in Chomsky (2001), where it is suggested that argument structure is associated with external merge; everything else with internal merge. Arguments of the verb are always introduced by pure merge and are semantically selected. As a result they represent thematic relations between the verb and the objects selected by it. Since the argument structure configurations are constructed solely by instances of pure merge and s-selection, they represent syntactic objects in terms of local relations. It was also proposed that predicate composition corresponds to only pure merge which involves both set merge and pair merge. The lexical VP consists of entities which are set merged or involve substitution. In case of ditransitives, since both the objects form the internal argument structure of the VP, they must be introduced by pure merge. However the crucial issue here pertains to the merge of the second object in ditransitives, given the fact that a hypothesis like SCH imposes a restriction on the internal argument structure of the verb.

Larson's (1988) view is of interest in this regard. It proposed a derivational structure for the ditransitives. The verb combines with its arguments on the basis of a thematic hierarchy: Agent > Theme > Goal > Oblique. It first combines with the lowest argument in the hierarchy, which becomes its complement and then takes the next argument as its specifier. This step is repeated until no arguments remain in the hierarchy. In case of ditransitives, the verb first combines with the goal, creating the Verb-Indirect Object (IO) configuration and then merging the Direct Object (DO) at the spec of it (2). The structure in (2) is strictly binary, obeys the SCH constraint and rightly exhibits the asymmetrical relation between the two objects.

(2)

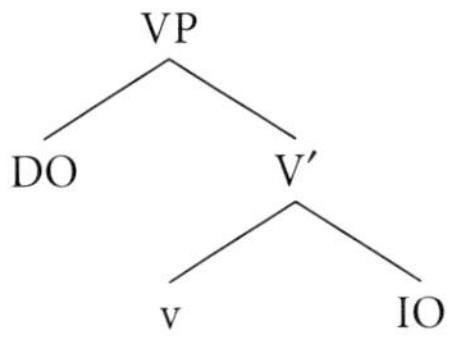

In verb-final languages like Hindi/Urdu, the issue related to the status of second object is more acute, as there are added complexities of the word order. In ditransitive constructions in Hindi/Urdu, for instance, the surface order of the arguments is IO>DO (3a). Hindi/Urdu also allows the DO>IO order (3b) but this one is marked. However in both the orders the dative case marker is attached to the Indirect Object.

(3) a. *jOn-ne merii-ko kitaab dii*
John-ERG Mary-DAT book gave
'John gave the book to Mary.'

b. *jOn-ne kitaab merii-ko dii*
John-ERG book Mary-DAT gave
'John gave the book to Mary.'

Furthermore, it is only the IO that can c-command the DO (4a) in Hindi/Urdu, and not the other way around (4b).

(4) a. *main-ne raam*$_i$*-ko [uskii*$_i$ *kitaab] dii* (Kidwai 2000)
I-ERG Ram-DAT his book gave
'I gave Ram$_i$ his$_i$ book.'

b. **main-ne us*$_i$*-ko raam*$_i$*-kii kitaab dii*
I-ERG he-DAT Ram's book gave
'I gave him$_i$ Ram$_i$'s book.'

Facts like these suggest that the IO is structurally higher than the DO in languages like Hindi/Urdu. In other words, the ditransitive structures in verb-final languages look like a mirror image of the English ditransitives. One approach adopted to solve this issue suggested that the thematic hierarchy of arguments in verb-final languages is opposite to that of English (Hoji 1985; Miyagawa 1997). The other approach is to assume that the Verb Phrase (VP) is universally constructed in the same manner and it's only later movements which obtain different orders in specific languages.

This chapter adopts the second approach to address the issues related to ditransitive constructions in Hindi/Urdu, and argues in favor of a universal theta hierarchy. Now the question is what is the underlying form of ditransitives in verb-final languages like Hindi/Urdu? and how is the surface form derived out of it? An answer to this requires a discussion on the argument structure of ditransitives. The following section provides some insight on that aspect.

3. The thematic structure of the ditransitive: Prepositional dative vs. the double object

The second issue with ditransitive constructions relates to the underlying argument structure of the ditransitives. The discussion of the argument structure of ditransitive often goes hand in hand with the two forms that ditransitives exhibit in languages like English. The two types of ditransitive constructions are characterized by distinct word-orders, different forms of the IO, a PP (5a) and a DP (5b).

(5) a. John gave [$_{DO}$the flowers] [$_{IO}$to Mary]. (Prepositional dative construction)

b. John gave [$_{IO}$Mary] [$_{DO}$the flowers]. (Double object construction)

The two constructions also exhibit different asymmetrical relations between the IO and DO. In prespositional dative constructions (henceforth PDC), the quantifier contained in the DO must c-command the pronoun in the IO (6), whereas in the case of double object constructions (henceforth DOC), the quantifier contained in the IO must c-command the pronoun in the DO (7).

(6) a. John gave every book$_i$ to its$_i$ owner (PDC)
b *John gave his$_i$ book to every owner$_i$

(7) a. John gave every child$_i$ his$_i$ book (DOC)
b *John gave his$_i$ book every child$_i$

There have been three kinds of approaches adopted to explain these facts. The first approach treats them structurally distinct but assumes the same underlying argument structure for both (Fillmore 1965; Baker 1988; Larson 1988 and many others). Larson (1988) is a leading view of this approach and argues for a derivational relation between the PDC and the DOC structures. The idea is that the PDC frame is the underlying structure from which the DOC frame is derived through a passive-like transformation involving two steps, (a) Withdrawal of Case from the IO through absorption of Case-assigning preposition, and (b) suppression of the thematic role assignment of the DO. As a consequence, the DO is demoted to an adjunct position, vacating the Spec, VP position to which the IO moves for Case reasons (8).

(8) **PDC**

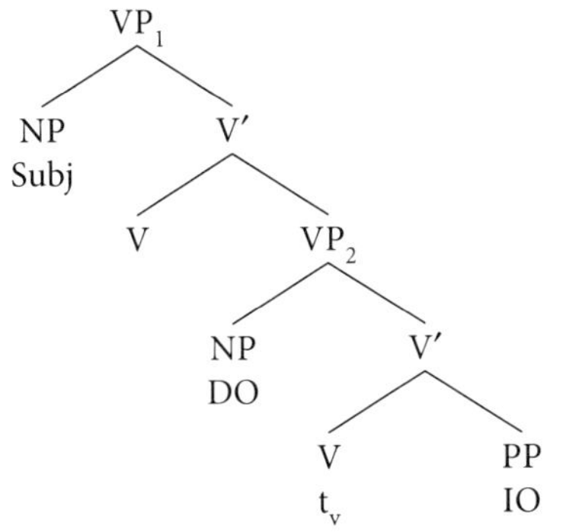

DOC

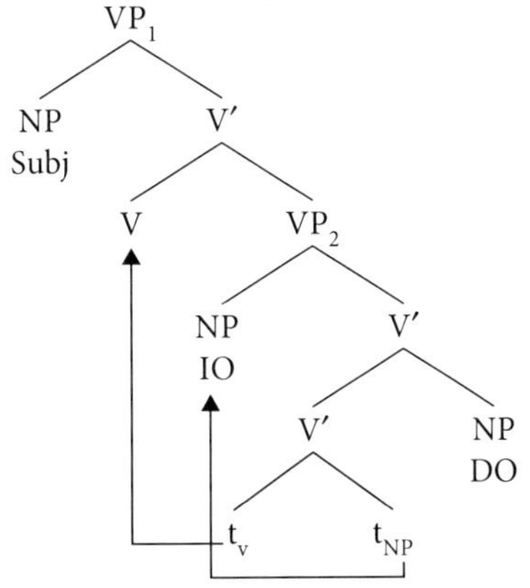

Many (Pesetsky 1995; Harley 1997; Bruening 2001; Richards 2001; Beck & Johnson 2004, among others) have argued against this option and provided evidence showing that PDC and DOC have completely different argument structures. One argument comes from nominalization, as deverbal nominalization allows the object of the verb to surface as either the genitive of the resulting NP, or inside an *of*-phrase. However, this is only possible if the object is the argument of the verb (9) and not when it is the subject of the small clause (10).

(9) Examine the problem (Beck & Johnson 2004)
  a. The examination of the problem
  b. The problem's examination

(10) believe Thilo handsome
  a. *the belief of Thilo handsome
  b. *Thilo's belief handsome

On this basis, Kayne (1984) argued that the IO (the first NP following the verb) in the DOC construction is not the argument of the verb because in nominalizations it behaves like a subject of a small-clause (11). In contrast, the DO (the first NP following the verb) in the PDC construction does behave like an argument (12).

(11) Present Satoshi a ball (Beck & Johnson 2004)
  a. *the presentation of the Satoshi a ball.
  b. *Satoshi's presentation a ball

(12) Present a ball to Satoshi (Beck & Johnson 2004)
  a. The presentation of the ball to Satoshi
  b. The ball's presentation to Satoshi

Apart from this there are various semantic differences between the two constructions. One difference is that it is only DOC (but not PDC) that is associated with a possession or causation meaning (13). These differences in semantics may indicate differences in thematic structure (Green 1974; Oehrle 1976; Harley 1995; Pesetesky 1995 etc.).

(13) a. The interview gave me a headache.
  b. #The interview gave a headache to me.

Another difference is the animacy restriction. The IO in the PDC can refer to both animate as well as inanimate goals (14) whereas the IO in the DOC can only refer to animate goals. As a result, the following sentences in (15) are good with an animate object (*Mary*) but not with an inanimate object (*Delhi*).[1]

(14) a. John sent a letter to Mary.
  b. John sent a letter to Tokyo.

(15) a. John sent Mary a letter.
  b. #John sent Delhi a letter.

1. One of the reviewers noted that (15b) would be okay if 'Delhi' is considered animate, which further supports the animacy requirement in DOC.

The requirement of the goal phrase to be animate in DOC arise out of the semantic nature of the of the goal phrase as a possessor.[2] This very nature of the IO advocates different underlying structures for the DOC. The thematic structure of PDC and DOC is different; the IO in the PDC is a receiver or the location whereas the IO in the DOC is a possessor. Marantz (1993) suggests that the IO in the DOC construction is introduced by an Applicative head that appears between the lexical V and the little v which introduces the external argument (agent>possessor>theme). The PDC, on the other hand, has the structure where both the goal and theme arguments are part of the same phrase (agent>theme>goal).

(16)

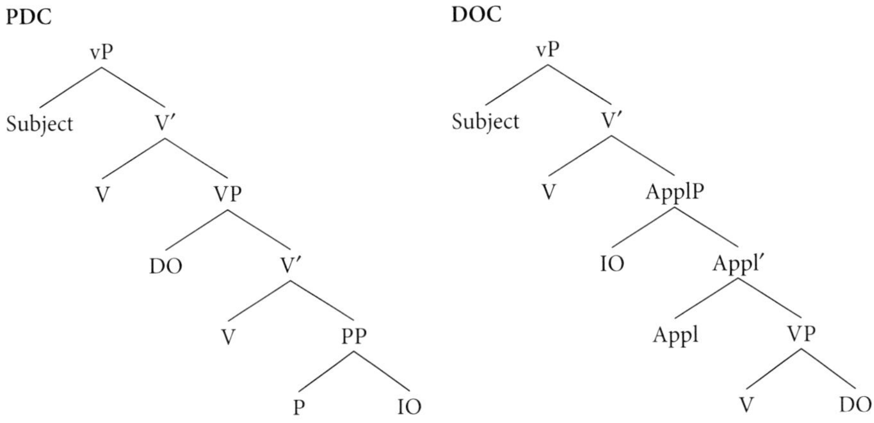

The third, and a recent, view on PDC and DOC structures has entertained the notion that the prepositional datives constructions and the double object constructions (henceforth DOC) are essentially the same, syntactically as well as semantically (Bresnan 2007; Bresnan & Nikitina 2009, among others). The leading idea in the third approach is that the two structures (PDC and DOC) have overlapping

2. One of the reviewers pointed out that the IO in DOC is not necessarily a possessor given that you can say "John sent Mary a letter but she never got it." This is a very surprise finding given that the speakers I checked with found this construction quiet odd (and contradictory). Moreover it is almost an established fact that DOC and PDC differ quiet clearly in terms of possession (Green 1974; Mazurkewich & White (1984); Larson (1988); Gropen et al. (1989) & Pinker (1989), among many others). Mazurkewich and White (1984) for instance talk about this contrast and suggest that verbs that show DOC adhere to certain rules that verbs in PDC don't. One of these rules is that the verb must entail a transfer of possession of the direct object from the subject to the indirect object and the indirect object must be capable of possession. Larson (1988) also mentions this in the context that the verbs that show DOC have a special quality of possession that lacks in PDC.

contextual use. The usage depends on factors like discourse flexibility, animacy, definiteness, the relative length of the two object NPs (full NPs Vs. pronouns), etc. Bresnan et al. argued that the way ditransitive alternations are used in natural contexts, shows that the mapping between the alternative syntactic constructions rests on probabilistic biases rather than strict grammatical categories.

Bruening (2010) provides arguments against this approach using scope interactions to show that the difference between the two are not just contextual, the grammar clearly distinguishes PDC from DOC. For instance, the second object in the DOC construction cannot take scope over the first (17a), whereas in PDC, inverse scope is possible (17b).

(17) a. I gave a different child every candy bar. (*every>a, a>every)
b. I gave a different candy bar to every child. (every>a, a>every)

With respect to verb-final languages like Hindi/Urdu, the question is, does Hindi/Urdu have PDC or DOC or both? At a surface level, Hindi/Urdu ditransitives look more like DOC. The IO in Hindi/Urdu is not a prepositional phrase but a Case-marked NP, i.e. ditransitive structures in Hindi/Urdu thus have an NP+NP frame instead of an NP+PP frame. Furthermore, the IO is structurally higher than DO, the IO asymmetrically c-commands the DO in Hindi/Urdu (4).

However, when it comes to the semantics, Hindi/Urdu ditransitives don't show a clear preference for DOC. For instance, ditransitive verbs like "bhej-naa" (to *send*) in Hindi/Urdu allow both the animate and inanimate goal phrases.[3] On the other hand, verbs like "dikhaa-naa" (to *show*) in Hindi/Urdu only allow an animate IO.

(18) a. *raam-ne dilli(*-ko) kitaab bhejii*
Ram-ERG Delhi-DAT book sent
'Ram sent Delhi a book.'

b. *raam-ne siitaa*(-ko) kitaab bhejii*
Ram-ERG Sita-DAT book sent
'Ram sent Sita a book.'

(19) a. *raam-ne siitaa-ko kitaab dikh-aa-yii*
Ram-ERG Sita-DAT book show-Caus-PST
'Ram showed a book to Sita.'

3. Even though a distinction between the inanimate and animate goal phrase is maintained in terms of the presence/absence of the dative Case marker in Hindi/Urdu, it is not restricted to ditransitives and thus not relevant for the purposes of current discussion.

b. **raam-ne dilli kitaab dikh-aa-yii*
Ram-ERG Delhi book showed
'*Ram showed a book to Delhi.'

Furthermore, some ditransitive verbs in Hindi/Urdu have a close relation to causatives, while others don't. Ditransitive verbs like "dikh-aa-naa" (*show*), paR-aa-naa (*teach*) etc. carry an overt morphological causative marker (*-aa*), and are of the form "caused to V". The causative marker licenses a dative argument which otherwise is not part of the argument structure of the verb (20). The animate IO in (20) is construed as the experiencer/beneficiary of the action (*Ram* caused *Sita* to experience the act of seeing a book)

(20) a. *raam-ne siitaa-ko kitaab dikh-aa-yii*
Ram-ERG Sita-DAT book see-Caus-PST
'Ram showed a book to Sita.'

b. *raam-ne (*siitaa-ko) kitaab dekhi*
Ram-ERG Sita-DAT book saw
'Ram saw the book (*to Sita).'

On the other hand, there are other ditransitive verbs like *bhej-naa* (*pass*) in Hindi/Urdu, which do not carry any overt causative morpheme.

(21) *raam-ne siitaa-ko kitaab bhej-ii*
Ram-ERG Sita-DAT book sent-AGR
'Ram sent a book to Sita.'

What seems to be happening in Hindi/Urdu is that verbs like *dikhaa-naa* pattern with DOC and verbs like *bhej-naa* pattern with PDC. However, the two types of verbs do not exhibit different word-order, unlike what we see in languages like English. The distinction that we see between ditransitive verbs like *show* and *send* in Hindi/Urdu has also been claimed to exist in Japanese.

Matsuoka (2003) claimed that different types of ditransitive verbs in Japanese have different base generated orders. Matsuoka investigated the inchoative variants of the Japanese ditransitive verbs like "pass" and "show" and suggested that the inchoative invariants are morphologically related to the ditransitive verbs. They do not project the external arguments of ditransitives, but instead promote one of their internal arguments to the subject position. There are two types of verbs that differ with respect to which argument they select for the subject of the inchoative variant. One type is represented by 'pass' which chooses the accusative argument over the dative for the subject and the other type is represented by 'show', which chooses the dative argument over the accusative one. It is argued that the difference in the alternation pattern between the two types of verbs reflects a difference in the base generated position of the dative argument and each type of verb promotes the second highest argument to the subject of the inchoative variant.

Hindi/Urdu also shows distinction between 'pass' type verbs and 'show' type verbs with respect to their inchoative variants. For instance, verbs like *dikhaa-naa* (*show*) have the inchoative form *dikh-naa* (*see*) and promote only the dative argument to the subject position (22).

(22) a. *siitaa-ko kitaab dikh-ii*
Sita-DAT book see-PST
'Sita saw the book.'

b. **kitaab siitaa-ko dikhi*
book Sita-DAT see-PST

Facts like these suggest that *show* type verbs in Hindi/Urdu have a structure similar to DOC; (a) they exhibit causative meaning and involve an overt causative marker, (b) they have restriction on the animacy of the goal phrase, and (c) they promote only the IO in the inchoative variant. These findings imply that the IO is higher than the DO (IO>DO) in *show* type verbs.

Verbs like *bhej-naa* (*send*) in Hindi/Urdu, on the other hand, have two inchoative forms *mil-naa* (*receive*) and *pahunCna* (*reach*), depending on the thematic role and animacy of the IO. The inchoative form *pahunCna*, occurs with locative and inanimate goal phrases and allows only its DO to be promoted to the subject position (23). The other form *mil-naa* occurs with recipient and animate goal phrases and allows only the IO to be promoted to the subject position (24).[4]

(23) a. *kitaab dilli pahunCii*
book delhi reached
'The book reached Delhi.'

b. **dilli kitaab pahunCii*
delhi book reached

(24) a. *merii-ko kitaab milii*
Mary-DAT book got
'Mary got the book'

b. **kitaab merii milii*
book Mary received

There seems to be two patterns for verbs like *send* in Hindi/Urdu. Similar to English, where the DOC and PDC distinction arises from the requirement

4. *mil-naa* (*receive*) in Hindi/Urdu takes dative subjects.

of the goal to be either construed as the recipient of the theme or the locative (Mazurkewich & White 1984), verbs like *send* in Hindi/Urdu maintain the possessor-locative distinction through animacy/inanimacy. Miyagawa and Tsujioka (2004) observed similar facts in Japanese and proposed that Japanese ditransitives like *send* have both the DOC and the PDC. They suggested that the order goal-theme may be the DOC if the goal is animate, but it must be the PDC if the goal is an inanimate that cannot be construed as the ultimate possessor of the referent of the theme.

They observed that in Japanese, two goal arguments (animate and inanimate) can exist in a sentence with verbs like *send*. However, the presence of the two goal arguments makes the word order rigid (the animate goal must precede the inanimate goal). We can notice the same facts in Hindi/Urdu as well (25).

(25) a. *raam-ne siitaa-ko dilli patr bhejaa*
Raam-ERG Sita-DAT Delhi letter sent
'Ram sent Sita a letter to Delhi.'

b. **raam-ne dillii siitaa-ko patr bhejaa*
Ram-ERG Delhi Sita-DAT letter sent

An important thing to consider here is that the meaning of this sentence in (25) is that *Ram* sent a package to *Delhi*, which is a location, with the intention that it will eventually end up in the possession of *Sita*. *Sita* is perceived to be the ultimate "possessor" of the theme *letter* whereas *Delhi* is only the location where the *letter* ends up. The two goal arguments in cases like (25) are associated with two dative positions, *high* and *low*. The animate/receipient goals are high dative whereas the inanimate/locative goals are low datives. The inanimate/locative goals are in the lower VP whereas the animate/receipient goals are in the higher VP. Miyagawa and Tsujioka (2004) showed that this seems to be the case as in Japanese, the lower VP containing the low goal and the theme can prepose, leaving behind the high goal. We see the same thing in Hindi/Urdu (26).

(26) a $[_{VP}$*dilli patr bhej-ne ka kaam*] *raam-ne siitaa-ko dii-yaa*
Delhi letter send-to of work Ram-ERG Sita-DAT gave
'Ram gave Sita the task of sending letter to Delhi.'

b *$[_{VP}$*siitaa-ko patr bhej-ne ka kaam*] *raam-ne dilli dii-yaa*
Sita-DAT letter send-to of work Ram-ERG Delhi gave

The scope-relations in Hindi/Urdu further distinguish the high goal from the low goal. The quantifier in the high Goal takes wider scope over the quantifiers in either low goal phrase or the theme, whereas the quantifier in the low goal and the quantifier in the theme can take scope over each other as in (27).

(27) a. *raam-ne kisi-ko har(-ek)-jagah-meN patr bhejaa*
Ram-ERG someone-DAT every-(one)-place-LOC letter sent
'Ram sent someone letter to every place.' (Some>Every)

b. *raam-ne kisi-ko dilli-meN har(-ek)- patr bhejaa*
Ram-ERG someone-DAT Delhi-LOC every-one- letters sent
'Ram sent someone every letter to Delhi.' (Some>Every)

c. *raam-ne siitaa-ko kisi-jagah-meN har(-ek) patr bhejaa*
Ram-ERG Sita-DAT some-place-LOC every-one- letter sent
'Ram sent Sita every letter to some place.' (Some>Every, Every>Some)

Verbs like *send* in Hindi/Urdu therefore seem to be associated with two different IOs (animate and inanimate) and two different structural configurations: IO (receiver)>DO and DO>IO (locative). *Send* type-1 (with high goal) take animate/receipient as their IOs, and promote the IO in their inchoative variant. *Send* type-2 verbs (with low goal) take inanimate/locative as their IOs and promote the DO in their inchoative variants.

The above-mentioned facts suggest that Hindi/Urdu has both DOC and PDC. An idea advocated for verb final languages like Japanese (Matsuoka, 2003) and Bangla (Bhattacharya & Simpson 2011). There are two different kinds of ditransitive verbs in Hindi/Urdu which involve these structures; the *show* type verbs which exhibit properties of DOC and the *give* type verbs which show properties of both DOC and PDC. The section below investigates the inner structure of the verb phrase in Hindi/Urdu in specific relation to these semantic classes of ditransitive verbs in the language. In this exploration, it also probes the licensing of the two objects in the verb phrase in connection with the asymmetrical relationship among them.

4. The structure of Hindi/Urdu ditransitive

In the previous section, we saw that there are three types of ditransitive verbs in Hindi/Urdu; the *show* type verbs, the *send* type-1 verbs and the *send* type-2 verbs. The three types of verbs are classified by the type of IO that they take; the *show* type verbs take an experiencer/benefactive, the *send* type-1 verbs take a possessor, and the *send* type-2 verbs take a locative.

Here, I adopt Pylkkänen's (2002) theory of applicatives to account for the above mentioned types of ditransitives in Hindi/Urdu. Pylkkänen's (2002) suggests that there are two types of applicatives, "high" and "low", which are associated with different lexical semantics. A high applicative (ApplH) denotes a relation between an event and an individual (thus simply adding another participant to the event described by the verb). It is located above VP but below the position of the external argument. A low applicative (ApplL), on the other hand, is located in the complement position of the verb root, and relates two individuals in a possessive relationship. In other words, the low applied (or indirect) argument bears no semantic relation to the verb but only bears a transfer of possession relation to the direct object (Theme). According to Pylkkänen (2002), because of this different semantics, ApplH head merges with an (eventive) VP complement and a DP specifier, and ApplL head with a DP complement and a DP specifier.

In this framework, the *show* type verb constructions like (28) can be understood to be composed of two events, a core event denoted by the lexical VP 'see a book', and an event of experience, combining the applicative argument 'Sita' and the lexical VP through the applicative head (Cause). The IO in this case, therefore, must be a high applicative, as it denotes a relation between an event and an individual. The *show* type verbs will thus have the following structure (29)

(28) *raam-ne siitaa-ko kitaab dikh-aa-yii*
Ram-ERG Sita-DAT book see-CAUS-PST
'Ram showed a book to Sita.'

(29)

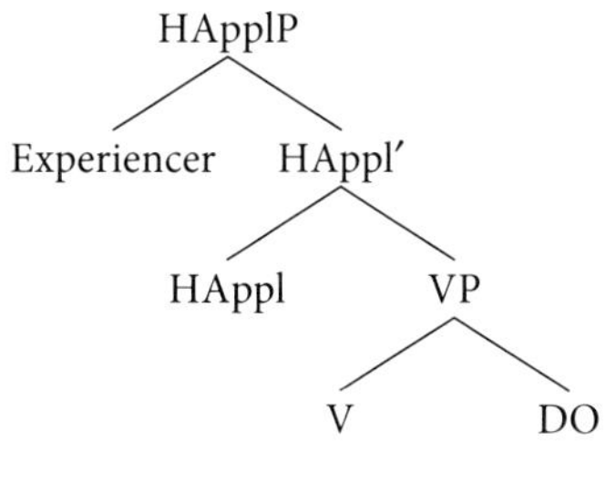

This structure also involves head movement. The lexical verb "see" first moves to the Appl head, and then the complex moves to v. The head adjunction between the V and the Appl head results in morphological fusion (*see*+caus=*show*). This fusion changes the argument structure of the verb and licenses a dative argument which otherwise was not part of the argument structure of the verb *see* (30).[5]

5. A similar idea has been proposed in Abraham (2010), which suggests a derivative relationship between verbs such that verbal derivatives can be derived from some basic verbs. These relationships are syntactic (in Hale & Keyser 1994 style), the lexicon only provides highly underspecified precategorical representations.

(30)

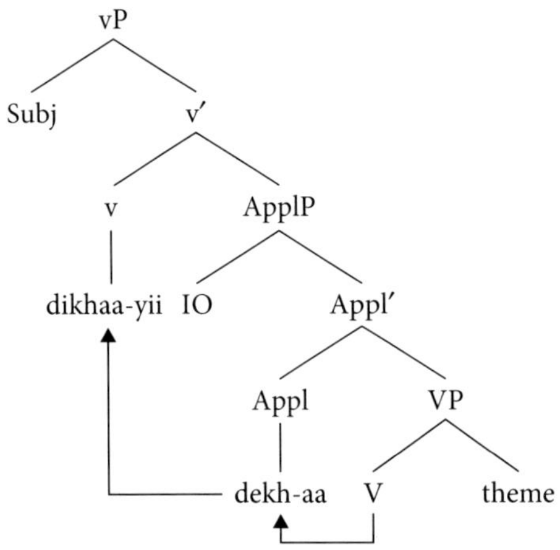

In *send* type-1 verbs, the IO is a possessor (31), and in Pylkkänen's model possession is attributed to the low ApplP. The low applicative denotes the relation between two individuals, and is located inside the lexical VP (32).

(31) *raam-ne siitaa-ko kitaab bhejii*
Ram-ERG Sita-DAT book sent
'Ram sent Sita a book.'

(32)

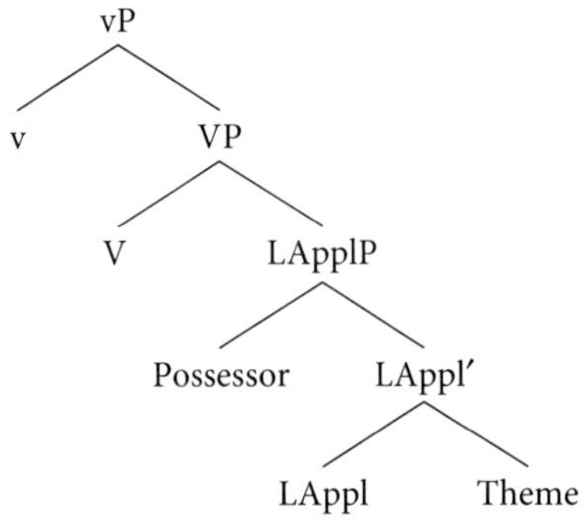

In contrast to the above structures, the low locative goal in *send* type-2 verbs would not be associated with an applicative (33). It can't be a low applicative because it lacks possession. This lack of possession relation that we see with the low goal is also present in the PDC which Marantz (1993), among others, suggests lacks a change of possession interpretation, and thus doesn't have an applicative head (34).

(33) *raam-ne dilli kitaab bhejii*
Ram-ERG Delhi book sent
'Ram sent a book to Delhi.'

(34)
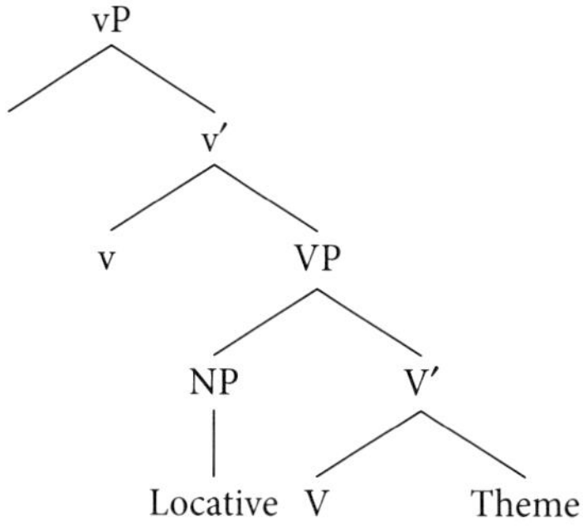

Notice that in the above structure, I assume a non-head final base generated structure for Hindi/Urdu. I suggest that the DO in Hindi/Urdu starts at the right of the verb but later in the course of the derivation moves to Specifier of the verbal projection for Case/Agreement reasons and results in a head-final structure, an idea also advocated in Kayne (1994), Mahajan (1997), Simpson and Bhattacharya (2003) and Malhotra (2011) (see Bhatt & Dayal 2007 among others for an alternative view). I use this assumption to address the issue of surface word order in Hindi/Urdu ditransitives in the following section.

5. Surface word-order and Asymmetrical relation between the objects

In the above section, I proposed that in *show* type verbs, the IO (experiencer) is higher than the DO (theme). In *send* type-1 verbs, the IO (possessor) is higher than the DO (theme), whereas in *send* type-2 verbs, the DO (theme) is higher than the IO (locative).

An obvious prediction of this proposal is that in Hindi/Urdu ditranstive passives, the *show* type verbs and the *send* type-1 verbs (with high goal) would promote their goal over the theme, as it is higher than the theme. Conditions like the minimal link condition (Chomsky 1995) would block the movement of the lower object across the higher object.[6] On the other hand, *send* type-2 verbs (with low goal) would promote their theme in ditransitive passive.

6. Minimal Link Condition: K attracts α iff there is no β, β closer to K than α, such that K attracts β.

In "send" *type-2* verbs, as expected, the theme gets passivized over the locative in Hindi/Urdu (35). Since the theme is higher than the locative in 'send' *type-2* verbs, the promotion of the theme over the locative is what we see.

(35) a. *patr dilli bhejaa gayaa*
letter Delhi send gone

b **dilli patr bhejaa gayaa*
Delhi letter send gone

The problem however comes from the *show* and the *send* type-1 verbs (with high-goal) where the possessor/experiencer is higher than the theme. In these constructions, contra expectations, it is the theme which can gets promoted and passivized and not the goal. Notice the contrast that (36a) shows with (36b) and (37a) with (37b).

(36) a. *kitaab merii-ko dikhaaii gayii*
book Mary-DAT showed went
'A book was shown to Mary.'

b. **merii kitaab dikhaaii gayii*
Mary book showed went

(37) a. *patr (siitaa-ko) bhejaa gayaa*
letter Sita-DAT send gone
'A letter was sent to Sita.'

b. **siitaa patr bhejaa gayaa*
Sita letter send gone

For ditransitive passives, Kidwai (2000) suggested that in Hindi/Urdu, only the structural Accusative Case is absorbed. The AgrO-head (the small v in modern terms) in ditransitive constructions bears two Case features, which must be checked by raising DPs into its checking domain. In ditransitive structures, both the goal and the theme arguments need to check their Case features structurally. As a consequence, the theme raises to [Spec, vP] to check structural Accusative Case and the goal adjoins to Spec, vP to check structural Dative Case.

Given this, I adopt a modified version of McGinnis (2003) theory of escape hatches in ditransitive passives. McGinnis proposes that the high applicative is a phase to talk about ditransitive passives in *show* type verbs and *send* type-1 verbs. Being a phase, the high applicative structure provides an escape hatch through the phase-EPP feature, which attracts an element to its edge (i.e. specifier). The low applicative, on the other hand, is not a phase and therefore doesn't allow an escape hatch.

With same variations with McGinnis approach, I assume that the High Applin Hindi/Urdu ditransitive verbs like *show* allow an extra specifier position. The DO in Hindi/Urdu carries two relevant features [–Case] and [+AGR]. In an attempt to check its features, it first moves to the specifier of the high APPL. This movement makes the DO and the IO equidistant from v. Both the DO and the IO then further move to Spec, vP. At [Spec, vP], the IO checks it structural Dative Case. The DO however only checks the Agreement features and not the Case features; passivization absorbs Accusative Case. Being at [Spec, vP], both the DO and the IO are equidistant from the T. Since it is the DO, which has the relevant features, it is the one that moves. Consider structure (38b) below.

(38) a. *kitaab* *merii-ko* *dikhaaii* *gayii*
book (DO) Mary-DAT (IO) showed went
'A book was shown to Mary.'

b.

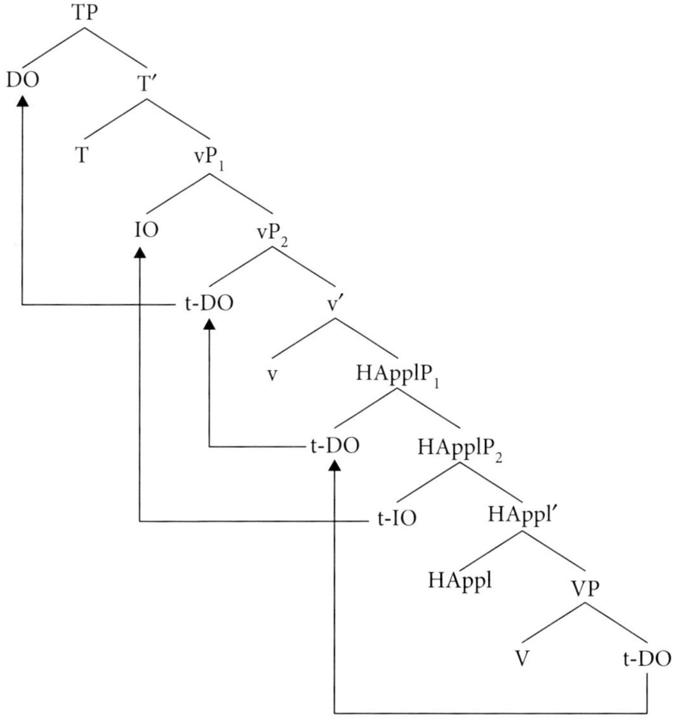

Ditransitive verbs like *send type-1*, where the goal is a possessor, include a low applicative structure. Here, I suggest that the phase-hoodness of the Low Appl is parametric, in the sense that it is a phase in Hindi/Urdu but not in English. Though this suggestion sounds pretty stipulative, it not only accounts for the ditransitive structures (and the incohative patterns) in Hindi/Urdu but also the facts we observe w.r.t ditransitive passives. Given the assumption that both the goal and the theme arguments need to check their Case features structurally in ditransitive structures in Hindi/Urdu, and as a consequence, raise to [Spec, vP], an obvious minimality violation can only be saved by an extra specifier/escape hatch position with the Low Appl. Consider the following structure (38). The movement of DO from inside the LAppl to Spec, vP is only possible if it moves via the extra specifier position at the LAppl. It otherwise will result in minimality violation given the presence of the intervening IO at [Spec, LApplP].

(39) a. *raam-ne siitaa-ko kitaab bhejii*
Ram-ERG Sita-DAT book sent
'Ram sent Sita a book.'

b.

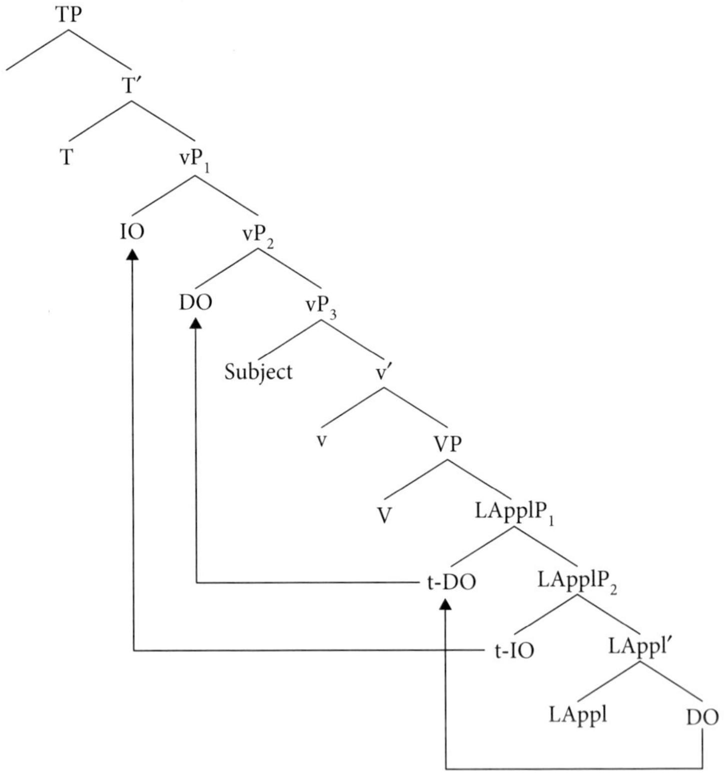

In passivization, the derivation, by which both the DO and IO reach [Spec, vP] to check their respective feature. This derivation, as in ditransitive structures, again is only possible if an extra specifier is available at LAppl. Once the DO and the IO reach [Spec, vP, the DO and the IO are equidistant from T, and since it is the DO which has the relevant Case feature, it moves further up to T (40).

(40) a. *kitaab (siitaa-ko) bhejii gayii*
book Sita-DAT send gone
'A book was sent to Sita.'

b.

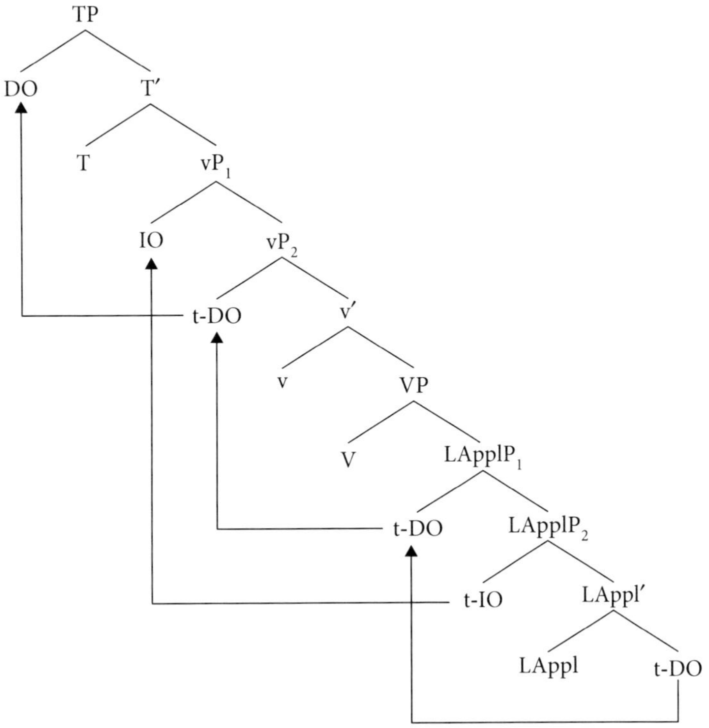

The proposal presented above differs importantly from Kidwai (2000), which places theme higher than the dative in Hindi/Urdu. One of the important assumptions in Kidwai (2000) is that the configurations from which PDC and the DOC are derived are identical, and the theme argument is always generated higher than the goal. However contra Larson (1988), it is the PDC, and not the DOC, which is derived by a rule of passive. In DOC, the theme raises to [Spec, AgrO] to check structural Accusative Case and the goal adjoins to Agro to check structural Dative Case (41).

(41)

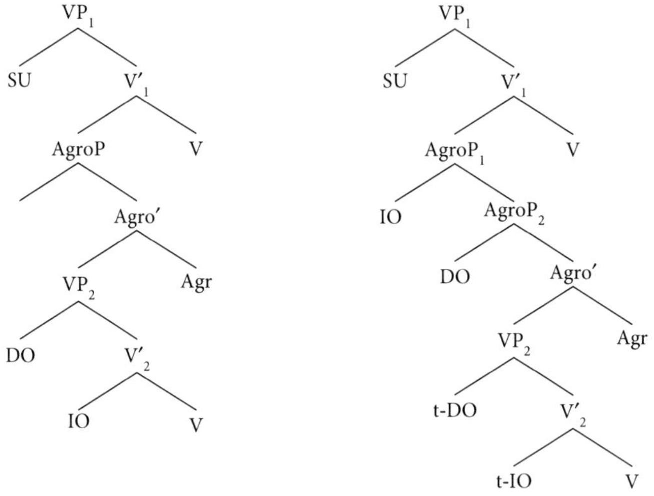

In PDC, passivization affects only the AgrO head, absorbing the Case feature of the goal. As a consequence, only the DO can raise to [Spec, AgrOP] and the IO remains in-situ. Preposition insertion takes place at PF as a last resort to save the derivation. According to Kidwai, Hindi/Urdu only exhibits DOC construction. It lacks *PDC* because it lacks the IO Case absorption mechanism due to the unavailability of preposition insertion at PF. Hindi/Urdu lacks IO passivization for the same reason. DO passivization on the other hand proceeds without problem, as sentential passive absorbs the Case feature of the DO on the AgrO head, triggering raising.

Though Kidwai (2000) makes a good attempt of capturing both DOC and *PDC* cross-linguistically while maintaining Larson's thematic hierarchy, it has certain disadvantages. First, it assumes that the PDC and DOC constructions are derived from an identical base structure. However as we have seen above, the work of Oehrle (1976), Marantz (1993) Harley (1995), Pesetesky (1995) among many others have shown that DOC and PDC differ distinctively from each other. Second, it suggests that Hindi/Urdu has only DOC, but we have seen in this section that Hindi/Urdu has both DOC and PDC and that these constructions have distinct properties. Third, it proposes that the direct object is base generated higher than the indirect object in ditransitive structures in Hindi/Urdu. Evidence from inchoatives however shows that the IO is higher than the DO and is the one that gets promoted in Hindi/Urdu.

6. Conclusion

This chapter suggested that Hindi/Urdu has three different kinds of ditransitive verbs; *show* type verbs, *send* type-1 verbs and *send* type-2 verbs. These verb types involve two different argument structures, which correspond to the PDC and the DOC constructions in English. The *show* type verbs take an experiencer as their IO and involve a high applicative structure. The *send* type-1 verbs have a possessor as their IO and involve a low applicative structure, whereas the *send* type-2 verbs take a locative and have a structure similar to PDC. The IOs and DOs in all the three types of verbs move via the extra specifier position of the applicatives to the specifier of the v for Case/Agreement reasons, and end up with a same surface word-order, thus making the difference between the three less apparent in Hindi/ Urdu.

The analysis proposed here for Hindi/Urdu has been shown to work for ditransitives in other verb-final languages like Japanese (Matsuoka 2003 and Miyagawa & Tsujioka 2004) and Bangla (Bhattacharya & Simpson 2011).

References

Abraham, Werner. 2010. Types of transitivity. Intransitive objects and untransitivity – and the logic of their de signs: Ways to keep apart derivation in syntax and the lexicon. In *Transitivity: Form, Meaning, Acquisition, and Processing* [Linguistic Aktuell/Linguistics Today 166], Patrick Brandt & Marco GarcíaGarcía (eds), 15–68. Amsterdam: John Benjamins.

Baker, Mark. 1988. *Incorporation. A Theory of Grammatical Function Changing*. Chicago, IL: University of Chicago Press.

Beck, Sigrid & Johnson, Kyle. 2004. Double objects again. *Linguistic Inquiry* 35: 97–123.

Bhatt, Rajesh & Dayal, Veneeta. 2007. Rightward scrambling as rightward Remnant movement. *Linguistic Inquiry* 38(2): 287–301.

Bhattacharya, Tanmoy & Andrew, Simpson. 2011. Diagnosing double object constructions in Bangla/Bengali. *Lingua* 121: 1067–1082.

Bresnan, Joan. 2007. Is syntactic knowledge probabilistic? Experiments with the English dative alternation. In *Roots: Linguistics in Search of its Evidential Base* [Studies in Generative Grammar], Sam Featherston & Wolfgang Sternefeld (eds), 77–99. Berlin: Mounton de Gruyter.

Bresnan, Joan & Nikitina, Tatiana. 2009. The gradience of the dative alternation. In *Reality Exploration and Discovery: Pattern Interaction in Language and Life*, Linda Uyechi & Lian Hee Wee (eds), 161–184. Stanford: CSLI Publications.

Bresnan, Joan, Cueni, Anna, Nikitina, Tatiana & Baayen, R. Harald. 2007. Predicting the dative alternation. In *Cognitive Foundations of Interpretation*, Gerlof Boume, Irene Kraemer & JoostZwarts (eds), 69–94. Amsterdam: Royal Netherlands Academy of Science.

Bruening, Benjamin. 2001. QR obeys superiority: Frozen scope and ACD. *Linguistic Inquiry* 32(2): 233–273.

Bruening, Benjamin. 2010. Double object constructions disguised as prepositional datives. *Linguistic Inquiry* 41(2): 287–305.

Chomsky, Noam. 1995. *The Minimalist Program*. Cambridge, Mass.: MIT Press.

Chomsky, Noam. 2001. Derivation by phase. In *Ken Hale: A Life in Language*, Michael Kenstowicz (ed.), 1–50. Cambridge, Mass.: MIT Press.

Fillmore, Charles J. 1965. Indirect Object Construction in English and the Ordering of Transformation. Monographs on Linguistics Analysis. Mouton: The Hague.

Green, Georgia M. 1974. *Semantics and Syntactic Regularity*. Bloomington: Indiana University Press.
Hale, Ken & Keyser, Samuel J. 1994. Limits on Arguments Structure. MIT Manuscript.
Harley, Heidi. 1995. Subjects, Events, and Licensing, PhD dissertation, MIT.
Harley, Heidi. 1997. If you have, then you can give. In: B. Agbayani and S.-W. Tang, eds. Proceedings of the 15th West Coast Conference on Formal Linguistics. Stanford, CA.: CSLI.
Hoji, Hajime. 1985. Logical Form Constraints and Configurational Structures in Japanese. Doctoral Dissertation, University of Seattle.
Kayne, Richard. 1994. *The Antisymmetry of Syntax*. Cambridge, Mass.: MIT Press.
Kidwai, Ayesha. 2000. *XP-adjunction in Universal Grammar: Scrambling and Binding in Hindi-Urdu*. New York: Oxford University Press.
Larson, Richard K. 1988. On the double object construction. *Linguistic Inquiry* 19: 335–392.
Mahajan, Anoop. 1997a. Against a rightward movement analysis of extraposition and rightward scrambling. In *Scrambling*, Shigeo Tonoike (ed.), 93–124. Tokyo: Kurosio Publishers.
Malhotra, Shiti. 2005. Asymmetry of Objects and the Larsonian VP-shell for Hindi/Urdu. M.Phil dissertation, University of Delhi.
Malhotra, Shiti. 2011. Movement and Intervention Effects. Doctoral dissertation, University of Maryland, College Park.
Marantz, Alec. 1993. Implications of asymmetries in double object constructions. In *Theoretical Aspects of Bantu Grammar*, Sam Mchombo (ed.), 113–150. Stanford, Calif.: CSLI.
Matsuoka, Mikinari. 2003. Two types of ditransitive constructions in Japanese. *Journal of East Asian Linguistics* 12: 171–203.
Mazurkewich, Irene & White, Lydia. 1984. The acquisition of the dative alternation: Unlearning over generalizations. *Cognition* 16: 261–283.
McGinnis, Martha. 2003. Lethal Ambiguity. *Linguistic Inquiry* 35: 47–95.
Miyagawa, Shigeru. 1997. Against optional scrambling. *Linguistic Inquiry* 28: 1–26.
Miyagawa, Shigeru & Tsujioka, Takae. 2004. Argument structure and ditransitive verbs in Japanese. *Journal of East-Asian Linguistics* 13: 1–38.
Oehrle, Richard T. 1976. The Grammatical Status of the English Dative Alternations. Doctoral dissertation, MIT.
Pesetsky, David. 1995. *Zero Syntax*. Cambridge, MA.: MIT Press.
Pinker, Steven. 1989. *Learnability and Cognition; the Acquisition of Argument Structure*. Cambridge, MIT Press.
Pylkkänen, Liina. 2002. Introducing Arguments. Doctoral Dissertation, MIT.
Richards, Norvin. 2001. An Idiomatic Argument for Lexical Decomposition. *Linguistic Inquiry* 32: 183–192.
Simpson, Andrew & Bhattacharya, Tanmoy. 2003. Obligatory overt *wh*-movement in a *Wh*-in situ language. *Linguistic Inquiry* 34: 127–142.

Is Kashmiri passive really a passive?

Richa Srishti & Shahid Bhat
Central Institute of Indian Languages Mysore

The present paper explores passives in Kashmiri, a Northwestern Dardic language of the Indo-Aryan family. Though Kashmiri has some special features like V-2 phenomenon, pronominal clitics etc. it has an analytic passive construction like its Indo-Aryan counterparts. The internal argument surfaces as the subject of the passive, where the participial/infinitival verbal form *-nI* is added to the verb root followed by a periphrastic auxiliary *yun* 'to come' in perfective form. The agent of the action is in the form of *athi* or *zaryi* (*by/through*) and is preferably omitted. This optionality casts a doubt on its status – whether it is an adjunct or an argument. The promotion of the internal argument to the subject position is another key issue. The present paper investigates the above issues and claims that the Kashmiri passive construction is also a kind of ACTIVE-Passive and not really passive as in English. It is argued that in Kashmiri passives, the underlying subject remains an active subject and the underlying object does not become the surface subject. To prove this claim, some tests based on anaphora binding, pronominal co-reference, control, etc. are applied.

Keywords: passivization; underlying subject; promotion; demotion; detransitivization

1. Introduction

Kashmiri is a Northwestern Dardic language of the Indo-Aryan family. It is spoken in the state of Jammu & Kashmir in India. It has several unique features making it quite different from other Indo-Aryan languages, e.g. presence of V-2 phenomenon, pronominal clitics, central vowels, palatalization etc. As in most modern Indo-Aryan languages (Gujarati, Punjabi, Hindi, Bengali, Assamese etc.), Kashmiri also has an analytic passive construction where the basic components are – a participial/infinitival verbal form and an auxiliary verb. First, let us consider the following examples from other modern Indo-Aryan languages.

– Perfective Participle and an Auxiliary Verb *go*:

(1) i. (*sashaa dwaaraa*) *kaam ki-yaa ga-yaa* (Hindi)
Sasha by work do-PRF go-PRF
'The work was done (by Sasha).'

ii. (*majdooraan vallon kamma ki:-taa ga-yaa* (Punjabi)
workers by work do-PRF go-PRF
'The work was done (by the workers)

– Infinitival form (ablative/locative) and an Auxiliary Verb *come*:

(2) (*raam waDe*) *kaam karawaa-maa aave che* (Gujarati)
Ram by work do.INF-LOC come be-PRS
'The work is done (by Ram).'

Returning to Kashmiri passive construction, there is an infinitival oblique verbal form *-nI* and a periphrastic auxiliary *yun* 'to come' in perfective form. The internal argument of the transitive verb surfaces as the subject of the sentence in the passive. For example,

(3) i. *faarooq-an khuul kuluf* Active
Farooq-ERG open-PRF lock
'Farooq opened the lock.'

ii. *kuluf aav khol-nI* Passive
lock came open-INF.OBL
'The lock was opened.'

The agent of the action is not overtly realized and preferably omitted. Therefore, the agent phrase is optional. However, if the agent is realized, it is either in the form of *-zaryi* or *-athi* phrase (a kind of *by* phrase).

(4) i. *farooq-ni zaryi aav kuluf khol-nI*
Farooq-GEN by came lock open-INF.OBL
'The lock was opened by Farooq.'

ii. *farooq-as athi aav kuluf khol-nI*
Farooq-DAT by came lock open-INF.OBL
'The lock was opened by Farooq.'

iii. *reyaaz-ni zaryi aav* (*farooq-as athi*) *kuluf*
Reyaz-GEN by came Farooq-DAT by lock
khol-na:v-nI (Causative Passive)
open-CAUS-INF.OBL
'Farooq was made to open the lock by Reyaz.'

This optionality casts a doubt on the status of the agent phrase – whether it is an adjunct or an argument (as it seems to be similar to *by* phrase in the English passive that is a PP). Another related issue is regarding the internal argument in Kashmiri passive. Is the internal argument actually promoted to the subject position or does it behave as it does in the active constructions? There is existing literature on Hindi-Urdu passives (cf. Mahajan (1994) and Richa (2011)) that attests the absence of canonical (English) passives in Hindi-Urdu. The claim is that this language has constructions which are only passive-like and not actually passives. Mahajan (1994) terms them ACTIVE Passive as he claims that the underlying object does not become the surface object and at the same time, the underlying subject remains an active subject. The present paper explores the aforementioned issues and compares the Kashmiri passive with canonical passives as well as with SAL passive constructions.

The paper is organized in seven sections. In section two, we discuss the features of canonical passives in the earlier literature. The behaviour of Kashmiri passives in different environments is looked at in section three. Section four examines the status of subject and object in Kashmiri passive constructions. The next section, i.e. section five, explores the status of the Implicit/Optional Agent in Kashmiri passive. Section six evaluates canonical passives, Kashmiri passive and other South Asian Languages' passive constructions. Section seven, the final one, presents the final remarks.

2. What is a passive construction?

Active and passive voices are kinds of grammatical voices (diathesis). When the subject is the agent or the doer of the action, the verb is in the active voice (5 i). On the other hand, when the subject is the patient, target or the undergoer, the verb is in the passive voice (5 ii).

(5) i. The man did the work
    ii. The work was done by the man

2.1 Approaches to passivization

Now let us look at structural, lexical and functional approaches to passivization. In the Generative Grammar framework, Chomsky (1957) postulated in the early transformational theory that active and passive were derived from the same structure, but later it was thought to be derived from two independent structures. But the passive transformational rule remained the main argument, a kind of noun-phrase movement. Bach (1980) regarded passive as a prototype of transformational relations. Chomsky (1965) argues that there does exist a difference between the underlying structures of actives and passives. This view was supported by other linguists (Ziff 1966; Robson 1972; Lakoff 1974). Hasegawa (1968) proposed that passivization is triggered by a structure that is a direct complement of the verb be. Jackendoff (1969) argues that both deep as well as surface structure contribute to the meaning in the transformation. Recent Minimalist Program (MP 1995) recognises that all movements are locality constraints and either active or passive voice is spelled out as required.

Another major structural approach was in the Relational Grammar framework where Perlmutter & Postal (1984) argue that in the passive construction, the agent has been demoted from the subject function and they termed it as *chômeur*.

In the framework of Lexical Decomposition Grammar (LDG), Kiparsky (2012) uses constraint-based theories which eliminate NP-movement and rely instead on argument structure representation. For him, the basic difference between the active and its passive is only that in the passive counterpart the logical subject is implicit and demoted, which can be expressed by an agent phrase, and, even if not so expressed, is visible to certain processes (e.g. construal and anaphora) in the same way as other demoted logical subjects.

Many linguists considered the structural approach to be inadequate as far as explaining passives was concerned. Freidin (1975) and Bresnan (1982) relate the active and the passive in the lexicon by means of a lexical rule. Both active and passive verbs are listed in the lexicon independently, i.e. both are base-generated and entail alternative mapping of the participants to grammatical functions. There is no transformational rule in this approach.

Functional approach to passivization focuses on information-structure/pragmatics. Shibatani (1985) states that passives may delete the agent for contextual reasons (first three reasons) – bring topical non-agents into subject position (fourth reason), or create a syntactic pivot for reasons such as co-referential deletion (fifth reason). In other words, the primary function of passive is 'agent defocusing' and not 'topicalizing'. He argues that this is the reason why passives generally do not have overt agents. It is further strengthened by the fact that passivization does not usually apply to non-agentive intransitive. According to him, 'true passives' are semantically transitive and syntactically intransitive, i.e. the agent is in the semantic frame but defocused at the level of syntactic encoding. Hence, he considers this the minimal condition for passives.

Siewierska (1988) argues that they are synonymous with regard to truth conditions, but they vary in other ways, e.g. passives are often stative, have scope and modal differences, and have differences of conversational implicature. She, too, regards passives as one of the topicalizing constructions where the object of the active sentence gets 'topicalized' in the passive one. In agentive passive like 'The book was bought by John,' two functions are fulfilled – (a) Topicalizing and,

(b) Focusing. 'The book' being 'the entity about which the predication predicates' becomes the topic and 'by John' being 'relatively the most important information between the speaker and the addressee' is the focus of the sentence. Keenan & Dryer (2007) consider passive as a foregrounding and backgrounding operation. For example,

(6) The cat ate the rat.

(7) The rat was eaten.

In sentence (6), 'rat' has been actually 'foregrounded' or in other words 'topicalized' towards which 'the attention has been drawn.' That is why, topic-prominent languages like Mandarin don't make use of passive as often as other languages. Hence, basic passives, according to Kennan & Dryer (2007) are defined as the ones which lack agent phrases and are formed from the transitive verbs denoting events.

Haspelmath (1990) claims that the basic function of the passive is to modify the event described by the verb through expressing inactivisation. Givon (1994) considers the agents in the passive to be the pragmatically suppressed arguments. All these linguists take the demotional approach to passivization.

Some linguists like Klaiman (1991) consider both promotional as well as demotional approaches suitable. She defines voice in terms of affectedness and control. She argues that the Patient nominal (of the active) does not actually acquire the agent role (in the passive) but the nominal linked to the Patient role assumes the grammatical relation basic to the nominal linked to the Agent role, i.e. a kind of subject relation. Croft (1994) states that the construal of events is represented in three ways: cause-become state, become-state, and state. Passive is a state, in other words it is the resultative view of an event with minimal control.

Based on the above approaches, we focus on some of the basic properties of passives. In World Atlas of Language Structures Online (April 2008), Siewierska classifies a construction as passive if it displays the following five properties:

i. it contrasts with another construction, the **active**;
ii. the subject of the active corresponds to a non-obligatory oblique phrase of the passive or is not overtly expressed;
iii. the subject of the passive, if there is one, corresponds to the direct object of the active;
iv. the construction is pragmatically restricted relative to the active;
v. the construction displays some special morphological marking of the verb.

Siewierska (1984) extensively review passives cross-linguistically and shows that passives cannot be defined universally in terms of word order, case-marking, verbal morphology or agentlessness. The only basis that is unquestionable is the relation between active and passive, i.e. the subject of a passive vs. non-subject in active and overt/implied agent of passive vs. non-subject of passive. Hence, it can serve as a basis for definition. It could either be through promotion of object or demotion of subject. Languages may have passives which have either subject promotion or object demotion or both.

The next section looks at the behavior of Kashmiri passives with light verb and modals, transitivity factor, choice between instrumental markers *-sI:t'* and *zaryi/athi* and (in)abilitative passives.

3. Kashmiri passives

3.1 Passive with light verb & modals

In Kashmiri complex predicates of VM + LV nature, the main verb appears in its participialized form and the light verb appears with the perfective marker. For example,

(8) *tam' os ni-mut su tsuunth khey-th*
He-ERG be-PST take-PRF that apple eat-PTCP
'He had eaten that apple (abruptly).'

In the passive counterpart of the above construction, too, the main verb is in its participialized form. It is the light verb that takes the infinitival verbal form (used for marking passive) *-nI*. For example,

(9) *farooq-ni zaryi os aa-mut su tsuunth*
Farooq-GEN by be-PST come-PRF that apple
khey-th ni-nI
eat-PTCP take-INF.OBL
'That apple had been eaten by Farooq (abruptly).'

In Kashmiri, unlike Hindi, we cannot have passive construction with modals. For example,

(10) *farooq dwaaraa yeh seb khaayaa jaa saktaa hai* (Hindi)
farooq by this apple eat-PRF go can-HAB be-PRS
'This apple can be eaten by Farooq.'

But, we cannot have the counterpart for the above sentence. We can only have the active sentence in Kashmiri. For example,

(11) *farooq chu su tsuunth hekaan khey-th* (Kashmiri)
farooq be-PRS that apple can-HAB eat-PTCP
'Farooq can eat that apple.'

3.2 Choice between *-sI:t'* & *zaryi/athi*

The instrumental marker *-sI:t'* is exclusively used to mark instruments in Kashmiri. For example,

(12) *farooq chu shrapch-i sI:t' tsuunth tsaTaan*
farooq be-PRS knife-OBL with apple cut-HAB
'Farooq cuts the apple with the knife.'

The other instrumental marker *zaryi/athi* cannot be used in the above example. It is exclusively used for animate agents. For example,

(13) i. **farooq chu shrapch-i zaryi/ shrapch-as athi tsuunth tsaTaan*
farooq be-PRS knife-OBL by/ knife-DAT by apple cut-HAB
'*Farooq cuts the apple by the knife.'

ii. *farooq-an karI-nA:v reyaz-ni zaryi/reyaz-as athi kA:m*
Farooq-ERG do-CAUS reyaz-GEN by/reyaz-DAT by work
'Farooq made Reyaz do the work/Farooq did the work through Reyaz (literal).'

But in passives of causatives, the causee agent is marked by *athi* and the matrix subject is marked by *zaryi.*

(14) *reyaaz-ni zaryi aav (farooq-as athi) kuluf*
Reyaz-GEN by came Farooq-DAT by lock
khol-na:v-nI Causative Passive
open-CAUS-INF.OBL
'The lock was made to open by Reyaz through Farooq.'

We cannot have,

(15) **reyaaz-ni zaryi aav (farooq-ni zaryi) kuluf*
Reyaz-GEN by came Farooq-GEN by lock
khol-na:v-nI Causative Passive
open-CAUS-INF.OBL
'The lock was made to open by Reyaz through Farooq.'

Similarly, we cannot have,

(16) **reyaaz-as athi aav (farooq-as athi) kuluf*
Reyaz-DAT by came Farooq-DAT by lock
khol-na:v-nI Causative Passive
open-CAUS-INF.OBL
'The lock was made to open by Reyaz through Farooq.'

It should be noted here that the *zaryi* phrase is always the matrix subject and the *athi* phrase is the causee.

(17) **reyaaz-as athi aav (farooq-ni zaryi) kuluf*
Reyaz-DAT by came Farooq-GEN by lock
khol-na:v-nI Causative Passive
open-CAUS-INF.OBL
'The lock was made to open by Reyaz through Farooq.'

3.3 Transitivity & passive

Unlike English where intransitives cannot be passivized (only transitives can be), Kashmiri intransitives as well as transitives can be passivized like most of the Indo-Aryan languages. But, only unergatives can be passivized not unaccusatives. For example,

(18) i. Ilya jumped over the fence. (English)
ii. *Ilya was jumped over the fence.
iii. The cat ate the rat.
iv. The rat was eaten by the cat.

(19) i. *farooq-an dits deyvaar-I peth' voth* (Kashmiri)
Farooq-ERG give-PRF wall-OBL above jump
'Farooq jumped over the wall.'

ii. *tati aayi di-nI voth*
there came give-INF.OBL jump
'There was jumped.'

iii. **tati aav fIT-nI*
there came break-INF.OBL
'*There was broken.'

iv. *braari kheyov gagur*
cat eat-PRF rat
'The cat ate the rat.'

v. *braari hind zaryi aav gagur khey-nI*
cat GEN by came rat eat-INF.OBL
'The rat was eaten by the cat.'

It should be noted here that though unegratives *can* be passivized in Kashmiri, the passive construction of unergatives is acceptable without specifying the agent, (see above Example (19ii)). Like in most of the Indo-Aryan languages, specification of the agent makes the construction slightly odd. For example,

(20) ??*tati aayi farooq-ni zaryi voth di-nI*
there came Farooq-GEN by jump give-INF.OBL
'??There was jumped by Farooq.'

Dative subject constructions in Kashmiri cannot be passivized, similar to most of the Indo-Aryan languages. For example,

(21) i. *farooq-as aav mushuq*
Farooq-DAT came smell
'Farooq smelled/To Farooq, the smell came (literal).'

ii. **farooq-ni zaryi aav mushuq yi-nI*
Farooq-GEN by came smell come-INF.OBL
'*This is smelled by Farooq.'

3.4 (In)abilitative[1] passives

(In)abilitative passive is another kind of passive construction that has been widely attested in the literature. It has other terms too, like, capabilitative passive (Balachandran 1973), passive of incapacity (Hook 1979), inability passive (Davison 1982) and capacity passive (Rosen & Wali 1989). It conveys the inability of an agent/initiator to initiate the event denoted by the predicate, hence it is called the inabilitative passive (Pandharipande 1981).

In Kashmiri, like other SALs, the (in)abilitative passives can be formed on eventive predicates intransitives and transitives both. For example:

(22) *farooq-ni zaryi aav-nI shong-nI*
Farooq-GEN by came-not sleep-INF.OBL
'Farooq was not able to sleep.'

(23) *faroo-ni zaryi aav-nI khey-nI*
Farooq-GEN by came-not eat-INF.OBL
'Farooq was not able to eat'

1. It should be noted here that we have deliberately used '(in)abilitative' instead of 'inabilitative' in this paper as in Kashmiri, it denotes both ability as well as inability, unlike other Indo-Aryan languages.

However, with stative predicates, we cannot have (in)abilitative passives as shown below:

(24) **farooq-ni zaryi aayi-nI bochi lag-nI*
Farooq-GEN by come-PRF-NEG hunger happen-INF.OBL
'Farooq was not able to be hungry.'

As various linguists (Pandharipande 1981; Kachru 1980; Davison 1982) have observed, despite similarities with the regular passive, the (in)abilitative passive differs significantly from it. We will examine this in the light of Kashmiri (in)abilitative passive construction.

Kashmiri, too, has (in)abilitative passives but it does not have any restrictions on the availability of the (in)ability reading, unlike other Indo-Aryan languages. In other words, Kashmiri (in)abilitative passives do not need affected environment (i.e. negation, conditional, question etc). For example,

(25) i. *??mujh-se ye kaam kiyaa jaaegaa* Hindi
I.OBL-INST this work do-PRF go-FUT
'I will be able to do this work.'

ii. *mujh-se ye kaam nahin kiyaa jaaegaa* Hindi
I.OBL-INST this work not do-PRF go-FUT
'I will not be able to do this work.'

iii. *myani zaryi yi-yi yi kA:m kar-nI* Kashmiri
I-GEN by come-FUT this work do-INF.OBL
'I will be able to do this work.'

iv. *myani zaryi yi-yi-nI yi kA:m kar-nI* Kashmiri
I-GEN by come-FUT-NEG this work do-INF.OBL
'I will not be able to do this work.'

As we have seen above, modals cannot appear in passive constructions in Kashmiri but we can have light verb with (in)abilitative passives in Kashmiri (unlike in Hindi). For example,

(26) i. *farooq-ni zaryi yiyi-nI su tsuunth*
Farooq-GEN by be-FUT-NEG that apple
khey-th ni-nI Kashmiri
eat-PTCP take-INF.OBL
'That apple could not be eaten by Farooq (abruptly).'

ii. **farooq-se ye seb khaa liyaa nahin jaega* Hindi
Farooq-INST this apple eat take-PFV not pass-FUT
'This apple could not be eaten by Farooq (completely).'

Another difference is in the choice of *zaryi* vs. *athi* phrase in (in)abilitative passives in Kashmiri. Unlike Hindi where the agentive phrase in inabilitative passives is marked by either the instrumental case marker *-se* or *-ke dwaaraa '-gen through/by'*, Kashmiri agentive phrase in (in)abilitative passive can only be marked by the instrumental case marker *-zaryi*. As seen in above examples, the matrix subject is always marked by *zaryi* and the causee agent is marked by *athi*, the agentive phrase of the (in)abilitative passives is also marked by *zaryi* and not *athi*. For example,

(27) **farooq-as athi yiyi-nI su tsuunth khey-th ni-nI*
Farooq-DAT by be-FUT-NEG that apple eat-PTCP take-INF.OBL
'That apple could not be eaten by Farooq (abruptly).'

To sum up, we have observed that Kashmiri intransitives (unergatives) as well as transitives can be passivized. Dative subject constructions in Kashmiri cannot be passivized. In Kashmiri, the (in)abilitative passives can be formed on eventive predicates intransitives and transitives both. Kashmiri (in)abilitative passives do not need affected environment (i.e. negation, conditional, question etc). Modals cannot appear in Kashmiri passives though we can have light verb with (in)abilitative passives. Kashmiri agentive phrase in (in)abilitative passive can only be marked by the instrumental case marker *-zaryi* and the causee agent is marked by *-athi*.

Now we will examine the status of subject and object in Kashmiri passive construction.

4. Status of the subject and the object in Kashmiri passive

It has been shown in many South Asian Languages (SALs) passives like Hindi (Mahajan 1994; Richa 2011), Oriya, Malayalam, Khariya, Meitei and Ao (Chandra & Sahoo 2013) that there is no object to subject promotion. Besides this, the subject retains its subject properties and the object its object properties.

The question is whether the subject and the object in the Kashmiri passive actually behave like other SALs passive subjects and objects? To attest this, some tests can be applied like anaphor binding, pronominal co-reference, control etc. (mostly based on Keenan 1976).

<u>**Subject in Kashmiri Passive:**</u>

Anaphor Binding:
Possessive reflexives in Kashmiri must be bound by the matrix subject. For example,

(28) *$arshid_i$ kari [$pann\text{-}is_i$ gar-as] mA:yinI*
arshid do-FUT self-GEN home-DAT examination
'$Arshid_i$ will examine $self's_i$ home.

Similarly, the *-zaryi* agentive phrase can bind the possessive reflexive.

(29) *farooq-ni$_i$ zaryi aav pann-is$_i$ gar-as mA:yinI kar-nI*
farooq-GEN by came self-GEN home-DAT examination do-INF.OBL
'Self's$_i$ house was examined by Farooq$_i$.'

In passive of causative, we find that the agentive phrase as well as the causee agent can bind the possessive reflexive.

(30) *farooq-ni$_i$ zaryi aav reyaaz-as$_j$ athi pann-is$_i$ gar-as*
farooq-GEN by came Reyaz-DAT by self-GEN home-DAT
mA:yinI kar-na:v-nI
examination do-CAUS-INF.OBL
'Reyaaz$_j$ was made to examine self's$_{i/j}$ house by Farooq$_{i.}$'

Antisubject Orientation of Pronouns:

(31) *farooq-an$_i$ kor tam-sInd-is$_i$ gar-as mA:yinI*
farooq-ERG do-FUT he-GEN-GEN home-DAT examination
'Farooq$_i$ will examine his$_{*i}$ home.'

Similarly,

(32) *farooq-ni$_i$ zaryi aav tam-sInd-is$_i$ gar-as*
farooq-GEN by came he-GEN-GEN home-DAT
mA:yinI kar-nI
examination do-INF.OBL
'His$_{*i}$ home was examined by Farooq$_i$.'

With passive of causative, we get the same result.

(33) *farooq-ni$_i$ zaryi aav reyaaz-as athi tam-sInd-is$_i$ gar-as*
farooq-GEN by came Reyaz-DAT by he-GEN-GEN home-DAT
mA:yinI kar-na:v-nI
examination do-CAUS-INF.OBL
'Reyaz made to examine his$_{*i}$ home was by Farooq$_i$.'

Control into Argument Clauses:
The agentive phrase in passive behaves as the subject does in the subject control constructions.

(34) i. *farooq$_i$ os [PRO$_i$ garI gatsun] yatsaan*
farooq be-PST home-OBL go-INF want-HAB
'Farooq wanted to go home.'

ii. *farooq-an$_i$ yotsh [PRO$_i$ garI gatsun]*
farooq-ERG want-PERF home-OBL go-INF
'Farooq wanted to go home.'

iii. *farooq-ni$_i$ zaryi aav [PRO$_i$ garI gatsun] yats-nI*
farooq-GEN by came home-OBL go-INF want-INF.OBL
'It was wanted by Farooq to go home.'

Control into Adverbial Clauses:

The agentive phrase in passive behaves similar to the subject as far as the control into adverbial clauses is concerned:

(35) i. *farooq$_i$ kari [PRO$_i$ garI gatsith]*
farooq do-FUT home-OBL go-CNJN PRTCP
reyaaz-as bevA:rii
reyaaz-DAT scolding
'Farooq will scold Reyaaz after going home.'

ii. *farooq-an$_i$ kAr bevA:rii reyaaz-as*
farooq-ERG do-PERF scolding reyaaz-DAT
[PRO$_i$ garI gatsith]
home-OBL go-CNJN PRTCP
'Farooq scolded Reyaaz after going home.'

Similarly,

(36) *nowsheen-ni$_i$ zaryi aayi [PRO$_i$ garI gatsith]*
nawsheen-GEN by come-PERF home-OBL go-CNJn prtcp
farooq-as bevA:rii kar-nI
farooq-DAT scolding do-INF.OBL
'Farooq was scolded by Nowsheen$_i$ after she$_i$ went home.

In passive of causative too, only the martix subject controls into adeverbial clause.

(37) *nowsheen-ni$_i$ zaryi aayi [PRO$_i$ garI gatsith]*
nawsheen-GEN by come-PERF home-OBL go-CNJn PTCP
reyaaz-as farooq-as athi bevA:rii kar-na:v-nI
reyaaz-DAT Farooq-DAT by scolding do-CAUS-INF.OBL
'Farooq was made to scold Reyaz by Nawsheen$_i$ after she$_i$ went home.

Object in Kashmiri Passive:

In Kashmiri, the accusative case is unmarked in constructions with ergative subject but can be marked in constructions with nominative subject.[2] In passives, the object is never marked for accusative case. For example,

---

2. Some linguists like Wali & Koul (1994, 1997) have mentioned about unmarked objects receiving nominative case in Kashmiri, in this paper, we have considered the nominative and the accusative both as structural cases, where the nominative is associated with subject

(38) i. *baadsha-an mA:r' jangal-as manz sA:riy sIh*
king-ERG kill-PERF forest-DAT in all lion
'The king killed all the lions in the forest.'

ii. *baadsha chu sIh-an maaraan*
king Aux lion-acc kill-HAB
'The king kills lions.'

iii. *raam-an mO:r su*
Ram-ERG kill-PERF him
'Ram killed him.'

iv. *raam-ni zaryi aav su maar-nI*
Ram-GEN by come-PERF him kill-INF.OBL
'He was killed by Ram.'

v. *baadsha-ni zaryi A:y jangal-as manz sA:riy*
king-GEN by come-PERF forest-DAT in all
sIh maar-nI
lion kill-INF.OBL
'All the lions in the forest were killed by the king.'

vi. *John-an mO:r bill*
John-ERG kill-PERF Bill
'John killed Bill.'

vii. *John-ni zaryi aav bill maar-nI*
John-GEN by come-PERF bill kill-INF.OBL
'Bill was killed by John.'

As the Examples (38 iii & iv) show, with pronouns too, in both the actives and passives, the accusative marking does not appear. Neither does it appear with the [+human] objects as (38 vi & vii) demonstrate. 'Bill' has accusative case neither in active nor in passive.[3]

Pronominal Coreference:

Kashmiri pronouns can corefer with the objects.

---

agreement and assigned/checked by the functional head T and the accusative is associated with object agreement and assigned/checked by the lexical head V.

3. A reviewer mentions object case as a counter-argument against our analysis. If passive objects are unmarked like nominative DPs, that should be counted as evidence for object promotion to subject position. However, note that object or accusative case is also unmarked in most cases, even for animate DPs. There is no object agreement observed, only the gender and number agreement (not person) on the auxiliary verb changes in the passive; the main verb that is in infinitival oblique form does not change – aav (sg.mas.), A:i (pl.mas.), aayi (sg. fem), aayi (pl.fem.).

(39) i. *reyaaz-an$_i$ suuz farooq$_j$ tohand$_{*i/j}$ garI*
reyaz-ERG send-PERF farooq his house
'Reyaz$_i$ sent Farooq$_j$ to his$_{*i/j}$ house.'

ii. *reyaaz$_i$ sozi farooq-as$_j$ tohand$_{*i/j}$ garI*
reyaz-ERG send-FUT farooq-DAT his house
'Reyaz$_i$ will send Farooq$_j$ to his$_{*i/j}$ house.'

Similarly, the pronoun in the passive also corefers with the object. For example,

(40) *reyaaz-ni$_i$ zaryi aav farooq$_j$ tohand$_{*i/j}$ garI soz-nI*
reyaaz-GEN by came farooq his house send-INF.OBL
'Farooq$_j$ was sent to his$_{*i/j}$ house by Reyaaz$_i$.'

In passive of CAUsative, we get the same result.

(41) *reyaaz-ni$_i$ zaryi aav farooq$_j$ nowsheen-as athi tohand$_{*i/j}$*
reyaaz-GEN by came farooz Nowsheen-DAT by his

garI soz-Ina:v-nI
house send-CAUS-INF.OBL

'Nowsheen was made to send Farooq$_j$ to his$_{*i/j}$ house by Reyaaz$_i$.'

Two relevant features of Kashmiri passives appear here – one is that the agentive phrase, though surfacing as a PP 'NP….zaryi' retains its subject properties and second, the object does not get promoted, it too retains its object properties. Though the case-less nature of the passive object casts a doubt whether it has moved to the specifier of the TP of not, we have shown above that it has not and control facts provide evidence that they raise high enough to c-command other arguments.

5. Status of the implicit/optional agent in passive

In canonical passives, the subject of the active corresponds to a non-obligatory oblique phrase of the passive or is not overtly expressed. It has been shown that the external argument in the passive is syntactically expressed, though in an alternative manner (Baker et al. (1989); Emonds (2000)). In other words, this syntactically suppressed argument is present in the argument structure (Roeper 1987; Grimshaw 1990), showing that passives do have an implicit argument. Now, the debate narrows down to whether this optional agent of the passive corresponds to the object of the active or not. We will argue that in canonical passives, this optional agent does and in Active-Passives it does not.[4]

4. Note here that the Active-Passive is different than the two other kinds of non-canonical passive constructions – one with only object promotion and the other with only subject demotion (See Ura 2000).

Let us examine the status of the implicit agentive phrase in Kashmiri passive. As it is marked by the preposition 'zaryi' or 'athi', it appears to be an adjunct but as we have provided evidences in the above section, it is actually an argument. Like other passive implicit agents (See Bhatt & Pancheva 2006), Kashmiri passive agent too is present in the structure as an implicit argument because (a) it is licensed by the 'zaryi/athi' phrase (b) has the ability to control and (c) its compatibility with adverbs like *deliberately*. First, we will see how the implicit agent is responsible for the licensing. For example,

(42) *zamrood-ni zaryi aav kul tsaTI-nI*
zamrood-GEN by came tree cut-INF.OBL
'The tree was cut by Zamrood.'

This implicit agent has the ability to control too. For example,

(43) *na:v aayi inshornIs ropyav khA:trI Duba:v-nI*
boat come insurance money for sink-INF.OBL
'The boat was sunk for insurance money' (to take insurance money)

Adverbs like 'deliberately' are taken to be agent-oriented and hence, the presence of an implicit agent can be attested. For example,

(44) *zA:nith mA:nith aayi na:v Duba:v-nI*
know-CNJPTCP accept-CNJPTCP came boat sink-INF.OBL
'The boat was sunk deliberately.'

In passive of causative too, it is the implicit agent that attests the presence of the implicit agent.

(45) *zA:nith mA:nith aav reyaz-as athi*
know-CNJPTCP accept-CNJPTCP came Reyaz-DAT by
kul tsaTI-na:v-nI
tree cut-CAUS-INF.OBL
'Reyaz was made to cut the tree was cut deliberately.'

The same phenomenon, i.e. implicit agent is noticed in causatives constructions too, where instrumental marked causee agents can also be implicit. For example,

(46) *reyaz-an ma:rI-na:vI-nov farooq (suhan-ni zaryi)*
reyaz-ERG kill-CAUS-PRF farooq sohan-GEN by
'Reyaz made Sohan kill Farooq.'

In the above Example (46), the instrumental marked causee, i.e. *suhan-ni zaryi* can be implicit.

Hence, we can predict that in passive of causative, both the matrix subject as well as the causee agent must be implicit. And that prediction is found to be true. For example,

(47) *farooq aav ma:rI-na:vI-nI (reyaaz-ni zaryi) (sohan-as athi)*
Farooq came kill-CAUS-pass Reyaz-GEN by Sohan-DAT by
'Farooq was made to be killed (by Reyaz through Sohan).'

This is not unique to Kashmiri. In other SALs too, like Hindi, the causative causee agents show this property. Due to this optionality, the causee agent has often been analysed as an adjunct (Mohanan 1994; Ramchand 2008, 2011) but Richa (2011) argues that it is an argument, quite different from *-se* adjuncts as the causee can easily control into the participial clauses (a property of arguments).

In Kashmiri too, the causee agent can control into the participial clauses. For example,

(48) *ma:shTar-an*$_i$ *vIRna:vI-nov [PRO*$_{i/j}$ *asa:n asa:n] shur-is*$_j$
master-ERG fly-CAUS-PRF laugh-HAB laugh-HAB child-DAT
athi patang
by kite
'The master$_i$ made the child$_j$ fly the kite while PRO$_{i/j}$ smiling.'

Furthermore, if we passivize the above sentence, the implicit agent can be the controller and also the implicit causee:

(49) *patang aav [PRO*$_{i/j}$ *asa:n asa:n] vIRI-na:v-nI*
kite came laugh-HAB laugh-HAB fly-CAUS-INF.OBL
'The kite was made to fly while PRO$_{i/j}$ smiling.'

Hence, Kashmiri passive agent is similar to the causee agent, both are syntactically real arguments present in the syntax, though not phonetically expressed sometimes.

6. Canonical passive vs Kashmiri passive vs SALs passive

If we compare a canonical passive with the Kashmiri one, we find that though there is a non-obligatory oblique agentive phrase in Kashmiri passive that may or may not be overtly expressed and though, on surface, it seems to correspond to the subject of the active; unlike canonical passive constructions, the subject of Kashmiri passive does not correspond to the direct object of the active as anaphor binding, pronominal co-reference and control tests above have confirmed that the oblique agentive phrase in Kashmiri passive remains a surface subject and the object too does not move to the subject position. In other words, there is no promotion of object or demotion of subject in Kashmiri passive. Interestingly, if we consider 'foregrounding', 'defocusing' or 'agent suppression' as the crucial property of passivization, Kashmiri passive does have this property.

As far as passive constructions in other SALs are concerned, we find mostly similarities and slight dissimilarities too. Chandra & Sahoo (2013) have considered languages from four different language families – Oriya (Indo-Aryan), Malayalam (Dravidian), Kharia (Austro-Asiatic), Ao & Manipuri (Tibeto-Burman). They find that unlike English-type passives, passives in all these languages (except Tibeto-Burman) are similar in preserving subject properties for their logical subjects and object properties for their logical objects.[5]

Tibeto-Burman passives are not similar to other SALs as they have no separate verbal morphology or 'by' agentive phrase but Chandra & Sahoo provide ample evidence that actives in Manipuri and Ao have passive counterparts with topicalized objects as well as dropped agents. Further, the topicalized object can control into the complement clause. Moreover, agent-oriented adverbials can also be used with the optional agent-sentences, proving that the agents in Ao and Manipuri are syntactically active (though phonetically absent).

Further, if we compare Kashmiri passive construction with SALs passives, we find that it also maintains subject properties for its logical subject and object properties for its logical object as observed in the above section. The only difference is that unlike Hindi, Oriya and Kharia passives, the object in Kashmiri passives is not overtly marked like its active object. In this regard, it is similar to Malayalam passive.

By examining the phenomenon of passivization cross linguistically, it is seen as a function of four linguistic features – (1) Optional Subject Suppression (OSS) (2) Object to Subject Movement (OSMv) (3) Separate Verbal Morphology (SVM) (4) Overt Marking on Object (OMO). (Note that the last feature OMO is not applicable for English as it is not morphologically rich like SALs; this feature has been considered to distinguish within the SAL group). We can contrast the presence or absence of these features in different SALs with canonical active and passive i.e. English active (A.) and English passive (P.), as done in the following table:

5. A reviewer comments that Malayalam passive objects are unmarked with nominative case and occupy sentence-initial positions. While further data is needed to substantiate this claim, it is also equally important to find out explanations for why agentive by-phrases and not objects show subject like properties in the language.

Table 1. Passive continuum

Language	OSS	OSMv	SVM	OMO	Feature value	Passiveness % age
English P.	+	+	+	*	3/3	100
Hindi	+	_	+	+	3/4	75
Urdu	+	_	+	+	3/4	75
Kashmiri	+	_	+	_	2/4	50
Malayalam	+	_	+	_	2/4	50
Kharia	+	_	+	_	2/4	50
Manipuri	+	_	_	_	1/4	25
Ao	+	_	_	_	1/4	25
English A.	_	_	_	*	0/4	0

On the basis of percentage of the defining features of the canonical passives, as shown in the above table, one can estimate the passiveness for each language in terms of numbers and there by a clear cut passive continuum can be traced & represented from canonical active to canonical passive (from 0% passiveness to 100% passiveness). By this way of estimation & representation, one can not only account for the differences between canonical passives and South Asian Languages' (SALs) passives but also the differences within SAL passives. Moreover, positing a passive continuum on the basis of numbers is a more empirical way rather than branding them collectively as complete passives, ACTIVE passives or half-passives.

6.1 Is passivization a Detransitivization/Intransitivization process?

Detransitivization is an operation that removes a complement DP from the selection features of the verb, suppresses that DP's theta role and neutralizes the verb's Case features. Therefore, the concept of passive as a valency-decreasing rule is also expressed as detransitivization, i.e. an argument suppression process, or a resultant state which removes a participant from the actual action (Siewierska 1984; Givón 1990; Thompson 1994).

The comparison of SALs passives and canonical passives also questions some basic aspects regarding the process of passivization. In canonical passives, as the external argument becomes an adjunct, i.e. it can be optionally represented and it goes to a different argument – the object, passivization has also been called as a detransitivization process. For Shibatani (1985), detransitivization and passivization are two different processes, though both involve valency decrease. In detransitivization, there is no agent conceived but in passivization, an agent is present in the semantic frame, though not in the syntactic frame. He argues that passivised transitives are detransitivised but passivised ditransitives are not – they must remain transitive to make sense of the clause. For example,

(50) The food was put on the shelf.

Klaiman (1991), too, considers passivization as a detransitivization process but distinguishes between two types of detransitivization – one that allows for the expression of the agent and one that does not. Kiparsky (2012) does not consider passivization as intransitivization and argues that it is the property of demotion to reduce the valency of a predicate (i.e. the number of its direct arguments) by one, hence, passives of ditransitives are transitive and passives of intransitives are subjectless/impersonal. Wunderlich (2012) considers passive as an affix that demotes/existentially binds the most prominent Theta-role which is not already demoted.

Hence, if we look at the passives in SALs, this very notion of passivization as a detransitivization operation fails to apply here. Moreover, in SAL passives, the agent is syntactically present too (though it may be not phonetically represented), unlike as claimed by Shibatani (1985) that it is only semantically present.

7. Final remarks

Adding to the passive controversy, the above investigation on Kashmiri passives shows that we cannot have a clear cut distinction between what is a passive or not, in terms of one specific set of features. Therefore, we have tried to illustrate the similarities as well as differences between the canonical passives and Kashmiri passive construction. In Kashmiri passive, the agent is encoded in an oblique case, i.e. it has been defocused to some extent, not complete, unlike the canonical passive where the agent is not syntactically encoded at all. Contrary to Keenan & Dryer (2007), we argued that the agent phrase, though in the form of an oblique NP, is an integral part of the passive construction and is the syntactic subject of the verb.

Therefore, in line with Shibatani (1985)'s view of passives forming as continuum with actives, we too consider that Kashmiri passive lies on the active/passive continuum – but slightly more towards the active side where though the subject is defocused to some extent, it retains its subject properties and object too retains its object properties.

Finally, we argue that despite lacking some of the features of canonical passives, Kashmiri has the passive voice that is one of the language universals.

References

Bach, Emmon. 1980. In defense of passive. *Linguistics and Philosophy* 3: 297–341.
Baker, Mark, Kyle Johnson & Ian Roberts. 1989. Passive arguments raised. *Linguistic Inquiry* 20: 219–252.
Bhatt, Rajesh & Pancheva, Roumanya. 2006. Implicit arguments. In *The Blackwell Companion to Syntax*, vol. II, 554–584. Oxford: Wiley-Blackwell.
Bresnan, Joan. 1982. The passive in lexical theory. In J. Bresnan (Ed.), *The mental representation of grammatical relations* (pp. 3–86). Cambridge, MA: MIT Press.
Chandra, Pritha & Sahoo, Anindita. 2013. Passives in south asian languages. *Acta Linguistica Asiatica* 3: 9–27.
Chomsky, Noam. 1957. *Syntactic Structures*. The Hague: Mouton.
Chomsky, Noam. 1965. *Aspects of the Theory of Syntax*. The MIT Press: Cambridge, Mass.
Croft, Willam. 1994. Voice: Beyond control and affectedness. In P. J. Hopper & B. A. Fox (Eds.), *Voice: Form and function* (pp. 89–117). Amsterdam: John Benjamin
Davison, Alice. 1982. On the form and meaning of Hindi passive sentences. *Lingua* 58(1–2): 149–179.
Freidin, Robert. 1975. The analysis of passives, *Language* 51: 384–405.
Givón, Talmy. 1990. *Syntax. A Functional Typological Introduction-II*. Amsterdam: John Benjamins.
Givón, Talmy (ed.). 1994. *Voice and Inversion*. Amsterdam/Philadelphia: Benjamins.
Grimshaw, Jane, 1990. *Argument Structure*. Cambridge: MIT Press.
Haspelmath, Martin. 1990. The grammaticalization of passive morphology. *Studies in Language* 14: 25–72.
Hasegawa, Kinsuke. 1968. The passive construction in English. *Language* 44: 230–243.
Hook, Peter Edwin. 1979. *Hindi Structures: Intermediate Level*. Michigan Papers on South and South-East Asia 16, Center for South and South-East Asian Studies, University of Michigan, Ann Arbor, Michigan.
Jackendoff, Ray, S. 1969. An Interpretive Theory of Negation. *Foundation of Language* 5(2): 218–241.
Kachru, Yamuna. 1980. *Aspects of Hindi-Grammar*. New Delhi: Manohar Publications.
Keenan, Edward. 1976. Towards a universal definition of 'subject.' In *Subject and Topic*, Charles N. Li (ed.), 303–34. New York: Academic Press.
Keenan, Edward L. & Dryer, Matthew S. 2007. Passive in the world's languages. In *Language Typology and Syntactic Description. Vol. I: Clause Structure*, Timothy Shopen (ed.), 325–361. Cambridge University Press: Cambridge.
Kiparsky, Paul. 2012. Towards a null theory of passives. *Lingua*. Nov. 2012.
Klaiman, Miriam. H. 1991. *Grammatical Voice*. Cambridge: Cambridge University Press.
Lakoff, George. 1974. Interview in H. Parret (Ed.), *Discussing language*, pp. 178–179. The Hague, Netherlands: Mouton.

Mahajan, Anoop. 1994. Active passives. In *Proceedings of the Thirteenth West Coast Conference on Formal Linguistics*, R. Aronovich, W. Byrne, S. Preuss & M. Senturia (eds). Stanford University: CSLI Publications.

Mohanan, Tara. 1994. Argument Structure in Hindi. Stanford: CSLI Publications.

Pandharipande, Rajeshwari. 1981. *Transitivity in Hindi.* 11(2): 161–179. University of Illinois, Urbana-Champaign.

Perlmutter, David M. & Postal, Paul M. 1984. The I-advancement exclusiveness law. In *Studies in Relational Grammar* 2, David M. Perlmutter & Carol Rosen (eds), 81–125. Chicago: University of Chicago Press.

Ramchand, Gillian. 2008. Verb Meaning and the Lexicon: A First Phase Syntax. Cambridge: Cambridge University Press.

Ramchand, Gillian. 2011. Licensing of instrumental case in Hindi/Urdu in Causatives. Working Papers on Language & Linguistics 38. Tromsø University: Septentrio Acdemic Publishing.

Richa. 2011. *Hindi Verb Classes and Their Argument Structure Alternations.* UK: Cambridge Scholars Publishers.

Robson, Roy Anthony. 1972. On the generation of passive constructions in English. Unpublished doctoral thesis, University of Texas, Austin, USA.

Roeper, Thomas. 1987. Implicit Arguments and the Head-Complement Relation. *Linguistic Inquiry* 18(2): 267–310.

Rosen, Carol & Wali, Kashi.1989. Twin passives, inversion, and multistratalism in Marathi. *Natural Language and Linguistic Theory* 7(1): 1–50.

Shibatani, Masayoshi. 1985. Passives and related constructions: A prototype analysis. *Language* 61: 821–848.

Siewierska, Anna. 1984. *Passive: A Comparative Linguistic Analysis.* Croom Helm: New Hampshire.

Siewierska, Anna. 1988. The passive in Slavic languages. In M. Shibatani (Ed.), *Passive and voice* (pp. 243–289). Amsterdam, Netherlands: John Benjamins.

Thompson, Chand. 1994. Passives and inverse constructions. In *Voice and Inversion*, T. Givón (ed.). 47–63. Amsterdam: John Benjamins.

Ura, Hiroyuki. 2000. *Checking Theory and Grammatical Functions in Universal Grammar.* New York: Oxford University Press.

Wali, Kashi. & Koul, Omkar Nath. 1994. Kashmiri clitics: The role of the case and CASE. *Linguistics* 32: 969–994.

Wali, Kashi & Koul, Omkar Nath. 1997. *Kashmiri: A Cognitive-Descriptive Grammar.* London: Routledge.

Wunderlich, Dieter. 2012. Operations on argument structure. In *Handbook of Semantics*, Claudia Maienborn et al. (ed.), Vol. 3. Berlin: Mouton de Gruyter.

Ziff, Paul. 1966. The Nonsynonymy of Active and Passive Sentences. *The Philosophical Review* 75: 226–232.

Middles in the syntax

Pritha Chandra
Indian Institute of Technology Delhi

It is well-known that while some languages mark middles and passives similarly, some others mark them differently. Researchers opine that this difference may ensue from the loci of middle generation; they can be generated either in the lexicon or in the syntax. I present some problems with the two-modular approach and propose a syntactic analysis for all middles, with the differences emanating from the choice of the non-active voice head. Languages like Hindi-Urdu which choose a middle non-active voice head fail to project a higher aspectual head hosting an external argument. The truncated structure makes the middles different from passives, in both morphological form and syntactic behavior.

Keywords: middles; passives; two-modular approach; aspect; voice

1. Introducing Hindi-Urdu middles

Hindi-Urdu has middle constructions like the following:

(1) *jahaaz aasaanise Dubte hain*
ships easily sink be
'Ships sink easily.'

(2) *kapRe aasaanise suukhte hain*
clothes easily dry be
'Clothes dry easily.'

The foremost characteristic defining them is that they are generic statements of some property of the arguments involved. Sentence (1) states a property of 'ships' being 'easily sinkable', while sentence (2) is about 'clothes drying easily'. A second and a related feature is that there are no external agents involved to accomplish these activities. 'Ships' don't need volitional agents to make them sink in (3), and 'clothes' can dry on their own, without help from an external agent in (4).

(3) **Dakaitone jahaaz aasaanise Dubte hain*
dacoits ships easily sink be
'Pirates sink ships easily.' (lit: *'Ships sink easily by pirates')

(4) **logone kapRe aasaanise suukhte hain*
people clothes easily dry be
'People dry clothes easily.' (lit: *'Clothes dry easily by people')

These characteristics define middles cross-linguistically and have placed them in a class distinct from other constructions like passives. However, it has been observed that in some languages, these two construction types lose their morphological distinction and even pattern similarly with regard to some syntactic features. We therefore have an interesting typological question here: middles in a given language may or may not be morphological look-alikes of passives. One possible solution already suggested in the literature is to allow two different modules to generate middles – albeit with distinct characteristics.

This paper demonstrates that a two-modular approach to middles is not right. All middles can be generated in the syntax, with cross-linguistic differences emerging from the choice of the non-active voice head and the clause structural representations underlying these constructions. Languages like Hindi-Urdu, where middles are different from passives select two different non-active voice heads for their middles and passives. They therefore look and pattern differently from each other. On the other end are languages like Serbo-Croatian, Romance languages that select a single non-active (passive) voice head for both constructions, which explains why their middles and passives overlap morphologically and syntactically.

2. Middle-passive overlap

Cross-linguistically, middles are marked morphologically in two ways: either with active morphology or with passive morphology. English middles, as is widely known, fall in the first category, with middles (5) marked differently from passives (6).

(5) The ship sinks easily.

(6) The ship was sunk easily.

Middles in the second category are morphologically similar to their passives. Take Greek, for instance:[1]

1. A reviewer suggests that semantic features of predicates play a role in deciding the construction types they can be involved in. That may explain why 'sink' but not 'read' can be taken in the following forms.

(i) The ship is sinking.
(ii) *The book is reading.

(7) *Afto to vivlio diavazete efkola*
This the book-nom read-nact easily
'This book reads easily.'

(8) *To vivlio diavastike*
The book read-nact
'The book was read.'

These sentences show a middle verb (7) marked with a non-active morpheme like a passive (8); see Tsimpli (1989), Sioupi (1998) and Alexiadou and Doron (2007) for more detailed descriptions of Greek. Similarly, many Romance and Slavic languages use the *si/se* passive morpheme to depict both middles and passives. The following examples are taken from Marelj (2004).

(9) *Questo tavolino si transporta facilmente* (Italian)
This table si transports easily
'This table transports easily.'

(10) *Questo giornalle si legge ogni mattina*
This newspaper si read every morning
'This newspaper is read every morning.'

(11) *Mrlje od crnog vina se ne skidaju* (Serbo-Croatian)
Smudges from black wine se not clean
'Red wine stains do not clean.'

(12) *kuca se gradi*
House se builds
'The house is being built.'

This cross-linguistic variation has been an ongoing domain of investigation. One repeatedly asked question is whether passive-like middles also share the syntactic properties of passives. Marelj (2004) has demonstrated that Italian *si/se* middles indeed have certain passive like syntactic features, such as the ability to license purpose clauses and agentive adverbials (13)–(14).

(13) *I bambini si lavano [per far piacere a Maria]*
The children si wash to give Maria pleasure

(14) *I bambini si lavano volentieri*
The children si wash willingly

These Italian middles pattern closely with English passives (15)–(16), but not with English middles, which are unacceptable with purpose clauses and agentive adverbials (17)–(18).

(15) The ship was sunk [to collect the insurance money].

(16) The ship was sunk intentionally.

(17) *The ship sinks easily [to collect the insurance money].

(18) *The ship sinks intentionally.

However, Marelj also notes that sentences (13) and (14) are instances of reflexive constructions, which may constitute a different class of constructions from middles. In order to confirm if the middle-passive correlation actually exists, one must instead consider predicates that are unambiguously middles. Some instances from Cinque (1988, 1995) help out in this regard. Consider the following constructions with predicates like 'sell' and 'bribe':

(19) **Il libro ha il pregio di vendersi voluntamente*
The book has the merit of selling voluntarily

(20) *Quelli'uomo politico hai il vantaggio di potersi corrompere facilmente*
[**per dimostare le propria influenza*]
That policeman has the advantage of si bribing easily to show one's influence

These middle constructions present a different picture from the one presented by sentences in (13) and (14). While the Italian middle with the predicate 'sell' in (19) is incompatible with an agentive adverbial, the 'bribe' middle disallows control into purpose clauses (20). This indicates that some Italian middles are very similar to English middles. The suggestion that they are more like passives is therefore not completely justified. Instead, the *si/se* passive/middle constructions need to be studied in more depth before one concludes whether they are middles, passives or a completely different class of constructions.

2.1 No middle-passive overlap in Hindi-Urdu

Hindi-Urdu middles, repeated in (21)–(22) are morphologically distinct from passives (23).

(21) *jahaaz aasaanise Dubte hain*
ships easily sink be
'Ships sink easily.'

(22) *kapRe aasaanise suukhte hain*
clothes easily dry be
'Clothes dry easily.'

(23) (*Dakaito dwaaraa*) *jahaaz Duboyaa gayaa*
(pirates by) ship sink go-PASS
'The ship was sunk (by the pirates).'

As illustrated above, middle verbs in (21)–(22) carry active verbal (habitual/imperfective) morphology. Passives (23) on the other hand, are marked with distinct passive morphology. Apart from morphology, these two construction-types also differ on syntactic grounds. Middles do not allow agentive adverbials (24) and purpose clauses (25), unlike passives (26)–(27).

(24) **jahaaz jaanbhuujkar aasaanise Dubte hain*
ships intentionally easily sink be
'*Ships intentionally sink easily.'

(25) **jahaaz [biimaa raashii paane ke liye] aasaanise Dubte hain*
ships insurance money get for easily sink be
'*Ships easily sink to collect the insurance money.'

(26) *jahaaz jaanbhuujkar Duboyaa gayaa*
ship intentionally sink be-PASS
'The ship was sunk intentionally.'

(27) *jahaaz [biimaa raashii paane ke liye] Duboyaa gayaa.*
ship insurance money get for sink go-PASS
'The ship was sunk to collect the insurance money.'

Differences between the two constructions also show up in other verbal paradigms. Bhatt and Embick (2003) classify causative-inchoative alternating verbs in Hindi-Urdu into a null-class (agentive and non-agentive) and an AA-class (agentive-non-agentive). In what they call the NULL-class of verbs owing to the lack of an overt affix in both members (causatives, inchoative/anti-causatives) of the alternation, we find while the verbal form of a regular transitive/causative (28) is retained in passives (29), the same is not the case with middles (30). Inchoatives (31) also have non-causative forms.

(28) *ram-ne jaaydaad baanT dii/baanTii.*
Ram-ERG. property divide give-PERF/divide-FEM.PERF.
'Ram divided the property.'

(29) *jaaydaad baanT dii gayii/baanTii gayii*
property divide give go-PASS/divide.FEM. go-PASS.
'The property was divided.'

(30) *jaaydaad asaaniise banTtii he/banT jaatii hain*
property easily divide-mid. be/divide go-mid. be
'Property gets divided easily.'

(31) *jaaydaad banTii*
Property divide
'Property got divided.'

For the AA-class of verbs too (where the causative form has an extra morpheme *-aa*), the causative morpheme (32) is retained in passives (33), but not in middles (34) and inchoatives (35).

(32) *Dakaitone makaan jalaa diyaa*
bandits house burn-CAUS. give
'Bandits burned the house.'

(33) *makaan jalaa diyaa gayaa/jalaayaa gayaa*
house burn-CAUS. give go-PASS/burn-CAUS. go-PASS.
'The house was burned.'

(34) *lakRiike makaan asaaniise jalte hain*
wooden house easily burn-MID. be
'Wooden houses burn easily.'

(35) *makaan jal rahaa hain*
house burn PROG. Be
'The house burns/is burning.'

If the causative has a *-vaa* verbal form (36), that form is as expected, retained in passives (37).

(36) *zamindaarne dakaito-se makaan jal-vaa diyaa*
landlord bandit-INSTR. house burn-CAUSE. give
'The landlord had the dacoits burn the house.'

(37) *makaan jal-vaa diyaa gayaa*
house burn-CAUS give go-PASS.
'The house was burnt.'

We see this pattern repeated on all predicates listed by Bhatt and Embick under the null-class and AA-class. These are illustrated below in Tables 1–4. The first table has encyclopedically agentive predicates from the null class (i.e. those that involve an agent in the encyclopedic semantics but not in the syntactic representation) and their transitive/causative, passive, middle and inchoative variants.

Table 1. Encyclopedically agentive predicates in the null class

Verb	Causative	Passive	Middle	Inchoative
Divide/banT-naa	baanT diyaa	baanT diyaa gayaa	banTtaa	banTaa
Tie/bandh-naa	baandh diyaa	baandh diyaa gayaa	bandhtaa	bandhaa
Print/chhap-naa	chhaap diyaa	chhaap diyaa gayaa	chhaptaa	chhapaa
Cut/kaT-naa	kaaT diyaa	kaaT diyaa gayaa	kaTtaa	kaTaa
Grind/pis-naa	piis diyaa	piis diyaa gayaa	pistaa	pisaa
Beat/piT-naa	piiT diyaa	piiT diyaa gayaa	piTtaa	piTaa
Weigh/tul-naa	tol diyaa	tol diyaa gayaa	tultaa	tulaa

For encyclopedically non-agentive verbs in the null class (i.e. those whose verb meanings are not contingent on the presence of an agent), the same pattern may be observed with only passives retaining the causative morphology. For some predicates like 'die' and 'emerge', however, there are neither any causatives nor passives, as these are essentially non-agentive. The causative and passive forms provided for these predicates in the table below are marked with a question mark since they fail to give the same interpretation as the verbal root.

Table 2. Encyclopedically non-agentive predicates in the null class

Verb	Causative	Passive	Middle	Inchoative
Fall/giR-naa	giR-aa diyaa/ giR-vaa diyaa	giR-aa diyaa gayaa/ giR-vaa diyaa gayaa	giRtaa	giRaa
Dissolve/ghul-naa	ghol diyaa	ghol diyaa gayaa	ghultaa	ghulaa
Die/mar-naa	?maar diyaa (to kill)	?maar diyaa gayaa (to be killed)	?martaa	maraa
Turn/muR-naa	mor diyaa	mor diyaa gayaa	murtaa	muraa
Emerge/nikal-naa	?nikaal diyaa (to throw out)	?nikaal diyaa gayaa (to be turned out)	nikaltaa	niklaa
Boil/ubal-naa	ubaal diyaa	ubaal diyaa gayaa	ubaltaa	ublaa

The same pattern shows up for encyclopedically non-agentive verbs in the AA-class (Table 3), where causatives and passives with 'flow', 'elapse', 'bloom', 'melt' are not allowed.

Table 3. Encyclopedically non-agentive predicates in the AA-class

Verb	Causative	Passive	Middle	Inchoative
Flow/bah-naa	?bahaa diyaa (to float X)	?bahaa diyaa gayaa (to be floated by X)	bahtaa/bah jaataa	bah gayaa
Elapse/bit-naa	?bitaa diyaa (to waste)	bitaa diyaa gayaa (to be wasted)	biittaa	biitaa
Shine/Chamak-naa	chamkaa diyaa	chamkaa diyaa gayaa	chamaktaa	chamkaa
Rock/hil-naa	hilaa diyaa	hilaa diyaa gayaa	hiltaa	hilaa
Bloom/khil-naa	*khilvaa diyaa	*khilvaa diyaa gayaa	khiltaa	khilaa
Melt/pighal-naa	*pighaal diyaa	*pighaal diyaa gayaa	pighaltaa	pighlaa

Finally, for a small class of encyclopedically agentive verbs in the AA-class, the same observations hold, as depicted in Table 4.

Table 4. Encyclopedically agentive predicates in the AA-class

Verb	Causative	Passive	Middle	Inchoative
Save/bach-naa	bachaa diyaa	bachaa diyaa gayaa	bach jaataa	bachaa
Entertain/bahal-naa	bahlaa diyaa	bahlaa diyaa gayaa	bahal jaataa	bahlaa
Unroll/bichh-naa	bichhaa diyaa	bichhaa diyaa gayaa	bichhtaa	bichhaa

In summary, I have illustrated here that Hindi-Urdu middles are not morphologically like passives. An ample amount of data was presented here from different classes to show that passives can also carry causative morphology, while middles and inchoatives cannot. This may indicate that while the former are underlying transitives, with covert external arguments or agents, the latter are derived intransitives, with no projected external argument. The next section is a brief detour on Hindi-Urdu passives, to help us understand these constructions in some more depth.

2.2 More on Hindi-Urdu passives

Passive-causative 'homonymy' is not uncommon cross-linguistically. Languages like Manchu (38)–(39), Chinese (40)–(41) among many others share this property.

(38) *bi* *morin* *be* *ule-bu-me*
1SG.NOM. horse ACC drink-CAUS-IPFV.CNV
'I let the horse drink (water)'.

(39) *tere* *inenggi* *mi-ni* *jakun* *morin* *hulha-bu-fi*
That day 1SG.GEN. eight horse-NOM steal-PASS-PFV.CNV.
'On that day my eight horses were stolen (by bandits)' (Schulze 2011)

(40) *wo* *gei* *ni* *cai* *ge* *miyu*
I give you-SG. guess CL riddle
'I (will) let you guess a riddle.'

(41) *fangzi* *gei* *tufei* *shao* *le*
house give hooligan burn ASP
'The house was burned down by the hooligans.' (Yap & Iwasaki 2003)

In Hindi-Urdu, the causative morphology is carried by the lexical verb in the passive construction, which also has a distinct passive light verb *gayaa* ('go'). Passives and causatives in this language are therefore partially homophonous. One reason for this similarity could be that passives are underlying transitives; they project (overt/covert) external arguments or agents. It has also been noted by Mahajan (1994) that Hindi-Urdu has 'active–passives' which differ from (canonical) passives in other languages in that their (optional) agents are the sentential subjects whereas their objects do not get promoted and remain within the verbal domain. In other words, they pattern more closely with actives rather than passives. Consider how.[2]

First, the external arguments of these constructions can bind anaphors, just like actives (42)–(43).

(42)	*Johnke*$_i$	*dwaaraa*	*apne*$_i$	*gharkaa*	*nirikshan*	*kiyaa*	*gayaa*
	John.GEN.	by	self's	house	inspection	do	go-PASS.

'John inspected his own house.'

(43)	*Johnne*$_i$	*apne*$_i$	*gharkaa*	*nirikshan*	*kiyaa*
	John.GEN.	self's	house	inspection	do

'John inspected his own house.'

Secondly, passives subjects must not co-refer to pronominal objects (44), just like active subjects (45).

(44)	*Johnke*$_i$	*dwaaraa*	*uske*$_{*i}$	*gharkaa*	*nirikshan*	*kiyaa*	*gayaa*
	John.GEN.	by	his	house	inspection	do	go-PASS.

'John inspected his house.'

(45)	*Johnne*$_i$	*uske*$_{*i}$	*gharkaa*	*nirikshan*	*kiyaa*
	John.GEN.	his	house	inspection	do

'John inspected his house.'

These similarities may indicate that 'active-passives' involve vP-structures with external arguments generated in the specifier of vP. These nominals are later moved to the specifier of TP for EPP reasons while the objects receive accusative case from v and remain in situ. A complete vP-structure may also be the reason why passives retain causative (transitive) morphology.

Hindi-Urdu middles (and inchoatives) on the other hand fail to carry causative morphology, suggesting that they are not underlying transitives. More specifically, they are intransitives that fail to host external arguments. If that is indeed true, it is pertinent to ask if the detransitivization operation leading to a middle formation is carried out in the lexicon or is a product of syntactic representations and operations. The first step towards answering this question is to trace the similarities and differences between middles in Hindi-Urdu and other languages. The next few sections address these questions in some detail.

2. Thanks to a reviewer for suggesting a more detailed comparison with 'active-passives'.

3. Middle formation in two modules

As already discussed, middles are of two types: those that stand apart as a class (English, Dutch), and those that look like passives (Romance languages, Greek). We discuss some of their defining characteristics below. Our primary task is to examine the type Hindi-Urdu middles best fit into.

We start with English and Dutch middles which do not resemble their passives. Their middles do not exhibit any special morphology (46)–(47). However, while English reflexives also remain unmarked (48), Dutch reflexives have a special deficient pronoun 'zich' (49).[3]

(46) This dress washes easily.

(47) *Dit hemd wast goed*
'This shirt washes well.'

(48) He washes.

(49) *Hij wast zich*
He washes himself
'He washes himself.'

Hindi-Urdu, as we have already seen, does not have any special middle morphology; middle verbs are marked with an imperfect, habitual *-taa* morpheme. It therefore patterns closely with English/Dutch type of languages, though when it comes to reflexive constructions, it requires a special pronoun (50).

(50) *usne apne aapko dhoyaa*
he-ERG self-ACC wash
'He washed himself.'

Note that in the second type of languages, where middles carry passive morphology, a reflexive *-si* morpheme is often used. An illustration from Italian is repeated in (51).

(51) *Questo tavolino si transporta facilmente*
this table SI transports easily
'This table transports easily.'

Secondly, in both Dutch and English, middles are unacceptable with recipient goals (see Hoekstra & Roberts 1993; Fagan 1992 for similar observations). Therefore while sentences (52)–(54) are good with locative goals or without goals in general, they are unacceptable with overt recipient goals (55)–(56).

3. See Abraham (1995) for interesting insights into West Germanic middles, where he also suggests a syntactic analysis for middle constructions in the language.

(52) Big presents don't sell easily.

(53) Big presents don't send easily to foreign countries.

(54) *Lange verhalen vertellen niet germakkelijik* (Dutch)
'Long stories don't tell easily.'

(55) *Big presents don't ship friends easily.

(56) **Lange verhalen vertellen niet gemakkelijik aan kinderen* (Dutch)
'Long stories tell not easily to children.'

Hindi-Urdu exhibits variations with different predicates. With a middle sentence involving a ditransitive 'sell' (57), while locative goals are fine (58), recipient goals yield unacceptability (59).

(57)

sunder	*khilone*	*aasaanii-se*	*(nahii)*	*bikte*	*hain*
beautiful	toys	easily	(not)	sell-mid.	be

'Beautiful toys (not) sell easily.'

(58)

sunder	*khilone*	*duusre*	*desho-me*	*aasaanii-se*	*(nahii)*	*bitke*	*hain*
beautiful	toys	foreign	nations-to	easily	(not)	sell-mid.	be

'Beautiful toys (don't) sell easily in foreign nations.'

(59)

**sunder*	*khilone*	*baccoko*	*aasaanii-se*	*(nahii)*	*bitke*	*hain*
beautiful	toys	children-to	easily	(not)	sell-mid.	be

'Beautiful toys (don't) sell easily to children.'

Middle formation is however infelicitous with ditransitives 'send' with or without locational goals (60). Ditransitives 'tell' and 'rent' are also barred from middle formation (61)–(62). These predicates cannot take middle forms.

(60)

**sunder*	*khilone*	*aasaanii-se*	*(baccoko)*	*(nahii)*	*bhejte*	*hain*
beautiful	toys	easily	(children-to)	(not)	send-mid.	be

'Beautiful toys don't send easily (to children).'

(61)

**lambii*	*kahaanii*	*aasaanii-se*	*(baccoko)*	*(nahii)*	*bataate*	*hain*
long	stories	easily	(children-to)	(not)	tell	be

'Long stories are (not) easily told (to children).'

(62)

**achche*	*ghar*	*aasaanii-se*	*(chhatroko)*	*(nahii)*	*bhaRte*	*hain*
good	houses	easily	(students-to)	(not)	rent-mid.	Be

'Good houses are (not) easily rented out (to students).'

The second type of middle-languages like Italian and Serbo-Croatian, on the other hand, allow middles with ditransitives, where the indirect (recipient goal) also surfaces overtly. The following Serbo-Croatian Example (63) taken from Marelj (2004) illustrates the difference.

(63) *Skupi stanovi se ne izdaju lako studentima*
expensive apartments se not rent easily students-dative
'Expensive apartments are not easily rented out to students.'

A third defining feature of the first type of middle-languages is that middle formation remains confined to a restricted set of predicates. Middles with statives are generally bad in English and Dutch as sentences (64)–(66) display.

(64) *Fierce enemies hate easily.

(65) *Good children love easily.

(66) **Zulke mensen haten germakkelijk*
'Such people hate easily.'

Hindi-Urdu too cannot form middles with stative predicates like 'hate', 'love', as illustrated in (67)–(68).

(67) **dushman aasaanii-se nafrate hain*
enemies easily hate-MID. be
'Enemies hate easily.'

(68) **bacce aasaanii-se pyaarte hain*
children easily love-MID be
'Children love easily.'

This restriction also ensues from the Affectedness Constraint, where the term 'affectedness' is understood as either change of location (i.e. motion) or change of state.; "(t)he argument that is specified as 'caused to change in the main event of a verb's semantic representation is linked to the grammatical object" (Gropen, et al. 1992, p. 159). In many works on middles, Jaeggli's (1986) account of affectedness plays a crucial role.

(69) Affectedness Constraint
If a complement of x is unaffected, it is impossible to eliminate the external theta role.

Jaeggli states that a thematic relation holding between an affected complement and its predicate is always 'well defined', by virtue of being independent of the thematic relation holding between the predicate and its external argument. Such a 'well-defined' thematic relation is absent when unaffected objects are involved, whose interpretation is thematically contingent on the interpretation of the subject. Both 'love' and 'hate' in English and Dutch have unaffected complements, and since middle formation involves elimination of the external role, the complements are left without any interpretation. This explains why stative predicates fail the middle formation rule in these languages. This restriction does not hold in the other set of languages. Take the Serbo-Croatian example in (70).

(70) *Dobra deca se lako vole*
nice children se love easily
'It is easy for one/people, in general to love good children.'

In summary, Hindi-Urdu seems to pattern very closely with the first type of middle languages, where middles and passives do not overlap morphologically. There are four crucial characteristics of these middles: (a) they are not marked with distinct middle morphology, (b) they are good with locational goals, but not with recipient goals, (c) stative predicates do not undergo middle formation and (d) only predicates with affected themes undergo middle formation.

3.1 A two-modular approach and its problems

Marelj (2004) suggests that differences between middle constructions emerge from the locus of the middle formation rule that detransitivizes the predicate. The two loci are the two modules – lexicon and syntax. Some languages manipulate the arity (middle) changing operation in the lexicon; others do it in the syntax. The lexicon languages (English, Dutch) have intransitive predicates introduced into the narrow syntax and hence display properties that are distinct from their passives which undergo detransitivization in the syntax. The syntax languages (Romance languages, Serbo-Croatian) on the other hand detransitivize both middle and passive predicates in the syntax, and hence the two show up with similar morphological forms. Lexicon middles and syntax middles also have varied syntactic behaviour. The technical details of the two-modular account are provided below, along with some of its problems.

Marelj observes that middles across languages have an implicit argument that is interpreted as ARB with a +human flavor, though the mechanisms for arriving at it are different for the lexicon and the syntax languages. Lexicon languages have a middle formation operation that utilizes the ARB role; the variable of ARB-role is not x but x-arb; i.e. the Arbitrarization is of a cluster.[4] Unlike lexical operations, syntax cannot manipulate the content of a cluster. Hence, for syntax languages, the ARB reading is obtained via a kind of variable binding or ARB-binding. The variable introduced by Arbitrarization comes with a built-in domain restriction,

4. Marelj follows Reinhart (2000, 2002) in claiming that arity operations are parametrized to occur either in the syntax or the lexicon. Further, theta-roles are constituted of formal features, which also govern theta-selection and linking/mapping operations. Each theta-role is taken as a feature cluster (of 'c' = cause, 'm' = has a mental state) as illustrated below.

(1) (a) [+c, +m] = agent
(b) [−c, +m] = experiencer
(c) [+c, −m] = instrument/cause
(d) [−c, −m] = affected patient/theme

indicated by a special subscript arb, which ranges over groups of people. ARB-saturation ensures that the saturated role in syntax languages is interpreted as ARB with a +human flavor. This operational difference for the two types of languages (English (71) versus Serbo-Croatian (72)) is illustrated respectively in (73)–(74).

(71) Tristram Shandy reads easily.

(72) *Tristram shendi se lako chita*
Tristram Shandy se ready easily.

(73) Gen, e, x-arb [reading (e) & [–c, –m] (e, Tristram Shandy) & [ ] (e, x-arb)] [easy (e, x-arb)]

(74) Gen, e, x-arb [reading (e) & [–c, –m] (e, Tristram Shandy)) & [+c, +m] (e, x-arb) [easy (e, x-arb)]

Therefore though English uses (73) for manipulating the internal content of the cluster [+c, +m], and Serbo-Croatian uses (74) with variable-binding, their middles are similarly interpreted as expressing the generic property of events of 'reading Tristam Shandy by any arbitrary person'. Syntax also cannot change saturated [+m] roles. Hence one may find the objects of stative verbs realized as in Serbo-Croatian with ARB-bound agents (see (75)). However, these middles would still be unable to license instrumental phrases since though the [+m] roles remain unavailable for syntactic purposes; they are interpretatively equivalent to their syntactically realized counterparts (76).

(75) *Neprijatni ljudi se lako mrzi (*nozem)*
'Unpleasant people se easily hate (*with a knife).'

(76) *Maks mrzi neprijatne ljude (*nozem)*
'Max hates unpleasant people (*with a knife).'

Further, the middle formation operation in the lexicon also manipulates the [/+c] cluster, creating an empty list, i.e., a [ ] which co-occurs only with fully specified clusters. A [–c] cluster is one of the instantiations of this unspecified cluster. Therefore the middle entries of verbs like 'teach' and 'sell' are different from their base entries, prompting arguments with the [–c] cluster from disappearing in middle constructions. Take for instance the following sentences (77)–(78), which can appear with all three arguments with their base (ditransitive) entries. Since lexicon languages manipulate [/+c] clusters, the goal arguments with these feature clusters cannot appear in middles, as shown by the unacceptability of (79)–(80).

(77) Peter taught children [–c] these ideas.

(78) Peter sold some sweets to Mary [–c].8

(79) *These children [–c] teach easily.

(80) *Sweets sell easily to children [–c].

Syntactic languages are incapable of manipulating feature clusters. Therefore the prediction is that all co-realizable clusters of the verb-entry can co-realize in the middle derivation as well. We have already witnessed that this is true; Serbo-Croatian, as many other syntax languages, allows arguments with [−c] feature cluster to co-appear with other arguments (81).

(81) *Skupi* *stanovi* *se* *ne* *izdaju* *lako* *studentima*
expensive apartments se not rent easily students-dative
'Expensive apartments are not easily rented out to students.'

Though appealing, the two-module approach to middle formation has its own problems. There is of course the 'methodological minimalism' question: why should the grammar allow two modules to undertake the same function? If middle formation can happen in the lexicon, why should syntax be given the extra burden of forming the same construction, albeit via different mechanisms? Secondly, there is the language acquisition problem: how do children learning different languages know which parameter to set for their respective languages. The parameter in question here is the one proposed by Reinhart and Siloni (2005), and stated below as in (82).

(82) The Lex-Syn Parameter
UG allows thematic arity operations to apply in the Lexicon or in Syntax.

A parameter like (82) works only when the child can glean from the positive data around her that verb alternations in her language are based in the lexicon and not in the syntax. That of course, is pretty difficult in this particular case since nothing in the morphological forms suggests anything different. One deciding factor could be the productive nature of middles, but that too is unclear since languages like Hindi-Urdu may be productive with one class of verbs, but not with another. Take for instance, the lack of Hindi-Urdu middles with stative predicates. This could be taken as an indicator that the language patterns closely with lexicon languages. Yet, if one were to look closely at the AA and null-class of causative-inchoative alternating verbs (Tables 1–4), a very different picture emerges. Middles are possible with most of the verbs listed in the four categories.

Moreover, though middle morphology may not surface on stative verbs, there are other ways of getting generic, property-like interpretations for the same predicates.

(83) *bacco-se* *aasaanii-se* *pyaar* *ho* *jaataa* *hain*
children-with easily love become go be
'It is easy to fall in love with children.'

(84) *dushmano-se aasaanii-se nafrat ho jaatii hain*
enemies easily hate become go be
'It is easy to hate enemies.'

These sentences, just like middles and unlike passives, also cannot control into purpose clauses and take agentive adverbials.

(85) **bacco-se [prashansaa paane ke liye] pyaar ho*
children-with praise get gen. for love become
jaataa hain
go be
'It is easy to fall in love with children in order to be praised by others.'

(86) **bacco-se jaanbhuujkar pyaar ho jaataa hain*
children-with intentionally love become go be
'It is easy to fall in love with children intentionally.'

These characteristics indicate that Hindi-Urdu middle/generic property statements can also be manifested without the proto-typical middle morphology. In that case, middle constructions are not as restricted in number in this language, as initially understood. We also find similar formations with verbs like 'translate' (87), which cannot otherwise have the canonical middle form (88).

(87) *Hindi-Urdu aasaanii-se anuvaad ho jaatii hain*
Hindi-Urdu easily translate become go be
'Hindi-Urdu gets translated easily.'

(88) **Hindi-Urdu aasaanii-se anuvaadtii hain*
Hindi-Urdu easily translate be
'Hindi-Urdu gets translated easily.'

Further, sentences like (89) show that these constructions can also host instrumental phrases, with the meaning that 'Hindi-Urdu poems have the property of being translated easily, not for any arbitrary person, but for John.' Compare this with the next sentence (90), which also displays an instrumental phrase 'with strong winds' with a canonical middle construction with the predicate 'sink', suggesting that even though certain predicates in Hindi-Urdu cannot appear with middle morphology, they can form property-like statements – albeit with different morphology – that share many syntactic properties with canonical middles.

(89) *Johnse Hindi-Urdu ki kavitaayen aasaanii-se anuvaad ho*
John-with Hindi-Urdu GEN. poems easily translate become
jaate hain
go be
'Hindi-Urdu poems are easily translated by John.'

(90) *tez hawaa-se jahaaz aasaanii-se Dubte hain/Dub jaate hain*
strong wind-with ship easily sink be/sink go be
'Ships sink easily with strong winds.'

A final problem with the two-modular approach is that it predicts that arguments with [–c] clusters in ditransitives will disappear in middles formed in the lexicon. This means that ditransitive middles are possible in lexicon languages, but without recipient goals. However, as we have seen, Hindi-Urdu disallows middle formation with most ditransitives. The only exception is the verb 'sell' which has a felicitous middle form (91), but without the recipient goal (92).

(91) *sundar khilone aasaanii-se (nahii) bikte hain*
beautiful toys easily (not) sell-mid. be
'Beautiful toys (not) sell easily.'

(92) **sundar khilone baccoko aasaanii-se (nahii) bikte hain*
beautiful toys children-to easily (not) sell-mid. be
'Beautiful toys (don't) sell easily to children.'

The same predicate can also appear with the non-canonical middle morphology (93).

(93) *sundar khilone aasaanii-se bik jaate hain*
beautiful toys easily sell go be
'Beautiful toys sell easily.'

Notice however that ditransitives like 'send', which are infelicitous with the canonical middle (94), also fail to appear with the non-canonical middle morphology (95).

(94) **sunder khilone aasaanii-se (baccoko) (nahii) bhejte hain*
beautiful toys easily (children-to) (not) send-mid. be
'Beautiful toys don't sell easily (to children).'

(95) **sundar khilone aasaanii-se bhej jaate hain*
beautiful toys easily send go be
'Beautiful toys are sent easily.'

Thus, the two-modular approach and the feature-cluster analysis fail to explain the restriction on ditransitive middle formation in Hindi-Urdu. There must be certain verb-specific features of 'sell' that make it acceptable to middle formation, which are absent in 'send' simply classifying them as ditransitive predicates in not enough. Wherever the detransitivization operation happens – whether in the lexicon or in the syntax – particular semantic features of these verbs must be taken into account, a topic I leave open for future research.

From the foregoing discussion, I conclude that relegating middle differences to the lexicon or the syntax is not a desirable analysis. First, it undermines concerns of methodological minimalism. Second, it is not clear that the characteristics of the lexicon middle constructions are completely at odds with those of the syntax middle constructions. What at least prima facie appear to be lexicon middle languages, on closer probe, turn out to have some overlapping properties with the syntax middle languages. In light of this, keeping a two-modular difference between middles does not seem to be completely justified.

4. A syntactic alternative

I now suggest a different analysis for middles, one which does not base itself on the lexicon-syntax dichotomy. It is a pure syntactic account, where middle formation is taken to follow from narrow syntactic operations. There are no lexicon-centric computations that give rise to a different sub-type of middles in some languages. As a prelude to the syntactic alternative, let me elaborate on some important structural properties of middles that usually go unnoticed in the literature. These are the telicity effects that indicate that subjects in middles are actually derived objects, much like canonical passives (as in English). Well-known differences between middles and passives must therefore arise from structural differences other than those concerned with derived subjects.

Let me begin with Borer's (2003) use of telicity diagnostics with direct objects. As one can observe below, (96) with a direct object has an accomplishment/telic interpretation and can co-occur with telicity phrases like 'in ten minutes', a reading that is impossible when the object appears as a PP (97).

(96) I ate the cake (in ten minutes).

(97) I ate at the cake (*in ten minutes).

Adding direct objects facilitates telicity readings in other sentences as well, as illustrated below.

(98) Bill ran for five minutes/*in five minutes.

(99) Bill ran the mile *for five minutes/in five minutes.

(100) Terry sang for an hour/*in an hour.

(101) Terry sang a ballad ?for an hour/in an hour.

Similar telicity effects are also available with middles, as illustrated below in the English (102)–(103) and Hindi-Urdu (104)–(105) sentences. Note that this reading is possible only when instrumental phrases are not present.

(102) The boat sinks easily in five minutes

(103) Latin texts read easily (*for Bill) in five minutes.

(104) *jahaaz *paanch minute tak/paanch minute-me samundar-me*
ships five minutes for/five minute-in ocean-in
aasaanii-se Dubte hain
easily sink-mid be
'Ships sink easily in the ocean *for five minutes/in five minutes.'

(105) *sundar khilone aasaanii-se *paanch minute tak/paanch minute-me*
beautiful toys easily *five minutes for/five minute-in
bikte hain
sell-mid be
'Beautiful toys sell easily *for five minutes/in five minutes.'

Interestingly, unergatives, which middles in some languages resemble (see Lekakou 2002, 2005), do not entertain telicity adverbials, as evidenced by the unacceptable sentences (106)–(107).

(106) *Babies laugh easily in five minutes.

(107) *Leopards jump easily in five minutes.

Hindi-Urdu unergatives show similar behavior, as can be attested by the following sentences.[5]

(108) *?bacce paanch minute-me has paRte hain*
children five minute-in laugh fall be
'Children start laughing in five minutes.'

(109) **bacce paanch minute-me kuud paRte hain*
children five minutes-in jump fall be
'Children start jumping in five minutes.'

5. A reviewer provides the following sentence to show that unergatives like 'laugh' can sometimes license telic adverbials.

(i) *bacce paanch minute me haste he, paanch minute me rote he.*
children five minute in laugh be, five minute in cry be
'Children start laughing in five minutes and start crying in five minutes.'

While (i) is felicitous, it may be one of the few exceptions with unergative predicates in the Hindi-Urdu variety/dialect I am considering. Unergatives like 'jump' cannot improve their acceptability by similar means/structures.

These sentences suggest that unergatives are pure intransitives in that they project only an external argument. There are no internal arguments in these constructions to license telic readings, unlike what we have already observed for middles.

Having established that middle predicates are not like unergatives and have internal arguments, we now proceed to an adequate representation for them. Consider Borer's (2003) underlying structure in (110) for all action verbs, which we wish to utilize for middles as well.

(110)

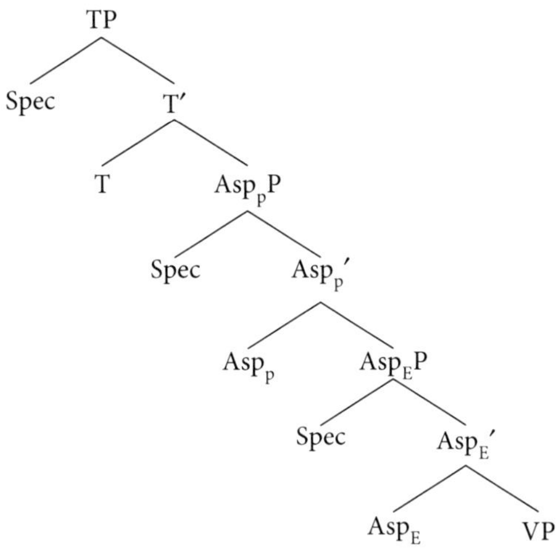

According to Borer, AspP projections are very significant determinants for the event semantics of action verbs. The specifiers of each of these heads (when projected) must be filled by some argument, which subsequently receives a specific type of event structure semantics. The argument that fills the specifier of the lower AspP head is attributed the 'object of result' reading; i.e. there is an event, which results into a state whose theme is the nominal occupying that position. The argument in the specifier of the higher AspP gets the 'object of process' reading, which most often coalesces with the subject argument of the sentence.

Following Borer, I posit two Asp heads for a middle representation (111). I assume that the object of the verb ('ship' as in 'the ship sinks easily') base-generates as sister to V and lands in the specifier of Asp$_E$P, receiving the 'object of result' (theme) semantics. This may be followed by a second instance of object-raising in some languages, this time targeting the specifier of Asp$_p$P to finally land in the specifier of TP position for case/agreement reasons. However, the higher Asp head is optional, with some languages choosing not to project it at all. In such languages, the object moves directly to the specifier of TP.

(111)

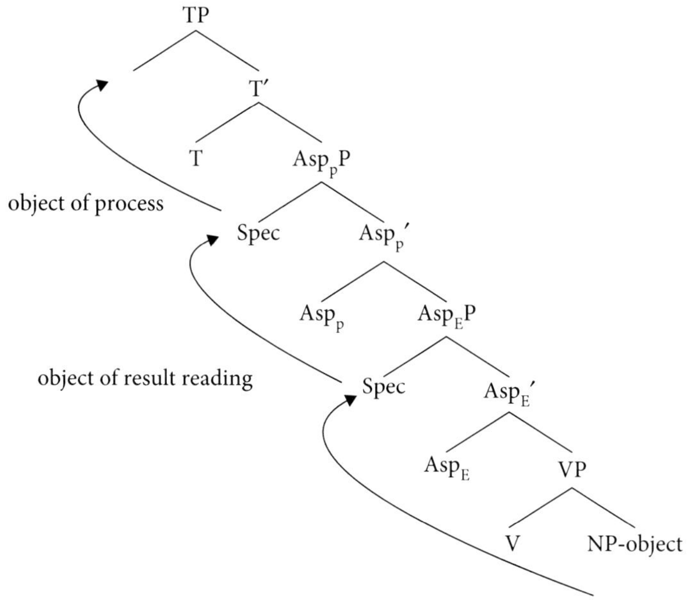

In effect, what I claim is that middle voice has two different manifestations – one with the double AspP projections and the other without the higher AspP head. Languages can choose one of these options and depending on the choice they make, their middle forms may resemble the passive forms. I provide the details below.

4.1 More on overlap with passives

I assume with Alexiadou and Doron (2007) that there are two kinds of non-active voice: middle and passive. The middle allows the non-insertion of v (Asp_pP), instead reclassifying the rootP (VP) with respect to its requirement for an external argument. Only an internal argument is introduced inside the rootP (112).

(112) $[_{TP}$ $[_{AspEP}$ $[_{VP}$ Internal Argument]]] → Middles

The passive voice head on the other hand, requires the insertion of v (Asp_p, hosting the en-morpheme), and modifies the thematic relation of Agent. It fails to manipulate the root, but instead modifies the head v introducing an additional external argument, and reclassifies such an argument as agent. Schematically, (113):

(113) $[_{TP}$ $[_{AsppP}$ External Argument $[_{Aspp}$ -en $[_{AspEP}$ $[_{VP}$ Internal Argument]]]]]
→ Passives

Note that these two (different) representations are allowed for languages that bar the projection of the higher Asp head for middles. Their middles will not be generated like passives, which are underlying structures like (113). These two constructions will therefore surface with different morphologies. Hindi-Urdu, English, Dutch are some of the languages that fall under this category.

Middles of this class of languages will have syntactic characteristics directly falling out from their underlying representations. Since the higher aspectual head is absent, they will not be able to license agentive adverbials. Their truncated clause structures will also disable them from hosting all three arguments of most ditransitives. Finally, statives may also be licensed with additional light verb heads (see Section 3.1 for a detailed exposition of alternative constructions with middle/generic/property interpretations).

Our analysis also has a simple answer for the passive-causative alternation we witness for Hindi-Urdu. Since the underlying form of a passive is a fully elaborated Asp_pP (vP) structure that hosts an external argument, just like any transitive construction, it carries with it the original transitive/causative morphology along with the extra passive light verb 'gayaa' (*go*). However for middles, this possibility does not arise – they fail to project the head that can host an external argument and hence they are structurally different from transitives/causatives.

For Hindi-Urdu passives (or more correctly, 'active-passives'), we can assume that the external argument hosted in the higher Asp projection blocks the movement of the lower argument or object. Since the external argument is closer to the T probe, it moves to its specifier for EPP reasons. This explains why active-passives in the language have their external arguments as subjects, unlike English passives where objects raise to the subject position. The passive 'gayaa' (go) is an independent light verb and generated on the higher aspectual head.

The difference between passives in English and Hindi-Urdu, following Collins (2005), Sahoo (in progress) and Chandra and Sahoo (2013), is that English smuggles the lower AspP involving the object over the external argument. This makes the object a closer goal to probe T, thus enabling it to move to T's specifier for EPP reasons. Suppose we also assume that there is an *en*-morpheme (adopted from Baker, Johnson & Roberts 1989, but without its argument status and theta/case receiving properties) that comes along on the higher aspectual head marking non-active passive voice. This *en*-morpheme will then move up to the verbal node (instead of lowering) since smuggling would have elevated the lower node to a higher position.

For the second class of languages (Romance languages, Greek, Serbo-Croatian) that involve an overlap between middles and passives, these two constructions will have underlying similarities. Unlike what we observe for the previous language class, all aspectual heads along with other relevant heads must be projected for both constructions. A single underlying representation must then give rise to these two different constructions and with different syntactic characteristics. Also note that they both have the non-active/passive -en morpheme. Schematically (114)–(115).

(114) $[_{TP} [_{AsppP} [_{Aspp}$ -en] $[_{AspEP} [_{VP}$ Internal Argument]]]] → Middles

(115) $[_{TP} [_{AsppP}$ External Argument $[_{Aspp}$ -en] $[_{AspEP} [_{VP}$ Internal Argument]]]]
→ Passives

As shown above, middles and passives have similar clause structures. In middles, the internal argument is introduced in the specifier of the lower AspP. The higher Asp head, though projected, is left empty and can be used by the lower argument as an intermediate landing site to move over the specifier of TP. The higher head will also have an *-en* morpheme. Passives have the same clause structure, with one crucial difference. They have an external argument base-generated in the specifier of the higher Asp head. Identical clause structures of middles and passives lie at the root of the homophonous morphology they share in this category of languages.

These languages derive their passives just like English. The internal argument will be smuggled over the external argument that enables it to move over to the specifier of TP. The *en*-morpheme will then move to the raised verbal head, giving rise to a passive construction. For their middles however, though the underlying representation will be that of a passive, there will be no external argument. Since the *en*-morpheme is not an argument, it fails to block the movement of the sole argument (object), which will eventually move over to T's specifier without the need to smuggle the entire RootP or VP. The *en*-morpheme can then lower down to the verbal head.

Importantly, it is the presence of the *en*-morpheme and the higher aspectual projection that dictates the morphology component to give a passive look to the middles in these languages. English and Hindi-Urdu do not have that extra aspectual projection for their middles and therefore create middles without passive morphology. Romance languages and Serbo-Croatian have it and therefore their middles are passive look-alikes. Underlying clause structural similarities also give way to variant syntactic behavior. While we have seen that middles in the first type of languages cannot support agentive adverbials and ditransitives due to truncated clause structures, those in the second type can do both. The higher Asp head that generally hosts external arguments, though empty for these languages, suffices to license agentive adverbials. Similarly, elaborate clause structures will be able to host all arguments of ditransitives.

5. Conclusion

To conclude, I have tried to show here that cross-linguistic differences in middle constructions do not find a proper explanation in the two-modular analysis. The thesis that languages which do not have productive middle formation must manipulate argument structures of their predicates in the lexicon, in contrast to those where middle formation is productive and hence must undertake the operation in the syntax, loses most of its appeal when we take up middles in Hindi-Urdu. This language seems to pattern more closely with the lexicon languages, and yet on closer probe, turns out to be quite productive in forming generic-middle like statements, using non-canonical middle morphology. Moreover, even though there is no middle-passive morphological overlap in this language, one can still adhere to pure syntactic processes to draw out the differences. The analysis presented above bases itself on a difference between non-active voices. Languages may opt for the same non-active voice (passive) for both middle and passive constructions or choose different non-active voices for them. This allows them to have either similar or different clause structural representations for both constructions. Similar clause-structural representations lead to middle-passive morphological overlaps in some languages. Hindi-Urdu is a language that goes for the second option and hence it produces middles that are not passive look-alikes.

References

Abraham, Werner. 1995. Diathesis: The middle, particularly in West-Germanic. What does reflexivization have to do with valency reduction? In *Discourse Grammar and Typolog*, W. Abraham, T. Givón & S. Thompson (eds), 3–47. Amsterdam: John Benjamins.

Alexiadou, Artemis & Doron, Edit. 2007. The syntactic construction of two non-active voices: Passive and middle. Paper presented at *GLOW XXX Workshop: Global Selective Comparison*, University of Tromso.

Baker, Mark, Johnson, Kyle & Roberts, Ian. 1989. Passive arguments raised. *Linguistic Inquiry* 20: 219–251.

Bhatt, Rajesh & Embick, David. 2003. Causative derivations in Hindi. http://people.umass.edu/bhatt/papers/bhatt-embick-caus.pdf (2003)

Borer, Hagit. 2003. Exo-skeletal and endo-skeletal explanations. In *The Nature of Explanation in Linguistic Theory*, J. Moore & M. Polinsky (eds), 1–35. Chicago: CSLI and University of Chicago Press.

Chandra, Pritha & Sahoo, Anindita. 2013. Passives in South Asian languages. *Acta Linguistica Asiatica* 3: 9–27.

Cinque, Guglielmo. 1988. On si constructions and the theory of arb. *Linguistic Inquiry* 19(4): 521–581.

Cinque, Guglielmo. 1995. *Italian Syntax and Universal Grammar*. [Cambridge Studies in Linguistics 77]. Cambridge: Cambridge University Press.

Collins, Chris. 2005. A smuggling approach to the passive in English. *Linguistic Inquiry* 36(2): 289–297.

Fagan, Sarah. 1992. *The Syntax and Semantics of Middle Constructions: A Study with Special Reference to German*. Cambridge: Cambridge University Press.

Gropen, Jess, Pinker, Steven, Hollande, Michelle & Goldberg, Richard. 1992. Affectedness and direct objects: The role of lexical semantics in the acquisition of verb argument structure. *Cognition* 41: 153–195.

Hoekstra, Teun & Roberts, Ian. 1993. Middle construction in Dutch and English. In *Knowledge and Language* 2, E. Reuland & W. Abraham (eds), 183–220. Dordrecht: Kluwer Academic Publishers.

Jaeggli, Osvaldo. 1986. Passive. *Linguistic Inquiry* 17: 587–622.

Lekakou, Marika. 2002. Middle semantics and its realization in English and Greek. *UCL Working Papers in Linguistics* 14: 399–416.

Lekakou, Marika. 2005. In the Middle, Somewhat Elevated. The Semantics of Middles and Its Crosslinguistic Realization. PhD Dissertation, University of London.

Mahajan, Anoop. 1994. Active passive. In Proceedings of the *Thirteenth West Coast Conference on Formal Linguistics*, R. Aronovich, W. Byrne, S. Preuss & M. Senturia (eds), Stanford University: CSLI Publications.

Marelj, Marijana. 2004. *Middles and Argument Structure across Languages*. Utretch: LOT.

Reinhart, Tanya. 2000. The theta system: Syntactic realization of verbal concepts. In *OTS Working Papers in Linguistics*. Utrecht: OTS.

Reinhart, Tanya. 2002. The theta system: An overview. *Theoretical Linguistics* 28: 229–230.

Reinhart, Tanya & Siloni, Tal. 2005. The lexicon-syntax parameter: Reflexivization and other arity operations. *Linguistic Inquiry* 36: 389–436.

Sahoo, Anindita. In progress. Passives in South Asian Languages: A Comparative Study. PhD Dissertation, Indian Institute of Technology Delhi.

Schulze, Wolfgang. 2011. On instances of causative/passive homonymy. http://schulzewolfgang.de/material/causative%20and%20passive.pdf (2011)

Sioupi, Athina. 1998. The typology of middle constructions, ergative verbs and passive voice: How similar are they after all? In Proceedings of the *12th International Symposium on Theoretical and Applied Linguistics*, S. Lambropoulou (ed.), 159–170. Thessaloniki: University Studio Press.

Tsimpli, Ianthi M. 1989. On the properties of the passive affix in Modern Greek. *UCL Working Papers in Linguistics* 1: 236–261.

Yap, Foong H. & Iwasaki, Shoichi. 2003. From causative to passive: A passage in some East and Southeast Asian languages. In *Cognitive Linguistics and Non-Indo-European Languages* [Cognitive Linguistics Research 18], E. Casad & G. Palmer (eds), 419–446. Berlin: Mouton de Gruyter.

Not so high

The case of causee in South Asian Languages (Hindi, Kashmiri, Punjabi & Manipuri)

Richa Srishti
Central Institute of Indian Languages Mysore

The status of the causee argument in Hindi and other South Asian Languages has been contentious in recent literature as it takes instrumental/ablative Case marker and hence, seems comparable to an instrumental/ablative adjunct (*-se* in Hindi, *athi* in Kashmiri, *tõ:* in Punjabi, and *-nə* in Manipuri). The question is whether the instrumental/ablative Case marker appearing on the causee and on an instrumental adjunct should only receive an analysis of accidental homophony or a more principled analysis between the two is possible? The paper here argues that such an analysis is certainly possible. The instrumental/ablative is an adjunct and in causatives, the causee argument is merged to the Voice head as its specifier (the position involving *-se/athi/tõ:/nə* being valued as a *structural,* rather than a lexical, Case). It is further argued that though, this position is υP-external, i.e. 'high' but not 'high' enough to count as the subject.

Keywords: causative alternation; voice; υP-external; argument/adjunct

1. Introduction

The present paper scrutinizes the status of causee in Hindi and other three South Asian languages – Kashmiri, Punjabi and Manipuri. Its marking by the instrumental/ablative marker has led to some analyses of the causee as an adjunct. Here it is illustrated that the causee in Hindi and in other three languages too is not an adjunct but an argument that occupies a subject-like position outside the υP by Spell-out, merged in the Specifier of VoiceP.

The paper is organized in five sections. The first section provides a brief description of the causative alternation phenomenon in Hindi and other languages. The second section examines the status of causee. The third section analyses the status of instrumental/ablative marked causee vs. pure instruments. The fourth section argues for a Voice analysis of the causative alternation. The fifth and last section concludes the paper with final remarks on the analysis.

1.1 Causative alternation

The causative alternation is a productive morphological construction in South Asian languages (SALs). It is derived by the addition of a suffix to the verb. The causee is introduced and surfaces as instrumental/ablative case marked.[1]

In Hindi, one of the modern Indo-Aryan languages, the causative alternation is a regular morphological process adding the *-wa* suffix to the transitive base and also introduces a causee. The Hindi causee surfaces as instrumental/ablative *-se*[2] marked. It shows reduced 'affectedness'/ little or diminished control over the action:

(1) *somi ru:na-se vanka-ko hə̃swaṯa hɛ*
Somi Runa-INS Vanka-ACC laugh-CAUS-HAB be-PRS
'Somi makes Runa make Vanka laugh.'

Here, though *Runa* is 'making Vanka laugh' but *Somi* is in direct control and *Runa* is only a sort of intermediary. Moreover, the causee can also be left unexpressed.

(2) *somi vanka-ko hə̃swaṯa hɛ*
Somi Vanka-ACC laugh-CAUS-HAB be-PRS
'Somi makes Vanka laugh (through somebody).'

In Kashmiri, another Indo-Aryan language and one of the most prominent Dardic languages, *-na:v* suffix is added to the intransitive base either to form transitive

1. Though, Saksena (1982) and Khokholova (1997) attest the presence of *-ko* causee in Hindi (as raised by a reviewer, too, regarding the study of *-ko* causee), the present paper does not deal with it as it is far too controversial. Consider the following examples,

(1) *maine makaan ko banwaayaa*
I-ERG house ACC make-CAUS-PRF
'I had a house built.' Saksena (1982)

(2) *maine larke ko darwaazaa khulwayaa*
I-ERG boy ACC door open-CAUS-PERF
'I helped the boy to open the door.' Khokholova (1997)

In the above Example (1), the *-ko* marked nominal is not the causee but the object as we can add the actual causee here – maine mohan se makaan ko banwaayaa 'I made Mohan make this house.' Here, the *-se* marked nominal is the causee. For majority of Hindi native speakers, sentence (2) is very awkward. The correct sentence should be with the *-se* causee again – 'maine larke-se darwaazaa khulwaayaa' where the meaning is 'I made the boy open the door.'

2. There does exist a historical reason for the homophonous nature of the relevant suffix (for causees and instrumental adjuncts). Traditionally, Hindi *-se* originally comes from Sanskrit *-səm* which meant 'with.' Generally, it is used as an ablative/instrumental in Hindi, meaning 'with/from' and so, marks the source or means of an action, as in many languages. Moreover, we can find this kind of homophony over and over again cross linguistically. (Miriam Butt, p.c.).

or to the pure transitive base to form the causative. To form causative from the already derived transitive as well as to form the double causative from the already derived causative, the suffix – *na:v* is added again. The causee surfaces as instrumental marked -*ət̪*^{h}*i* and can be left unexpressed too. For example,

(3)	a.	*ram-ən*	*kərɪ-na:v*	*mili*	*ət̪*^{h}*i*	*g*^{h}*ənʈi*
		Ram-ERG	do-CAUS-PFV	Mili	INS	bell
		'Ram made Mili ring the bell/did the bell.'				

b.	*somi*	*chu*	*mohən-əs*	*əsɨ-na:v-an*	
	Somi	be-PRS	Mohan-DAT	laugh-CAUS-PROG	
	'Somi makes Mohan laugh.'				

c.	*somi*	*chu*	*(jokər-əs*	*ət̪*^{h}*i)*	*mohən-əs*	*əsɨ-na:v-an*
	Somi	be-PRS	Jokar-DAT	INS	Mohan-DAT	laugh-CAUS-PROG
	'Somi makes the joker make Mohan laugh.'					

In Punjabi, an Indo-Aryan language, the causative suffix is *-wa* and the causee is marked by the ablative marker *tõ:*.

(4)	*runa-ne*	*mili-tõ:*	*ƙə̃nʈi:*	*vaj-va-yi:*
	Runa-ERG	mili-ABL	bell	ring-CAUS-PRF
	'Runa made Mili ring the bell.'			

Manipuri, a Tibeto-Burman language, employs a uniform strategy for forming causatives by suffixing a morphological causative suffix- hən\-həl to the transitive base. -nə marker is used as an agent as well as an instrumental marke (i.e. thaŋ-nə 'with sword').

(5)	*runa-nə*	*mili-nə*	*bell*	*khiŋ-həl-le*
	Runa-AG	Mili-INS	bell	ring-CAUS-PRF
	'Runa made Mili ring the bell.'			

These facts have prompted a discussion about the grammatical status of the causee as argument or adjunct.

2. The status of the causee

As pointed out in the earlier section, the causee is marked by the instrumental/ablative marker. According to Indian traditional grammarian Panini, there are instances when a *karaka*[3] other than an agent is treated as an agent due to any

3. *Karaka* is a term used to denote a thing which brings about an action and *apadana* denotes point of departure. There are six *karakas* (apadana, sampradana, karana, adhikarana, karman and kartr).

additional meaning it expresses. This can also be equated to the concept developed by DeLancey (1989a) indicating that instrumental marker may be used as an agentive marker through a metaphorical extension of its primary meaning. Hence, we may infer that the instrumental (karana)/ablative (apadana) in causative constructions has such a status. It can express the usual meaning of 'instrument/source' or an additional meaning of 'agent' as well. It can denote manner too.[4] The agentive meaning is expressed in causatives and inabilitative constructions[5] too.

Now we look at the agentive meaning of instrumental/ablative marker in different SA languages.

2.1 Hindi

-se, the instrumental/ablative marker in Hindi appears on the causee as well as the inabilitative passive[6] agents apart from its instrumental and ablative meaning. For example,

(6) a.

ram	*mili-se*	*sonu-ko*	*khilwat̪a*	*hɛ*
Ram	Mili-INS	Sonu-ACC	eat-CAUS-HAB	be-PRS

'Ram makes Mili feed Sonu.'

b.

ram-se	*sonu-ko*	*mara*	*nə̃hĩ*	*gəja*
Ram-INS	Sonu-ACC	beat-PRF	not	PASS-PRF

'Ram was not able to beat Sonu.'

c.

ram	*caku-se*	*kek*	*kat̪t̪a*	*hɛ*
Ram	knife-INS	cake	eat-HAB	be-PRS

'Ram cuts cake with a knife.'

d.

ram	*ghar-se*	*bahar*	*jata*	*hɛ*
Ram	home-ABL	outside	go-HAB	be-PRS

'Ram goes out of home.'

---

4. Ahmed (2009) attests that this is not a fluke of Urdu/Hindi, but that other South Asian languages also use the instrumental for this range of meanings. It seems to be an areal feature in the South Asia *Sprachbund*.

5. The agentive meaning can also be seen in middles (in Sanskrit).

ra:meɳ	*a:mram*	*kʰa:d̪jət̪e*
Ram-INS	mango	eat-MID-PRS

'Ram eats mango.'

6. Hindi and several SALs have another passive construction which conveys the inability of an agent/initiator to initiate the event denoted by the predicate – inabilitative passive (Pandharipande 1981). Other terms for this are – capabilitative passive (Balachandran 1970), passive of incapacity (Hook 1979), inability passive (Davison 1982) and capacity passive (Rosen & Wali 1989).

In the above Example (6a), though *-se* marked, *Mili* is behaving as an intermediate agent to accomplish the particular action of feeding *Sonu* and the causer is *Ram*. (6b) is an example of inabilitative construction where *Ram* is an agent. In Example (6c), the usual meaning of 'instrument' is expressed by *-se* and it denotes the point of departure in (6d).

2.2 Kashmiri

In Kashmiri, there are three instrumental markers – *zaryi/athi* and *sI:t'* but there is clear cut distinction between them. The use of the instrumental *athi/zaryi* is restricted to the animate set as there is the other instrumental marker *sI:t'* that is exclusively used for instruments. For example,

(7) a. *farooq chu shrapch-i sI:t' tsuunth tsaTaan*
Farooq be-PRS knife-OBL with apple cut-HAB
'Farooq cuts the apple with the knife.'

b. *farooq-an karI-na:v reyaz-as athi/*sI:t' ka:m*
Farooq-ERG do-CAUS reyaz-DAT by /*with work
'Farooq made Reyaz do the work/Farooq did the work through Reyaz (literal).'

In (in)abilitative passives, the agent is marked by the instrumental too.

c. *farooq-ni zaryi aav-nI shong-nI*
Farooq-GEN by came-not sleep-INF.OBL
'Farooq was not able to sleep/It was not slept by Farooq (literal).'

2.3 Punjabi

In Punjabi, there is a clear-cut distinction as far as the instrumental and dative are concerned and the important thing to note here is that the causee and the inabilitative passive agents are marked by the ablative marker *tõ:*. For example,

(8) a. *sarbi-ne ram-tõ: kam kar-va-ya*
Sarbi-ERG Ram-ABL work do-CAUS-PRF
'Sarbi made ram do the work.'

b. *sarbi-tõ: kam nai kita gaya*
Sarbi-ABL work not do-PRF go-PRF
'Sarbi was not able to do the work.'

c. *ram ghar-tõ: bahar nikalya*
Ram ghar-ABL outside come-PRF
'Ram came out of/from (literal) the house.'

2.4 Manipuri

In Manipuri, too, the extended use of the instrumental marker -*nə* is attested. For example,

(9) a. *oja-nə angang-nə telangga pai-hal-lam-mi*
teacher-AG child-INS kite fly-CAUS-EVI-DECL
'The teacher made the child fly the kite.'

b. *ram-nə thabaktu touba ngam-lam-de*
Ram-AG work do-to able- EVI-NEG
'Ram was not able to do the work.'

c. *ai-nə heijrang-nə kek kak-le*
I-AG knife-INS cake cut-PRF
'I cut the cake with the knife.'

2.5 Previous analyses of Hindi causative: Causee as an adjunct

Bhatt & Embick (2004) analyze Hindi causatives within the Distributive Morphology framework. They assume that there is no lexicon where the transitive verb could be derived from an intransitive as the basic one and vice-versa. Hence, the verbal alternation for them is syntactic and the existing differences between transitivization and causativization are only due to locality considerations.

Bhatt & Embick (2004) argue that the Hindi causatives involve a passive substructure that is based on the corresponding transitive. In their causative structure, there is an addition of an agent-licensing head *v*[AG] with an external argument in its specifier. This head *v*[AG] takes a passive *v*P as its complement. The passive υP complement is a υP containing a υ[AG] without a Case feature and thus, no DP in the specifier of this head) (see Embick 1997). The reason they state is that since Hindi causee is not obligatory, i.e. not explicitly realised in the embedded event, the embedded *v*[AG]P lacks an external argument. Furthermore, when overt, it has the same case marker that is found in passive agents and hence, it is a passive υP complement.

Bhatt & Embick (2004)'s analysis invites comparisons of Hindi causee with the demoted agent analysis of English *by*-phrases. It also resonates with the earlier view of Hindi causee as an instrumental *se*-marked adjunct that is licensed with an 'intermediate agent/causee' interpretation in the indirect morphological causative using the suffix -*wa* (Masica 1991; Saksena 1982; Kachru 1980; Hook 1979).

Though Ramchand (2008, 2011) too suggests that Hindi causee is an adjunct as it is interpreted as an intermediate agent and is always optional, she argues against the demoted agent analysis of -*se* marked causee in Hindi. She states that in Hindi passive the -*se* phrase does not express the intermediate agent intrepretation and hence, is independent of passivization. According to her, "instrumental marked adjuncts are actually nearly always possible with all verbal forms (interpreted as instruments), it is just their interpretation as intermediate agents that is at stake" in causatives. Ramchand (2011) further refines her analysis of *-se* causee in Hindi and equates it with the standard interpretation of other adverbial modifiers. She claims that "the *-se* adjunct is linguistically always a subevent modifier which introduces a direct, non-volitive cause, the different interpretations it gets is a matter of semantics: implicit encyclopaedic content from a root verb provides conceptual information that makes an intermediate agent interpretation possible/felicitous."

3. Position of the causee

The position of the causee would naturally depend on the fact whether it is considered as an adjunct or an argument. If it is considered as an adjunct, it must not have any role in the argument structure but if it is an agrument, it is present in the argument structure of the causative. As seen above, Bhatt & Embick (2004) and Ramchand (2008, 2011) consider the Hindi causee as an adjunct, hence, no place in the argument structure. Contrary to the previous analysis of Hindi causee, I argue that it is an argument, not an adjunct, occupying a subject-like position in the specifier of VoiceP. Zeroing in to this point, we first examine the control diagnostic by Mohanan (1994) based on her observation that "participial adjuncts in Hindi require their controllers to be grammatical subjects":

(10) A nominal that can control a participial adjunct clause with an obligatory control must be a SUBJ.

(11) *ram-ne mohan-ko [PRO*$_{i/*j}$ *muskurate hue] mara*
Ram-ERG Mohan-ACC laugh-HAB be-PRF hit-PRF
'Ram$_i$ hit Mohan$_j$ while $_{i/*j}$ smiling.'

In the above sentence, the obligatory control is with the subject 'Ram' and not the object 'Mohan.'

Now, let us consider the following example:

(12) *ram-ne ravi-se vijay-ko [___ muskurate hue] bitḤvaya*
Ram-E Ravi-I Vijay-A smile-IMPERF be-NF sit-C-C-PERF
'Ram$_k$ made Ravi$_i$ seat Vijay$_j$ while $_{\_k/*i/*j}$ smiling.' (Mohanan 1994: 128)

As seen in the above example, the *-se* marked causee cannot control into the participial adjunct clause and hence, one can argue that it is an adjunct not an argument according to the Control Diagnostic by Mohanan. But if we probe deeper we find that this inference is erroneous. I will provide evidence that though, the objects cannot control into the participial adjunct clause, it is not only the subject that can control into it, the causee in the causative constructions can also control into the participial adjunct clause:

(13) a. *ram$_i$-ne mina$_j$-se mohən$_k$-ko [PRO$_{i/j/*k}$ k^{h}aṯe*
Ram-ERG Mina-INS Mohan-ACC eat-PRS.PTCP

hue] piʈwaja Hindi
be-PFV hit-CAUS-PRF

'Ram$_i$ made Mina$_j$ hit Mohan$_k$ while PRO$_{i/j/*k}$ eating.'

b. *ram$_i$-ən layɪ-nov mohən$_k$-əs mina$_j$ əṯ^{h}i*
Ram-ERG hit-CAUS-PRF Mohan-DAT Mina INS

[PRO$_{i/j/*k}$ k^{h}eyvan k^{h}eyvan] Kashmiri
eat-PROG eat-PROG

'Ram$_i$ made Mina$_j$ hit Mohan$_k$ while PRO$_{i/j/*k}$ eating.'

c. *Ram-ne$_i$ mina-tõ:$_j$ mohan-nũ:$_k$ [PRO$_{i/j/*k}$ khandya:$_{i/k}$*
Ram-ERG mina-ABL mohan-ACC eating.PTCP

hoya:] kut-va-yaa Punjabi
be-PRF beat-CAUS – PRF

'Ram$_i$ made Mina$_j$ hit Mohan$_k$ while PRO$_{i/j/*k}$ eating.'

d. *ram-nə mina-nə mohan-bu*
Ram-ERG Mina-ERG Mohan-ACC

[PRO$_{i/j/*k}$ ca-ri-ngaida phu-hal-lam-mi Manipuri
eat-PROG-PTCP beat-CAUS-EVI-DECL

'Ram$_i$ made Mina$_j$ hit Mohan$_k$ while PRO$_{i/j/*k}$ eating.'

(14) a. *masʈər ne bəcce se pəṯəŋg [PRO$_{i/j}$ muskuraṯe*
teacher-ERG child-INS kite smile-PRS.PTCP

hue] uɽwai Hindi
be-PRF fly-CAUS-PRF

'The teacher$_i$ made the child$_j$ fly the kite while PRO$_{i/j}$ smiling.'

b. *masʈər$_i$-ən vɨɽɨ-na:v-nav bəccəs$_j$ əṯ^{h}i ganʈɨ brar*
teacher-ERG fly-CAUS-CAUS-PRF child INS kite

[PRO$_{i/j}$ əsan əsan] Kashmiri
smile-PROG smile-PROG

'The teacher$_i$ made the child$_j$ fly the kite while PRO$_{i/j}$ smiling.'

c. *ti:car-ne$_i$ bacce-tõ:$_j$ [PRO$_{i/j}$ muskura:nde hoya:]*
teacher-ERG child-ABL smiling.PTCP be-PRF

pəṯəŋg ud-va:-yi: Punjabi
kite fly-CAUS-PRF

'The teacher$_i$ made the child$_j$ fly the kite while PRO$_{i/j}$ smiling.'

d. *oja-du-nə* *əŋaŋ-du-nə* *teləŋga-du-bu*
teacher-ERG child-INS kite-DST-ACC
[*PRO*$_{i/j}$ *nok-li-ŋəidə* *pai-həl–ləm-mi* Manipuri
smile-PROG-PTCP fly-CAUS-EVI-DECL
'The teacher$_{i}$ made the child$_{j}$ fly the kite while PRO$_{i/j}$ smiling.'

Hindi

(15) a. *ram-ne* *kəmre* *mẽ* *gʰusṱe* *hue* *somi-se* *hə̃sṱe*
Ram-ERG room in enter-PTCP be-PFV Somi-INS smile-PTCP
hə̃sṱe *məheʃ-ko* *piʈwaja*
smile-PTCP Mahesh-ACC hit-CAUS-PRF
'Ram$_{i}$ made Somi$_{j}$ hit Mahesh$_{k}$ while PRO$_{i/j/*k}$ entering the room while PRO$_{i/j/*k}$ smiling.'

Kashmiri

b. *ram*$_{i}$*-ən* *layɪ-na:v-nov* [*PRO*$_{i/j/*k}$ *əsan* *əsan*]
Ram-ERG hit-CAUS-PRF smile-PROG smile-PROG
somi$_{j}$*-əs* *əṱʰi* *məheʃ*$_{k}$*-s* *kəmbrəs* *mənz* *əṱsiṱʰɨy*
Somi-DAT INS Mahesh-DAT room-DAT in enter-PTCP
'Ram$_{i}$ made Somi$_{j}$ hit Mahesh$_{k}$ while PRO$_{i/j/*k}$ entering the room while PRO$_{i/j/*k}$ smiling.'

Punjabi

c. *ram-ne*$_{i}$ *kamre-vicc* [*PRO*$_{i}$ *vaRdeya:* *hoya:*] *somi-tõ:*$_{j}$
ram-ERG room-in entering.part be-PRF somi-ABL
[*PRO*$_{i}$ *hasde* *hasde*] *Mahesh-nũ:* *kut-va-yaa*
smile-PTCP smile-PTCP Mahesh-ACC beat.CAUS.PERF.M.SG
'Ram$_{i}$ made Somi$_{j}$ hit Mahesh$_{k}$ while PRO$_{i/j/*k}$ entering the room while PRO$_{i/j/*k}$ smiling.'

In all the sentences above (13–15), both subject and causee can control into the participial adjunct clause. Furthermore, if we passivize (14), the sentence turns out to be ambiguous – on one interpretation it is the implicit agent which is the controller and on the other, it is the implicit causee:

(16) a. *pəṱəŋg* [*PRO*$_{i/j}$ *muskuraṱe* *hue*] *uɽwai* *gəji* Hindi
kite smile-PRS.PTCP be-PFV fly-CAUS-PFV PASS-PFV.F
'The kite was made to fly while PRO$_{i/j}$ smiling.'

b. *ganʈɨ brar* *ayi* *vɨɽɨ-na:v-na:v–nɨ*
kite come-PST fly-CAUS-PASS
[*PRO*$_{i/j}$ *əsan* *əsan*] Kashmiri
smile-PROG smile-PROG
'The kite was made to fly while PRO$_{i/j}$ smiling.'

c. [PRO$_{i/j}$ *muskura:nde hoya:*] *pət̪əŋg ud-va:-yi: gayi:* Punjabi
smiling.PTCP be-PRF kite fly-CAUS-PRF go-PRF
'The kite was made to fly while PRO$_{i/j}$ smiling.'

Now, I will illustrate that in Hindi as well as in Kashmiri, Punjabi and Manipuri causative constructions, there are three mutually distinct theta positions – agent, causee and patient/theme. Note here that the instrumental/ablative marked causee can *only* be licensed when there is a causative morphology on the verb.

(17) a. **runa-ne mili-se gʰənʈi bəɟa-i* Hindi
Runa-ERG Mili-INS bell ring-TR-PRF.F
'Runa made Mili ring the bell.'

b. *runa-ne mili-se gʰənʈi bəɟ-wa-i*
Runa-ERG Mili-INS bell ring-CAUS-PRF.F
'Runa made Mili ring the bell.'

(18) a. **farooq-an reyaz-as athi khuul kuluf* Kashmiri
Farooq-ERG Reyaz-DAT by open-PRF lock
'Farooq made Reyaz open the lock.'

b. *farooq-an kholI-nov reyaz-as athi kuluf*
Farooq-ERG open-CAUS Reyaz-DAT by lock
'Farooq made Reyaz open the lock.'

(19) a. **runa-ne mili-tõ: ʈ̃ənʈi: vaj-a-yi:* Punjabi
Runa-ERG mili-ABL bell ring-TR-PRF
'Runa made Mili ring the bell.'

b. *runa-ne mili-tõ: ʈ̃ənʈi: vaj-va-yi:*
Runa-ERG mili-ABL bell ring-CAUS-PRF
'Runa made Mili ring the bell.'

(20) a. **runa- nə mili-nə bell khiŋ-le* Manipuri
Runa-ERG Mili-INS bell ring-PRF
'Runa made Mili ring the bell.'

b. *runa-nə mili-nə bell khiŋ- həl-le*
Runa-ERG Mili-INS bell ring-CAUS-PRF
'Runa made Mili ring the bell.'

In all the (a) sentences in (17–20) above, there is the transitive suffix on the verb and a causee as an intermediate agent. These sentences are ungrammatical. On the contrary, all the (b) sentences in (17–20) have a causative suffix on the verb and also a causee, but the sentences are prefectly grammatical. This contrast in grammaticality and the absence/presence of causative morphology on the verb shows that given the dependence of the causee on causative morphology, it does not seem to be an adjunct but actually a part of the argument structure. In other words, the causee is attested only in the presence of the causative suffix, not in the presence of the transitive suffix. The causee is essential as it is needed for the intermediate agent interpretation in the causative construction.

Next, the elision of the causee is not sufficient to guarantee its adjunct status as arguments can also be omitted in Hindi. As (21) shows, the object of the verb 'pəɽʰna' *study* can also be omitted.

(21) *ram (kiṯabẽ) pəɽʰṯa hɛ*
Ram books study-HAB be-PRS
'Ram studies/reads (books).'

Therefore, Mohanan (1994)'s observation that "participial adjuncts in Hindi require their controllers to be grammatical subjects" is attested to be incorrect; at the same time, as we have seen, objects cannot be the controllers. Hence, the diagnostic in (10) should be as below:

(22) A nominal that can control a participial adjunct clause with an obligatory control must be a high argument.

High argument, here, is an argument that is "high" in position, occupying a subject-like position outside the *v*P but below TP.

Now, let us ponder over the agent-like properties of the causee.[7] Dowty (1991) introduced some proto-agent properties of 'agents' –

→ volitional involvement in the event or state
→ sentience (and/or perception) causing an event or change of state in another participant
→ movement (relative to the position of another participant)
→ exists independently of the event

If we consider the above properties, the causee has at least first three properties. Let us consider the following sentences:

(23) *ram ne mohan se sohan ko marwaya*
Ram ERG Mohan INS Sohan ACC kill-CAUS-PRF
'Ram made Mohan kill Sohan.'

(24) *ram ne mohan se sohan ko zabardasti marwaya*
Ram ERG Mohan INS Sohan ACC unwillingly kill-CAUS-PRF
'Ram made Mohan unwillingly kill Sohan.'

7. Richa (2003, 2008) compares Hindi causee agent to Manning (1994)'s 'a-subject.' Manning suggests that we need a class of all arguments that are first on some level of argument structure – he terms these 'a-subjects.' All logical subjects are 'a-subjects', but the compound argument structures that result from derivational operations, like passive and causative, yield additional 'a-subjects.'

If we compare both the sentences above, we will observe that in (23) though the causee is not completely volitional as the matrix subject, there does exist some extent of volitionalty on causee's part. Otherwise, the meaning of the sentence (24) and the sentence (23) will not have much difference as in (24), the causee is 'unwilling' to do the action of 'killing.' Hence, we can infer that the volitionality may not be complete but to a great extent it is present in the event. The causee 'Sohan' also changes the state of the other participant 'Mohan' as 'Sohan' does the action of killing 'Mohan.'

Moreover, the role of the causee in the event is integral (though not always overtly present) and its thematic role is very much needed to the interpretation of the event.

4. The status of instrumental/ablative marked causee vs. instrument

4.1 Hindi

It is also essential to make a distinction between instrumental/ablative marked causee and instrument. Consider the following examples:

(25) *ram-ne caku-sẽ mina-ko mara*
Ram-ERG knife-INS Mina-ACC kill-PRF
'Ram killed Mina with a knife.'

(26) **ram-ne mohən-sẽ mina-ko mara*
Ram-ERG Mohan-INS Mina-ACC kill-PRF
'Ram killed Mina through Mohan.'

(27) *ram-ne mohən-sẽ mina-ko mərwaja*
Ram-ERG Mohan-INS Mina-ACC kill-CAUS-PRF
'Ram made Mohan kill Mina.'

(28) *ram-ne mohən-sẽ caku-sẽ mina-ko mərwaja*
Ram-ERG Mohan-INS knife-INS Mina-ACC kill-CAUS-PRF
'Ram made Mohan kill Mina with a knife.'

The *-se* marked instrument is possible with all verbal forms, whereas the *-se* marked causee is possible only with causatives and (in)abilitatives. Apparently, it seems that the distinction between *-se* marked causee and *-se* marked instrument is along the lines of [± animate], but it is not, as Examples (29–33) below confirm:

(29) *t̪um-ne kəmpjuʈər-se əpni ãnkʰẽ pʰuɽwa lĭ*
You-ERG computer-INS self's eyes break-CAUS take-PRF
'You spoiled your eyes because of the computer.' (Khokhlova 1997: 12)

(30) *t̪um-ne ram-se əpni ãnk^{h}ẽ p^{h}uɽwa li*
You-ERG Ram-INS self's eyes break-CAUS take-PRF
'You got your eyes spoiled through Ram.'

But we cannot say,

(31) **t̪um-ne kəmpjut̪ər-se əpni ãnk^{h}ẽ p^{h}oɽ li*
You-ERG computer-INS self's eyes break-TR take-PRF
'You spoiled your eyes through the computer.'

Neither,

(32) **t̪um-ne ram-se əpni ãnk^{h}ẽ p^{h}oɽ li*
You-ERG Ram-INS self's eyes break-TR take-PRF
'You spoiled your eyes through Ram.'

At this juncture, we can envisage that if we place *-se* marked instrument in place of the *-se* marked causee, it would render the causative construction ungrammatical, not the transitive one.

(33) a. **t̪um-ne sui-se əpni ãnk^{h}ẽ p^{h}uɽwa li*
You-ERG needle-INS self's eyes break-CAUS take-PRF
'You got your eyes spoiled because of/through the needle.'[8]

b. *t̪um-ne sui-se əpni ãnk^{h}ẽ p^{h}oɽ li*
You-ERG needle-INS self's eyes break-TR take-PRF
'You spoiled your eyes with the needle.'

This undoubtedly proves that despite having the same marker *-se*, the causee and the instrument[9] in Hindi are different interpretively, one is an argument and the other is an adjunct. Reflexive binding in Hindi provides syntactic evidence in favour of this argument. It is known that an adjunct cannot bind the reflexive:

(34) *zu:bi-ne [ram-se milkər] əpni kit̪ab li:*
Zoobi-ERG Ram-INS meet-CONJ.PTCP self's book take-PRF.F
'Zoobi took her/*his book after she met Ram.'

8. Ungrammatical only under a causee reading of *sui-se*.

9. The true instrumentals should be the first merge after υ is merged, though the actual surface evidence will be tricky to find. We need to go by the semantic considerations i.e. if an adverb makes reference to agents, it should come in after the agent has been introduced syntactically by the right kind of υ head. But due to so much scrambling present in Hindi, it is trickier to find it (Rajesh Bhatt, p.c.).

On the other hand, the causee can bind the possessive reflexive:

(35) a. *mina$_i$-ne miku$_j$-se əpna$_{i/j}$ d̪ərwaza kʰulwaja*
Mina-ERG Miku-INS self's door open-CAUS-PRF
'Mina made Miku open her/his door.'

b. *ʃivani$_i$-ne rica$_j$-se əpna$_{i/j}$ kəmra saf kərwaja*
Shivani-ERG Richa-INS self's room clean-CAUS-PRF
'Shivani$_i$ made Richa$_j$ open self$_{i/j}$ room.'

This behaviour is not entirely unexpected. It has been observed that arguments that originate in the VP are unable to bind the possessive reflexives – only subjects/external arguments may (Kidwai 1995, 2000; Richa 2003).

(36) *ram$_i$-ne moni$_j$-ko əpni$_{i/j}$ kit̪ab lɔʈai*
Ram-ERG Moni-ACC self's book return-TR.PRF.F
'Ram returned Moni his/*her book.'

As the causee can also bind the possessive reflexive,[10] it appears that these arguments must also be "high" in position. But, the interesting point is that the anti-subject orientation does not hold with the causee arguments, suggesting that it is not really in the "subject" position.

(37) *sara$_i$-ne moni$_j$-se mili$_k$-ko uske$_{*i/j/k}$ gʰər mẽ mərwaja*
Sara-ERG Moni-INS Mili-ACC her house in kill-CAUS-PRF
'Sara$_i$ made Moni$_j$ kill Mili$_k$ in her$_{*i/j/k}$ house.'

This provides substantive evidence that though the causee is in the "high" position, it is not as high as the subject position. In other words, it occupies a "subject-like" position outside the υP by Spellout.

4.2 Kashmiri

As discussed in Section 2.2. Kashmiri has three instrumental markers and one of them (*sI:t'*) is restricted to be used only with instruments and the other two *zaryi/athi* are used exclusively with animate agents. The only difference between *zaryi* and *athi* is that in the passive of a causative construction, the causee agent is marked by *athi* and the matrix subject is marked by *zaryi*.

(38) *reyaaz-ni zaryi aav (farooq-as athi) kuluf khol-na:v-nI*
Reyaz-GEN by came Farooq-DAT by lock open-CAUS-INF.OBL
'The lock was made to open by Reyaz through Farooq.'

10. This sensitivity of binding domain to argument structure is somewhat similar to languages like Inuit (one of the Eskimo-Aleut languages) and Turkish, where both causer and causee can bind the reflexive. In these languages too, first, the transitive stem is causativized and the causee is expressed via some oblique role (See Manning 1994).

Though, the instrument vs agent distinction is present there in Kashmiri, the oblique phrase and its optionality renders its status doubtful as the causee in other languages.

4.3 Punjabi

In Punjabi, the instruments are marked with *na:l* and the ablative can be used for the extended agentive meaning. For example,

(39) a. *ram-ne mina-nũ: cakku-na:l ma:r-ya:*
ram-ERG mina-ACC knife-INS kill-PRF
'Ram killed Mina with a knife.'

b. *ram-ne mohan-tõ: mina- nũ: cakku-na:l mar-va:-ya:*
ram-ERG mohan-ABL mina-ACC knife-INS kill-CAUS-PRF
'Ram made Mohan kill Mina with a knife.'

4.4 Manipuri

In Manipuri, the problem is complex as *-nə* is the ergative marker as well as the intrumental marker. Beside this it can be used with causee too.

(40) a. *ram-nə mina-bu həijraŋ-nə hat-khi*
Ram-ERG Mina-ACC knife-INS kill-CERT
'Ram killed Mina with a knife.'

b. *ram-nə mina-nə mohan-bu hat-həl–ləm-mi*
Ram-ERG Mina-ERG Mohan-ACC kill-CAUS-EVI-DECL
'Ram made Mohan kill Mina.'

Hence, we cannot have

c. **ram-nə mohan-nə mina-bu hat-khi*
Ram-ERG Mohan-ERG Mina-ACC kill-CERT
'Ram killed Mina through Mohan.'

Like Hindi, adjuncts in Manipuri, too cannot bind the reflexives but the causee can.

(41) a. *zoobi-nə məsa-gi lairik-tu ram-bu*
Zoobi-ERG self-GEN book-DST Ram-bu
unə-rəgə lau-rəm-mi Manipuri
meet-CONJ.PTCP take-EVI-DECL
'Zoobi took her/*his book after she met Ram.'

b. *ram-nə moni-nə məsa-gi məmə-bu phu-həl–ləm-mi*
Ram-ERG Moni-INS self-GEN his mother-ACC beat-CAUS-EVI-DECL
'Ram made Moni hit his/her mother.'

5. Voice in the analysis of causative

In the present analysis of the causative configuration, the Voice-based transfer/inheritance proposals of Roberts (2008) has been adopted. Capturing traditional insights (Whorf 1945; Nikolaeva & Tolskaya 2001; Yeon 2002) that hold causative to be a Voice, and assuming the arguments of Pylkkänen (2002) that causativization adds an event layer as well as another argument, it is proposed that causatives like (42) instantiate the configuration in (43) where the Voice head takes a υP as its complement. As argued above, the causee is not an adjunct but an argument in Hindi causatives, and in (43) it is licensed by Voice head in Spec, VoiceP – i.e. an argument position (see Richa 2008):

(42) *somi-ne* *ru:na-se* *vanka-ko* *hə̃swaja*
Somi-ERG Runa-INS Vanka-ACC laugh-CAUS-PRF
'Somi made Vanka make Runa laugh.'

(43)

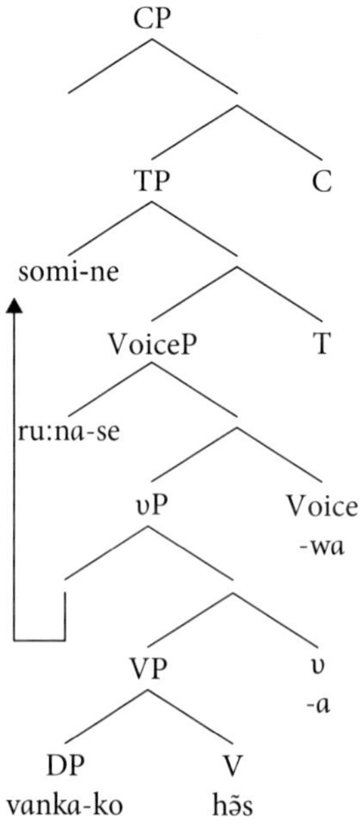

Under this analysis, Voice has two kinds of features: argumental features and Case (i.e. an uninterpretable φ-set). As argumental features, it has not only the [AG] feature, which licenses the external argument, but also that of causee, i.e. the *-se* argument. In actives, both the accusative Case feature as well as the [AG] feature are transferred to υ; however, the Causee is systematically licensed in the specifier of Voice.

This analysis predicts that in a passive of a causative, the *-se* argument should remain unaffected, as it is not Case-marked by υ but by the Voice head. This is true, given that in (44b), passivisation affects the external argument, not the *-se* argument:

(44) a. *somi-ne ru:na-se vanka-ko piʈwaja*
Somi-ERG Runa-INS Vanka-ACC hit-CAUS-PRF
'Somi made Runa hit Vanka.'

b. *ru:na-se vanka-ko piʈwaja gəja*
Runa-INS Vanka-ACC hit-CAUS-PFV PASS-PRF
'Vanka was hit (through Runa).'

Moreover, if we form inabilitative passives of causatives, the prediction is that the *-se* argument of the causative should remain unaffected, and it is indeed true:

(45) *somi-se runa-se vanka-ko piʈwaja nə̃hi gəja*
Somi-INS Runa-INS Vanka-ACC hit-CAUS-PRF not PASS-PRF
'Somi was not able to make Runa hit Vanka.'

Here, inability is on the part of the external argument *Somi* and not the *-se* causee as predicted.

6. Conclusion

With this analysis, the *-se* marked cause argument must be υP-external, and it is this property that explains the perplexing binding properties of the causee. As shown above, though Hindi (see also Richa 2003) causee can bind possessive reflexives in lower categories, anti-subject orientation does not hold in this position. Following Mahajan (1990) and Kidwai (2000) in analysing anti-subject orientation as holding of arguments in [Spec, TP], this indicates that though the causee is in a subject-like position, it cannot be the specifier of TP. [Spec, Voice P] is indeed such a position. Hence, this is a 'high' argument but not 'high' enough to count as the subject (while possessive reflexive binding makes reference just to height in terms of υP-externality, anti-subject orientation refers to height alone).

The fact that causee argument can act as binder for possessive reflexives suggests that when Voice is Causative, a higher head, other than υ, may serve to value the j-set of possessive reflexives. In the present proposal above, Voice transfers its features to υ in actives, identifying υP as a phase. For reflexives embedded in arguments lower than the external argument, the only available binder that is υP-external and it is the subject that has raised to [Spec, TP]. In causative Voice, on the other hand, Voice withholds its features from υ – in other words, the category headed by υ is j-incomplete. Consequently, just like other defective categories, it is transparent to Agree Probes from higher heads in the clause, such as Voice and T.

Thus, feature transfer is always from a phase head to a non-phase head. Now, let us compare Voice-υ feature-inheritance with C–T feature inheritance. In the present proposal, where the insights of Roberts (2008) have been followed, just as TP cannot appear in isolation without C, υP cannot appear without Voice. Therefore, in cases where υ appears to be the phase head, it must be the case that Voice has transferred the relevant features to υ. This proposal, therefore, takes issue with Collins' (2005) conclusion that Voice head is present only in the passives, and through the analysis of causatives that has been built here, lends support to Roberts' (2008) claim that Voice is uniformly present.

Acknowledgements

I am much indebted to Rajesh Bhatt and Miriam Butt for their frequent academic insights. Special thanks to Pritha Chandra for her consistent encouragement and academic interactions. For language-specific data, I am grateful to Shahid (Kashmiri), Gurmeet & Sarabjeet (Punjabi) and Nandaraj & Premila (Manipuri).

References

Ahmed, Tafseer. 2009. Spatial Expressions and Case in South Asian Languages. Doctoral Dissertation, University of Konstanz.

Balachandran, Lakshmi Bai. 1970. A Case Grammar of Hindi with Special Reference to Causative Sentences. Doctoral Dissertation, Cornell University, Ithaca.

Bhatt, Rajesh & Embick, David. 2004. Causative Derivations in Hindi. Ms. University of Texas & University of Pennsylvania.

Collins, Chris. 2005. A smuggling approach to the passive in English. *Syntax* 8(2): 81–120.

Davison, Alice. 1982. On the form and meaning of Hindi passive sentences. *Lingua* 58(1–2): 149–179.

DeLancey, Scott. 1989a. Verb agreement in Proto-Tibeto-Burman verb. *Bulletin of the School of Oriental & African Studies* 52(2): 315–333.

Dowty, David. 1991. Thematic proto-roles and argument selection. *Language* 67(3): 547–619.

Embick, David. 1997. Voice and the Interfaces of Syntax. Doctoral Dissertation, University of Pennsylvania.

Hook, Peter. 1979. Hindi structures: Intermediate level. Michigan Papers on *South and South East Asia* 16, University of Michigan, Ann Arbor.

Kachru, Yamuna. 1980. *Aspects of Hindi Syntax*. Manohar Publications: Delhi.

Khokholova, Ludmila. V. 1997. Infringement of morphological and syntactic operations' pairing in "Second causative" formation. Paper presented at the *XVIII South Asian Language Analysis Round Table*, JNU, New Delhi.

Kidwai, Ayesha. 1995. Binding and Free Word Order Phenomenon in Hindi-Urdu. PhD thesis, Jawaharlal Nehru University.

Kidwai, Ayesha. 2000. *XP-Adjunction in Universal Grammar: Scrambling and Binding in Hindi-Urdu*. New York: OUP.
Mahajan, Anoop. 1990. *On the A/A-Bar Distinction and Movement Thoery.* PhD Thesis, MIT.
Manning, Christopher. 1994. Argument Structure as a Locus for Binding Theory. Ms. University of Sydney.
Masica, Colin P. 1991. *The Indo-Aryan Languages*. Cambridge: Cambridge University Press.
Mohanan, Tara. 1994. *Argument Structure in Hindi*. Stanford: CSLI Publications.
Nikolaeva, Irina & Tolskaya, Maria. 2001. *A Grammar of Udihe*. Berlin: Mouton de Gruyter.
Pandharipande, Rajeshwari. 1981. Transitivity in Hindi. 11(2): 161–179. University of Illinois, Urbana-Champaign.
Pylkkänen, Liina. 2002. Introducing Arguments. Doctoral Dissertation, MIT.
Ramchand, Gillian. 2008. *Verb Meaning and the Lexicon: A First Phase Syntax*. Cambridge: Cambridge University Press.
Ramchand, Gillian. 2011. Licensing of instrumental case in Hindi/Urdu in Causatives. *Working Papers on Language & Linguistics* 38. Tromsø University: Septentrio Acdemic Publishing.
Richa. 2003. Possessive Reflexives and Pronominals in Hindi-Urdu and Indian sign Language: A Minimalist Analysis. M.Phil. Dissertation, Jawaharlal Nehru University.
Richa. 2008. Unaccusativity, Unergativity and the Causative Alternation in Hindi: A Minimalist Analysis. Doctoral Dissertation, J.N.U. Delhi.
Roberts, Ian. 2008. Smuggling, Affectness and Argument Structure Alternation. Ms. University of Cambridge.
Rosen, Carol & Wali, Kashi. 1989. Twin passives, inversion, and multistratalism in Marathi. *Natural Language and Linguistic Theory* 7(1): 1–50.
Saksena, Anuradha. 1982. *Topics in the Analysis of Causatives with an Account of Hindi Paradigms*. Los Angeles: University of California Press.
Yeon, Jaehoon. 2003. *Korean Grammatical Constructions: Their Form and Meaning*. London: Saffron Books.
Whorf, Benjamin Lee. 1945. Grammatical categories. *Language* 21(1): 1–11. Linguistic Society of America.

Agreement and verb types in Kutchi Gujarati*

Patrick Grosz & Pritty Patel-Grosz
Universität Tübingen

This paper explores the ϕ-agreement system in Kutchi Gujarati, focusing on canonical transitive cases and on non-canonical cases involving psych predicates and modal auxiliaries. Based on the agreement pattern in the future perfect, we argue that ϕ-agreement in Kutchi Gujarati involves two agreement probes, a higher (number/person) probe in *T*, and a lower (gender/number) probe in the *v*/*Asp* area. After showing how such a system derives the split-ergative agreement pattern in canonical transitive constructions (Section 2), we extend our analysis to other types of verbs, specifically to psych predicates (such as *gam* 'like') and to constructions that involve modal auxiliaries (such as *par* 'have to'), both of which require a dative-marked subject (Section 3).

Keywords: split-ergativity; future perfect; Gujarati; psych predicates; modals

1. Background on ϕ-agreement in Indo-Aryan languages

ϕ-agreement in Indo-Aryan languages (such as Gujarati and Hindi) is generally assumed to exhibit a so-called aspectually conditioned *split ergative* pattern (cf. Dixon 1994), instantiated by (1) for Standard Gujarati (abbreviated as *SG*): In the 'imperfective' aspects (e.g. habitual and progressive), the transitive subject is not case marked, and the verb agrees with the subject, (1a). Contrastively, in the 'perfective' aspects (e.g. simple past and future perfect),[1] the transitive

* For helpful feedback and detailed discussion we would like to thank Jonathan Bobaljik. We would also like to thank the following for numerous comments: Rajesh Bhatt, Pritha Chandra, Alice Davison, Ad Neeleman, David Pesetsky, Neil Smith, Richa Shristi, and an anonymous reviewer.

1. For now, we follow the usual simplification from work on Indo-Aryan languages, which collapses the notions of imperfective, habitual and progressive into 'imperfective' on the one hand, and the notions of perfective and perfect into 'perfective' on the other hand. Naturally, this glosses over the fundamental differences between perfective and perfect, but this is nevertheless justified, since each of these groups patterns uniformly with respect to the directionality of agreement.

subject bears the ergative case marker *-e*, and the verb agrees with the direct object, (1b).

(1) Standard Gujarati (Mistry 2004: 3–4)

a. ***šilaa*** *kaagaL lakh-t-**i**.* past habitual
Sheela(F) letter(M) write-IPFV-F
'Sheela used to write a letter.'

b. *šilaa-e* ***kaagaL*** *lakh-y-**o**.* past perfective
Sheela(F)-erg letter(M) write-PFV-M
'Sheela wrote a letter.'

Morphological alignment (i.e. case marking and ϕ-agreement) in Standard Gujarati) is summarized in (2), where *DOM* stands for 'differential object marking', an affix *-ne* on the direct object that generally marks specificity (cf. Mistry 1997 for Standard Gujarati).

(2) **morphological alignment in Standard Gujarati**

a. *past imperfective*

i. intransitive

ii. transitive

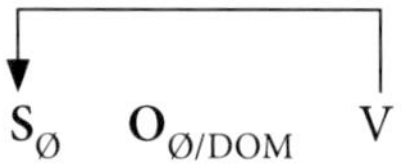

b. *past perfective*

i. intransitive

ii. transitive

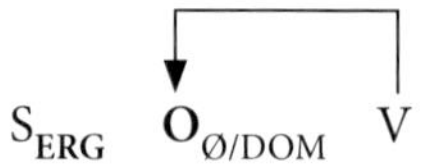

Many recent approaches to Indo-Aryan languages such as Standard Gujarati and Hindi-Urdu generally assume a single ϕ-agreement probe, usually on *T* (cf. Bhatt 2005, and more recently Bhatt & Walkow 2013). This ϕ-agreement probe targets the subject when it is not case marked; if the subject is case-marked, it becomes unavailable for agreement and the ϕ-agreement probe must probe further and target the object. In the same vein, Bobaljik (2008) argues that ϕ-agreement always targets the structurally highest DP in a ϕ-probe's agreement domain, while tracking morphological case. For the pattern in (2), a single probe approach could be modeled as follows. On the one hand, the ϕ-probe on *T* agrees with the subject if it can, and with the (structurally lower) object otherwise. On the other hand, ergative-marked subjects cannot trigger agreement, which means that ergative-marking (in the perfective aspect) gives rise to object agreement.

Furthermore, Bhatt (2005: 800–801) argues that subject agreement and object agreement are not fully symmetrical. Based on data from Standard Gujarati, he shows that object agreement lacks person features. In the intransitive, (3a), the present tense auxiliary exhibits person and number agreement (2nd plural) with the intransitive subject; by contrast, in the transitive, (3b), the present tense auxiliary lacks person agreement (3rd singular and 3rd plural being identical forms in Gujarati). The underlying idea that (3b) involves object agreement both on the participle (*māryā* 'struck') and on the auxiliary (*che*) directly follows from a view that assumes a single ϕ-probe in Standard Gujarati.

(3) Standard Gujarati (Bhatt 2005: 801, (3b) from Magier 1983a: 324)

a. ***tEhme*** *aw-yā* ***cho***. present perfect
you.PL come-PFV.M.PL be.PRES.2.PL
'You have come.'

b. *mãĩ* ***tam-ne*** *mār-yā* *che*.
I.ERG you.PL-DOM strike-PFV.M.PL be.PRES.3
'I have struck you.'

In the following section, we discuss data from Kutchi Gujarati and Marwari, which challenge a *single probe* view on ϕ-agreement for these languages. Since Kutchi Gujarati, Marwari and Standard Gujarati are closely related languages, it follows that a single probe analysis should also be questioned for Standard Gujarati.

2. A dual probe system for Kutchi Gujarati and Marwari

2.1 The basic alignment patterns

In the remainder of our paper, we focus on Kutchi Gujarati, an Indo-Aryan language spoken in the Kutch district of the Gujarat state in North-West India.[2] Other languages spoken in this area include Kachchi (an Indo-Aryan language related to Sindhi) and Kachi Koli. As shown below, Kutchi Gujarati exhibits systematic similarities to Marwari (Magier 1983a, 1983b) in its ϕ-agreement system. This should not come as a surprise; while Marwari and Gujarati are geographically close, allowing for contact phenomena, it is also generally assumed (cf. Tessitori 1913, 1914–16) that both languages evolved from Old Western Rajasthani, sometimes called Old Gujarati (spoken approximately between 1000 CE and 1500 CE), cf. Magier (1983a), Desai & Ramsay-Brijball (2004).

The basic ϕ-agreement pattern in Kutchi Gujarati and Marwari is similar to that of Standard Gujarati. We find split-ergativity that correlates with aspect. However, both Kutchi Gujarati and Marwari exhibit this split only in their agreement systems, not in their case systems.

2. Our language consultants are based in different locations within the Kutch district, including its capital city Bhuj, and the port city Mandvi.

Consider first the Kutchi Gujarati data in (4).[3] In intransitive constructions, verbal ϕ-agreement targets the subject both in the imperfective, (4a), and in the perfective, (4b).

(4) a. ***Reena*** *naach-th-**i**.* past habitual intrans.
Reena(F) dance-IPFV-F
'Reena used to dance.'

b. ***Reena*** *naach-**i**.* past perfective intrans.
Reena(F) dance-PFV.F
'Reena danced.'

Contrastively, we encounter the familiar agreement split in the transitive constructions; ϕ-agreement targets the transitive subject in the imperfective, (5a), but it targets the transitive object in the perfective, (5b). However, in Kutchi Gujarati, the case pattern in the imperfective and the perfective are identical.[4] The intransitive and transitive subject is unmarked, whereas the direct object can be unmarked or bear a semantically triggered differential object marker *-ne*, cf. (5a) and (5b).[5,6] The differential object marker, if present, does not block object agreement (a core difference between Kutchi Gujarati/Standard Gujarati/Marwari on the one hand and Hindi-Urdu on the other hand).

(5) a. ***Reena*** *kutro(-ne)* *mar-th-**i*** past habitual trans.
Reena(F) dog(M)-DOM hit-IPFV-F
'Reena used to hit a/the dog.'

3. Examples throughout this paper are from Kutchi Gujarati, unless noted otherwise.

4. This is a difference between Kutchi Gujarati and Standard Gujarati, where transitive subjects carry an ergative marker *-e* in the perfective. It is worth emphasizing that there are many varieties of Gujarati, and little descriptive work has been carried out at this point. To illustrate the current state, the *UCLA Language Materials Project* ⟨http://www.lmp.ucla.edu/profile.aspx?langid=85&menu=004⟩ lists 8 key dialects, for which little descriptive and theoretical linguistic work is available. See also Magier (1983a) for an extensive discussion of the dialect problematic for Marwari.

5. We depart from standard notation, e.g. Butt & Ahmed (2011), Butt (2012), where *-ne* is glossed as *acc*(*usative*) whenever it attaches to the direct object, and gloss it as *dom* instead (for *differential object marking*); we follow convention and gloss *-ne* as *dat*(*ive*) whenever it attaches to DPs other than the direct object, e.g. to indirect objects or to oblique subjects.

6. Note that *-ne* in Kutchi Gujarati only has the dative/accusative use, whereas *-ne* in Hindi/Urdu only has an ergative use. Nevertheless, Kutchi Gujarati *-ne* and Hindi-Urdu *-ne* are historically connected: Butt & Ahmed (2011) argue that Hindi/Urdu *-ne* was a loan from neighboring languages such as Haryani, in which *-ne* has both a dative/accusative use and an ergative use (Butt & Ahmed 2011: 562). (Butt & Amhed 2011 argue that *-ne* originally derived from Old Rajasthani *kanhaïN* 'aside, near', cf. Tessitori 1913, 1914–16.)

b. *Reena* ***kutro**(-ne)* *mar-y-**o*** past perfective trans.
Reena(F) dog(M)-DOM hit-PFV-M
'Reena hit a/the dog.'

The perfective pattern in (4b) and (5b) is illustrated for perfective clauses in Marwari, in (6) and (7) respectively, as documented by Magier (1983a, 1983b). The intransitive verb *ā* 'come' in (6a–b) agrees with the subject, whereas the transitive verb *jīml* 'eat' in (7a–b) agrees with the object, *lāpsī* 'wheat gruel' in (7a), and *ek sogro* 'one piece of millet-bread' in (7b). As in Kutchi Gujarati, Marwari lacks the morphological ergative case marking found in Standard Gujarati and Hindi-Urdu.

(6) Marwari (Magier 1983b: 248)
a. ***rām*** *aṭhe kāle* *ā-**iyo*** past perfective intrans.
Ram here yesterday come-PFV.M
'Ram came here yesterday.'

b. ***sītā*** *aṭhe kāle* *ā-**ī***
Sita here yesterday come-PFV.F
'Sita came here yesterday.'

(7) Marwari (Magier 1983b: 248)
a. *rām* ***lāpsī*** *jīml-**ī*** past perfective trans.
Ram wheat-gruel.F eat-PFV.F
'Ram ate wheat gruel.'

b. *sītā* ***ek sogro*** *jīml-**īyo***
Sita one millet.bread.M eat-PFV.M
'Sita ate one (piece of) millet-bread.'

To sum up, we have seen that Kutchi Gujarati and Marwari have a ϕ-agreement split that correlates with aspect; nevertheless, these languages lack overt morphological structural case, i.e. we do not find ergative marking or accusative marking, but differential object marking (*dom*).[7,8] The core question can be stated as follows: How do we best derive the ϕ-agreement pattern in Kutchi Gujarati and Marwari?

7. Later on, we will see examples of inherent/lexical dative marking, which occurs in indirect objects and certain subjects in Kutchi Gujarati and other Indo-Aryan languages.

8. Since both languages (Kutchi Gujarati and Marwari) developed from Old Western Rajasthani, it can be assumed that Kutchi Gujarati and Marwari evolved from a system that had split-ergativity both in its case system and in its agreement system (as is still found in Standard Gujarati). Remnants of ergative marking are still found in the Kutchi Gujarati focus marking-system, e.g. *-e* can be used as a focus marker, similar to the use of Standard Gujarati *-e* as a (synchronically non-ergative) inclusive marker that means 'also', as documented by Mistry (1997: 437).

In Sections 2.2–2.4, we argue that agreement in Kutchi Gujarati and Marwari involves a *dual probe* ϕ-agreement system (as opposed to a *single probe* ϕ-agreement system); specifically, ϕ-agreement involves a probe on T and a second probe in the *v*/Asp domain (cf. Bobaljik 1993; Laka 1993, 2000, and Rezac 2003, 2008b). We argue that the lower probe (in the *v*/Asp domain) is responsible for the Kutchi Gujarati agreement split. In fact, the higher probe lacks an *overt* reflex in all examples that we discussed above.

2.2 Future perfect, present perfect and dual probes

Most *single probe* ϕ-agreement analyses of Indo-Aryan languages adopt the view that subjects in the perfective are unavailable for ϕ-agreement. This is reflected by Bhatt's (2005) assumption that the present tense auxiliary in (3b), repeated in (8), agrees with the object (*tam-ne*), and fails to do so with respect to the object's person features.

(8) Standard Gujarati (Bhatt 2005: 801, from Magier 1983a: 324)
mā̃ī ***tam-ne*** *mār-yā* *che.* present perfect
I.ERG you.PL-DOM strike-PFV.M.PL be.PRES.3
'I have struck you.'

Kutchi Gujarati and Marwari exhibit a very different pattern, first observed for Marwari by Magier (1983a, 1983b), which has largely gone unnoticed in the formal syntactic literature on Indo-Aryan agreement. While the perfective participle exhibits agreement with the direct object (as expected), the tense auxiliary exhibits agreement with the subject.[9] This nested agreement pattern is illustrated for the Kutchi Gujarati future perfect in (9).

(9) a. *Hu chokra-ne jo-y-**a*** *ha-**is**.* future perfect
I boys-DOM see-PFV-PL aux-FUT.1SG
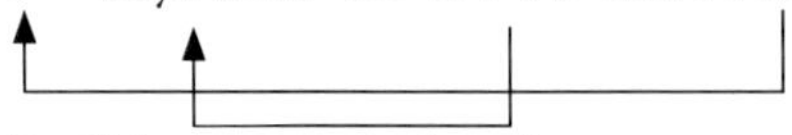
'I will have seen the boys.'

b. *John mane jo-**i*** *ha-se.*
John me.DOM see-PFV.F.SG aux-FUT.3SG
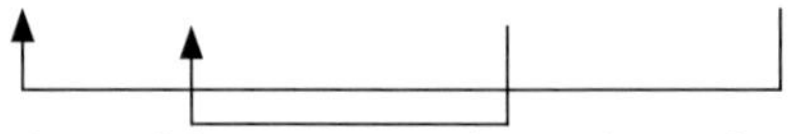
'John will have seen me.' (*speaker is female*)

9. Of course, this is a surprisingly 'normal' pattern in Indo-European, which we also find in French participle agreement; cf. Magier (1983a, 1983b).

Crucially, the aspectually triggered agreement split still holds in the future tense, between the future perfect in (9), where the aspectual participle agrees with the direct object, and the future imperfective in (10), where both the aspectual participle and the tense auxiliary agree with the subject.

(10) a. *Hu chokra-ne jo-th-**i** ha-**is**.* future imperfective
I boys-DOM see-IPFV-F.SG aux-FUT.1SG

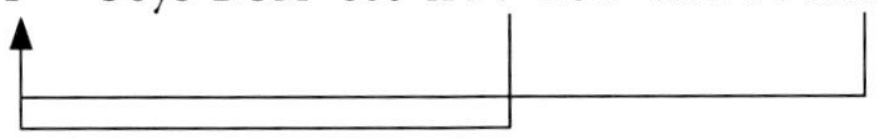

'I will see the boys.' (*speaker is female*)

b. *John amne jo-th-**o** ha-**se**.*
I us.DOM see-IPFV-M.SG aux-FUT.3SG

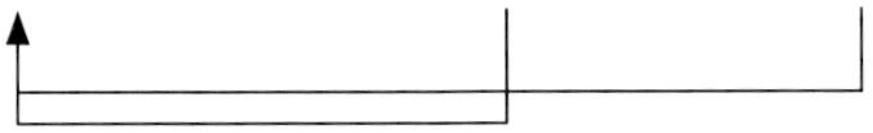

'John will see us.'

In Marwari, we find a ϕ-agreement pattern identical to the pattern in (9) in the present perfect, given in (11).

(11) Marwari Magier (1983b: 250)
a. *mhāī sītā-ne dekhī hū.* present perfect
I Sita-DOM saw.F am.1SG

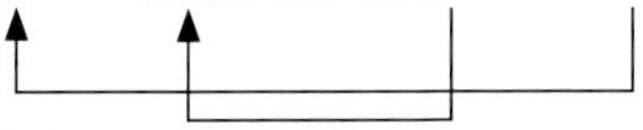

'I have seen Sita.'

b. *āp sītā-ne dekhī ho.*
you(PL) Sita-DOM saw.F are.2PL

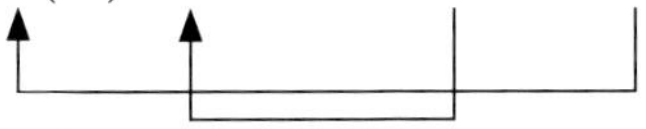

'You have seen Sita.'

c. *mhe sītā-ne dekhī hā.*
we(excl) Sita-DOM saw.F are.1PL

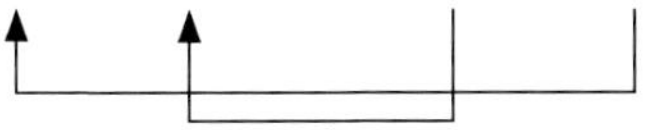

'We have seen Sita.'

d. *ve sītā-ne dekhī hai.*
they Sita-DOM saw.F are.3SG/PL

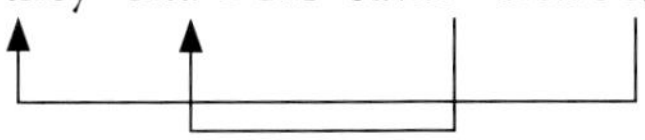

'They have seen Sita.'

The nested patterns in Kutchi Gujarati and Marwari sharply contrast with the Standard Gujarati example in (8). A plausible explanation for this difference derives from the observation that Standard Gujarati, as opposed to Kutchi Gujarati and

Marwari, requires morphological ergative case marking in the perfective aspect, which can be assumed to block the auxiliary agreement found in (9) and (11), in accord with Bobaljik (2008).

Based on these languages' future perfect and present perfect patterns, we propose that Kutchi Gujarati and Marwari involve two ϕ-agreement probes, a higher number/person probe that is located in *T* and a lower number/gender probe that is located in the *v/Asp* domain. To derive the split-agreement pattern, we propose the following, illustrated in (13) below. The lower *v/Asp* probe always agrees with the direct object and the higher *T* probe always agrees with the subject. In the future perfect, both probes have an overt reflex, giving rise to the nested agreement pattern. However, in the imperfective, the two probes share one agreement domain, which causes the two probes to act as *one* complex *v/Asp/T* probe (cf. D'Alessandro 2011 for the concept of complex probes). This *v/Asp/T* probe has established an Agree relationship with both the direct object (via *v/Asp*) and the subject (via *T*). In the spirit of Bobaljik (2008), PF then spells out morphological agreement with the structurally higher argument, i.e. with the subject. To account for the agreement split, we assume that the formation of such a complex *v/Asp/T* probe requires a local relationship between *v/Asp* and *T*, which is interrupted by an additional head that is present in the perfective and absent in the imperfective. For mnemonic reasons, we call this the *Perf* head. (The idea that split-ergativity is due to such a structural asymmetry is due to Coon & Preminger 2011, and Coon 2013, though they assume the opposite of our analysis, namely that the imperfective involves an additional head lacking in the perfective.)

Our analysis of (12a–b), repeated from (9a) and (10a) is given in (13a–b). The four arrows indicate agreement between *v/Asp* and the direct object and between *T* and the subject respectively.[10,11] In (13b), the dotted oval marks the unification of the *v/Asp* probe and the *T* probe, which has the consequence that object agreement on *v/Asp* will not be spelled out at PF, while all verbal elements spell out subject agreement. (We adopt standard assumptions such as the view that the subject originates in Spec, *v*P; cf. Chomsky 2001, 2004. For expository ease, we omit traces in this illustration.)

---

10. Our analysis does not depend on whether the probe that is responsible for object agreement is active on v^0 or Asp^0 or on both (or another functional head in the lower area of the clause). For arguments that a higher probe is associated with *T* and a lower probe with *v*, see Bobaljik (1993), Laka (1993, 2000) and Rezac (2003, 2008b).

11. The idea that there is a *Perf* head (possibly encoding the meaning of the Perfect) above the clausal *Asp* head (which encodes perfectivity *vs* imperfectivity) is inspired by Iatridou et al. (2003: 181).

(12) a. *Hu chokra-ne jo-y-**a** ha-**is**.* future perfect
I boys-DOM see-PFV-PL aux-FUT.1SG
'I will have seen the boys.'

b. *Hu chokra-ne jo-th-**i** ha-**is**.* future imperfective
I boys-DOM see-IPFV-F.SG aux-FUT.1SG
'I will see the boys.' (*speaker is female*)

(13) a. Perfective pattern b. Imperfective pattern

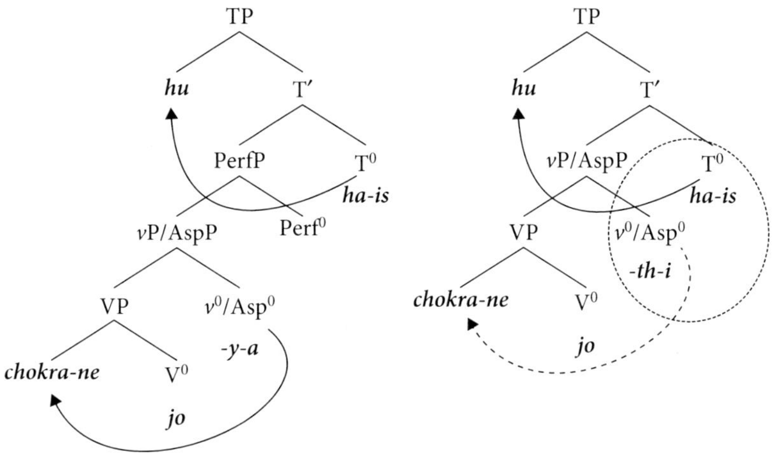

It is beyond the scope of this paper to include a formal implementation of how *v/Asp* and *T* are united into a single probe in (13b), and why this is interrupted by an additional intervening head in (13a). See Grosz & Patel-Grosz (2013) for an analysis based on D'Alessandro's (2011) idea of complex probes. The following section addresses the question of whether this analysis can also be applied to the more familiar agreement patterns in the past tense. We provide arguments that the same dual probe analysis should be applied there, arguing that past *T* simply remains unpronounced.

2.3 Past *vs* future

One obvious concern at this point seems to be that the future is more complex than the past, i.e. the future contains an additional auxiliary, *ha-*. This holds equally for the perfective cases in (14) and for the imperfective cases in (15), i.e. the additional structure cannot cause the agreement split.

(14) a. *Hu chokra-ne jo-y-**a** ha-**is**.* future perfect
I boys-DOM see-PFV-PL aux-FUT.1SG
'I will have seen the boys.'

b. *Hu chokra-ne jo-y-**a**.* past perfective
I boys-DOM see-PFV-PL
'I saw the boys.'

(15) a. *Hu chokra-ne jo-th-**i** ha-**is**.* future imperfective
I boys-DOM see-IPFV-F.SG aux-FUT.1SG
'I will see the boys.' (*speaker is female*)

b. *Hu chokra-ne jo-th-**i**.* past habitual
I boys-DOM see-IPFV-F.SG
'I used to see the boys.' (*speaker is female*)

Nevertheless, two questions arise: First, can the analysis in (13) also derive the agreement split in the past perfective *vs* past imperfective if *T* does not have an overt realization? Second, should we worry that the future examples in (14) and (15) involve some type of biclausal structure absent in the past?

To answer the first question, we propose that this is indeed the case. We treat past tense in Kutchi Gujarati as the unmarked tense whenever aspect is overtly marked (compare Dahl & Velupillai 2011 for a general discussion of similar tense/aspect interactions). As a consequence, past tense does not need to be (and in fact cannot be) overtly expressed in these basic cases.[12] In analogy with the future tense examples, we then treat (14b) and (15b) as involving a null *T*-head that covertly agrees with the subject, cf. (16a–b).

(16) a. *Hu **chokra**-ne jo-y-**a** Ø.* past perfective
I boys-DOM see-PFV-PL aux.PAST.1SG
'I saw the boys.'

b. ***Hu** chokra-ne jo-th-**i** Ø.* past habitual
I boys-DOM see-IPFV-F.SG aux.PAST.1SG
'I used to see the boys.' (*speaker is female*)

The second question (i.e. whether the future is biclausal) is more difficult to answer, since the mere presence of an additional auxiliary *may* be taken to indicate a biclausal structure (cf. Coon 2013). However, based on the following observations, we argue that this is not the case. The driving force for inserting an auxiliary

12. Interestingly, the past progressive seems to be more marked than the past habitual in that it requires an additional auxiliary, as in (i). However, this auxiliary differs from future and present tense auxiliaries in that it lacks person agreement; therefore, we do not treat it as a spell-out of *T*.

i. ***Hu** chokra-ne jo-th-**i** th-**i**.*
I boys-DOM see-IPFV-F.SG aux.PROG-F.SG
'I was watching the boys.' (*speaker is female*)

in (14) and (15) does not seem to be the future tense, but the fact that aspect is explicitly marked by the imperfective *-th-* morpheme or the perfective *-y-* morpheme. As opposed to languages such as English and German, which require a periphrastic future (e.g. *he will sleep*), the future tense in Kutchi Gujarati can be expressed on the main verb unless the main verb combines with an aspectual affix, as shown in (17).

(17) a. ***Hu*** *chokra-ne* *jo-**is**.* simple future
I boys-DOM see-FUT.1SG
'I will see the boys.'

b. ***John*** *mane* *jo-**se**.*
John me.DOM see-FUT.3SG
'John will see me.'

The insertion of an additional *ha-* auxiliary can then be derived as follows. First, we have seen that [+past] *T* is unpronounced, (16), whereas [+future] *T* must be spelled out in the shape of the agreeing *-is*/*-se*/… affix that we see in (17). Second, we have argued that *-y-* and *-th-* are overt realizations of perfective and imperfective aspect, respectively, which combine with a *v*/*Asp* agreement marker. We propose that (like many other languages, including English) Kutchi Gujarati does not generally allow aspectual and temporal affixes on the same verb, i.e. a combination such as *jo-y-a-is* is excluded in (14a). As a consequence, we can assume, following Bjorkman (2011), that the auxiliary *ha-* is some sort of pleonastic form, which is inserted in order to serve as an attachment host for the future tense affix whenever aspectual information is overtly expressed, occupying the unique affix slot on the main verb.

2.4 On the optionality of aspectual information

We now conclude Section 2 by addressing one more question with respect to our analysis. We have argued above that *T* always agrees with the subject, even if *T* does not have any overt reflex (i.e. in the past tense). By analogy, the question arises whether the lower probe in the *v*/*Asp* layer always agrees with the object as well. No part of our proposal hinges on the answer to this question, but the following facts indicate that the answer is affirmative.

Kutchi Gujarati (on a par with Standard Gujarati, Mistry 1997, and the Ripano dialect of Italian, D'Alessandro 2011) exhibits adverb agreement, which tracks the participle agreement that exhibits the agreement split, i.e. we find subject agreement on adverbs with intransitive subjects, (18a–b), and with transitive subjects in the imperfective, (19a); and we find object agreement on adverbs with transitive objects in the perfective, (19b).

(18) a. *Khimji vel-**o** av-th-**o** ha-se.* future imperf.
Khimji early-M come-IPFV-M aux-FUT.3
'Khimji will arrive early.'

b. *Khimji vel-**o** av-y-**o** ha-se.* future perfect
Khimji early-M come-PFV-M aux-FUT.3
'Khimji will have arrived early.'

(19) a. *Hu chokra-ne vel-**i** jo-th-**i** ha-is.* future imperf.
I boys-DOM early-F see-IPFV-F aux-FUT.1SG
'I will see the boys early.' (*speaker is female*)

b. *Hu chokra-ne vel-**a** jo-y-**a** ha-is.* future perfect
I boys-DOM early-PL see-PFV-PL aux-FUT.1SG
'I will have seen the boys early.'

It is a plausible assumption that adverb agreement is due to the lower *v/Asp* probe, since it always patterns together with *v/Asp*-agreement. Therefore, examples like (20), which lack *v/Asp*-agreement on a participle, indicate that some lower head in the *v/Asp* domain is also active when there is no aspectual participle to exhibit the relevant ϕ-agreement.

(20) a. *Khimji vel-**o** av-se.* *simple future*
Khimji early-M come-FUT.3
'Khimji will arrive early.'

b. *Hu vel-**i** av-is.* *simple future*
I early-F come-FUT.1SG
'I will arrive early.' (*speaker is female*)

2.5 Interim summary

In this section, we have argued for a dual probe analysis of split ϕ-agreement in Kutchi Gujarati and Marwari (focusing our discussion on Kutchi Gujarati). We have argued that these languages involve a higher probe on *T*, which always agrees with the subject, and a lower probe in the *v/Asp* domain, which always agrees with the object. Both instances of agreement can remain unpronounced, e.g. in the unmarked past tense, Section 2.3, and if there are no aspectual participles, Section 2.4; nevertheless, we have argued that both agreement relations are always established. The split agreement pattern arises from an interaction between these two agreement processes. In the imperfective aspect, *T* and *v/Asp* combine into a single probe, yielding agreement with the structurally highest argument (i.e. the subject) at the PF interface. Contrastively, in the perfective aspect, such a unification of *T* and *v/Asp* does not take place, and the two probes are spelled out independently (unless one of them is unpronounced); this gives rise to the nested agreement pattern in the Kutchi Gujarati future perfect and in the Marwari present perfect.

3. Extension to non-canonical agreement configurations

3.1 Lexical case interacts with agreement in Kutchi Gujarati

In the previous sections, it has become clear that the ϕ-agreement system of Kutchi Gujarati and Marwari does not seem to be sensitive to any notion of structural/dependent case. While the perfect in Standard Gujarati involves an ergative subject that cannot trigger verbal agreement, (21a), Kutchi Gujarati and Marwari exhibit subject agreement on the tense auxiliary in the future perfect, (21b), and present perfect, (21c), respectively. (This auxiliary agreement occurs in addition to the object participle agreement found in all three languages). We have also seen that the differential object marker *-ne* does not block object agreement (where applicable); this is also illustrated in (21).

(21) a. *mãĩ tam-ne mār-yā che.* [Standard Guj.]
I.ERG you.PL-DOM strike-PFV.M.PL be.PRES.3
'I have struck you.' (Magier 1983a: 324)

b. *hu chokra-ne jo-y-a ha-is.* [Kutchi Guj.]
I boys-DOM see-PFV-PL aux-FUT.1SG
'I will have seen the boys.'

c. *mhe sītā-ne dekhī hā.* [Marwari]
we(excl) Sita-DOM saw.F are.1PL
'We have seen Sita.' (Magier 1983b: 250)

However, this is not the full story. While structural case does not seem to affect agreement, lexical/inherent case does. Specifically, the non-structural dative case[13] on the Experiencer argument of *gam* 'like' does not allow for agreement, i.e. *gam* 'like' always exhibits agreement with the argument that lacks case marking. Example (22) contrasts with the regular transitive example in (5) in that the agreement pattern is identical in the imperfective, (22a), and in the perfective, (22b),

13. The label *dative* is arbitrary and should not be understood as a technical term. We follow the usual convention of calling non-differential-object-marking uses of the Gujarati *-ne* marker *dative* to indicate that it differs from the use of *-ne* as a differential object marker. (The latter is often labeled *accusative*.) As a diagnostic, while DPs with the DOM marker *-ne* can trigger verbal agreement, this is impossible for DPs with the *dative* marker *-ne*.

always targeting the argument that lacks case marking. The question arises whether the properties of this construction also fall out of our analysis of ϕ-agreement, as proposed above. We argue that they do, and analyze this pattern in Section 3.2. Specifically, we will see evidence, in the spirit of Baker (2008), that the person probe on *T* requires a more local relationship to its goal than the lower probe in *v*/*Asp*, which lacks person features, agreeing only for number and gender.

(22) a. *Reena-ne* ***kutro*** *gam-th-**o*** — *past habitual psych verb*
Reena(F)-dat dog(M) like-IPFV-M
'Reena used to like a/the dog.'

b. *Reena-ne* ***kutro*** *gam-y-**o*** — *past perfective psych verb*
Reena(F)-DAT dog(M) hit-PFV-M
'Reena liked a/the dog.'

3.2 Agreement with psych predicates in Kutchi Gujarati

From the perspective of our analysis, we expect that psych verbs like *gam* 'like' behave on a par with intransitives, i.e. neither of the two arguments qualifies as an external argument. This view is supported by the fact that the unmarked word order is one where the dative argument precedes the unmarked argument (both of which are located inside the VP, as has been proposed for psych predicates in many other languages, e.g. Bobaljik & Wurmbrand 2003). This becomes clear if we consider binding facts (see also Mistry 2004: 15 for similar observations in Standard Gujarati). While the Experiencer argument of *gam* 'like' can bind a reflexive in possessor position, as shown in (23a), the scrambled direct object of *mar* 'hit' cannot do so, as shown in (23b).[14]

(23) a. ***Ene***$_i$ [*eno* ***potha**-no*$_i$ *dikro*] *gam-yo.* — psych verb
3.DAT 3.GEN.M self-GEN.M son like-PFV.M
'She liked her own son.' (lit. 'She liked herself's son.')

b. ??***Ene***$_i$ [*eno* ***potha**-no*$_i$ *dikro*] *mar-i.* — transitive verb
3.DOM 3.GEN.M self-GEN.M son hit-PFV.F
'Her own son hit her.' (lit. 'Herself's son hit her.')

We now encounter the following facts, which may seem puzzling at first. On the one hand, in the cases without person agreement (i.e. if the agreeing DP is in

14. The fact that (23b) is marked '??' rather than '*' reflects the observation that reflexive in possessor position can sometimes be contextually licensed without being syntactically bound. We cannot test cases with psych verbs where the non-case-marked element is a reflexive, since reflexives in Kutchi Gujarati must be case-marked.

the unmarked 3rd person), the underlying word order must be preserved. This is shown in (24a–b).

(24) a. *Reena-ne i gam-se*
Reena-DAT 3SG/PL like-FUT.3
b. **i Reena-ne gam-se*
3SG/PL Reena-DAT like-FUT.3
'Reena will like them/him/her.'

On the other hand, once we introduce first or second person arguments, the order obligatorily reverses, as shown in (25) and (26).

(25) a. **Reena-ne ame gam-se/si*
Reena-DAT 1PL like-FUT.3/1PL
b. *ame Reena-ne gam-si*
1PL Reena-DAT like-FUT.1PL
'Reena will like us.'

(26) a. **Reena-ne hu/tu gam-se/is/is*
Reena-DAT 1SG/2SG like-FUT.3/1SG/2SG
b. *hu/tu Reena-ne gam-is/is*
1SG/2SG Reena-DAT like-FUT.1SG/2SG
'Reena will like me/you.'

Due to their behavior in (24)–(26), psych verbs allow us to refine our analysis of agreement in Kutchi Gujarati. Specifically, such a pattern follows under a view like Baker's (2008), who assumes that person agreement, as opposed to gender/number agreement, requires a local (Spec-Head) relationship between the agreeing DP and the probe. Kutchi Gujarati exhibits person agreement on its future tense and present tense auxiliary, which we have localized in *T*. For psych predicates, we thus find two configurations, one in which *T* exhibits default agreement (3rd singular/plural *-se*), in (24), and one in which *T* attracts the non-case-marked DP to its specifier in order to agree for person (possibly in connection with licensing of a structural nominative case, as we will see later). This difference is illustrated in (27). Since perfective and imperfective do not give rise to split-agreement with psych predicates (or, more generally, intransitives), we only illustrate for the imperfective case; also, we remain agnostic as to whether psych predicates project a *v*P or not. It is worth pointing out the following. If movement in (27b) is parasitic on licensing of structural nominative case, as conjectured in Section 3.3.7 below, then the driving force for movement cannot be an EPP feature, but it must be the (first and second) person features of the nominative argument.

(27) a. 3rd person pattern

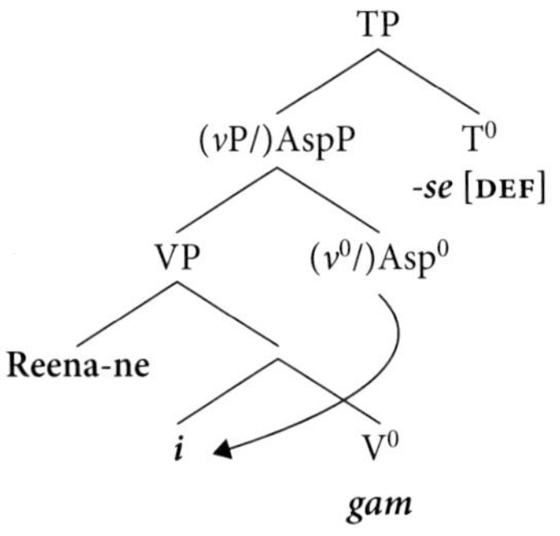

b. 1st/2nd person pattern

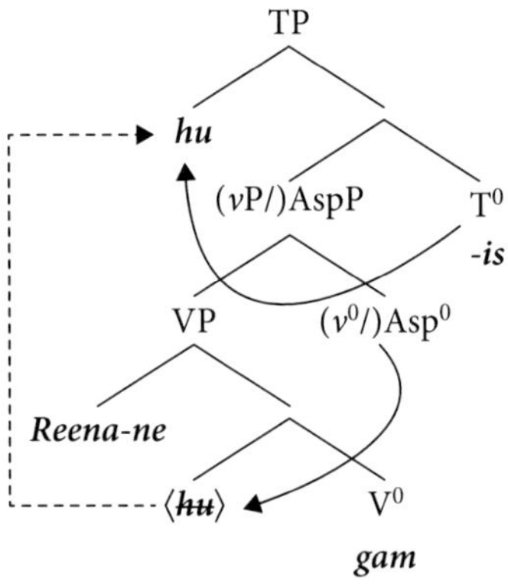

We can thus summarize the difference between transitive verbs like *mar* 'hit' and psych predicates like *gam* 'like' as follows. Much in the spirit of the standard analyses for languages such as English and German (e.g. Bobaljik & Wurmbrand 2003), *mar* 'hit' is a true transitive predicate, (28a), the subject of which is generated in Spec*v*P, whereas *gam* 'like' is an unaccusative predicate with two internal arguments, (28b).

(28) a. [$_{vP}$ SUBJ [$_{VP}$ DO$_{DOM}$ ***mar***] *v*]
b. [$_{VP}$ IO$_{DAT}$ [$_{V'}$ DO ***gam***]]

The next section extends our proposal to an apparent case of *long distance agreement* (*LDA*) with the modal *par* 'have to'. What we find is that LDA in Kutchi Gujarati also seems to involve the *v/Asp* probe rather than the *T* probe (possibly in contrast to Hindi-Urdu LDA, Bhatt 2005; Chandra 2007).

3.3 'Long distance agreement' in Kutchi Gujarati

Another type of construction that appears to involve dative-marked subjects is the modal construction with *par* 'have to', illustrated in (29).[15,16] Here, the embedded

15. The verb root *par* has three uses: It occurs as a main verb *par* 'fall', as a light verb *par* 'sudden initiation of an event' (gloss based on Cardona 1965: 130 for Standard Gujarati) and as a modal *par* 'have to'. Following Ramchand (2008b), we assume that the main verb use and the light verb use draw on the same lexical entry. However, we assume that the modal use *par* 'have to' (which we discuss in this section) uses a distinct lexical entry, though it plausibly originated from *par* 'fall' (cf. Magier 1983a: 176, who glosses Marwari *par* as 'befall', i.e. in its modal use, *par* may have originated as *par* 'it befalls someone to do something').

16. Note that Kutchi Gujarati does not seem to have many verbs that allow for such long distance agreement; all the ones that do seem to require a dative-marked subject.

verb (which occurs with an apparent infinitive affix-*v*-) as well as the apparent matrix verb (*par* 'have to') agree with the direct object.

(29) a. *Khimji-ne* ***Reena**-ne* *jo-v-**i*** *par-th-**i**.* past habitual
Khimji.M-DAT Reena.F-DOM see-INF-F have.to-IPFV-F
'Khimji used to have to watch Reena.'

b. *Khimji-ne* ***Reena**-ne* *jo-v-**i*** *par-**i**.* past perfective
Khimji.M-DAT Reena.F-DOM see-INF-F have.to-PFV.F
'Khimji had to watch Reena.'

In the absence of a direct object, default agreement (neuter singular) arises, as shown in (30).

(30) a. *Khimji-ne* *su-v-**u*** *par-th-**u**.* past habitual
Khimji.M-DAT sleep-INF-N have.to-IPFV-N
'Khimji used to have to sleep.'

b. *Khimji-ne* *su-v-**u*** *par-**u**.* past perfective
Khimji.M-DAT sleep-INF-N have.to-PFV.N
'Khimji had to watch Reena.'

The question that this section addresses is how to integrate the LDA patterns in our analysis of ϕ-agreement in Kutchi Gujarati.

3.3.1 *Two possible analyses of the modal* par

Constructions with *par* 'have to' raise two questions in light of the discussion above. First, given the superficial similarity to psych predicates (experiencer subject and no agreement split), why can the object carry the differential object marker *-ne*? This question arises since such differential object marking is ruled out with psych predicates like *gam* 'like', (31b).

(31) a. *Reena* ***kutro**-ne* *mar-y-**o*** past pfv. transitive
Reena(F) dog(M)-DOM hit-PFV-M
'Reena hit the dog.'

b. *Reena-ne* ***kutro**(*-ne)* *gam-y-**o*** past pfv. psych verb
Reena(F)-DAT dog(M)-DOM hit-PFV-M
'Reena liked the dog.'

Second, we observe that person agreement with the direct object is excluded, as shown in (32b) versus (32c), which is reminiscent of Bhatt's (2005) *Person Generalization* originally proposed in connection with examples like (3b).[17]

17. Note that it does not seem to be possible to embed *gam* 'like' under *par* 'have to', with a reading such as 'Reena will have to like me'.

(32) a. *Reena-ne* ***mane*** *mar-v-**o*** *par-y-**o**.* past perfective
Reena.F-DAT me.DOM hit-INF-M have.to-PFV-M
'Reena had to hit me.' (*speaker is male*)

b. *Reena-ne* ***mane*** *mar-v-**o***
Reena.F-DAT me.DOM hit-INF-M

par-se/-**is**.* simple future
have.to-FUT.DEF/*1SG

'Reena will have to hit me.' (*speaker is male*)

c. ***hu*** *Reena-ne* *gam-**is***
1SG Reena-DAT like-FUT.1SG
'Reena will like me.'

In the spirit of Bhatt's (2005) analysis of Hindi-Urdu long-distance agreement, we can argue that the Kutchi Gujarati construction involves restructuring (cf. Cinque 2004; Wurmbrand 2001), one core indication for restructuring being the long distance agreement on the apparent matrix predicate *par* 'have to' (cf. Bhatt 2005: 779). We can also show that embedded objects can take scope over *par* 'have to' (cf. Bhatt 2005: 799), as in (33b), which further corroborates a restructuring analysis.

(33) a. *Valji-ne* [[*amukaj* *chopri*] *vanch-v-i*] *par-i.*
Valji.M-DAT some book-F read-INF-F have.to-PFV-F
'Valji had to read some of these books.'

b. OK *some » have to (de re):*
For some specific books, Valji had to read them.

c. OK *have to » some (de dicto):*
Valji's need: to read some books (no matter which ones).

However, the fact that psych predicates do not allow for differential object marking indicates that differential object marking (on a par with accusative marking in nominative-accusative languages) requires a transitive *v*. As a consequence, a restructuring analysis must allow for the presence of a transitive *v*P in constructions with *par* 'have to'. At this point, it becomes crucial to consider Wurmbrand's (2001, 2004) distinction between functional restructuring and lexical restructuring. An analysis in terms of functional restructuring would treat *par* 'have to' as a modal auxiliary; contrastively, an analysis in terms of lexical restructuring would treat *par* 'have to' as a main verb, which selects an infinitival complement that is smaller than a CP or TP. We could thus posit the two competing analyses in (35) and (36) for the construction in (34). (We omit *Asp* in these illustrations, which is plausibly located above *Mod*.)

(34) *Khimji-ne* [***Reena**-ne* *jo-v-**i***] *par-th-**i**.*
Khimji.M-DAT Reena.F-DOM see-INF-F have.to-IPFV-F
'Khimji used to have to watch Reena.'

A functional restructuring analysis, (35), would treat the 'infinitival' affix on the main verb as a marker of modality (i.e. similar to 'affix hopping' in English, cf. Chomsky 1957, the auxiliary *par* would trigger the affix form -*v* on the next lower verbal element). Similarly, the apparent *Experiencer* dative on the subject would not be an instance of theta-related case, since *par* 'have to' as an auxiliary would not assign any theta roles; rather, it would be an instance of differential subject marking (Butt & Ahmed 2011 and Butt 2012), abbreviated as *DSM* in (35). As indicated, we assume that *v* licenses differential object marking, possibly in connection to structural accusative licensing.

(35) *Functional restructuring analysis*

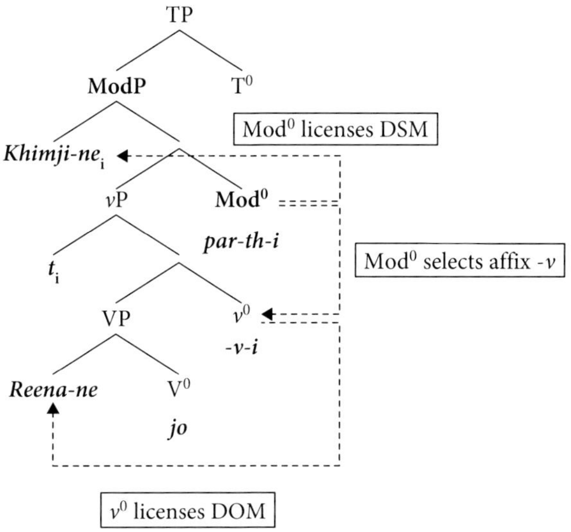

In contrast to (35), if we assume a lexical restructuring analysis, *par* 'have to' is analyzed as a matrix verb that selects a *v*P complement, as shown in (36) (at least if the lower verb is transitive). In this case, it would be plausible that the dative marking on the subject is an instance of θ-related case (cf. Woolford 2006; Rezac 2008a), due to an *Experiencer* θ-role assigned by *par* 'have to'. Since the embedded verb *jo* 'see, watch' would assign an *Agent* θ-role, the construction would be expected to have the properties of a control construction, which we indicate by means of the PRO in (36).

(36) *Lexical restructuring analysis*

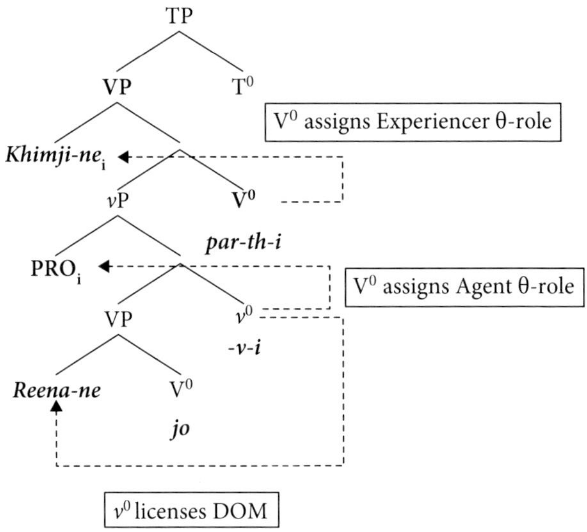

We now proceed by discussing arguments in favor of the functional restructuring analysis in (35), which treats *par* 'have to' as a modal auxiliary, i.e. as a functional restructuring predicate as opposed to a (lexical restructuring) main verb.

3.3.2 par *does not assign a theta role*

The first argument concerns the fact that *par* 'have to' does not seem to assign an *Experiencer* theta role (by virtue of which it would require its dative subject to be animate), even though it appears to assign lexical/inherent dative to its subject; its dative argument can be inanimate, (37a). In this respect, *par* 'have to' clearly contrasts with *gam* 'like', which does require its dative argument to be an animate *Experiencer*, (37b).

(37) a. *Dablu-ne* *par-v-u* *par-y-u*
container-DAT fall-INF-N have.to-PRF-N
'The container had to fall.'

b. #*Dablu-ne* *par-va* *gam-y-u*
container-DAT fall-OBL.INF like-PRF-N
'The container liked/enjoyed to fall.'

3.3.3 par *does not combine with light verbs*

The second argument concerns the fact that main verbs in Kutchi Gujarati can generally be combined with aspectual light verbs, such as *ja* 'go', (38b), or *le* 'take', (39b), both of which indicate completion of an event; *ja* 'go' and *le* 'take' are amongst the most productive light verbs in Kutchi Gujarati, and combine quite freely with a wide range of matrix verbs (cf. Cardona 1965 for Standard Gujarati, which is similar in this respect). In line with Butt (1995) and Ramchand (2008a, 2008b, 2012), we assume that light verbs are *not* auxiliaries, but serve to fine-tune the event structure of a verbal predicate, i.e. they contribute to the core verbal meaning. This is reflected by the fact that light verb constructions do not exhibit agreement on lower verbal elements, as opposed to constructions that involve genuine auxiliaries, cf. Section 3.3.6. In a light verb construction, agreement is only reflected on the (highest) light verb, and not on the main verb. The main verb (and potential intermediate light verbs, which we do not discuss here) show up with the uninflected linking morpheme -*i*, as shown in (38b)/(39b).

(38) a. ***Khimji*** *par-y-**o**.*
Khimji fall-PRF-M
'Khimji fell.'

b. ***Khimji*** *par-i* *g-y-**o**.*
Khimji fall-link[18] go-PRF-M
'Khimji fell down.'

(39) a. ***Khimji*** *naach-y-**o**.*
Khimji dance-PRF-M
'Khimji danced.'

b. *Khimji* *naach-i* *li-dh-**u**.*
Khimji dance-link take-PRF-N
'Khimji finished dancing.'

Based on the distribution of these light verbs, we infer that there is a high probability that a main verb in Kutchi Gujarati is compatible with the light verb *ja* 'go' or *le* 'take' or both. Contrastively, we expect a modal auxiliary to be incompatible with any light verbs, since light verbs only combine with main verbs. The prediction is that a main verb like *gam* 'like' should combine with light verbs, whereas *par* 'have to' may be unable to do so. This is exactly what we find. (40) shows that *gam* 'like' is compatible with both *ja* 'go' and *le* 'take' (and possibly with other light verbs as

18. Throughout this paper, we gloss -*i* as 'link' for 'linking element', much in the spirit of the label 'compound verbs', which is sometimes used for Indo-Aryan light verb constructions, e.g. Kachru (2006). This linking element is invariable/uninflected. It is attached to any verb root if the verb combines with a light verb (cf. Cardona 1965: 134 for Standard Gujarati); e.g. *par* 'fall' becomes *pari* when combining with *ja* 'go'.

well). Contrastively, *par* 'have to' is not compatible with either, (41), and as far as we can tell, *par* 'have to' cannot combine with any light verb at all.[19]

(40) a. *Khimji-ne su-va gam-i g-y-u*
Khimji-DAT sleep-OBL.INF like-link go-PRF-N
'Khimji eventually liked sleeping.'

b. *Khimji-ne su-va gam-i li-dh-u*
Khimji-DAT sleep-OBL.INF like-link take-PRF-N
'Khimji stopped liking to sleep.'

(41) a. **Khimji-ne su-v-u par-i g-y-u*
Khimji-DAT sleep-INF-N have.to-link go-PRF-N
(*intended:* 'Khimji eventually had to sleep.')

b. **Khimji-ne su-v-u par-i li-dh-u*
Khimji-DAT sleep-INF-N have.to-link go-PRF-N
(*intended:* 'Khimji stopped having to sleep.')

3.3.4 par *constructions cannot passivize*

Our third argument for treating *par* 'have to' as a modal auxiliary rather than a main verb is based on the observations that the infinitival argument of *gam* 'like (to)' can become the subject of a passive construction, as in (42), which is not the case for the VP embedded by *par* 'have to' in (43).[20] This follows if the infinitival that expresses the *Subject Matter of Emotion* (cf. Pesetsky 1991, 1996) has the status of a verbal complement in constructions with *gam* 'like', (42), whereas no such thing holds in constructions with *par* 'have to', (43).

(42) Kutchi Gujarati
a. *mane su-va gam-y-u*
me.DAT sleep-OBL.INF like-PFV-N
'I liked to sleep.'

b. *su-va gam-a-i g-y-u*
sleep-OBL.INF like-pass-link go-PFV-N
'Sleeping/To sleep was liked.'

(43) Kutchi Gujarati
a. *mane su-v-u par-y-u*
me.DAT sleep-INF-N have.to-PFV-N
'I had to sleep.'

19. The full set of light verbs in Kutchi Gujarati is yet to be determined.

20. To create the passive, an affix *-(v)a* is adjoined to the verb stem, followed by the linking affix *-i*, and the light verb *ja* 'go' is added. The alternation between *-a* and *-va* is phonologically determined (*-va* occurs after a vowel). (See also Cardona 1965: 116 for Standard Gujarati.)

b. **su-v-u par-a-i g-y-u*
sleep-INF-N have.to-pass-link go-PFV-N
(intended: 'Sleeping/To sleep was necessary.')

3.3.5 par *does not exhibit selectional variability*

A fourth (though weaker) argument can be construed from the fact that *par* 'have to' does not exhibit any selectional variability. In contrast to English *need* and *like*, which can take infinitival complements (*I need/like to eat*) as well as DP complements (*I need/like food*), Kutchi Gujarati *par* 'have to' only ever occurs in combination with an 'infinitival' *v*P, (44a), and never with a noun phrase, (44b). Contrastively, true infinitival complements of main verbs generally appear to have the distribution of nominals (cf. Cardona 1965 for Standard Gujarati, and Magier 1983a for Marwari), as illustrated in (45a–b); (45) shows that *gam* 'like' not only combines with infinitivals (*su-va* 'to sleep'), but also with noun phrases (*saak* 'curry').

(44) a. *mane su-v-u par-y-u*
me.DAT sleep-INF-N have.to-PFV-N
'I had to sleep.' (or: 'I needed to sleep.')

b. **mane saak par-y-u*
me.DAT curry have.to-PFV-N
(intended: 'I needed curry.')

(45) a. *mane su-va gam-y-u*
me.DAT sleep-OBL.INF like-PFV-N
'I liked to sleep.'

b. *mane saak gam-y-u*
me.DAT curry.N.SG like-PFV-N
'I liked the curry.'

3.3.6 *Agreement with* par *is not long distance*

'Long distance agreement' on *par* 'have to' can now be simply viewed as an instance of auxiliary agreement; as we see in (46b) and (46c), the number/gender agreement that we see in the lower part of the clause (and which we attribute to a *v/Asp* probe) spreads onto auxiliaries and modals. We can treat this as an agreement chain that is established between a functional *Asp/Mod* head (spelled out by the respective auxiliary) and the next lower head in the clausal spine (cf. also Bhatt 2005 for similar assumptions).

(46) a. past habitual
Reena *kutro(-ne) jo-th-**i**.*
Reena.F dog.M-DOM see-IPFV-F
'Reena used to watch a/the dog.'

b. past progressive
Reena *kutro(-ne)* *jo-th-**i*** *t-**i**.*
Reena.F dog.M-DOM see-IPFV-F aux.PROG-F
'Reena was watching a/the dog.'

c. past progressive with modal
Reena-ne ***kutro**(-ne)* *jo-v-**o*** *par-th-**o*** *t-**o**.*
Reena.F-DAT dog.M-DOM see-INF-M have.to-IPFV-M aux.PAST-M
'Reena used to have to watch a/the dog.'

3.3.7 *The lack of person agreement in modal constructions*

Having argued for a functional restructuring analysis of constructions with *par* 'have to', we can now address the second problem outlined at the beginning of this section, namely the lack of person agreement in such modal constructions, repeated in (47).

(47) *Reena-ne* ***mane*** *mar-v-**o*** *par-se/*-**is**.* simple future
Reena.F-DAT me.DOM hit-INF-M have.to-FUT.DEF/*1SG
'Reena will have to hit me.' (*speaker is male*)

The relevant configuration that we have argued for in the previous sections is given in (48) (omiting *Asp*, which is plausibly located between *Mod* and *T*). Here, the lower probe (which is connected to *v*, see above) agrees with the direct object *mane* 'me', as indicated. However, 'true' direct objects (which we can define as direct objects that can carry differential object marking) cannot move to SpecTP, and thus cannot trigger person agreement on T, in concurrence with Baker's (2008) proposal, yielding a configuration very much like (27a).

(48) *Functional restructuring analysis*

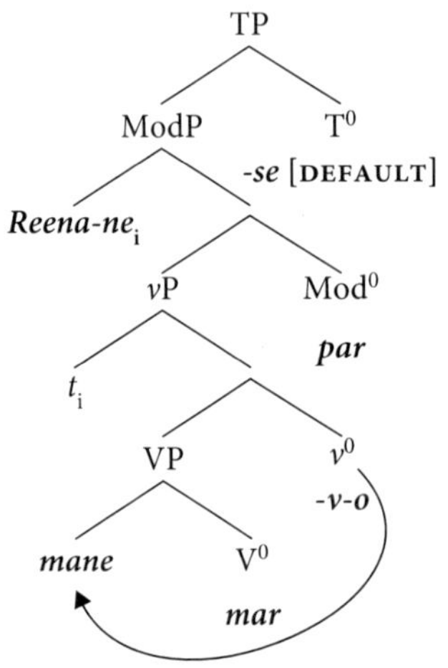

The question now arises why arguments that can carry differential object marking are unavailable for movement to *SpecTP*. The explanation seems to be as follows. We have discussed above (in Section 3.3.1) that differential object marking appears to be connected to abstract (accusative) case licensing by *v*. If we assume that movement to *SpecTP* in Kutchi Gujarati is parasitic on abstract nominative/absolutive case licensing by *T*, we derive that an accusative-licensed object cannot move to *SpecTP* and thus cannot trigger person agreement on *T*.

4. Conclusion

In this paper, we have explored three types of verbal elements in Kutchi Gujarati: Canonical transitive predicates such as *mar* 'hit', the psych verb *gam* 'like' and the modal *par* 'have to'. Focusing on the agreement patterns in the respective constructions, we argued that ϕ-agreement in Kutchi Gujarati involves two probes, a number/gender probe in the *v/Asp* domain, which always agrees with the transitive object (or intransitive subject), and a number/person probe in *T*, which always agrees with the (transitive/intransitive) subject. We have shown that the higher ϕ-probe in *T* requires a local relation with the intended agreement trigger; this is possible in the case of psych verbs in spite of their unaccusative structure (as long as the non-case-marked argument moves to *SpecTP*), but it is not possible in the case of modal constructions with *par* 'have to', since transitive direct objects are barred from moving to *SpecTP*.

References

Baker, Mark. 2008. *The Syntax of Agreement and Concord*. Cambridge: Cambridge University Press.

Bhatt, Rajesh. 2005. Long distance agreement in Hindi-Urdu. *Natural Language and Linguistic Theory* 23: 757–807.

Bhatt, Rajesh & Walkow, Martin. 2013. Locating agreement in grammar: An argument from agreement in conjunctions. *Natural Language & Linguistic Theory* 31: 951–1013.

Bjorkman, Bronwyn. 2011. BE-ing Default: the Morphosyntax of Auxiliaries. PhD dissertation, MIT.

Bobaljik, Jonathan. 1993. On ergativity and ergative unergatives. In *Papers on Case and Agreement II. MITWPL volume 19*, Colin Phillips (ed.), 45–88. Cambridge, MA: MITWPL.

Bobaljik, Jonathan. 2008. Where's Phi? agreement as a post-syntactic operation. In *Phi-Theory: Phi Features across Interfaces and Modules*, Daniel Harbour, David Adger & Susana Béjar (eds), 295–328. Oxford: Oxford University Press.

Bobaljik, Jonathan & Wurmbrand, Susanne. 2003. Long distance object agreement, restructuring and anti-reconstruction. In *Proceedings of the North Eastern Linguistics Society Annual Meeting 33 (NELS 33)*, Makoto Kadowaki & Shigeto Kawahara (eds), 67–86. Amherst: University of Massachusetts, GLSA.

Butt, Miriam & Ahmed, Tafseer. 2011. The redevelopment of Indo-Aryan case systems from a lexical semantic perspective. *Morphology* 21: 545–572.
Butt, Miriam. 2012. From spatial to subject marker. Handout for *Workshop on Non-Canonically Case-Marked Subjects*.
Butt, Miriam. 1995. *The Structure of Complex Predicates in Urdu*. Stanford: CSLI Publications.
Cardona, George. 1965. *A Gujarati Reference Grammar*. Philadelphia: The University of Pennsylvania Press.
Chandra, Pritha. 2007. (Dis)Agree: Movement and Agreement Reconsidered. PhD Dissertation, University of Maryland, College Park.
Chomsky, Noam. 1957. *Syntactic Structures*. The Hague: Mouton.
Chomsky, Noam. 2001. Derivation by phase. In *Ken Hale: A Life in Language*, Michael Kenstowicz (ed.), 1–52. Cambridge, MA: MIT Press.
Chomsky, Noam. 2004. Beyond explanatory adequacy. In *Structures and Beyond. The Cartography of Syntactic Structures*, Adriana Belletti (ed.), 104–131. Oxford: Oxford University Press.
Cinque, Guglielmo. 2004. "Restructuring" and functional structure. In *Structures and Beyond. The Cartography of Syntactic Structures*, Adriana Belletti (ed.), 132–191. Oxford: Oxford University Press.
Coon, Jessica & Preminger, Omer. 2011. Towards a unified account of person splits. In *Proceedings of* 29th *West Coast Conference on Formal Linguistics (WCCFL 29)*, 310–318. Somerville, MA: Cascadilla Press.
Coon, Jessica. 2013. TAM split ergativity, Part I. *Language and Linguistics Compass* 7: 171–190.
D'Alessandro, Roberta. 2011. Agreement, Ergativity, and the Parameterization of Probes. Ms. Leiden University.
Dahl, Östen & Velupillai, Viveka. 2011. The past tense. In *The World Atlas of Language Structures Online*, Matthew S. Dryer & Martin Haspelmath (eds). Munich: Max Planck Digital Library, Chapter 66, ⟨http://wals.info/chapter/66⟩ (30 May 2013).
Desai, Usha & Ramsay-Brijball, Malini. 2004. Tracing Gujarati language development philologically and sociolinguistically. *Alternation* 11: 308–324.
Dixon, R.M.W. 1994. *Ergativity*. Cambridge: Cambridge University Press.
Grosz, Patrick & Patel-Grosz, Pritty. 2013. Structural Asymmetries. The View from Kutchi Gujarati and Marwari. Handout for *GLOW 36*, Lund University.
Iatridou, Sabine, Anagnostopoulou, Elena & Izvorski, Roumyana. 2003. Observations about the form and meaning of the Perfect. In *Perfect Explorations*, Artemis Alexiadou, Monika Rathert & Arnim von Stechow (eds), 153–204. Berlin: de Gruyter.
Kachru, Yamuna. 2006. *Hindi*. Amsterdam: John Benjamins.
Laka, Itziar. 1993. Unergatives that assign ergative, unaccusatives that assign accusative. In *Papers on Case and Agreement I. MITWPL volume 18*, Jonathan Bobaljik & Colin Phillips (eds), 149–172. Cambridge, MA: MITWPL.
Laka, Itziar. 2000. Thetablind case: Burzio's generalisation and its image in the mirror. In *Arguments and Case: Explaning Burzio's Generalisation*, Eric Reuland (ed.), 103–129. Amsterdam: John Benjamins.
Magier, David S. 1983a. Topics in the Grammar of Marwari. Ph.D. dissertation, University of California, Berkeley.
Magier, David S. 1983b. Components of Ergativity in Marwari. *CLS 19. Papers from the 19th Regional Meeting*, 244–255. Chicago, IL: Chicago Linguistic Society.

Mistry, P. J. 1997. Objecthood and specificity in Gujarati. In *The Life of Language: Papers in Linguistics in Honor of William Bright*, J. Hill, P. J. Mistry & L. Campbell (eds), 425–442. Berlin: Mouton de Gruyter.

Mistry, P. J. 2004. Subjecthood of non-nominatives in Gujarati. In *Non-nominative Subjects*, vol. 2, Peri Bhaskararao & Karumuri Venkata Subbarao (eds), 1–32. Amsterdam: John Benjamins.

Pesetsky, David. 1991. Zero Syntax: Vol. 2: Infinitives. Ms., MIT.

Pesetsky, David. 1996. *Zero Syntax*. Cambridge, MA: The MIT Press.

Ramchand, Gillian. 2008a. *Verb Meaning and the Lexicon: A First Phase Syntax*. Cambridge: Cambridge University Press.

Ramchand, Gillian. 2008b. Lexical Items in Complex Predications: Selection as Underassociation. *Nordlyd, Tromsø Working Papers in Linguistics*.

Ramchand, Gillian. 2012. Indexical vs. Anaphoric Modals. Ms. University of Tromsø/CASTL.

Rezac, Milan. 2003. The fine structure of cyclic agree. *Syntax* 6: 156–182.

Rezac, Milan. 2008a. Phi-agree and theta-related case. In *Phi Theory: Phi-Features across Modules and Interfaces*, Daniel Harbour, David Adger & Susana Bejar (eds), 83–129. Oxford: Oxford University Press.

Rezac, Milan. 2008b. The syntax of eccentric agreement: The person case constraint and absolutive displacement in Basque. *Natural Language and Linguistic Theory* 26: 61–106.

Tessitori, Luigi. 1913. On the origin of the dative and genitive postpositions in Gujarati and Marwari. *Journal of the Royal Asiatic Society of Great Britain and Ireland* 45: 553–567.

Tessitori, Luigi. 1914–16. Notes on the grammar of the Old Western Rajasthani with special reference to Apabhramsa and to Gujarati and Marwari. *The Indian Antiquary* volumes 43–45.

Woolford, Ellen. 2006. Lexical case, inherent case, and argument structure. *Linguistic Inquiry* 37: 111–130.

Wurmbrand, Susi. 2001. *Infinitives: Restructuring and Clause Structure*. Berlin/New York: Mouton de Gruyter.

Wurmbrand, Susi. 2004. Two types of restructuring – lexical vs. functional. *Lingua* 114: 991–1014.

Markedness and syncretism in Kashmiri differential argument encoding

Emily Manetta
University of Vermont

The pronominal clitic system in Kashmiri takes the form of set of verbal suffixes conditioned by the case of the coreferent DP. This system interacts in unexpected ways with differential argument encoding (DAE) in Kashmiri, in which the case-marking of objects in non-perfective aspects is dependent on a person hierarchy. I will follow in spirit Aissen's (2003) approach to DAE as adapted to Kashmiri in Sharma (2001), however I will argue that the particulars of the Kashmiri clitic system force us to adopt an account couched not in the syntax, but in the post-syntactic component of the grammar. Keine and Müller (2008) propose that DAE is a phenomenon of the morphology-syntax interface, employing harmonic alignment of scales within framework of Distributed Morphology (Halle & Marantz 1993, 1994). I argue here that an otherwise mysterious set of clitic syncretisms in Kashmiri, including the overlap in the marking of ergative subjects and accusative objects, find explanation if we consider Kashmiri DAE not as an instance of differential marking in the narrow syntax, but instead as a as a non-zero/non-zero alternation resulting from the interaction of morphological processes and a system of optimization at the morphology-syntax interface.

Keywords: Kashmiri; clitics; distributed morphology; differential argument encoding; syncretisms

1. Introduction

The pronominal clitic system in Kashmiri takes the form of set of verbal suffixes conditioned by the case of the coreferent DP. This system interacts in unexpected ways with differential argument encoding (DAE) in Kashmiri, in which the case-marking of objects in non-perfective aspects is dependent on a person hierarchy. In essence, in the less-marked scenario in which the subject is of higher grammatical person than a pronominal object (I>II>III, I>III) (Hale 1972; Silverstein 1976), the object is morphologically bare, yet the clitic otherwise used to corefer with ergative subjects appears obligatorily suffixed to the verb, as in (1).[1]

(1) *bɨ* *vuch-a-**th*** *tsɨ* (I>II)[2]
1SG.NOM see-1SG-**2SGPS** 2SG.ACC
'I will see you.' (Wali & Koul 1997: 228)

In the more-marked scenario in which the subject is of lower/equal person relative to the object, the object is in the dative case, and a corresponding dative clitic may appear on the verb, as in (2a), but in many contexts may also be omitted, as in (2b) (Wali & Koul 1997).

(2) a. *su* *vuch-iy* *(tse)* (III<II)
3SG.NOM see-**2SGPS** 2SG.DAT
'He will see you.'

b. *su* *vuch-i* *təmis* (III=III)
3SG.NOM see-FUT 3SG.DAT
'He will see him.'

This creates DAE scenario in which the case-marking paradigm appears to fit the pattern the Hale-Silverstein hierarchy would lead us to expect. The object is unmarked when the person hierarchy is respected, but is marked dative otherwise. However the corresponding clitic marking does not seem to follow the pattern. Instead, in the less-marked scenario an unusual ergative clitic obligatorily appears corresponding to the person of the nominative object, but in the more-marked scenario the dative clitic may appear corresponding to the dative object in a limited number of situations, or no clitic morphology at all may be present.

In this paper, I will follow in spirit Aissen's (1999, 2003) approach to DAE as adapted to Kashmiri in Sharma (2001), in which a range of constraints built from the alignment of universal hierarchies interspersed with markedness constraints punishing morphological structure derive DAE. However, I will argue that Sharma's

1. For reasons that will become clear below, I have chosen to gloss this morphologically bare nominal as "accusative". Note that the form the pronoun takes in (1) is identical to the nominative form. Following Legate (2008), Keine and Müller (2008), and Calabrese (2008), the present account maintains that the absence of distinct morphological paradigms for accusative does not indicate the lack of accusative in the morphosyntax. See Sections 4–5 (in particular 5.2) for detailed discussion.

2. Glossing in this article is in large part consistent with the Leipzig glossing rules. Of particular note are pronominal enclitics suffixed to the verb, glossed with person and number plus PS for "pronominal suffix" (e.g. -1SGPS), following Wali and Koul 1997. Agreeing morphemes that are not pronominal suffixes will be glossed with person and number information but without the additional PS (e.g. -1SG).

syntax-based system is not sufficiently nuanced to account for the complete pattern. I show that Kashmiri DAE must in fact be considered a special case of the non-zero/non-zero alternation in which we account simultaneously for not only the presence/absence of morphological clitic marking on the verb, but also case marking patterns on the nominal. Keine (2007) and Keine and Müller (2008) illustrate that an Aissen-style syntax-based approach cannot be easily extended to contexts in which the DAE alternation is between two overtly case-marked candidates. They propose that DAE be considered a phenomenon of the morphology-syntax interface, employing harmonic alignment of scales within framework of Distributed Morphology (Halle & Marantz 1993, 1994). Under this approach, DAE does not indeed represent differential case assignment in the narrow syntax. Instead, a combination of underspecification of vocabulary items and impoverishment via an optimality-theoretic competition employing constraints targeting specific subfeatures of syntactic heads conspire to produce DAE effects.

Empirically, this paper suggests that the intricacies of the highly complex Kashmiri case/cliticization system, which to this point has received only partial treatment (Wali & Koul 1994; Sharma 2001), can be best understood as the result of the interaction of morphological processes and a system of optimization at the morphology-syntax interface. Further, the Kashmiri data expands our understanding of non-zero/non-zero DAE alternations, and the present analysis supports an approach to DAE phenomena couched not in the narrow syntax, but in the post-syntactic morphological component. Indeed, the analysis of Kashmiri DAE presented here suggests that the syntactic treatment of the triggering configuration be uniform, instead attributing differential encoding to post-syntactic operations, including impoverishment and the insertion of underspecified vocabulary items.

Overall this article addresses several broader, vital questions concerning the organization of the grammar. How do we best account for the syncretic patterns of morphological exponents? How and where (in what component) are typologically-motivated universal markedness hierarchies implemented in the grammar? And finally, how do we best characterize the relationship between the grammatical function of an argument and the morphological encoding of that function?

2. Kashmiri case marking and clitic systems

Kashmiri is a language with a rich inflectional system and a relatively complex set of conditions on the appearance of case and clitic morphology. In this section I provide an overview of these systems with an emphasis on the sets of most relevance to this analysis.

Kashmiri is a split-ergative language by aspect, featuring ergative marking on subjects in perfective transitive clauses. Objects in perfective transitive clauses are unmarked.

(3) *Mohn-an* *chəl'* *palav*
Mohan-ERG washed.MPL clothes.MPL
'Mohan washed the clothes'

Subjects of intransitive verbs and subjects in non-perfective aspects are typically unmarked, except for a small collection of psych predicates that require dative subjects (i.e. *sharaarath khasIn* 'to be angry'). In non-perfective clauses, the case on the object alternates between unmarked and dative case, determined by the person hierarchy. If the subject is of higher person than the object (I>II>III, I>III), the object is morphologically bare; otherwise, it is marked with dative case.[3]

(4) *tsɨ* *chi-han* *su* *par-ɨnaav-aan* (II>III)
2SG.NOM AUX-3SGPS 3SG.ACC learn-CAUSE-PART
You are teaching him.'

(5) *su* *chu-y* *tse* *par-ɨnaav-aan* (III>II)
3SG.NOM AUX-2SGPS 2SG.DAT learn-CAUSE-PART
'He is teaching you'.

(6) *su* *chu* *Aslam-as* *par-ɨnaav-aan* (III=III)
3SG.NOM AUX Aslam-DAT learn-CAUSE-PART
'He is teaching Aslam.

The following are the nominal case-marking morphemes in Kashmiri:

(7) <u>Kashmiri case morphemes</u>[4]

	MASUCLINE		FEMININE	
	SING	PLUR	SING	PLUR
Nom/Acc	∅	∅	∅	∅
Ergative	an/'	av	i	av
Dative	is/as	an	i	an
Ablative	ɨ/i	av	i	av

3. DAE in Kashmiri has been sometimes called "case lifting" in the literature (perhaps originating in Hook & Koul 1984), referring to the notion that in certain configurations the object that would otherwise be in the dative case appears bare. Notice that this implies that the marked/non-canonical scenario is the one in which the object is bare ("lifted"), when in fact this the configuration that respects the person hierarchy (I>II>III, I>III).

4. Once again, adding "accusative" to both the case and clitic paradigms is not a neutral choice. Kashmiri has no distinctly marked accusative case, but the designation of a set of morphemes as accusative will prove important both to Sharma's (2001) account and to the account developed here. This choice is discussed in greater detail in Section 5.

Kashmiri tensed verbs obligatorily exhibit primary gender and number agreement with the unmarked nominal in all tenses and aspects. Following the primary agreement morphology suffixed to the verb stem are pronominal enclitics, which vary by case and agree with the person and number features of their corresponding arguments.

(8) Kashmiri clitic sets

PERSON	NOMINATIVE		ERG/ACC		DATIVE	
	SING	PLUR	SING	PLUR	SING	PLUR
I	-s	∅	-m	∅	-m	∅
II	-kh	-v(i)	-th	-v(i)	-y	-v(i)
III	(-n)	-(kh)	-n	-kh	-s	-kh

The nominative set is used to mark the person and number of the most prominent unmarked argument, irrespective of its grammatical role. Similarly, the dative set corresponds to the person and number of dative arguments, in any role. The set of suffixes I have labeled ergative/accusative marks the person and number of both ergative subjects of perfective transitive clauses and, importantly for the present account, nonperfective bare objects surfacing as a result of the person hierarchy described above.

(9) a. *tse* *vodu-**th***
2SG.ERG cry-**2SGPS**
'You cried'.

b. *bɨ* *chu-s-**ath*** *tsɨ* *par-ɨnaav-aan*
1SG.NOM AUX-1SGPS-**2SGPS** 2SG.ACC learn-CAUSE-PRS
'I am teaching you.'

Whether or not the clitics are obligatory and whether or not they can co-occur with an overt pronominal (clitic doubling) is variable. The nominative set is obligatory, and the unmarked argument is optionally null. First and third-person ergative suffixes are optional if the arguments are overt, but obligatory if they are null. Second person ergative suffixes are obligatory, but the corresponding argument may be overt or null. The optional presence of the dative suffixes requires null corresponding arguments in first and third person. Dative second person arguments are obligatorily marked, but doubling is optional. Bare nonperfective (accusative) objects must be marked with the ergative/accusative clitics (Wali & Koul 1997). In this paper I will not present a complete account of these obligatory marking and doubling conditions (nor does Sharma 2001), though this will be a topic of discussion in Section 5. I will primarily focus on the clitic forms themselves when they do surface, and the workings of the morphology-syntax interface.

Let us return now to the core empirical puzzle. Although in nonperfective clauses in which the subject is of higher person than the object the object bears no case morphology, it is marked by the ergative clitic suffixed to the verb.

(10) *bɨ* *vuch-a-**th*** *tsɨ* (I>II)
1SG.NOM see-1SG-**2SGPS** 2SG.ACC
'I will see you.'

On the other hand, in the scenario in which the object is of lower/equal person, it appears with dative case morphology, and under certain conditions, marked by the dative clitic.

(11) *su* *vuch-i* *təmis* (III=III)
3SG.NOM see-FUT 3SG.DAT
He will see him.'

In what follows, I will show that the account developed by Sharma (2001), modeled on Aissen's approach to DAE, cannot account for the complete non-zero/non-zero nature of this alternation. Instead, I will build on this body of work but shift the locus of the analysis to the morphological component, allowing us to simultaneously understand the deep syncretism visible in the case-marking and clitic morphology in (7) and (8) above, as well as the nature of DAE in Kashmiri.

3. Sharma 2001: An analysis of Kashmiri DAE

Following the account of differential argument encoding (DAE) developed in Aissen (1999, 2003), Sharma (2001) proposes a system of ranked syntactic constraints derived from the alignment of universal markedness hierarchies and local conjunction (Prince & Smolensky 1993). Competition between candidates then produces the interaction between person-marking, case, and ergativity in Kashmiri. Importantly, the goal of her analysis is to account only for the verbal clitic marking in Kashmiri, and not for the pattern of case assignment. In this section I will review the essential components of Sharma's account, highlighting the points of departure for the approach presented in this paper.

Sharma's analysis develops three separate sets of subhierarchies in an effort to account for Kashmiri DAE: one to account for person hierarchy effects in non-perfective clauses, one for case selection, and one for perfective subject marking. The person hierarchy effects derive from the harmonic alignment of constraints based on universal scales of markedness of person and of grammatical relation.

(12) *Creating constraints from markedness of person and grammatical function*

SCALE	HARMONIC ALIGNMENT	CONSTRAINT ALIGNMENT
Su > Obj	Su/1 ⊃ Su/2 ⊃ Su/3	*Su/1 >> *Su/2 >> *Su/3
1 > 2 > 3	Obj/3 ⊃ Obj/2 ⊃ Obj/1	*Obj/3 >> *Obj/2 >>*Obj/1

From these scales, Aissen (2003) then derives constraints that favor certain combinations of subjects and objects via local constraint conjunction (Smolensky 1995), which combines each member of one alignment pairwise which each member of the other. The highest constraint in the first alignment is conjoined with the highest constraint in the second, then with the next highest, and so on. The end result is nine constraints partially ranked with respect to one another:

(13) *Su/3 & *Obj/1 >>
{*Su/2 & *Obj/1, *Su/3 & *Obj/2} >>
{*Su/1 & *Obj/1, *Su/2 & Obj/2, *Su/3 & *Obj/3} >>
{*Su/1 & *Obj/2, *Su/2 & Obj/3} >>
*Su/1 & *Obj/3

Finally, when each of the constraints in (13) is conjoined with a markedness constraint targeting lack of case morphology, as in (14), some case morphology is required to mark the respective configuration. An example is in (15):

(14) $*\varnothing_C$ Avoid absence of morphological case (Aissen 2003)

(15) [*Su/3 & *Obj/1] & $*\varnothing_C$ Avoid absence of morphological case when a clause involves a third person subject and a first person object

As in Aissen (2003), the entire set of conjunctions of the form in (15) is then interspersed with a markedness constraint that prohibits structure as in (16):

(16) *STRUC$_C$ Avoid (case specification) structure

For Kashmiri specifically, Sharma determines that in order to obtain the scenario in which the object is marked only when the subject is of lower or equal person compared to the object, *STRUC$_C$ must be ranked below all the conjoined constraints featuring a subject of lower or equal grammatical person. *STRUC$_C$ must in turn dominate all conjoined constraints in which the subject is of higher grammatical person. The overall ranking we are looking for is therefore schematized in (17), with the family of conjoined constraints such as those in (15) abbreviated for clarity.

(17) [*Su ≤ Obj & $*\varnothing_C$] >> *STRUC$_C$ >> [*Su > Obj & $*\varnothing_C$]

This ranking alone will derive the fact that in those contexts in which the subject is of lower or equal person compared to the object, case marking must arise – but what marking on which argument? To answer this question, Sharma relies on the notion of core vs. non-core arguments and core vs. non-core case (Wierzebicka 1981). In essence, instead of just $*\varnothing_C$, which is violated when an argument is not case-marked, the analysis requires a constraint that is violated when a core argument (subject, object) is marked with a non-core case (dative, ergative) (see Woolford

2001). Sharma calls this constraint $*\varnothing_{NC}$, and it requires non-core cases in the given context. The conjunctions in (17) are refined by replacing $*\varnothing_{C}$ with $*\varnothing_{NC}$.

Sharma then presents constraint subhierarchies based on the relative markedness of perfective subjects over nonperfective subjects and nonperfective objects over perfective objects (Greenberg 1966). The constraint conjunctions in (18), when ranked with respect to *STRUC$_C$, require that perfective subjects and nonperfective objects must be marked.

(18) *SU/PERF & $*\varnothing_{C}$, *OB/PERF & $*\varnothing_{C}$ >> *STRUC$_C$ >>
*SU/NONPERF & $*\varnothing_{C}$, *OB/PERF & $*\varnothing_{C}$

Sharma combines the rankings from the three different sets of subhierarchies in the following way to produce the case-marking patterns in Kashmiri.

(19) *SU/PERF & $*\varnothing_{C}$, *SU≤OJ & $*\varnothing_{NC}$, *OJ/NONPERF & $*\varnothing_{C}$ >>
*STRUC$_C$ >> *C-ARG/NC-CASE >>
*SU/NONPERF & $*\varnothing_{C}$, *SU > *OJ & $*\varnothing_{NC}$, *OB/PERF

The ranking in (19) indicates that in Kashmiri, both the perfectivity system and the relative person markedness system are split across *STRUC$_C$. Those configurations described by constraints ranked higher than *STRUC$_C$ will require morphological marking. Those below will not.

Because in this account I am primarily concerned with the outcome for nonperfective inputs (and the accompanying DAE effect), I will exclude Sharma's perfective tableaux here. The tableau in (20) represents the competition between candidates with a less-marked input, such as when the subject is in the first person and the object is in the second person.

(20)
Input: V(nonperf)-S1–O2

	*SU/PERF	*SU≤ OJ	*OJ/NONPERF	*STRUC$_C$	*C-ARG/NC-CASE	*SU/NONPERF	*SU > *OJ	*OBJ/PERF
a.			*!			*	*	
☞b.				*		*	*	
c.			*!	*	*			
d.				*	*!	*		
e.				**!	*			

a. V-1.NOM-2.NOM
b. V-1.NOM-2.**ACC**
c. V-1.**ERG**-2.NOM
d. V-1.NOM-2.**DAT**
e. V-1.**ERG**-2.**ACC**

In the tableau in (20), the pattern in which the subject is nominative and the object is accusative emerges as the winner. Losing candidates (a) and (c) fail to provide any marking of a non-perfective object (note that the accusative clitic required in (b) allows it to satisfy this constraint).[5] Candidate (e) features too much marking (two clitics) and runs afoul of *STRUC$_C$. Candidate (d) loses because a core argument is marked with non-core case (dative), leaving (b) the winner.

The second relevant tableau is the one in which the input is more marked: the subject is of lower grammatical person than the object.

(21)
Input: V(nonperf)-S2–O1

	*SU/PERF	*SU≤ OJ	*OJ/NONPERF	*STRUC$_C$	*C-ARG/NC-CASE	*SU/NONPERF	*SU > *OJ	*SU > *OJ
a.		*!	*			*		
b.		*!		*		*		
c.			*!	*	*			
☞d.				*	*	*		
e.				**!	*			

a. V-1.NOM-2.NOM
b. V-1.NOM-2.**ACC**
c. V-1.**ERG**-2.NOM
d. V-1.NOM-2.**DAT**
e. V-1.**ERG**-2.**ACC**

5. There seems to be some inconsistencies in the way in which the constraint *OJ/NONPERF & *$\varnothing_C$ functions in this account. Since it evaluates only clitic markers, then both **nom** and **acc** object inputs may have associated clitics (so candidate (c) should not necessarily receive a violation). If (contrary to fact) it evaluated case-marking, then candidate (b) would violate the constraint, because the accusative object is bare (see Sharma (2001), Footnote 15).

In tableau (21), the candidate with dative marking on the object emerges as the winner. Candidates (c) and (e) are ruled out for the same reasons as in the tableau in (20). Candidates (a) and (b) both violate the constraint requiring non-core case marking in a configuration in which the subject is of lower or equal person to the object. Importantly, the accusative clitic obligatorily suffixed to the verb in candidate (b) satisfies this constraint because accusative is a core case in this account.

This syntax-based analysis attempts to account for the two distinct case-marking configurations in the nonperfective in Kashmiri that are conditioned by the person hierarchy. Sharma invests significant effort in defending the universal hierarchies that underlie the constraints and the potential for constraint re-ranking to result in other familiar patterns crosslinguistically. That said, the complete empirical puzzle of Kashmiri DAE has not been addressed here. I explore this shortcoming below, and show that once we consider it carefully, the account of Kashmiri no longer stands as Sharma has presented it.

In Sharma's (2001) account, she considers *only* clitic morphology, which appears suffixed to the verb. The clitic morphology serves to exempt a candidate from violations of constraints such as *OJ/NONPERF & $*\varnothing_C$ in the tableau in (20). That is, candidate (b) does not violate *OJ/NONPERF & $*\varnothing_C$, crucially, because this candidate does provide overt morphological marking of the nonperfective object, in the form of the accusative clitic. Following the same reasoning, the candidate receives only a single violation of $*\text{STRUC}_C$, for the single clitic morpheme.

What is problematic under this view is candidate (d) in the tableau in (21). Recall that in certain configurations the dative-case-marked argument is not doubled by a dative clitic suffixed to the verb, as in (2b), repeated here.

(2b)	*su*	*vuch-i*	*təmis*	(III=III)
	3SG.NOM	see-FUT	3SG.DAT	
	'He will see him.'			

Therefore candidate (d) in (21), in which the object is marked dative, could potentially fail to have the dative clitic present. In the tableau in (21), this will mean that candidate (d) will violate the highly ranked constraint *SU<OB & $*\varnothing_{NC}$, requiring non-core case marking in a configuration in which the subject is of lower or equal person to the object. This would eliminate candidate (d), incorrectly leaving candidate (e) the winner. In other words, in scenarios in which the subject is of lower/equal person to the object, this constraint ranking will not consistently yield dative-marked objects, contrary to fact.

The analysis fails precisely because the DAE effects in Kashmiri are an instance of an alternation significantly more complex than the zero/non-zero patterns Aissen's approach was designed to account for. If one considers clitic morphology *alone*, as Sharma has done here, then this is at best a non-zero/non-zero alternation in which the more-marked and less-marked configurations receive precisely the same quantity of morphological exponence (either the accusative clitic or the dative clitic). At worst, this is a situation in which the less-marked configuration is marked with the ergative/accusative clitic, but the more-marked configuration has no morphological exponence at all (when the dative clitic fails to appear). Moreover, DAE in Kashmiri certainly exists independent of the pronominal system (and pronominal clitics) entirely. Animate third person direct objects must be marked dative if the subject is of equal person (III = III).

(22)	*su*	*za:ni*	*nəziir-n-en*	*tr-en*	*doost-an.*
	3SG.NOM	knows	Nazir-GEN-DAT	three-DAT	friend-DAT

'He knows three friends of Nazir'.

It is only once we consider the totality of the morphological pattern, including both case and clitic morphology, that we develop a satisfactory account of DAE in Kashmiri.

A further problem has to do with the way in which Sharma has set up the paradigms for both case marking and clitic morphemes. Recall that Sharma does not provide a set of case markers for the accusative case, as these would be null, identical to the nominative set. However, she does provide a set of accusative verbal clitic suffixes, even though these are identical to the ergative set. This distinction proves critical to the analysis, as can be seen in the tableaux above. If what Sharma calls the accusative clitic were instead considered the ergative clitic, then candidate (b) in (21) would not receive a violation of *SU<OB & *$\varnothing_{NC}$. This is because ergative is a non-core case in Sharma's account, and would suffice to satisfy this constraint. It is only because she has labeled the set of clitics marking bare nonperfective objects "accusative" that the competition in (21) can (modulo inputs like (2b), above) select (d) as the winner. Sharma suggests that the ergative/accusative overlap in the clitic system is a result of surface syncretism, not deep neutralization. If this were so, would it be surprising to see surface syncretisms between nominative and accusative in the case-marking paradigm?

Grammars and analyses of Kashmiri over the past century are mixed in their treatment of accusative case. While some posit accusative case markers as distinct (e.g. Bhatt 1999), others do not (Wali & Koul 1997; Koul & Wali 2006). Notably, Grierson (1916) is alone in identifying a distinct accusative clitic set, as far as I am aware. As Sharma's account operates over syntactic (as opposed to morphological) structures, the status of accusative as a core, structurally-assigned case needs to be clarified. Further discussion of the nature of accusative case and its role in DAE follows in Section 5.

In sum, in Kashmiri, the less-marked scenario is not one entirely lacking in morphological marking, and the more-marked scenario may not always exceed the less-marked in the quantity of morphological exponence. For this reason, DAE in Kashmiri must be understood as an instance of non-zero/non-zero alternation, falling into the wider set of patterns that Keine and Müller (2008) identify as less/more alternations. In the account I will present below, the morphological markedness of configurations not conforming to the person hierarchy will be lodged in the level of specification of the morphemes themselves, not necessarily the quantity of morphological exponence.

In the remaining sections of this paper I provide a new approach to these facts that accounts for both the core empirical puzzle of Kashmiri DAE and the linked deep syncretisms visible in the morphology of the case and clitic paradigms. In order to accomplish these two goals, we will need to shift the optimality-theoretic mechanism underlying this account from the syntax into the morphological component.

4. Non-zero/non-zero alternations

Keine and Müller (2008) bring a new set of empirical facts to the fore in order to demonstrate that the account of DAE phenomena as developed in Aissen, while essentially correct, will not be sufficient to account for non-zero/non-zero markedness alternations. They address examples of DAE in Hindi-Urdu, Dyirbal, Mannheim German, Trumai, Cavineña, and Finnish that exhibit alternations between two or more overt markers. And yet, as they show, in each of these scenarios less and/or lighter marking is placed on the canonical object and more and/or heavier marking is placed on the non-canonical object. For this reason, they argue that both the zero/non-zero and the non-zero/non-zero cases are part of a broader less/more pattern, and expand Aissen's original approach to encompass this larger set of DAE phenomena.

Keine and Müller's alternative adopts the harmonic alignment of markedness scales and local conjunction with faithfulness constraints (blocking deletion of case). As in Aissen's core approach, these are then interspersed with markedness constraints. The major difference is that Keine and Müller implement this account at the morphology-syntax interface so that primitive case features can be targeted by the optimality-theoretic competition. They argue that the selective deletion of case features post-syntactically through the interaction between conjoined faithfulness constraints and markedness constraints derives the process of *impoverishment* as it is understood in the framework of Distributed Morphology (DM). We may therefore unify our explanation of hierarchical markedness and syncretisms in morphological marking occurring in the broader less/more pattern of DAE.

Keine and Müller's approach is situated in DM, which assumes that Vocabulary Insertion takes place post-syntactically and is subject to the *subset principle* and *specificity*. The subset principle requires that the vocabulary item must have at least a subset of the morpho-syntactic features of syntactic head where it is inserted. Further, if more than one vocabulary item meets this requirement, it is the most specific (the one with the most features) that is inserted (Halle 1997). Crucial to their approach is the decomposition of syntactic case into primitive features (justified elsewhere; see Bierwisch 1967), permitting the optimality-theoretic system to allow partial deletion of features. Vocabulary Insertion will then cause these partially expressed sets of formal features to be realized based on the properties of the relevant set of markers.

Let us briefly review how their approach accounts for a less/more DAE scenario in Mannheim German. In this variety of German, although nominative and accusative non-pronominal DPs are indistinguishable, masculine personal pronouns are marked differently in nominative and accusative contexts. The pronoun is either marked with the accusative exponent *-n* or the nominative exponent *-r*. Further, determiners for non-pronominal DPs in object position exhibit non-zero nominative case marking (*-r*). Thus a non-zero/non-zero alternation emerges for governed objects (as it is unlikely that pronominal objects are assigned structural accusative case and DP objects are not).

The analysis Keine and Müller propose assumes that case and gender/number are decomposed as follows:

(23) Case/Gender/Number

NOM: [–obl,–gov]	MASC: [+masc,–fem]
ACC: [–obl,+gov]	FEM: [–masc,+fem]
DAT: [+obl,+gov]	NEUT: [+masc,+fem]
GEN: [+obl,–gov]	PL: [–masc,–fem]

Making use of these decompositions, the relevant vocabulary items then have the following feature specifications:

(24) *Vocabulary Items for Mannheim German*

/n/ ↔ [+masc,+gov]	(ACC.MASC.SG.)
/r/ ↔ [+masc]	(NOM.MASC.SG.)

Turning now to the markedness scales at work in this example, pronouns outrank non-pronominals on the definiteness scale:

(25) Definiteness scale
Pro(noun) > Name (PN) > Def(inite) > Indefinite Specific (Spec) > NonSpecific (NSpec)

When this scale is harmonically aligned with the grammatical function scale (Subject>Object) we arrive at a set of constraints that can then be conjoined with faithfulness constraint MAX-CASE (MAX_C) that penalizes deletion of case features from input to output. For instance, **Obj/Pro & MAX_C* is violated if a case feature of an object pronoun is deleted.[6] A markedness constraint, *[+gov], can be ranked just below the faithfulness constraint for object pronouns, resulting in lack of distinction in nominative/accusative marking in all non-pronominal contexts. Consequently the ranking of constraints that govern the marking of objects in the post-syntactic domain in Mainheim German is as follows:

(26) *Ranking in Mannheim German*
*Obj/Pro & MAX_C >> *[+gov] >> {*Obj/PN & MAX_C, *Obj/Def & MAX_C, *Obj/Spec & MAX_C, *Obj/NSpec & MAX_C }

This means that pronominal objects will maintain the specification [+gov], and will therefore receive overt accusative marking in the form of *-n*. All other types of non-pronominal objects will emerge with impoverished feature inventories, lacking [+gov]. These pronominals and the relevant full DP determiners, though structurally accusative, will appear with overt nominative marking (*-r*).

As Keine and Müller point out, this non-zero/non-zero alternation cannot be captured within Aissen's original account. However, when the optimality-theoretic evaluation is shifted from the syntax into the morphological component, and when more specific subfeatures of syntactic case are targeted by markedness constraints, we can capture instances in which DAE is a gradient phenomenon. It is clear that something like this approach is needed to account for the facts of Kashmiri DAE. In what follows I propose a new analysis of the non-zero/non-zero alternation in Kashmiri along these lines, building on Sharma's (2001) account and shifting that account to the morpho-syntactic interface.

5. Underspecification and syncretism: A revised approach to Kashmiri DAE

5.1 Orientation

The syntax-based approach to Kashmiri DAE pursued in Sharma (2001) has two shortcomings. The first is purely empirical. The account does not completely address the contribution to morphological markedness made by both the clitic

6. Keine and Müller have replaced the markedness constraint $*\varnothing_C$ in these conjunctions with the faithfulness constriaint MAX_C. The conjunction functions more or less equivalently, penalizing any deletion of case features on arguments with the appropriate qualities.

and the case marker. For this reason, the correct winner cannot be predicted in those contexts in which the dative clitic fails to surface (for reasons independent of DAE). Further, since there is DAE in Kashmiri even with non-pronominal objects, nominal case must also be included in the analysis.

The second reason is a theoretical one. It is certainly possible to overhaul the account pursued in Sharma such that specific case subfeatures are targeted by markedness constraints and both clitics and case marking are evaluated by these constraints. But such a revision would prompt us to ask whether this kind of competition occurs in the narrow syntax at all. More broadly, is DAE in fact a competition between the syntactic features of a construction or the way in which those features are marked morphologically? I will argue, along with Keine and Müller (2008), that it is the latter. In a context in which there are many fewer morphological exponents than combinations of syntactic features, shifting the burden of this account to the morphology-syntax interface makes possible an explanation of how those exponents are ultimately assigned (and why underspecification would exist in the first place). As Calabrese (2008) points out, there is no reason to assume that emergence of syncretic patterns has a syntactic motivation – that is, there is no clear reason that syntax should play any role in the (possibly idiosyncratic) variation observed in morphological exponents of the clitic and case-marking system.

5.2 Kashmiri case decomposition and case/clitic vocabulary items

In order to develop a more complete account of Kashmiri DAE along the lines of the approach proposed in Keine and Müller, we must first define the decomposition of the syntactic case features in Kashmiri. I will follow Keine and Müller (making use of subfeatures presented in Jakobson 1936 and Bierwisch 1967) in assuming the following decompositions of the relevant cases:

(27) *Decomposition of case*[7]

Nominative	[+subj, –gov, –obl]
Accusative	[–subj, +gov, –obl]
Dative	[–subj, +gov, +obl]
Ergative	[+subj, –gov, +obl]
Ablative	[–subj, –gov, +obl]

7. Wali and Koul (1994) offer a syntactic approach to cliticization in Kashmiri using Spec-head agreement via movement to successive Agreement Phrases. In addition, they propose a feature decomposition of the clitic types using the features [±absolutive, ±oblique]. While I do not adopt any specific trappings of this analysis here, I follow this aspect of their approach in spirit, in that they have attempted to designate feature specifications which align ergative clitics with clitics marking nonperfective bare nominals (both are [–absolutive, –oblique]).

Crucially, I assume the existence of structural accusative case in the syntax, assigned by transitive *v* in non-perfective aspects to the DP complement of V, and with the basic feature decomposition above. Following Legate (2008), Keine and Müller (2008), and Calabrese (2008) (inter alia), the present account maintains that the absence of distinct morphological paradigms for accusative does not indicate the lack of accusative in the morphosyntax. In fact, much as Legate argues for Hindi-Urdu, I will claim that nonperfective objects in Kashmiri are assigned abstract accusative case, later realized differentially in the morphology. Accusative case in Kashmiri is characterized by completely syncretic morphological exponents, and the goal of the account below will be to provide an explanation for the marking given to syntactically accusative objects.

I will further assume here, that clitics in Kashmiri arise as the result of an Agree operation in the syntax between a probe on a functional head and a goal nominal. Some version of this approach is adopted in a range of other work on Kashmiri including Subbarao (2001), Wali and Koul (1994), and Manetta (2006, 2011). In this way, the functional head that generates secondary agreement (a clitic head) will carry the same feature specification as the goal nominal just as the functional head that generates primary agreement (the Tense head) carries the feature specification of its goal (the highest unmarked nominal). Primary and secondary agreement in Kashmiri then arise on distinct functional heads, but crucially via the same mechanism, the Agree operation, in the syntax.

I claim here that underspecification of clitic and case morphemes in Kashmiri allows us to understand an otherwise mysterious set of syncretisms in the language, including the overlap in the clitic marking of ergative subjects and bare non-perfective objects. I repeat here the set of verbal enclitics in Kashmiri. As you can see in (28), beyond the complete overlap in ergative and accusative marking, there are a number of other shared exponents. All plural clitic sets are identical. Further, the clitics used to encode ergative/accusative and dative first person singular and nominative and ergative/accusative third person singular are shared.

(28) Kashmiri clitic sets

PERSON	NOMINATIVE		ERG/ACC		DATIVE	
	SING	PLUR	SING	PLUR	SING	PLUR
I	-s	∅	-m	∅	-m	∅
II	-kh	-v(i)	-th	-v(i)	-y	-v(i)
III	(-n)	-(kh)	-n	-kh	-s	-kh

I claim that these syncretisms arise because a number of these vocabulary items are underspecified. Therefore the heads in which they may be inserted may have a superset of the features specified on the marker.

(29) *Vocabulary Items for Kashmiri clitics*[8]

-s	↔ [+first, +sing, −gov]	NOM 1st SING
-kh	↔ [+second, +sing, −gov]	NOM 2nd SING
-y	↔ [+second, +sing, +gov]	DAT 2nd SING
-s	↔ [+third, +sing, +gov]	DAT 3rd SING
-m	↔ [+first, +sing]	DAT/ERG/ACC 1st SING
-th	↔ [+second, +sing]	ERG/ACC 2nd SING
-n	↔ [+third, +sing]	ERG/ACC 3rd SING
-v(i)	↔ [+second, +plur]	NOM/DAT/ERG/ACC 2nd PLUR
-kh	↔ [+third, +plur]	NOM/DAT/ERG/ACC 3rd PLUR
∅	↔ [ ]	NOM/DAT/ERG/ACC 1st PLUR

The plural markers in (29) lack specification for case entirely, as they are identical across the paradigm. Crucially for this discussion, *-m, -th,* and *-n* are underspecified for case.[9] As we will see below, the subset principle and specificity will then work in concert to cause this set of clitics to mark singular ergative subjects and non-perfective bare (accusative) objects.[10]

I have repeated the markers of the Kashmiri nominal case system below. Once again, we see significant overlap. Nominatives and accusatives are completely unmarked. The plural paradigms are identical irrespective of gender, and all oblique feminine singular markers are *-i*.

(30) *Kashmiri case markers*

	Masculine		Feminine	
	Sing	Plur	Sing	Plur
Nom/Acc	∅	∅	∅	∅
Ergative	an/'	av	i	av
Dative	is/as	an	i	an
Ablative	ɨ/i	av	i	av

8. There is one overlap here that this account does not treat as a systematic syncretism: the *-s* marking first person nominative singular and the *-s* marking third person dative singular.

9. Although the sets of feature specifications for both clitics and case marking are at least in part in accordance with the Iconicity Meta-Principle, I will not pursue a detailed account of the relative phonetic complexity of these markers here.

10. The first person clitic in both the ergative/accusative and dative paradigms is the same (*-m*), however whenever this morpheme appears in the context of a nonperfective object it must be the dative clitic. This is because the ergative/accusative first person clitic will never arise in the context of unmarked nonperfective objects, since these objects only appear in the scenario in which the subject is of higher person than the object. If the object is first person, this configuration cannot be generated and we will see only dative-marked objects with corresponding dative clitics.

The feature specifications for each case marker of Kashmiri, employing the feature decompositions above in (31), are below. Note that just as in the clitic markers above, the null marker is radically underspecified.

(31) *Vocabulary Items for Kashmiri case markers*

an/'	↔	[+masc, +sing, +obl, +subj]	ERG M. SING.
ɨ/i	↔	[+masc, +sing, −gov, +obl]	ABL M. SING.
is/as	↔	[+masc, +sing, +gov]	DAT M. SING.
i	↔	[+fem, +sing, +gov]	DAT F. SING.
i	↔	[+fem, +sing, +obl]	ERG/ABL F. SING.[11]
av	↔	[+plur, −gov, +obl]	ERG/ABL M/F PLUR.
an	↔	[+plur, +gov]	DAT M/F PLUR.
∅	↔	[ ]	NOM/ACC M/F SING/PLUR

In the analysis that follows in Section 5.3, I will show how impoverished outputs serve as the input for morphological realization, resulting in the insertion of the correct case and clitic markers in DAE contexts.

5.3 A DM-based account of Kashmiri DAE

This approach to the clitic and case system syncretisms then permits us to adopt the analysis of non-zero/non-zero DAE alternations pursued in Keine and Müller (2008). In essence, Kashmiri falls into the less/more marking pattern (of which the zero/non-zero pattern is a proper subset), in the sense that the clitic inserted in the less marked scenario (in which the subject is of higher person than a pronominal object) is in fact the less specified morpheme. The ergative/accusative set of clitics and the accusative case markers in fact have no specification for case at all, and hence will prove to be the best match for impoverished outputs. In the more highly marked scenario, requiring dative case on the object, the clitic and case marker inserted are the more highly specified morphemes, marked with dative case subfeatures.

An account modeled after that in Keine and Müller is situated in the post-syntactic morphological component, prior to vocabulary insertion. The competition is one of markedness vs. faithfulness – it is this interaction that ultimately derives DAE. The faithfulness constraints in essence encode the fact that certain marked configurations (in our case, those which fail to obey the person hierarchy) require greater faithfulness to input than less marked configurations.

11. Again here we have an overlap that cannot quite be captured (-*i* is the exponent for both the specifications [+fem, +sing, +gov] and [+fem, +sing, −obl]).

Markedness is relativized to certain syntactic subfeatures. In particular, I will adopt two markedness constraints employed by Keine and Müller for a range of DAE scenarios. These constraints are *[+gov] and *[−obl], violated by each instance of the feature [+gov] or [−obl] on a syntactic head, whether that head is a verbal clitic or nominal case marking. Unless a higher-ranking constraint is violated, these markedness constraints will favor impoverished candidates for which these features have been deleted. That is, the optimality-theoretic competition is one that reduces the syntactic inputs for morphological realization. This process will in turn cause less specific morphemes to be inserted. The refinement of markedness I pursue here permits us to derive the full range of DAE effects in Kashmiri.

Sharma's syntax-based account features the conjoined constraint: *s ≤ OB & *$\varnothing_{NC}$. The constraint requires that if the subject is of lower person than object, non-core case features ([+erg], [+dat]) be morphologically realized (this includes case-marking and clitics). The new account I develop here relies on a slightly different and somewhat simpler constraint. I follow Keine and Müller in conjoining the harmonically aligned constraint *s≤OB with the faithfulness constraint MAX$_C$. The conjoined constraint *s≤OB & MAX$_C$ requires that if the subject is of lower/equal person than the object then the candidates must be faithful to the case marking specifications of the input. There are two desirable implications of this change. First, we no longer need to refer to the category of "non-core" case at all. Instead we may target specific case subfeatures, as needed. Second, and more importantly, DAE now becomes a competition between markedness of specific syntactic features (in this instance, [+gov] and [−obl]) and faithfulness to the input.

The relevant faithfulness constraints have a fixed, invariable ranking (Aissen 1999, 2003; Sharma 2001): *s≤OB & MAX$_C$ >> *s>OB & MAX$_C$. Interpolated in between these two constraints are the two markedness constraints *[gov] and *[−obl]. The two markedness constraints are not ranked with respect to one another. This results in an overall ranking that requires faithfulness to the input in the more-marked scenario, but otherwise allows markedness to determine the optimal candidate.

(32) s≤OB & MAX$_C$ >> *[gov], *[−obl] >> *s>OB & MAX$_C$

Let us now return to the core empirical contrast of interest. In (33), we see the less-marked scenario in which the subject is of higher grammatical person than the object, and the ergative/accusative clitic appears suffixed to the verb:

(33) *bɨ* *vuch-a-**th*** *tsɨ* (I>II)
1SG.NOM see-1SG-**2SGPS** 2SG.ACC
'I will see you.'

The syntactic case on the object in (33) is in fact accusative, decomposed as [+gov, −obl, −subj]. As discussed above, the clitic arises as the result of an Agree operation in the syntax, and will have the identical syntactic features. I have eliminated all but the person, [+gov], and [−obl] specifications in the tableau for clarity, as the other features (e.g. gender) are not targeted here.

(34) *Less-marked input, impoverished output*

INPUT: SU[1ST] OB[2ND, +gov, −obl] CL[2ND, +gov, −obl]	*S≤OB & MAX_C	*[+gov]	*[−obl]	*S>OB & MAX_C
a. OB[2ND, +gov, −obl] CL[2ND, +gov, −obl]		*!*	**	
☞ b. OB[2ND] CL[2ND]				****

In tableau (34), neither candidate incurs a violation of the highest ranked faithfulness constraint, as it does not apply – the subject is not of lower or equal grammatical person than the object. The winner is then determined by markedness constraints, punishing all instances of the feature [+gov] and the feature [−obl] in the input. The optimal output is thus the impoverished candidate (b), in which the features [+gov] and [−obl] have been eliminated. Notice that any partially impoverished candidate, in which some of the [+gov] and/or [−obl] specifications remained, would have incurred violations of the markedness constraints, and candidate (b) would still emerge as the winner.

This candidate then serves as the input for morphological realization. For the case marker on the object, the only marker that would be in compliance with the subset principle is the null marker, which has no subfeature specification at all. All other second person singular markers are overspecified for this output. We therefore correctly expect to see no case-marking morphology. For the clitic suffixed to the verb, two markers comply with the subset principle, the null marker [ ], and the ergative/accusative marker [+second, +sing]. In this scenario *specificity* dictates that the more specific marker must be chosen, and so the ergative/accusative exponent, with the specification [+second, +sing], will surface. The process of vocabulary insertion is schematized in (35).

(35) OB[+second, +sing] ↔ ∅ [ ]
CL[+second, +sing] ↔ *-th* [+second, +sing]

Thus we arrive at precisely the case-marking and clitic configuration in the sentence in (33).

In the more-marked scenario in which the subject is of lower/equal person relative to the object, the object appears in the dative case, and a corresponding dative clitic may appear on the verb.

(36) *su* *vuch-i-y* *tse* (III<II)
3SG.NOM see-FUT-**2SGPS** 2SG.DAT
'He will see you.'

In the syntax, the case assigned to the object in (36) is still accusative, as it is in precisely the same syntactic configuration. Accusative case decomposes into the following subfeatures: [+gov, −obl, −subj]. Once again, the clitic arises as the result of an Agree operation in the syntax, and will have the identical syntactic features. In the second tableau in (37) I have eliminated all but the person, [+gov], and [−obl] specifications in the tableau for clarity.

(37) *More-marked input, fully-specified output*

INPUT: SU[3RD] OB[2ND, +gov, −obl] CL[2ND, +gov, −obl]	*S≤OB & MAX_C	*[+gov]	*[−obl]	*S>OB & MAX_C
☞ a. OB[2ND, +gov, −obl] CL[2ND, +gov, −obl]		**	**	
b. OB[2ND] CL[2ND]	*!***			

In tableau (37), since the subject is in fact of lower grammatical person than the object, the impoverished candidate incurs multiple violations of the highest ranked faithfulness constraint – one for each case specification subfeature in the input not present in the output. The fact that the optimal output, the fully-specified candidate (a), incurs a number of markedness violations is of no consequence. Once again, any partially impoverished candidate would still incur some violations of the highest ranked faithfulness constraint, so candidate (a) would still emerge as the winner.

This candidate then serves as the input for morphological realization. For the case marker on the object, the null marker and the dative marker will compete for insertion, as both markers comply with the subset principle. However the dative marker, with the specification [+masc, +sing, +gov], is more specific than the null marker [ ], and will therefore win. For the clitic suffixed to the verb, dative clitic [+second, +sing, +gov] is more specific than the ergative/accusative clitic [+second, +sing]. The process of vocabulary insertion for this more marked output is schematized in (38).

(38) OB [+second, +sing, +gov, −obl] ↔ *-as* [+masc, +sing, +gov]
CL [+second, +sing, +gov, −obl] ↔ *-y* [+second, +sing, +gov][12]

12. I have chosen the example in (36) to serve as the input in the more-marked scenario somewhat carefully. Clitic doubling of the dative argument is only permitted with the second person, so in order to present a context in which the impoverishment of both the clitic and the NP yield the appropriate exponent we must use a third-person subject and second-person object. The endings for the pronominals are not precisely the same as the case endings for full

To see the masculine singular dative case marker arise as predicted by (38), we need to look at a full DP object:

(39) *su* *chu* *Aslam-as* *par-ɨnaav-aan* (III=III)
3SG.NOM AUX Aslam-DAT learn-CAUSE-PART
'He is teaching Aslam.'

5.4 Conditions on cliticization

The conditions on cliticization and clitic doubling in Kashmiri are complex and idiosyncratic. In particular, the dative clitic is required only when the dative argument is second person, and doubling is optional, but first and third person arguments may not be doubled. In this account, I will assume that the processes that govern these properties of clitics and the arguments they mark are indeed lodged in the morphological component, yet are distinct from those governing DAE. Clitic appearance and clitic doubling are completely independent of the person hierarchy and the relative markedness of grammatical function, and so I will argue that the morphological mechanisms conditioning clitic appearance, whatever they may be, are in fact separate.

This points to a crucial difference between the syntax-based approach and the account developed here. As we saw in Section 3, an empirical problem with the syntax-based approach arose when the dative clitic fails to appear (and since the clitic is always optional except in marking the second person, this is significant). Because in the syntax-based approach the dative clitic itself is a syntactic object and its markedness can only be evaluated when it is overt, its absence (irrespective of what conditions it) causes the wrong winner to be chosen by the optimality-theoretic competition regulating DAE. However, when the competition is shifted to the morphological component, this problem no longer arises. The formal syntactic features of both the NP argument and the clitic are fixed by syntactic processes before the morphological realization is at issue. It is those syntactic heads that serve as the input for the optimality-theoretic competition prompting impoverishment and ultimately deriving DAE. Following that competition, further conditions may be placed on the ways in which vocabulary items are inserted or

DPs. For reasons of space/time, I cannot provide here a detailed exploration of the feature compositions and syncretisms of the entire pronominal system of Kashmiri, though I will note that, as Sharma points out, "the pronoun system corresponds broadly to the NP pattern" (2003: 227). For this reason I will assume that the pronominal vocabulary items would have specifications very similar to the full NP case markers and that the analysis would function in a nearly identical way.

the way in which exponents are realized at PF. These conditions need not interact with or affect the realization of DAE.

According to the present analysis, DAE in Kashmiri is not a syntactic process, but instead a morphological one. More precisely, in less-marked scenarios (in which the person hierarchy is respected), a less specific set of exponents is inserted – one that corresponds to the syntactic case assigned to the argument. But in marked scenarios (in which the person hierarchy is not respected), a more specific set of exponents is inserted – and this set superficially appears to be mismatched with the syntactic structure. In the account I have developed here, impoverishment operations (via an optimality-theoretic competition) and underspecification of vocabulary items conspire to derive non-zero/non-zero DAE effects.

6. Conclusion

The account of Kashmiri DAE developed here provides a more complete analysis of the case marking and pronominal clitic systems than was previously available, including a unified explanation for both the morphological syncretisms and the non-zero/non-zero nature of Kashmiri DAE. In addition, it provides a clear path to account for DAE patterns that differ only slightly from that of Kashmiri. As with any optimality theoretic approach, we would expect re-rankings of the interpolated markedness constraints with respect to the universally ranked faithfulness constraints to generate other attested patterns. Taking a micro-comparative approach to morphological typology, we see that the closely related language Poguli exhibits DAE, with an important difference: there is a separate set of distinct clitic markers for the accusative case.[13]

In Poguli, DAE proceeds as in Kashmiri, in the sense that in nonperfective transitives direct objects are bare when the person hierarchy is respected, but marked dative when it is reversed. However, there is a separate set of accusative clitic suffixes, distinct from those used to mark ergative subjects, as in (40) and (41).

(40) *aaU* *tu* *tyeer*
1SG.NOM 2SG.ACC there
pyeen-mi-s (*pyeen-mi-t)
send.FUT-1SPS-2SG.ACC (*send.FUT-1SPS-2SG.ERG)
'I will send you there.' (adapted from Hook 1987: (3))

13. Thanks to Rajesh Bhatt for raising the question of accounting for Poguli.

(41) Poguli singular clitic sets

PERSON	NOM SING	ERG SING	ACC SING	DAT SING
I	-us/is	-m	N/A	-m
II	-us/is	-t	-s	-t
III	-u/i	-ni/nyE	-m	-s

The account developed here for Kashmiri DAE can be easily adjusted to account for the separate set of accusative markers in Poguli. First, since there is an additional set of vocabulary items, the specifications for each marker will shift slightly to accommodate the greater complexity of the paradigm. In particular, an accusative clitic marker like *-s* will be differentiated from the ergative marker *-t* [+second, +sing], with a specification [+second, +singular, –obl]. The dative clitic marker will be specified [+second, +singular, -subj, +gov]. In each case, these clitics are slightly more specific (have more features) than their Kashmiri counterparts, and this is to be expected in a more crowded morphological space in which more distinctions must be made. Notice, though, that they are still in the same relative relationship with respect to specifity; the dative clitic is more highly specified than the accusative.

Poguli is a language in which the accusative clitic marker arises in an impoverished context, but not as completely impoverished as in the case of Kashmiri (because the clitic paradigm is less syncretic). For this reason, only the markedness constraint [+gov] will be ranked between the two relevant faithfulness constraints, yielding the following ranking for Poguli:

(42) S≤OB & MAX_C >> *[+gov] >> *S>OB & MAX_C >>... *[–obl]

In the less-marked configuration, in which the highest-ranked faithfulness constraint is not active, only the feature [+gov] will be eliminated from the output, yielding a partially impoverished winning candidate with the case subfeatures [–subj, –obl]. The accusative marker will be the better insertion here, as it is more specific than the ergative marker, and since the dative marker is overspecified for this feature set and therefore does not comply with the subset principle. On the other hand, in the more-marked configuration in which the faithful output emerges with the case subfeatures [–subj, –obl, +gov], the dative clitic marker is now the more specific and better match.

I will not attempt to account for the many intricacies of the Poguli clitic system here, nor the various ways in which Poguli constrasts with Kashmiri. Instead, I bring this example to the fore to point out that it is just this type of microvariation that the post-syntactic, optimal theoretic account would lead us to expect.

Ongoing work should continue to address the typological variation in DAE predicted to exist by the account proposed here.

In conclusion, the present account suggests clear responses to important questions about the way the grammar is structured. First, large-scale syncretic patterns in the morphology are not motivated by syntactic processes (see Calabrese 2008), but are instead a product of underspecification of morphological exponents and the way in which they are inserted in the post-syntactic morphological component. Second, as Keine and Müller (2008) suggest, the typologically-motivated universal markedness hierarchies that drive DAE are not best understood as operating in the syntax, but instead in optimality-theoretic competitions in the morphological component that serve to reduce the syntactic input to morphological realization. Finally, as Kashmiri effectively demonstrates, the relationship between the grammatical function of an argument, its structural case assigned in the syntax, and the morphological encoding of that function is by no means one-to-one (Legate 2008). When non-zero/non-zero DAE arises, the present account suggests that the syntactic treatment of the triggering configuration be uniform, instead attributing differential encoding to post-syntactic operations, including impoverishment and the insertion of underspecified vocabulary items.

References

Aissen, Judith. 1999. Markedness and subject choice in optimality theory. *Natural Language and Linguistic Theory* 17: 673–711.

Aissen, Judith. 2003. Differential object marking: Iconicity vs. Economy. *Natural Language and Linguistic Theory* 21: 435–483.

Bhatt, Rakesh.1999. *Verb Movement and the Syntax of Kashmiri*. Kluwer: Dordrecht.

Bierwisch, Manfred. 1967. Syntactic features in morphology: General problems of so-called pronominal inflection in German. In *To Honor Roman Jakobson* (ed.), vol. 1, 239–270, The Hague/Paris: Mouton.

Calabrese, Andrea. 2008. On the shyness of the first person: Investigations on markedeness and under specification in morphology. *MUMSA Conference*, Harvard University, March 1–3, 2008.

Greenberg, Joseph. 1966. Language Universals. The Hague: Mouton.

Hale, Ken. 1972. A new perspective on American Indian linguistics. In: *New Perspectives on the Pueblos*, Alfonso Ortiz (ed.), 87–103. Albuquerque: University of New Mexico Press.

Halle, Morris & Marantz, Alec. 1993. Distributed morphology and the pieces of inflection. In *The View from Building 20: Essays in Linguistics in Honor of Sylvain Bromberger*, Ken Hale & Samuel Jay Keyser (eds), 111–176. Cambridge, Mass.: MIT Press.

Halle, Morris & Marantz, Alec. 1994. Some key features of distributed morphology. In *Papers on Phonology and Morphology*, Andrew Carnie, Heidi Harley & Tony Bures (eds), Cambridge, Mass.: MITWPL, MIT Working Papers in Linguistics. 21, 275–288.

Halle, Morris. 1997. Distributed morphology: Impoverishment and fission. In *Papers at the Interface*, Benjamin Bruening, Yoonjung Kang & Martha McGinnis (eds), Cambridge, Mass.: MITWPL, MIT Working Papers in Linguistics 30: 425–449.

Hook, Peter Edwin & Koul, Omkar N. 1984. Pronominal suffixes and split ergativity in Kashmiri. In *Aspects of Kashmiri Linguistics*, Omkar N. Koul & Peter Edwin Hook (eds), 123–135. Delhi: Bahri.

Hook, Peter. 1987. Poguli syntax in the light of Kashmiri: A preliminary report. In *Studies in the Linguistic Sciences* 17(1): 63–71.

Jakobson, Roman. 1936. Beitrag zur allgemeinen Kasuslehre: Gesamtbedeutungen der russischen Kasus. *Travaux du Cercle Linguistique de Prague* 6: 240–288, reprinted 1966 In *Readings in Linguistics II*, Eric Hamp, Fred Householder & Robert Austerlitz (eds), 51–89, Chicago: University of Chicago Press.

Keine, Stefan. 2007. Reanalysing Hindi split ergativity as a morphological phenomenon. In *1 2 Many*, Jochen Trommer & Andreas Opitz (eds), Universität Leipzig, Linguistische Arbeitsberichte 85, 73–127.

Keine, Stefan & Müller, Gereon. 2008. Differential argument encoding by impoverishment. In *Scales*, M. Richards & A. Malchukov (eds), 83–136. Berlin: de Gruyter.

Legate, Julie Anne. 2008. Morphological and abstract case. *Linguistic Inquiry* 39: 55–101.

Manetta, Emily. 2006. Peripheries in Kashmiri and Hindi-Urdu. PhD dissertation. University of California, Santa Cruz.

Manetta, Emily. 2011. Peripheries in Hindi-Urdu and Kashmiri. Amsterdam: John Benjamins.

Sharma, Devyani. 2001. Kashmiri case clitics and person hierarchy effects. In *Formal and Empirical Issues in Optimal Theoretic Syntax*, Peter Sells (ed.), 225–256. Stanford, CA: CSLI.

Silverstein, Michael. 1976. Hierarchy of features and ergativity. In: *Grammatical Categories in Australian Languages*, R. M. W. Dixon (ed.), 112–171. Canberra: Australian Institute of Aboriginal Studies.

Subbarao, Kārumūri V. 2001. Agreement in south Asian languages and minimalist inquiries: The framework. In *The Yearbook of South Asian Languages*, P. Bhaskararao & K. V. Subbarao (eds), 457–492. London/New Delhi: Sage Publications/Thousand Oaks.

Wali, Kashi & Koul, Ashok. 1994. Kashmiri clitics: The role of case and CASE. *Linguistics* 32: 969–994.

Wali, Kashi & Koul, Omkar N. 1997. *Kashmiri*. New York: Routledge.

Woolford, Ellen. 2001. Case Patterns. In Optimality-Theoretic Syntax. Eds. Geraldine Legendre, Jane Grimshaw, and Sten Vikner. Cambridge, MA: The MIT Press, 509–543.

Author index

Subject index